# *Always* CEDAR POINT

## A Memoir of the Midway

### *by* H. JOHN HILDEBRANDT

▶ **40 YEARS** *of* stories from the world's greatest amusement park

**Casa Flamingo Literary Arts**
NASHVILLE, TENNESSEE, USA

Published by Casa Flamingo Literary Arts, Nashville, Tennessee, www.casaflamingo.com

Paperback first printing, October, 2018

ISBN: 978-0-9967504-1-7

Library of Congress Control Number: 2018952579

Cover Artwork and Interior Design: Jennifer Wright

Editor and Production Director: Tim O'Brien

Distribution: Ingram Global Publisher Service

For additional copies of "Always Cedar Point – A Memoir of the Midway" ask your local bookstore to order or purchase online at www.alwayscedarpoint.com or www.amazon.com. Distributed by Ingram and available throughout the US, Canada, Australia, United Kingdom, European Union, and Russia.

*This book is dedicated to the employees*
*of Cedar Point – past, present and future.*
*You are the heart and soul of the park.*

# Always CEDAR POINT
## Contents

# Introduction

### *Hold on tight!*

John Hildebrandt has taken us on the ride of his life, giving us an insider's view of working at the worlds' greatest amusement park, Cedar Point. From his time as a ride operator on the Frontier Lift at age 20 to becoming the park's general manager 35 years later, John brings us inside the fascinating world of what it takes to market and operate a destination built on fun.

John's love for the park is felt on every page. His devotion to the park's heritage is loud and strong. His Cedar Point story is also a tribute to his colleagues and co-workers who bring joy to millions of guests every season. "Always Cedar Point" is a love poem to an extraordinary place.

At Cedar Point John developed the marketing skills to create campaigns to introduce the greatest collection of roller coasters on earth. In the marketing and advertising of Corkscrew, Gemini, Magnum, Millennium Force, and Top Thrill Dragster, there are stories told and lessons learned.

This is one of the best books yet written about life inside an amusement park. There is humor, history, disappointment, thrills, and excitement on the Cedar Point midway. In 30 years as a marketer and 10 as a general manager, John was witness to the park's, and the company's, amazing growth. In his own words: "I saw a lot." John tells a good story, and there are plenty to tell.

"Always Cedar Point" reveals the ups and downs involved in the park becoming the economic powerhouse it is today, an anchor attraction for Ohio but also for the Great Lakes region, and with a growing national awareness.

In the words heard every day on the Cedar Point midway... "Welcome Magnum riders, are you ready to RIDE?"

Yes!

**Melinda Huntley**
*Executive Director*
*Ohio Travel Association*

*Always* **CEDAR POINT**
**A Memoir of the Midway**

# Foreword

When you spend 40 years doing something, you ought to have something to say about it. This is the story of my time in the amusement park business. In all of that time, even when I worked seasonally in the summer of 1969, I was employed by Cedar Point or its parent organization, Cedar Fair Entertainment Company, so this is really the story of my time at Cedar Point, save one year when I worked at a sister park, Dorney Park and Wildwater Kingdom, in Allentown, Pennsylvania.

For most of the time I have been here on earth I have worked in the amusement park business. I started full time when I was 24 in 1974, and I retired when I was 64, in 2014. Open to Close, or in amusement park jargon, OC, means that on any given day you are working from the time the park opens until it closes. This story starts when the gate opened in 1974, and it ends when it closed on January 1, 2014.

My life has thus far been largely conventional. I have accomplished no great deeds. I have not achieved three of the goals I set for myself when I was 21: write a great novel; sail across the Atlantic; and walk the length of the Appalachian Trail. However, I have managed to accomplish a few things I never dreamed about doing when I was 21. And I have written a novel (two actually, and part of a third). I have sailed Lake Erie and Sandusky Bay, and once, for a few hours, the spot where San Francisco Bay meets the Pacific Ocean. I have hiked the Grand Canyon from rim to rim and many parts of the Appalachian Trail. I have caught bonefish in the Florida Keys and trout in the Rocky Mountains.

When I was 18 and graduating from high school, I wrote that I wanted to be a writer and a lecturer. I loved giving speeches, something I had discovered as a member of the debate team at St. Edward High School, and I knew I wanted to be a writer one September afternoon my freshman year in Brother Michael Hauser's class in English Composition. Words were magical things and could be put to work to tell stories. I wanted to tell stories.

My business card now reads "freelance writer," and in truth I am one. I also give presentations to various groups on local and state history subjects, and so I am a lecturer, too. Some people start fresh in retirement or in later age and embark on new adventures; and

Always CEDAR POINT
A Memoir of the Midway

some return to what they were originally. I am now 18 or 21 again. In between there was the park business, more specifically Cedar Point, the framework for much of my life.

The story is part autobiography, part memoir, part history, but it all comes winding back to the park, which is a powerful piece of geography in my mind, and in my heart. Everything seems to be connected to it. It's a little scary at times.

This is not a history of Cedar Point. The park's history, from its beginnings in the years after the Civil War through about 2010, has been well told by the late David Francis and Diane DeMali Francis, authors of three editions of "Cedar Point: Queen of American Watering Places." They tell the story of Cedar Point very well. And they loved the park. When David died in 2006 he was buried wearing a Cedar Point tie. David was a great friend. I think of him often.

So, there is no need to cover a lot of plowed ground on the history of Cedar Point. Still, the history of the park is part of the story of my life at the park and so it's always there moving around in the background.

This is not a corporate history, either. It's not sponsored by Cedar Point or Cedar Fair and it does not purport to tell the story of the business or its corporate transformations the past half century.

For 30 of my 40 years with Cedar Point I was a marketer, and for the last 10 years I was a general manager. My perspective and my experiences were certainly heavily influenced by the roles I played. I believe I was fortunate to work both as a specialist and a generalist.

When I started at Cedar Point in February 1974, the company was just Cedar Point with revenues of less than $30 million. When I retired in January of 2014, the company was Cedar Fair Entertainment Company with 11 parks and a billion dollars in revenue. I saw a lot.

I believe Cedar Point is the world's best amusement park. I'm not alone in that belief—it has received every major award in the industry including the Golden Ticket as the World's Best Amusement Park a record 16 times in a poll sponsored by Amusement Today magazine. In 1996, Cedar Point received the Applause Award, an international award sponsored by Liseberg, a famous Swedish theme park, which is given every two years to an amusement park whose "management, operations, and creative accomplishments have inspired the industry."

Cedar Point has been around since 1870 and will undoubtedly continue long after I am riding the roller coaster in the sky. Its best years may well be ahead of it. I hope that's the case, but of course no one knows. In 1900, when he was about to launch Cedar Point into its first golden age, did George Boeckling foresee a parking lot for 10,000 cars, online ticketing, Top Thrill Dragster, and female guests wearing yoga pants on the midway? If George Boeckling were to look back a similar time frame, say 115 years to 1785, Cedar Point was then a howling wilderness, Ohio was 18 years short of statehood, the population of the area was nearly 100 percent Native American, and George Washington was 57 years old and the office of president of the United States had yet to be created.

Cedar Point is a hybrid, part resort and part amusement park. Two different businesses which can function very successfully on their own but when paired together like Cedar Point (or Disney World) can create a sum that's far greater than its two parts. Cedar Point is located in a small town, Sandusky, Ohio, 60 miles west of Cleveland and 60 miles east of Toledo. In the 2010 census it had a population of about 24,000. The park occupies the tip of the Cedar Point Peninsula (technically a barrier island connected by two causeways), which in turn forms the eastern boundary of Sandusky Bay.

Its location on Lake Erie is beautiful—yes, even in winter—and a great part of its appeal, and a reason it still exists today. Cedar Point came of age as a true amusement park in the late 19th and early 20th centuries, at a time when all the great urban parks were in their heyday, from Coney Island in New York City to Riverview in Chicago to Euclid Beach in Cleveland. For a variety of reasons, most did not survive. However, Cedar Point was a survivor; perhaps the only old-time park to make the transition to modern super-park. It is a remarkable comeback story, legendary within the amusement park industry.

Cedar Point has grown organically over nearly 150 years. It was not created on a drawing table. I believe that is one of its strengths. It is authentic. If you look closely, you can see amazing things.

Like all businesses, Cedar Point is also the story of the individuals who made it what it was, and is. A few local dreamers, Louis Zistel, Jacob Kuebler, and W.F. Dwelle among others, took a chance and got it started in the 1870s and 1880s. A huge dreamer, also a very talented builder and operator, George Boeckling, took over in 1897 and created the first golden age for Cedar Point. What he built managed to survive the 1930s and 1940s and 1950s until two new men, Emile Legros and George Roose, undertook its transformation starting in the late 1950s. In the mid-1970s and into the mid-1980s Bob Munger drove the Cedar Point agenda, and then in the late 1980s and the 1990s and through the first decade of the Millennium, it was Dick Kinzel. Take these people out of the picture and the story would read quite differently. In fact, there might not be a story to tell. The actions and decisions, the biases and beliefs, the loves and hates, of individuals matter. People make history. History is very much alive.

I apologize in advance for any errors that I have unwittingly brought to life. I realize that many people will no doubt remember certain events and people differently than I do. I can't help that. As a student of the Civil War, I have read many old soldier memoirs in which modern day editors, writers, and readers have pointed out errors in memory. We are not as good as a computer when it comes to storing facts. I have done my best to remember as accurately as I can. I have fact-checked certain things, e.g. the height of the Blue Streak roller coaster and the year Frontier Trail opened and the cost to build Top Thrill Dragster, but much of this story is my perception of what happened and why. It's proudly subjective, not objective. I'm not running from it.

I did read a lot of old stuff as I was writing this book. My wife and I are at an age where on poor weather days we retreat to the basement and go through boxes of stuff, sorting by child, by parent, by life experience. When I read old letters I had written to my parents when I was a freshman in college, or my letters to my sister, I sometimes get an electric-like shock as I do not recognize myself in the words or the actions described. We are many different people in our lifetimes, which is largely a good thing, even a blessing. A visit to your past life is like a trip to a foreign country, as many others have observed. I disagree: it's more like a visit to Jupiter.

For 40 years I was paid to help people have fun. It was a very good gig. If not the best job in the world, it was certainly in the top one percent. I know this to be true... as I have been told so by lots of 11 year-old boys, and girls. The roller coaster and the carousel were my brothers in arms, my friends, my companions. I was proud to be their spokesperson, ever their champion. In our time together, Cedar Point earned space in the hearts of millions.

**H. John Hildebrandt**
*Sandusky, Ohio*
*Summer 2018*

## Chapter 1

# The Midway
### I Made My Living in Crowds

I knew every inch of it. I usually didn't need a watch: I knew what time it was by the way the sun looked on the Corkscrew loop, the way the sun painted it at 6 p.m.; the way the sun was squeezed from a ball to a square between the bracing on the Mean Streak at 8 p.m.; the way the east side of the Coliseum and Kiddy Kingdom were bathed in light at park opening. I knew it from my office window, looking out and down at the midway fountain and the green track of the Raptor rising behind it. I knew it from the stampede of guests down the midway at opening. For the fastest guests it meant a shorter wait time for Millennium Force. We called it "The Running of the Bulls," but it was different than Pamplona, as guests were running to, not from, something big and fast and scary.

I made my living in crowds.

I sometimes fancied myself a Shawnee Indian tracking sign. I could look at certain ride lines and know within 500 guests the current park attendance. The length of Scrambler line was another sign, almost infallible. I could walk along the midway and know by the spaces between guests about what the attendance was. The attendance signs changed over the years. My first years, the Blue Streak line snaked across the main midway in the morning almost to the water fountain, an indicator of a 25,000 attendance day. The Blue Streak line hasn't reached the main midway in more than 30 years and likely never will again, even on huge attendance days. The signs have changed.

As the day wore on the main midway lightened, the great mass of people migrating to the center and back of the park. Then in the evening it went the other way. Frontier Town, even after Maverick opened in 2007, started emptying at 8 p.m., and conversely the main midway at the front of the park started filling up again. I used to imagine the park as a giant teeter-totter, floating up and down always searching for the perfect balance.

The perfect balance meant the optimization of the guest experience—the shortest lines possible for rides and food stands given the relative park attendance—and the optimization of the corporate experience, which meant all points of sale open and generating lots of revenue. In management, we used to talk about the

ideal size crowd. Given a choice, the company would always opt for maximum attendance, and the guests would always opt for minimum attendance (short lines for everything). The most realistic scenario was attendance in the 30,000 – 35,000 range, a number, assuming adequate staffing, that could generate significant revenue but still provide a great guest experience. It would have been nice to have had predictable attendance, day after day, especially in that range, but of course it's not reality. There would always be 8,000 and 12,000 days when we'd send employees home, and there would always be 45,000 days with very long lines and not enough employees. But we did have 33,000 days when everybody won; we had quite a few of them.

Like airports, fairgrounds, train stations, bus depots, malls, college and professional sports venues, the midway presents an opportunity to look at significant numbers of your fellow human beings in a relatively short period of time and in a controlled space. The midway crowd is a unique blend, different from a Cleveland Indians game or the concourse at JFK. You don't see packs of teenage girls wandering the airport concourse, and there are more female guests on the midway than you would find in the right field seats in Progressive Field. Wading through tens of thousands of people over a period of several hours is a unique experience.

It's a good place to observe clothing trends, especially among the young. And T-shirts with messages. I used to write down the good ones in my notebook. I don't remember them now. Faces. Body types. All manner of both.

In the nine years of walking the midway as GM of Cedar Point, I used to think about the fact that I was in charge of this party. Mostly it was a good feeling and I welcomed it. After all, it was a voluntary assignment.

Cedar Point is known for its wide midways. They are a signature feature of the park, part historical accident and part design. The overall park presentation is very simple, especially for a guest entering from the main entrance, which is probably 80 percent of guests. The main midway extends about a quarter of a mile straight ahead, to the spot where the Sky Ride station and the Corkscrew helix are close together. At that point the midway splits, one section going under the Corkscrew toward Top Thrill Dragster on the lake side of the park, the other headed to the train station and Millennium Force on the bay side. Take either path and you eventually arrive in Frontier Town. There are nooks and crannies, some significant like the Beach midway and the Blue Streak/Valravn midway, others much smaller like Camp Snoopy.

For most of its length, the main midway is wide open with massive, and beautiful, flower beds running down the center.

What it means is that as a guest you can see where you're going. It means groups can walk together horizontally, even on busy days.

Cedar Point's original midway ran more north-south, from the boat dock on the bay side across the peninsula to the beach and lake. Today's main midway dates from the early 1960s, which is now half a century ago, and so it is the only midway nearly all current guests know or remember.

## Welcome to Cedar Point

For nearly all my career, Cedar Point had a very low-key front gate, basically a row of ticket booths and then a row of turnstiles anchored at each end by a small building. It may have been attractive when it was built, in the 1960s, but even a decade hence it was quite underwhelming. Newer parks made a bold statement at the front entrance, which makes good sense from just about every perspective. The Marriott parks each had a two-decked carousel at the front gate. At Kings Island, there was a restaurant overlooking the main entrance.

As a GM, I was expected to be at the main gate in the morning when the park opened. It was an unwritten rule, but still very much a rule. Dick Kinzel, the CEO for most of the years I was GM, had started the tradition back when he was director of operations at Cedar Point. He wanted his GMs up at the front to welcome guests, assess the crowd, and make sure the opening went smoothly. It wasn't a bad rule. When Dick or Jack Falfas, our COO from 2005 - 2010, were in town, they usually made it a point to come to the front for opening. Lots of business was discussed just out of earshot of the guests, some very serious and some not serious at all. And there was baseball and football talk, too. Sometimes Dick and Jack would step away to have a private conversation.

Our goal was to get everyone into the park as quickly and efficiently as possible. Anything that could speed up the process was considered. Balancing staffing between the ticket booths and the turnstiles was always tricky. On one level we all loved to see the crowd backed up like salmon before a waterfall—it was proof we were loved—but on another it screamed inefficiency and poor guest service.

Guests have questions. We were conspicuous, by design, of course, in our shirts and ties, and guests sought us out for answers. But it was not wearisome work. Most issues were easily resolved. Occasionally Dick Kinzel was recognized by a coaster enthusiast or an investor, and guests would stop to talk to him or even get their picture taken with him. He always obliged.

Cedar Point, the world's greatest amusement park, surrounded by
Lake Erie and Sandusky Bay, about 2012. CEDAR POINT ARCHIVES

He didn't stay at the front long, soon he was walking back to
his office. Most days, especially Saturdays, he would remerge in mid-
afternoon and walk most of the park and especially the resort areas.

I listened to my park radio to hear the codes that meant the big
rides were opening. My instructions to the Park Operations staff was
that I was to be notified by phone any time a major ride did not open
on time or any time a major ride went down during the operating day
for anything that might take longer than 10 or 15 minutes to fix.

Alone, I would wander out front by the flagpole, by the fringes
of the parking lot. I had two missions. One was to look for trash,
the other was to look at guests. The edges of the main parking lot
were a kind of no-man's land. Guests tended to bring things with
them, especially cigarettes and soft drink cans and cups, and dump
them when they left the lot and approached the front gate. They
especially liked throwing them in our landscaping. Technically, we
were covered—we had a sweep whose responsibilities included the
transition zone—but often they could get overwhelmed, especially
when a large group moved through the area. Sometimes, it was the
trash cans that needed attention more than the midway. I would pick
up what I could, and I notified the area supervisor. We had to respond
quickly: first impressions count.

The guests were excited. Even if they had risen before dawn to drive four hours from Pittsburgh or Grand Rapids, they had now reached the holy place and they were energized. I looked to make eye contact and said, "Good Morning" or "Welcome to Cedar Point" and always got a smile back and a nod of the head, even on rainy days.

All branches of American humanity were represented: men, women, children, teens, babes in strollers, thin and heavy, well dressed and not, clean shaven and not, tall and short, with hats and not, obvious grandparents, all races and ethnicities. But it was not a random slice. We were an amusement park and therefore by definition we leaned young. There were gaps, e.g. adults over 30, unless, of course they were there as parents. The demographics of our guests were very specific, and we knew them well and worked hard at noticing any changes.

I seldom walked out into the parking lot. If I had, I would have seen more trash, I'm sure. The tightly packed cars hid much of it. There was a reason we scheduled two big trash trucks to clean the parking lots every night after the park closed. I checked license plates. The majority were Ohio and neighboring states, especially Michigan, but on any given day you would spot more than a few exotics: Alabama, Vermont, Texas, Florida, North Carolina, South Dakota, Maine, New Jersey. To determine where our guests were coming from we collected zip codes, which allowed for more precise advertising, but it was still fun to look at license plates.

Throughout my time at Cedar Point, both as marketing vice president and as GM, I worried very little about the parking lot. I knew it was managed very well. Using systems and protocols developed over many seasons, I believed we were always prepared. The credit went to Jack Falfas, John McClure, Bill Spehn, Dave Bauer, Jack Baus, and Candy Frankowski, who believed the guest experience started and ended with the parking lot and that doing it right was extremely important. We directed vehicles to specific spots, and there was a method to how we did it. It was administered by a large team of seasonal employees. Traffic was something we just accepted as one of the activities that was staff heavy. The alternative, especially on lighter attendance days, was to let guests self-park. Not going to happen. We were convinced the main lot would be a mess and certainly less safe. It would not be Cedar Point.

Big attendance days were a challenge for Traffic, but a welcome challenge. Our full-time staff was energized by it, as was the seasonal staff.

Getting cars out was the bigger challenge, especially given the unique geography of the park and the fact we had two large public parking areas, the main lot and the lot by Soak City, our water park, in the back of the park. On big attendance days, the kids working Traffic earned their pay, especially at closing. In the cars, the kids were tired and fighting in the back seat. Mom was figuring out how much money they'd spent. Dad was behind the wheel and the car wasn't moving and it was nearly midnight and it was at least two hours to get back to Detroit. Other cars were jockeying for position to cut him off. And in front of him was a young guy with a whistle and a twirling flashlight telling him what to do. There was the occasional expletive.

As the marketing guy for so many years, I kept an interest in the Group Sales Booth. I often stopped inside and talked to the supervisor and watched the kids work. Group leaders came up to the booth to pick up and pay for tickets for their groups, most often in the 25 – 300 range. With last-minute additions and subtractions, it often ended up being a complex transaction; in fact, I considered it the most complex guest transaction which took place at the park. The seasonal supervisor running the Group Sales Booth had a lot of financial responsibility. They were among the best and brightest of our seasonal staff. Several times I went through the training myself and serviced group customers. I gave myself a B- (good attitude, average skills.) From the Group Sales Booth I wandered through Guest Services, until my final season as GM located on the lake side of the turnstiles and talked to the supervisor for a few minutes. Guest Services was the catch all: complaints (about anything), questions (about everything), ticket pick up. I watched the guest interactions with the staff. Mostly I refrained from getting involved, but occasionally I did step in and resolve an issue.

The supervisor during my time as GM was Nancy Otto, then in her early 60s, who could play the role of good cop/bad cop as well as anyone. I know I trusted her to make the right call when a guest had a problem. She could be mom, or she could be a drill sergeant, depending on what was needed. She was mostly mom.

## Jack Aldrich

Then I was inside the park, on the midway. The Midway Carousel was in front of me and I had to decide to pass it on the right or the left, the lake side or the bay side. Mostly, I opted for the bay side, which almost immediately took me past the Jack Aldrich Theater. On the front of the theater was a bronze plaque with information about Jack. I had written it in 2006, after Jack died and Dick Kinzel had decided to honor Jack's memory and his impact on the park's live entertainment program by re-naming the Centennial Theater the Jack Aldrich Theater. It was the right thing to do. Dick later told me that he had waited too long, that he should have done it when Jack was alive. I told him what mattered was that he had done it.

Jack had been one of my best friends in the company. We shared a love of baseball. His knowledge of the game was prodigious. He was about 20 years my senior and he had clear memories of players like Ted Williams, Satchel Page, Bob Feller, Lou Boudreaux, Jackie Robinson, and Joe DiMaggio. He was an Indians fan, of course, and hated the Yankees and the Tigers with a passion. Jack's father had been a fan, too, and Jack had often described to me going to Sunday double headers at both League Park and Cleveland Stadium. It was a long day, starting with a 60-mile drive into Cleveland. They brought their own food. No matter the score, they stayed until the last out.

One summer Jack spent most of his time in the Cleveland Clinic with an infection that originated from gall bladder surgery. He nearly died several times. He joked afterward that listening to the Tribe games that summer saved his life because he knew the Indians were worse off than he was, and they kept playing.

Jack was a man of considerable wit, a good judge of musical talent, a good company politician, a devout Mormon, highly intelligent, a Sandusky native. His wit was on display at every company Christmas party. He re-wrote the lyrics to several traditional Christmas songs and carols to poke fun at senior management. They were hilarious; even senior management had to laugh. He led the entire room in song.

To the tune of "Jingle Bells":

*People want to know*
*Do you work in winter, too*
*When it starts to snow*
*Is there stuff for you to do*
*I know it makes you mad*
*But there's lots of things to say*
*Just keep your cool and they'll be sad*
*If you answer them this way, say*

*We don't work, we don't work*
*We just rest all day*
*We play cards and watch TV*
*And they give us double pay, hey*
*We don't work, we don't work*
*We just rest all day*
*Sleeping hours are eight to five*
*'Til we open up in May!*

When Jack retired in 1994, I arranged to get an unvarnished Albert Belle bat from the Louisville Slugger factory in Kentucky. Belle was the bad boy slugger of the Cleveland Indians at the time. I took it around to every department in the company and had it signed by his fellow employees. We presented it to him at the Cedar Point Christmas party a few weeks before he retired.

When I walked by the theater I always checked to see the condition of the plaque. If there were cobwebs or dirt, or gull droppings on it, I immediately went in search of a sweep. If I couldn't find one, I got on the phone and called for one and stayed until the sweep arrived. Every season I talked to the zone leader and told her about Jack. This wasn't just a bronze plaque, a piece of Cedar Point inventory like a bench or a window or a fence. This was Jack Aldrich, my friend.

## The Raptor Flight Deck

I loved going up on ride platforms, especially the coasters. The first one I would hit coming back from the front gate was the Raptor. My route was through the gate in the back of the ride which took me up the spiral steps to the main ride platform. The view of the Cedar Point Marina and behind it Sandusky Bay, and then behind the bay the city of Sandusky, was one of the best in park. You looked directly southwest, where much of the park's weather originated. In the days before weather radar had become ubiquitous, and even when it had become so, the Raptor platform at the top of the winding staircase was a great weather outpost for Park Operations.

The marina was always full of boats, the docks filled, even on beautiful summer Saturdays and Sundays. I never understood it. Why weren't they all out on the lake? It remains one of my eternal mysteries of Cedar Point.

My goal on the platforms was to show the colors, to let the ride crews know I was interested in what they did and to let them know it was important work. I did watch them work, as they loaded and unloaded trains and then dispatched them into coaster heaven. I watched the guests, too. Train after train. The eagerness, the nervousness, sometimes the abject fear. It was all there. At several coasters, including Raptor, riders who had backpacks or who carried plush or had large purses, had to cross through the train to the exit side of the platform and deposit their belongings in a wooden bin, and then go back onto the ride and get in a seat and secure their seatbelts. You had to move fast. It always reminded me more than a little of the loading and unloading of a New York City subway train during the 5 p.m. hour.

The bins were there because the ride couldn't accommodate riders holding large objects, really while holding any objects, especially phones. Frankly, it would be dangerous to try. The ride forces were "dynamic" as we liked to say. On the Raptor, you flew at 57 mph, you went upside down six times, and you went through a 360-degree vertical loop. It was better to hold on with both hands. Riders who wore unsecured sandals and flip-flops had to put them in the bin as well. If worn on the ride, they ended up flying off into the air.

Our biggest worry was the flying cell phone. Phones tended to slip out of hands and disappear into the air and go wherever the laws of physics dictated. No one wanted to be whacked in the head by a flying phone. Of course, a few riders took their phones out as soon as they left the station and assumed they were out of sight and began taking pictures or video of their ride experience. If this action was observed by a ride operator, the ride was stopped, and the guest was warned and told to put away the phone.

The ground below the ride was canvassed regularly for objects from the train, including right after the ride closed for the day, and the ride crews regularly brought back to Lost and Found cracked and broken phones, hats, car keys, sunglasses, wallets, pens, and, at least once every few years, some type of dental appliance.

Some guests threw their belongings into the bin without any thought—the ride awaited—while others were hesitant. You could see it in their faces. We did our best to secure the bins. The bins were matched to the three Raptor trains so that only one bin was open at a time (the two others were locked). When a train left the station, the ride operator closed and locked the bin. It was not opened again until that train was back in the station and guests were exiting the ride. Despite our best efforts, there were still thefts. Very few, infinitesimally few if you matched thefts—perhaps a half dozen over the course of a season— against 1.3 million rides—but a punch in the stomach if it was your backpack (with a wallet or car keys inside). It did take nerve to steal things out of the bins. The owner of the backpack you are reaching for might be standing next to you and about to reach for it, too.

In three train operation, which was pretty much the norm for the Raptor, the loading area was controlled chaos. Everything happened quickly in support of the objective of delivering the most rides possible within the parameters of safe operation.

I made eye contact with the ride operators and waived acknowledgement. In the brief time between trains I spoke a little with the person on the exit side of the platform. The usual topics: weather, hometown and/or college, how they liked working the Raptor. If I could, I tried to talk with the team leader and complimented him or her on the crew's performance. I was very conscious of not getting in the way or distracting the crew. I tried hard not to induce stress. That certainly wasn't my intent. I wanted to give them the chance to show their stuff to the boss. I wanted them to know they were valued.

Occasionally, a ride supervisor would appear on the platform, most likely on a tip the GM was on the platform of one of his or her rides. The front-line supervision really ran the park. The Cedar Point full time staff was small. We relied on a number of 19, 20, and 21-year-olds to make a host of decisions every day that made a difference in the business. We asked much of them, including long hours, and expected much of them, including a personal commitment to giving their best. It's not easy supervising your peers at any age but I believe it's even more of a challenge when you are all under 21. I had great admiration for our seasonal supervisors whatever their division: Park Operations, Food Services, Accommodations, Merchandise, Games.

The Raptor queue held hundreds of riders. From the platform I could look down on almost all of them.

Unless I got a phone call, my visits were short, less than 10 minutes. There were lots of rides to visit in a two to three-hour park tour.

From the Raptor stairs I could easily slip into the Park Services lot and the adjacent employee break area by the Park Services warehouse. This area was ground zero for managing the cleanliness of the park and the conditions in the parking lot. There was a lot of coming and going in a small area.

I entered back into the park through a gate between the Park Services warehouse and the Blue Streak. The Blue Streak operated in the shadow of Raptor, both literally and figuratively. It is a traditional coaster in every way, including its signature cupola which tops the first hill. The Blue Streak queue, easily visible from Perimeter Road, was another measure of park attendance.

I watched the crew as they checked lap bars and seatbelts. Lots of bending. A job for young backs.

Sometimes I entered the park from Park Services through the kitchen of the Silver Dollar aka Game Day Grille aka Chickie's & Pete's restaurant. The kitchen was a different world: hot, greasy (fries were on the menu), slippery, crowded, noisy, monochromatic (gray, hard-used stainless steel). I usually didn't stay long. I exited into the dining room and walked slowly through the restaurant. I nodded and smiled to guests. I looked around to find Jeanie, the restaurant manager, to say hello.

In the fall, I used to find excuses to go to the Game Day Grille and check on sports scores, especially football. The bartenders always had the Notre Dame, Ohio State, Indians or Browns game on at least one TV.

As I walked down the steps of the restaurant, I had my choice of a left turn to the Blue Streak, Turnpike Cars, and Super Jets, or right to the main midway. I usually turned right.

## Cleanliness is Godliness

As always, I was looking for trash. I was looking for trash for 40 years. I found more of it my early years, less of it my later seasons. Why? We got better at keeping the park clean, and so did our guests.

The park's cleanliness obsession (and it was, and is, an obsession in many ways) goes back to the days of George Roose and Emile Legros in the early 1960s. They, in turn, got it from Walt Disney. A hallmark of Disneyland was, and is, its cleanliness. Walt's vision of a magical alternative to the real world had no allowance for squashed cigarette butts or ketchup-stained napkins on the midway. He wanted a clean break from the old paradigm where a certain amount of trash blowing around was part of the charm of a traditional American amusement park. Not in Walt's world. No. Not ever. Ever.

Roose and Legros were of the same mind, even though they operated a traditional amusement park. Both were wealthy men, and in late middle age, when they acquired Cedar Point. From my perspective, Legros was a man of patrician habits. I doubt he had picked up much trash before his Cedar Point days. But he picked up plenty at Cedar Point. So much in fact that he was dubbed "Mr. Clean" by the employees. Dick Kinzel told me the story of Legros interviewing a young man for a job. While they were walking the midway, Legros bent over and picked up a piece of paper. He stopped, looked at the young man (Lee Weiber, who would go on to a very successful career with Key Bank) and simply said: "Get the idea?"

George Roose picked up his share of trash, too. They both knew that for park cleanliness to be taken seriously they had to set the example at the top. Dick Kinzel picked up trash. Jack Falfas picked up trash.

The cleanliness standard has been a part of Cedar Point's brand for more than 60 years. It is the core of the apple.

When I started full-time in 1974, the cleanliness standard was well established. But guests could still appreciate it as something new. Many remembered visiting the Cedar Point of the 1940s and 1950s, as well as other amusement parks and county and state fairs and similar attractions, where the cleanliness standard was weak or even non-existent. When I talked to guests on the midway or in out of park settings, we were often complimented for being such a clean park. It was a big deal, in part because these folks had been through the alternative experience at other places.

Over time, the cleanliness standard became more and more a given, an expectation. Guests who first came to the "clean" Cedar Point as children in the early 1960s are now senior citizens. They only know clean amusement parks and theme parks. Cleanliness is a given. We no longer receive as many glowing compliments—even though the park is cleaner now than ever before—simply because a very clean park is a core expectation of the Cedar Point experience.

Not everyone bought into picking up trash. There were a few full-time employees, and some seasonal employees, who glazed over or suffered a lightning bolt of temporary blindness when confronted by a Popsicle stick, a smashed soft drink cup, a used napkin, or a candy wrapper laying there on the ground in front of them. They treated such objects as highly radioactive material.

For the cleanliness thing to work, there has be 90% or more buy-in by employees.

I'm sure their rationale for not picking up trash—in addition to the fact that it meant bending over and touching something potentially pretty yucky—was that it wasn't their job to pick up trash, it's why we had sweeps and Park Services; or that they were running late on their way to somewhere and that precluded running down that napkin blowing across the midway.

But those were not acceptable excuses.

One of my fantasies was to secretly videotape employees, both seasonal and full-time, walking past trash on the midway and then use it as a training aid. When I did see an employee going out of his way to pick up trash, I made sure to compliment him or her. I liked doing it. The great majority of employees bought into Cleanliness. It was one of the Cedar Point Cornerstones of guest service, in addition to Safety, Courtesy, Service, and Integrity. These were our principles, our code of conduct, and our promise to our guests.

When I talked to the seasonal supervisors before the start of the season, I ended my talk with a few thoughts on cleanliness. I told them cleanliness was everyone's job, including mine. I told them they would set the example for the people who worked for them. If they walked past trash, so would their staffs. I told them I would call them out if I saw them walk past trash. But I also told them I expected them to call me out if they ever caught me doing it.

I told them the story of the father in the focus group in Pittsburgh. The moderator had asked the group some questions about park cleanliness. One man slammed his fist on the table and announced: "At Cedar Point they even clean the dirt!" Made my day.

I carried sanitary wipes in my front pocket every time I left the office to walk the midway.

The last three or four years of my career I carried a picker. Great invention. It not only saved my back, it allowed me to get to places I couldn't get to otherwise. I wish I had started using one many years earlier. I think over the years I developed amusement park back syndrome. I still have it.

If guests see trash on the ground, they are being sent a message that it's okay to join the party and drop stuff on the ground. The converse is also true: most guests will refrain from this behavior if the ground around them is clean AND there is a trash can only a few feet away. One of the big keys to making the system work is the right number and the right placement of trash cans. In my seasons as a GM, Cedar Point had about 2,000 trash cans in the park, including the water park but excluding the resort areas. There was science to their placement. In general, Park Services wanted a trash can every 25 feet, or four or five strides. After that, even conscientious guests started looking for bushes or benches to drop trash. There were aesthetic considerations, too. Trash cans were in rows, like soldiers, and should to be pleasing to the eye. Jack Falfas was famous for constantly fine tuning the position of trash cans as he walked the midways. I did it, too, but I did not have Jack's eye.

Depending on location and time of day, some trash cans filled much quicker than others. Some cans needed emptying daily (or even more frequently) others weekly. When an employee, including the GM, observed a full to overflowing trash can we were expected to contact Park Services immediately.

Doing garbo runs was not an easy job. It was all about the application of human muscle. The only mechanical advantage was the fact that the bin you pushed up the midway from can to can until it was filled with several hundred pounds of trash rested on wheels. Individual bags might weigh up to 50 pounds or more, depending on how many half full Pepsi cups and/or water bottles they held. Many had holes and liquids would seep out of the bag before you tossed it in the bin, staining the midway, a constant problem.

I got a letter once from a guest from Illinois which included a $20 bill. In the letter he wrote that he and his family had been recent visitors to the park, staying at Hotel Breakers for three nights. It was July and the weather was hot and muggy. He said he was impressed with how clean the park was. He said he observed the same young man on several occasions moving a cart up the midway emptying trash cans. It was tough work, but he was doing it well. The guest noted he believed in rewarding good guest service and that he had a soft spot for back of the house employees. He offered the Park Services kid $20. The kid refused to accept it. He offered it again, and again it was refused. He asked me in the letter to get the money to the seasonal employee. He remembered his first name from his name tag. We found him easily enough and got him his $20. I wrote back to the guest and thanked him for being a fine human being.

## Sweeps

When I walked the midway I looked for sweeps. When I started at Cedar Point the employees who walked the midways with brooms and pans were called sweeperettes. All were female. Nearly all were college students. They were physically fit. They wore bright yellow jumpsuits. Management wanted them to be noticed, both because we wanted to send the message we were working hard to keep the park clean, but also because sweeps also served as a mobile information service, especially in the pre-internet/cell phone era.

The park began recruiting males as well as females and sweeperettes became sweeps. The males did not have to wear yellow jumpsuits. The jumpsuits were retired and replaced by standard beige pants/shorts and a logo golf shirt. When Jack Falfas became chief operating officer in 2005 he brought the yellow jumpsuits back for a few seasons, but it was a losing battle. The jumpsuits were very unpopular with female sweeps, especially those who wore larger sizes.

A good sweep might walk eight or nine miles in a shift. If you weren't in good shape to start, you soon would be—or you would be offered another position. Sweeps were assigned to specific zones and while they were often moved about short term to wherever they were needed, they were encouraged to develop ownership of their zone. It was home base, their base. They came to know it well. The tools of their trade were a small broom and a metal dustpan, also a pair of metal tongs. One of the trademark sounds of the Cedar Point midway was the clang of a dustpan hitting the concrete on the midway. You worked outside your entire shift, no matter the weather. Good sweeps were always on the move, which helped on cold and windy days and nights. They did more than keep the midway clean. They cleaned the midway plaques, knocked down spider webs from light fixtures, climbed into landscaping to get trash from behind bushes, and they were the ones tasked with cleaning bodily fluids, primarily vomit, which occasionally found their way onto the midway.

They were also expected to be mobile information centers. Sweeps interacted with guests a great deal, usually answering questions about the location of rides and attractions but also where to get candy apples or Cedar Point Fries or a certain kind of T-shirt or simply what time it was. Their primary job was keeping the midway clean, but the best ones were great ambassadors for the park.

I had great respect for sweeps. I always greeted them on the midway.

I always carried a pen and a notebook with me. I made short notes on every midway walk. Most managers and supervisors did the same. Some notes were frivolous: I used to copy down what I thought were particularly clever or humorous T-shirt phrases. I can't remember them now (I wish I could, however, because some of them were quite good). Some notes were notes of serious self-inspiration. But most were the amusement park version of the "to do" list. I looked for anything I thought didn't look or feel right. A good GM has to have at least an average "eye" for things out of whack: trash, backed up ride queues, the train station clock displaying the wrong time, employees missing name tags, midway signage in the wrong place, sound system problems, trash cans in the wrong places, burned out lights just about anywhere (a pet peeve of Matt Ouimet, the CEO my last two seasons). I did not have the best GM eye in the company, but I think I was competent.

I did many midway walks alone, as did Dick Kinzel, Don Miears (GM of Cedar Point 1994 – 2000), and Larry MacKenzie (the GM of Valleyfair for many years) among others. I liked the time to think and to go wherever I wanted in the park. Other GM's liked to have companions and would conduct walking meetings with one or more staff members. Dan Keller, GM of Cedar Point 2001 – 2004, liked to conduct roving staff meetings on Saturday afternoons, theoretically the busiest time of the week. He invited all his direct reports to meet him at the flag pole in front of the park at a specific time. Attendance was not mandatory, and we were all free to come and go as the need arose, but most of us reported to the flagpole.

The tour/meeting would cover most of the park and last up to three hours. We drew a few gawks and stares from guests: seven or eight men and women (all the men wearing ties) in a scrum coming down the midway. We were quite a sight. Discussion covered a wide range of subjects, but most had an operational focus. We also played what-if games in terms of new rides or attractions. Dan would stop and point out an area and ask us what we thought its future might be. What might work better than what was there now?

I thought it was a worthwhile exercise.

Of course, you are never alone on the Cedar Point midway. In the time I was a GM I always carried a radio and a cell phone. The main thing I did with the radio was listen. I used the phone to talk.

When I started at Cedar Point in 1974 there were land lines and there were pagers (roughly the size of an iPhone but with the thickness of a good ham sandwich). Pagers were ubiquitous. Most managers and supervisors were authorized to carry one. You got a signal followed by a beep, then a number flashed on a tiny screen, and you went in search of a land line to return the call. Land lines were ubiquitous, too. Every ride, every food stand, every store, every out of the way building had at least one phone. This was by design. It was of immense help when you got paged on the midway. You knew you could duck into the closest food stand or gift shop and return the call.

Cedar Point Police and Safety operated with radios, as did their counterparts outside the park.

In the late 1970s, hand-held radios began to pop up everywhere in the park. It started in Park Operations, then spread to Foods, Merchandise, Traffic (parking lot), Admissions, Maintenance, even to Marketing. Each group had its own channel and its own system of signals and codes. Staff members had a number, usually but not always based on seniority or rank within the division, so that a typical exchange might go:

"One to four . . ."

"One, go . . ."

"Four, please get another sweep to the area in front of Millennium Force. It's looking bad here."

"Will do."

"One, clear . . . "

"Four, clear . . . "

The catalog of signals for a variety of situations was long. Park Operations had 37 signals covering everything from a guest getting ill on a ride to ride down for maintenance to call me immediately. I memorized most of them, but I took no chances and always a carried in my shirt pocket a laminated card with all the signals.

The benefits of radios were immediate and direct. If you are the division head, you can listen to all the chatter on the channel and know pretty much what's going on in your area in real time. It's a huge benefit. You can also address everyone in your management group at the same time. Radios could be a dangerous tool in the hands of a micro-manager. It was now very easy, at times too easy, in my opinion, to insert yourself into every decision. Pagers forced a certain amount of decision-making down because sometimes it was impossible to locate your boss in the time you had to make a decision. But there was no going back. Radios were here to stay.

Radios were a status indicator, like the color of your name badge or where you were authorized to park your car. Everyone wanted one, even though they hung on your belt with the weight of metal hammer. Females devised lots of creative ways to carry their radios.

Division heads carried the Cadillac of radios, those with multiple channels.

In my Marketing days I seldom carried a radio. There just wasn't the need. In fact, I resisted wearing one. That changed when I became a GM. I had to know what was going on in the park and the best way to do that was to listen to the Park Operations channel. It allowed you to know the operational status of every ride, any weather updates, any cleanliness issues, and any park-wide emergencies. When I was on the midway, I almost always listened to the Park Operations channel. Even if I was alone in my office it was always on in the background.

The radio chatter was almost constant. Marcia Frankart was the voice of Park Operations the years I was a GM, and very good at managing the Park Op channel. Her voice was distinctive and had a touch of attitude when needed. I liked it. It cut through the air like Sherman through Georgia.

So, I listened mostly, and then followed up with a phone call when I needed to talk to someone. All my direct reports carried cell phones. It was easier and better to talk on the phone than on the radio, even allowing for the privacy issue. My biggest phone problem on the midway was hearing the person on the other end of the call. The Cedar Point midway is a noisy place, the main midway especially. It's a cacophony of sound. It is the sound that creates such great positive energy, but it is the enemy of two-way conversation. I should have worn an earpiece, but I didn't.

Anxiety? Anxiety is when you get a call from your boss in California, specifically Jack Falfas, and the connection is not all that great and Jack is known to mumble a bit and he is speaking from a midway at Knott's Berry Farm with its own sound issues and you are walking past the Raptor. At best, you get every fifth word. But you can't risk pretending you know what he's saying. We managed a serious business.

The first option:

"Jack, I'm under the Raptor. I can't hear you very well." Hopefully, he repeats to you what was important.

The second option:

"Jack, please repeat. I can't hear you very well." Hopefully, Jack repeats again. But you can hear the frustration in his voice.

Do you try one more time?

The other cell phone issue was light. Possibly by the time you read this Apple or Samsung will have solved the problem of looking at phone screens in bright sunlight and seeing nothing but sun spots or a Jason Pollok painting. Vast riches await the person who figures this out.

## Engine House

At the end of the main midway, where the path diverges, one path continuing under the Corkscrew to Top Thrill Dragster and the other continuing past the Iron Dragon, the Cedar Point & Lake Erie Railroad (CP&LE), to Millennium Force, I would have to make a decision. Sometimes there was a specific reason to go one way or another, other times it was just whim. Looking back, I probably walked toward Millennium Force more often than toward Top Thrill.

I often stopped at the CP&LE Railroad engine house. I took a back way in between the restrooms and the Wildcat. Once inside I was in a unique world, almost a return to the 19th century. It smelled wonderful: soot and steel, wood and grease, coal dust and dirt.

Randy Catri ran the CP&LE. He was the superintendent. A big man with dark hair and a rambling gait, we were close in age and he liked it that I had known Mike Hetrick, his predecessor. His face was clean but little else. It was impossible to work on steam trains and stay clean. He was very safety conscious. He and his guys handled lots of different tools that had the potential to hurt people in horrible ways if used improperly. They worked with fire. They worked with steam. Boilers were unforgiving things. Randy kept a picture on the engine house bulletin board of the four men killed at a fair in Ohio in the 1990s when the boiler on their antique farm tractor exploded.

Randy always seized the opportunity to use one of my impromptu visits to lobby me for something, and the something usually involved spending money. He was not going to let an opportunity to go one-on-one with the boss get away from him. I respected him for that. His pitches were calm and rational, never any doomsday stuff, and never on behalf of anything wacky. He might want the go-ahead to use some part-time hours to replace railroad ties in the fall rather than waiting until the spring when his crew was busy getting the locomotives ready to go. He might want approval to get more painting done on the passenger cars.

His staff was unique. They wore coveralls and engineer scarves and caps and were as dirty as Randy was, probably worse, since they worked in the cab and shoveled coal.

There was always at least one locomotive in the shop. The locomotives were narrow gauge size but seemed enormous resting indoors. They filled the building, huge animals asleep.

One of the great perks—I certainly thought of it as a perk—the GM of Cedar Point enjoyed was that just about any time you got the inclination you could wander down to the engine house and climb aboard a genuine steam-powered locomotive and go for a ride. Much of the time I chose to ride in the cab with the engineer and the fireman. I had to be careful where I put my hands, as the risk of getting burned was real. You are surrounded by hot metal, steam, fire. The fireman would often shovel coal into the boiler just a foot or two from my feet. I did my best not to brush against things, but often I got off with soot on my pants or shirt. I enjoyed talking to the engineer on the ride to Frontier Town.

I asked lots of questions about what the gauges meant, how to read them properly. They were always happy to answer my questions. The train guys were a brotherhood; they watched out for one another. The train thing got into your blood. Most of them worked three or four summers for the park, several worked five or six. It was the work, the chance to be around working trains that brought them back along with the camaraderie. The engineers were a tight group.

The view from the fireman's seat going out to Frontier Town was spectacular: Sandusky Bay. Sometimes it was as still as a farm pond at sunset and empty of boats; other times it was a froth. On summer weekend afternoons there were boats everywhere, all shapes and sizes. Occasionally you'd see a big lake freighter, 800 or 1,000 feet in length, moving through Moseley Channel headed to the coal docks on the west side of Sandusky, several miles to the southwest.

From the cab perspective, the track was not as straight and true as you would expect. The locomotive rattled and rocked on the rails (they were not a product of CAD).

The best fun—and it was little kid fun, pure and simple—was the chance to pull the cord and blow the whistle. The engineer always asked me if I wanted to do it and I always said yes. Each train whistle was unique. The railroad guys had no trouble matching whistles to locomotives. I could not do it. I was a great feeling of power to pull the cord and hear the screech. It was like the locomotive was talking to the guests waiting at the Frontier Town Station: "Here I am. I'm coming. I'm big and I'm beautiful."

Depending on where I wanted to go next or how much time I had, I would either get off the train in Frontier Town or stay aboard and ride back through our Wild West town, called Boneville, populated by about 50 animated skeletons (mostly human). Not much changed in Boneville in my 40 seasons with the park. I don't think many of our guests expected or wanted to see much change in Boneville. They liked it just the way it was. So did the inhabitants.

If I was doing the full midway tour, I stayed on the train and rode it back to the main station, blowing the whistle, ringing the bell, and waving to guests as the train pulled into the station. When I got off the cab, I walked back through the engine house and thanked Randy for the ride.

There are three spots in the park where the train crosses the midway. At these locations all that separates the guest from several thousand pounds of moving steel (albeit slowly moving steel) is eight or ten feet and two sets of wooden gates. At each location, one near the main station, one near the entrance to Mean Streak, and the other where the Gemini midway crosses over into Frontier Town, we stationed an employee whose job it was to verbally announce to the guests the train was coming and to make sure they remained beyond the yellow line on the midway, and to make sure the gates did indeed come down.

It was a minor inconvenience for park guests but especially on busy days guests would get antsy and some would step very close to the gates. The employee at the crossing was trained not to allow it and to get on his microphone and walk people back. It was my job, too, if I was there. The worst offenders were teenage boys. I would motion them back and usually, but not always, they would comply. There were times when I felt like yelling at them, but I never did. When I had to, I used my eyes and my GM voice to move them back.

## Too Big to Ride

After the crossing near the main station, the midway opens into a plaza before continuing as the Frontier Trail. The plaza always hummed because of the nearby entrance and exit to Millennium Force. I used to watch our employees greet guests at the entrance to Millennium Force. They measured guests to make sure they met the height requirement, which was 48 inches. They turned away guests who attempted to bring backpacks, basketballs, or other large objects onto the ride and directed them to put the items in a locker or to give to a friend to hold. This never went down well with guests but was essential for the safe operation of the ride.

An even bigger issue with guests was the suggestion by one of our employees that they should try out the test seat next to the ride entrance to make sure they could ride safely. Millennium Force, the world's greatest roller coaster, was not perfect: it was not designed for large people. What this meant in practical terms was that riders who were large, especially through the waist and thighs, but not necessarily obese, could not ride. Height and weight did not automatically rule a rider in, or out; rather it was how the weight was distributed, and its density, that made the critical difference. The ride manufacturer designed the ride to accommodate most people, sacrificing those under 48 inches and those at the other end of the spectrum who were too big, either too tall or too heavy.

The test seat was located a few feet from the ride entrance, in plain, public view. Some potential riders were clearly uncomfortable with being singled out by their size and did not look happy getting into the test seat. Others, I think, appreciated it that we gave them the option of finding out now, versus after a 90-minute wait in line, if they could safely ride, or not. The make or break was the seatbelt. Maintenance went to great lengths to make sure the seatbelt used on the test seat was exactly the same length as the seatbelts on the ride. The length of the belt was determined by the manufacturer. The maintenance staff measured all the belts at least once a week and adjusted accordingly. Slight variation did occur because of stretching, UV light, humidity. What we wanted to avoid was a situation where a guest fit on the test seat but not in an actual seat. That was a bad situation for both the park and the guest. It happened, but very rarely.

Much more common was the situation where a guest assumed they would fit, passed on the test seat, and then discovered in the station they did not fit.

"I was able to ride last year" was a common statement. Perhaps the 10-12 pounds they gained over the winter was just enough to disqualify them from riding. Another was that they had ridden similar rides at other parks. Our ride operators did everything they could to fit guests into the seats. They pulled hard on the seatbelt straps; they advised the guest on how best to sit in the seat. But many times on every operating day guests would be forced to get out of the train and walk off the ride in full view of hundreds of other guests waiting to ride. No fun for anyone.

One of the things I wanted to do was quantify the impact of "too big to ride" on total ridership of the park but especially on major coasters like Millennium Force, Top Thrill Dragster, and Raptor. I do not recall the specific data points now, but I remember it was a significant number. Potentially, Cedar Point was losing tens of thousands of visits every year because many large guests could not safely ride many of our best rides.

We communicated all this information to the major ride manufacturers. They were sympathetic—up to a point—but acknowledged there was little that could be done in terms of modifying existing rides. Several indicated they would try to accommodate larger guests in new rides. All agreed it was in everyone's best interests to accommodate as many physical types as practical.

Some guests got very upset when they couldn't ride Millennium Force. They berated the ride operators or the supervisor or manager they ended up talking with. A handful of times I approved a refund for large guests who convinced me they had only come to the park to ride the signature rides and wanted to leave the park when they discovered they could not. If this happened shortly after opening, I was much more likely to honor the request.

Other guests took a different approach. My first year as GM I had to deal with a very angry airline pilot who had flown up from Houston, Texas, with his adult daughter (mid 20s) to do a two-day father/daughter coaster trip. The daughter had been turned away from Raptor, Millennium Force, and Top Thrill Dragster and had experienced the walk of shame on two of them. She was mortified, in tears, and her father, as any father would be, was ready to go to war for his daughter. He took his issue up the chain until he got to me. We talked a long time on the midway in front of the Coliseum. He was a tall man, I recall, with close-cropped white hair. He looked to be in his late 40s or early 50s. His daughter hung back a little and let him do the talking. She was tall as well, but her torso and the Millennium Force seat were not compatible. Ultimately, he understood our position: we are bound by state law to operate the rides as the manufacturer dictates; guest safety is our prime concern. He understood, but he still didn't like it. He had made a significant investment in time, money and heart in this trip, all for his daughter, and he felt cheated. I sensed there was an interesting backstory to their visit, but I didn't pursue it.

About a year later, the same man and his daughter stopped me on the midway. As soon as he said, "I'm the pilot from Texas—we talked last year when my daughter couldn't ride your big rides," I knew who he was. His daughter was with him. He was smiling (they both were smiling), so I was pretty sure she had ridden Top Thrill Dragster and Millennium Force.

The pilot explained to me that when they got home to Texas his daughter decided she was going to lose enough weight so that she would be able to ride the big rides. She joined a gym. She went on a weight loss program. She changed her life. They told me that a return trip to Cedar Point was her motivation. She pinned up pictures of Millennium Force and Top Thrill Dragster in her cubicle at work and in her apartment. She didn't volunteer how much weight she'd lost—and I didn't ask—but whatever it was it was enough that her body changed enough to allow her to ride.

And ride they did. For the next several minutes I listened to the recap of their riding adventures. I was genuinely happy for them. Sometimes, life just works out for the best. I thanked them for coming back to the park.

It was mid-summer, a busy day in the park. Lines for the big rides were probably 90 minutes. I offered to get them immediate boarding on any three coasters of their choice. They acted like they had just won the lottery.

That all happened nearly 15 years ago. I wonder if they still visit Cedar Point.

Being able to ride the coasters at Cedar Point as a successful weight loss motivator is not uncommon. The Rides staff all have stories to tell like the pilot and his daughter. Millennium Force is indeed a force.

## Millennium Force

When I visited the platform of Millennium Force I often went in behind Panda Express, walking underneath the ride toward the steps that led to the platform and entrance queues for the trains. I would occasionally pass a guest, almost always alone, who was coming from the platform and headed toward the regular exit. They were on this path for one of two reasons: they could not fit on the ride, or they had succumbed to fear and could not make themselves get in the coaster train. Sometimes it was obvious which reason it was, sometimes not. I sympathized with them either way.

The view of the first hill is spectacular from the small platform just outside the back of the station. I would sometimes stand there for several minutes and marvel at the structure, Sandusky Bay in the background, the train popping out of the station and engaging on the lift hill. I listened for the sound of the catch car as it slid back down from over 300 feet above and got into position to engage the next train.

There was just enough space to stand in front of the queue for the first row. We allowed guests who wished to ride in the first row the option of standing in a separate line. It was a longer wait, but in my opinion well worth it. I took the opportunity to talk to guests waiting for the front row. Usually, they were eager to talk. Although they skewed young (under 30), there was a wide age range overall. Most were from our traditional marketing areas, but some were from more exotic places like Rapid City, South Dakota or Spartanburg, South Carolina, or even Bristol, England. There were a lot of first-time riders who were in the company of a ride veteran who served as a kind of ride sponsor or guardian, talking the ride experience up but at the same time trying to keep the rookie relatively calm. When I talked to guests I was mostly in selling mode and congratulated them on the wisdom of investing their time in waiting for the first row because it was a much better ride experience (which it was). I sometimes joked that the ride gives over a million rides a year—how bad could it be? I asked how many other big coasters they had ridden, and what was their favorite? I would occasionally uncover an American Coaster Enthusiasts member who would then launch into a detailed review of his top 10 steelies, but most first row riders had ridden relatively few big coasters.

On warm days, the station smelled of sweat and sunscreen. The returning train as it flew past the station created its own gut punch of air followed by the sound of vibrating steel screens in the station. It announced itself with fury.

At night it was flashing lights and flashing faces, the reoccurring metallic sounds created by the action of the ride, the loud (by design) techno soundtrack that cut through everything. It still plays in my head sometimes.

I usually ducked into the control booth before I left. The sound level was much less, and the AC was most welcome. I nodded to the operator and watched him or her work, making the announcements in the station, working the control buttons, launching a couple thousand pounds of steel and 36 human beings up a 310-foot hill. I checked the

DOR (Daily Operational Report), which recorded ride downtime on an ongoing basis with a code for the reason for the downtime. The DOR also recorded the number of rides given every hour of operation. I had a good feel for what were good numbers and what were bad numbers. If numbers were good, I said something to the team leader and thanked them for their efforts. I looked around to see how the crew had personalized the control booth. There was usually a small bulletin board full of call-outs for crew birthdays, personal notes to one another, pictures, and crew performance awards. Lots of stuff on the walls was an almost sure indicator of a good crew.

## The Red Garter

When I exited the ride, I turned left and headed to the Red Garter Saloon, the start of the Frontier Trail. The Garter was the most seriously themed building at Cedar Point. I used to tell people that with little change to the interior you could film a Western movie in the Garter. It had it all: long wooden bar with a mural featuring a frontier era canal boat; a tin ceiling, western-style tables and chairs; wood floor, one big room open to a second-floor balcony on one side and row of rooms on the other; lots of themed objects like the heating stove by the front door; antique lighting fixtures. There were two staircases, one in front which led to the balcony and a second just behind and to the right of the stage. The second staircase was used by the cast during performances. The bartenders and servers wore period costumes. It was a small venue, including the balcony, which meant on busy days a standing room crowd gathered just inside the door and along the bar.

The Red Garter had a substantial pass-through crowd, guests who would hear the music on the Trail and decide to pop in to see what was going on. They stood in the back for a song or two, then headed back to the Trail.

The Garter opened in 1971, so it has had a long history and has been home to a variety of musical acts from Dixieland bands to both traditional and new country bands, to straight rock and roll. In my years as GM it seemed to rotate between new country and rock. Acts were usually four or five singers/dancers plus three or four musicians. The music was live, a great virtue in the eyes of Jack Aldrich, director of park attractions, and Marje Rody, manager of live entertainment (and me). Many other theme parks used recorded music for most of their shows. It was cheaper than hiring musicians.

The performers were all young, mostly in their late teens or early 20s; some were cruise ship veterans and a little older. Many came from musical theater departments from colleges in the Midwest and the Middle Atlantic states.

The servers were mostly college students since we served beer at the Garter. For two seasons our goddaughter, Cynthia Greene Ragona, worked there as a server while she attended college.

The room was not really designed for the audio level produced by most Garter shows. Outside it was beckoning; inside it sometimes drove you back outside. I often told Live Entertainment the sound was too hot and we ran the risk of driving guests away, but my comments were mostly ignored. But with a smile.

My routine was to stand by the back of the bar to watch the performance. The bartenders always offered me a cup of water, which I always accepted. By mid-season, I knew the song progression very well and knew if I wanted to stay longer or make a polite exit.

I was no great judge of musical talent or performance. I did not appreciate the nuances. In fact, I did not know what the nuances were. I can remember sitting in the Garter in pre-season rehearsals with Marje Rody, and later with Charles Bradshaw and Lisa Jones (her successors following her retirement in 2009), watching them take notes and conferring together in whispers. Afterward, they would apologetically comment on all the things the performers did wrong and explain how they were going to fix the problems. Problems? What problems? I thought the kids were fantastic and ready to go.

The choice of what type of show or music to feature in any given venue in any given season was partly political. Not always, but sometimes. The available range was broad in theory—there is a lot of musical space in between the Rolling Stones and Lawrence Welk—but senior management had musical likes and dislikes, as all of us do. As I remember, Dick Kinzel liked beach music, Dixieland, early rock and roll, movie and TV show themes, and some traditional country. Jack Falfas liked Broadway, pop, traditional rock and country, and 1960s rock, including Janis Joplin (Jack had met her at a concert at West Virginia University). Don Miears, who was GM of the park in the mid to late '90s, liked country. Me? I liked classic rock, new country, folk rock, and pop. I was always looking for an excuse to suggest a Bob Dylan song, but I don't think Bob ever made the cut at the Red Garter.

We are all in danger of thinking the rest of the world, including visitors to Cedar Point, share our musical tastes. They do not. Basic musical identity is usually set by ages 18-20 and doesn't change much after that. Nothing wrong with that, of course, you just need to be aware of it in trying to match music and audiences.

I confess I am in awe of musical talent. I have none myself. Still, I love music very much and have very specific, and eclectic, musical likes and dislikes. I sneaked in a few favorites every year.

For HalloWeekends, we covered the Garter in Halloween theming. It looked weird to me—Wyatt Earp meets Frankenstein—but it worked, and the guests seemed to like it fine. We put together a special show for HalloWeekends each year, which naturally gravitated to heavy metal and dark rock. Loud, too. The performers were costumed and made up appropriately.

## Frontier Trail

A right turn out of the Garter put me on Frontier Trail. The Trail opened in 1971, primarily the brainchild of George Roose. His vision was a unique guest experience: a trip back to frontier America by seeing how craftspeople of the time—blacksmiths, potters, woodcarvers, candle makers, glassblowers—created the necessities of life in late 18th and early 19th century America. Craftspeople worked in barns and cabins along the Trail. Several cabins date back to the 1820s and were purchased in southern Ohio and relocated to Cedar Point. The Trail also contains a replica of Fort Sandusky, a Colonial era fort which was burned to the ground in the Pontiac Conspiracy in 1763. There is also a working gristmill purchased in North Carolina and brought to Cedar Point. Carved out of thick woods, the Trail was quiet, peaceful, and beautiful.

However, it was far from an immersive 18th century experience. It was in an amusement park. There was a petting farm for kids, a candy shop, a glass-blowing theater with an attached gift shop, a few frontier-themed food stands, and wandering music groups.

At the western terminus of the Trail, when it opened in 1971, just before the bridge that led into Frontier Town, was a wooden building called the Paddock, which was divided up into stalls for visiting craftspeople. In 1986, the Paddock was razed, and Thunder Canyon was built on the spot.

Guest interest in the Trail as an attraction peaked in the early 1970s, in the years just after it opened. I believe there were several flaws in the concept of the Trail, the biggest being that the majority of park guests came to ride rides and see shows and were really not interested in getting educated about frontier America. Cedar Point was not Colonial Williamsburg. There was also no way to really measure its success as an attraction. There was no gate, no turnstile, and no separate admission fee. Until the Gemini midway opened in 1978, the Frontier Trail was the only pedestrian access to Frontier Town. There was no practical way to separate the Trail-goers from those guests who were on a mission to get to the Cedar Creek Mine Ride.

The appeal of the Trail skewed old. Go to your local crafts festival and you'll know what I mean. You will also see families with young kids at crafts and arts festivals. However, the kids at crafts festivals live in a closed universe; there is no competition from roller coasters. Put the kids at Cedar Point, where they have the option of riding the Blue Streak—or watching a glass blower—and the history lessons don't stand a chance.

People don't come to Cedar Point to buy things. Buying stuff happens, but it's a sidelight. They come to be entertained. They certainly don't come to Cedar Point to buy high end crafts. In the mid-'70s the merchandise and games division organized a week-long event in July for visiting craftspeople. We marketed it as a promotional event. It was a great show, attracting top level talent. The Trail was transformed with everything from dulcimer-making to quilting and portraiture. I remember walking the Trail and being quite impressed. I also remember interviewing some of the craftspeople to help publicize future events and hearing first hand that they hadn't sold much and likely wouldn't be back.

I think over the many seasons we all accepted that the Trail would never be much of an attendance-builder or a revenue-producer, but it would always be a part of Cedar Point. Employees had great affection for it. Guests, too. It was emotional space to many, including me. Over the years, the Frontier Trail had surrendered much of its physical charm. It started with Thunder Canyon in 1986. It continued with Millennium Force in 2000, which flew right above it and over it (twice), Shoot the Rapids in 2010, and other construction.

In 2009, we draped much of the Trail in LED lights and electrical illuminations of various kinds for a nighttime experience, complete with sound and music, we called "Starlight Experience," an attraction we hoped would boost nighttime attendance at the park. The visual effect was quite impressive, but LED meets mountain dulcimer is just not right. Same with Asian food in the former home of Aunt Em's, which originally featured freshly made pies. And of course, the "family dryer" unit next door to Grist Mill Refreshments (now Frontier Fold-overs).

Our first HalloWeekends Fright Zone was located along the middle section of the Trail, anchored by Fort Sandusky and the cabins. It worked very well. The trees and the other vegetation helped hold the fog and the many small buildings provided mystery and great scare angles for our Screamsters.

Even in my GM years there were nooks and crannies along the Trail where George Roose would have felt at home, places where the right look took you back to 1825. You just squeezed your eyes a little.

As the GM, I looked at the revenue numbers for the Trail every day, and there were few surprises. The revenue generated by Frontier

Trail paled in comparison to our midway stores. I never felt that Merchandise gave up on the Trail. They kept trying new things, like a gold panning attraction for kids, and bringing in concessionaries to sell leather goods and house signs.

I liked to drive the Trail in the off-season. In the fall, I would occasionally stop and get out of my car and take a picture of the Blacksmith Shop, or one of the other cabins, enveloped by yellow and red leaves, looking, in the camera's eye, like it was 1825 and a young Abraham Lincoln was indoors by the fireplace. It could be even more beautiful after the leaves were gone and were replaced by snow.

I got to know several craftspeople over the years. Two stand out. The first was Granny Weatherall, better known as just Granny, whose hook was spinning dog hair into yarn. It was a good gig. Granny was from West Virginia and in her frontier costume and dry drawl she both looked and sounded the part. Her age was anyone's guess; mine was early 70s (in the mid-1970s). She taught spinning at the state prison for women in West Virginia. I never knew how she developed the practice of spinning dog hair into bags, sweaters, hats and jackets. It always raised eyebrows, though approached logically it shouldn't have. Her favorite breed for spinning was Samoyed. This breed was from Russia and was used mainly in Siberia for herding and occasionally pulling sleds. Its coat had two layers of thick, soft, white hair.

Granny was a talker. Her famous opening line: "You ain't spinning yarn if you're not spinning a yarn." She loved to talk to people, including the press, and always provided good copy. The PR staff took her on the road quite a bit, and she represented the park well. TV loved her. Granny was a natural storyteller. She loved the attention.

My wife, Marie, enjoyed talking with her quite a bit and missed her when she left the park after the 1977 season.

My other Trail buddy was Paul Koerner, a woodcarver. When I did my rounds as GM I always stopped by the Woodworking Shop to say hello. Paul was one of the friendliest men I have ever met. Not a back-slapper, not a born storyteller, not overtly gregarious, he won people over with a soft smile, an easy way of talking, a pleasant face, and the rare quality of making you feel like you always have one hundred percent of his attention.

He is a first-rate carver and always had a long backlog of commissioned pieces, many of them carousel horses. At the park, he also did a good business in carved and painted replicas of Cedar Point rides. These small, representational pieces retailed under $50 and thus had a chance to sell. His trick was to work on one of his larger commission pieces out on the porch to draw people in. While he talked to mom and dad, junior was free to wander the shop. More often the kid or kids would find something to buy. It was a good strategy.

Paul talked to everyone, guest and employee. He knew what was going on.

## Frontier Town

A beautiful stone bridge connects the Frontier Trail to Frontier Town, Cedar Point's only real themed area. In my mind, Dinosaurs Alive on Adventure Island, Frontier Trail, Camp Snoopy, and Planet Snoopy are too small to qualify as themed areas and are attractions rather than areas. Frontier Town, as the name implies, is Western themed, circa 1870s or 1880s. I have no insight into why that theme was chosen for the expansion of the park, which began in 1967. However, the Western theme is relatively easy to execute. There were lots of successful models around, including Ghost Town at Knott's Berry Farm and Frontier Land at Disneyland. The look of Frontier Town begins and ends with the building façades which run from the train station to the Palace Theater to the Jitney Arcade and the Trading Post. The visual is Old West, reinforced by a thousand TV shows, movies, and book covers.

## Town Hall Museum

The bridge over the lagoon connecting the Trail to Frontier Town was one of the crossroads of the park. On one side the Maverick trains flew by just over the lagoon, air jets shooting water into the air pop-pop-pop. On the opposite side the boats from Snake River Falls came thundering down and sent a wall of water over the exit bridge soaking whoever was standing there. Depending on the strength and the direction of the wind, the over spray might get you a little wet crossing the stone bridge. The day Snake River Falls opened in 1993 our carpenters were still nailing up safety signage in the station as the ride opening ceremonies began. It was our tightest fit. All the VIP riders were given blue rain ponchos to wear. They all wore them. They all got wet. I rode in the second row, sitting next to our Sandusky City Manager, Frank Link. We got wet, too.

After crossing the bridge, I usually walked into the Town Hall Museum. The doors were open and inviting. On hot days, the cool air was welcome. The water fountain near the front entrance had some of the coldest water in the park. On busy days, there was a line.

Not much changed in the Town Hall Museum year to year. It opened in 1968, along with most of Frontier Town. It was designed as a museum of mostly 19th century objects: antique fire-fighting equipment, the façade of a drug store, ship models, and farm implements. Over the years the park had added vintage arcade games, a major display of Cedar Point memorabilia, a gigantic hand carved wooden clock made by a local Sandusky man named Steinle, and a display case with the park's Golden Ticket Awards. Created by Amusement Today and patterned after the Academy Awards, the Golden Ticket recognizes excellence in the amusement park industry, both nationally and internationally. Awards are voted on annually by a select group of knowledgeable park-goers. Over the years Cedar Point had been voted a Golden Ticket in several different categories, from Best Steel Coaster to Best Games Area to Best Park, and in some categories we had received the award many times. Cedar Point employees were very proud of their Golden Ticket Awards, especially since they were peer awards, voted by people who knew the park business.

The Cedar Point history exhibit in Town Hall was the creation of the late Tom Layton, who started working at the park in the 1960s as a sign painter and restoration artist. He left in 1978 to work full time doing carousel horse restoration. Our time at the park overlapped for only four years, and Tom was more than 20 years my senior, but we shared a passion for the park's history and became good friends.

Tall and thin, strong, with a drooping moustache, he had been given a full allotment of the artistic temperament. He fiercely loved wooden carousel horses, his "ponies," as he called them, and the carousels themselves. His commitment was total, and it showed in the quality of his work. He believed strongly that carousels should never be broken up and the individual horses sold, as often happened as individual horses increased in value, recognized as magnificent examples American folk art. Wooden carrousel restoration is a specialty business, a feast and famine way of life. In the 1990s Tom and his wife moved from Sandusky to Arizona to be closer to family. I saw him occasionally when he came back to Sandusky to visit; he was in a wheelchair the last time I remember seeing him at the park. He of course did an inspection of our carousels (and we got a passing grade). I talked to him about a week before he died. He had made his peace and had come home from the hospital to be with family and call old friends. I was one of them. His voice was still strong, and we talked of many things.

## Stan the Man

The entrance to Skyhawk was only several yards from the Town Hall Museum. Like a lot of other rides, it was based off a simple design: it was essentially a giant mechanical swing, although a swing

103 feet high with the capacity for hundreds of rides per hour and powered by a pneumatic system. I thought it was a pretty thrilling ride and a good addition to the park when it opened in 2006. Stan Checketts, the owner of S&S Power, the Utah company that designed and manufactured the ride, attended media day ceremonies for Skyhawk. It was not Millennium Force or Magnum, but we had a good media turn out. I knew there was no way I could get out of riding Skyhawk, especially with Stan there. Checketts was an interesting guy, the closest thing to a true wild man within the small fraternity of ride designers and manufacturers.

He took risks in everything he did: snowmobiles, ATV's, motorcycles, pickup trucks, cars. He lived and worked in Utah.

Stan was no kid, white-haired and probably in his late 50s or early 60s when I knew him. He and his company had built Power Tower at Cedar Point in 1998, a 300-foot tower with both a take-you-up and a shoot-you-down option (the shoot-you-down option was the most frightening experience in the park, in my opinion). As part of the effort to help publicize the ride in its inaugural year, Stan had volunteered to stand at the top of the tower, anchored only by straps around his shoes, and wave to the camera. We took him up on his offer. It went off without a hitch and the picture ran everywhere. It was a very big deal from a publicity perspective. Stan was a willing and able marketing partner—I had to give him that. He understood the need for promotion.

On Media Day 2006, after the speeches and the ribbon-cutting, I found myself seated next to Stan getting ready for my first ride on Skyhawk. I had watched it being built and had seen others ride it during the testing period, so I knew what to expect. Sort of. Nothing quite like the real thing.

The ride experience, especially at the apex of swing, either forward or backward, at a height of 125 feet, was a great combination of exhilaration and terror. My hands had a death grip on the bar, but Stan had both his arms and his legs sticking straight out so the only thing touching the seat was his skinny butt. He kept telling me: "This is how the kids like to ride!" Well, screw them all, Stan included, I was holding onto the bar.

Skyhawk is a relatively short ride. I survived. I had to admit, after I got off, that it was an excellent ride experience and would do well for the park. Good screams.

On bright sunny days I used to station myself against the fence in front of the ride and watch the individual swings soar up over me until they reached near vertical. They looked magical with the deep blue sky behind them.

## Toilet Time

I always looked in on the men's restroom beneath the old entrance to the Frontier Lift and next door to Skyhawk. It was the largest restroom in Frontier Town and the only one with changing stalls for guests coming off Snake River Falls. The floor was almost always wet, especially on warm summer days.

My eyes always went to the floor, looking for white, for paper. As much as we had a love/hate relationship with our brown paper towels, and the fact that many in front-line management preferred one hundred per cent air drying for washing hands, you had to have white toilet paper in the stalls. No one expects to wipe his ass with brown toilet paper. By design, the amount of space between floor and partition was considerable. You had enough privacy, but not too much. Paper on the floor was easily seen by both guests and employees. Nothing looks worse than a lot of white toilet paper on the floor in one or more stalls. If I saw any, I investigated. Much of the time the toilet just needed a flush, which I made happen with my foot to avoid having to touch anything. If it looked like a true plumbing problem, I called Park Services or Maintenance, so they could take care of the situation.

The motion-activated automatic flush is one of the great inventions in history; certainly if you are the GM of a large amusement park it is, or if you are responsible for restrooms at a ball park or other facility where large numbers of people gather for a significant period of time. As great as they are, they don't, as they say, "get everything." You still must clean the toilets. At Cedar Point, our restrooms were set up at several different levels, mainly depending on when they had been built. The newest had hot water, automatic flushing, non-slip floors, the latest in towel-dispensing equipment, more effective hand dryers, bright lights, automatic systems for dispensing soap and water in sinks, and larger mirrors.

Using automated hand dryers goes back decades. The pitch is based on two main benefits: less paper to deal with, both logistically and monetarily, and better hygiene (fewer germs). There are lots of studies—I assume industry sponsored (though I do not doubt their results)—which show clear benefits in terms of cutting down on germs. However, there are also studies—also industry sponsored, I'm sure—which point out that the air blasting out of the hand dryer does a pretty good job of spraying some nasty germs into the local atmosphere.

Some automated hand dryers come with a noise that rivals a fighter jet at takeoff. I hate them.

From the guest perspective—are the bathrooms clean? —the first deal-breaker was paper on the floor. The second was fecal matter and paper floating around in unflushed toilets. The third was smell. A restroom can go bad in a matter of minutes. It can be shiny and clean with a spotless floor and gleaming sinks, and then someone forgets to flush or misses the garbage bin with some paper towels and it crosses over the perception line to "dirty."

If a restroom had air conditioning, it made a huge difference. The restroom smelled better, felt better. One of the unique problems for restrooms at Cedar Point was the presence of muffleheads, especially from late May until early July. In appearance, they were the benign twin to the common mosquito. They did not bite and lived much shorter lives. They loved to fly around the lights in the ceiling, then die and cover toilet seats, sinks, and urinals. Most of our guests saw these creatures and mosquitos as one in the same.

Cleaning bathrooms is not fun. There is no glory in it. It is no one's first choice on a job application. Guests using public bathrooms consider those cleaning them to have no other job options. They avoid eye contact.

The key to clean bathrooms is a motivated staff—and having enough staff. In theory, every restroom in the park should be checked and evaluated every 15-20 minutes. That was our goal, allowing for the number of people in the park, the weather, and the time of day.

Many seasonal employees stated in job interviews that they would do any job but restrooms.

Our restroom staff was an interesting group: locals from Sandusky, international students, older folks. Some did it because they liked the fact they were doing something no one else wanted to do. Others were attracted by the hourly rate (restroom attendants got a premium). Some got talked into it by friends. The international kids did it to get extra hours.

I think our Park Services staff did a good job of recruiting and motivating the restroom staff. It was a tough job. Jack Baus and Dave Huff were the front-line managers of restrooms for most of my Cedar Point years. Their best motivating approach was ownership: this is your restroom. Also, that clean bathrooms were a critical part of the guest experience, and you were responsible for that part of the guest experience. You were important. You owned it, as much as any ride host on Top Thrill Dragster.

In the 1958 film comedy, "No Time for Sergeants," the late actor Andy Griffith, playing a hayseed Air Force recruit, is given the "critically important" job of cleaning the barracks latrine. The character believes what his sergeant has told him, not realizing he's the butt of a joke, and attacks the job with an over the top enthusiasm. When it comes time for inspection, the character smiles and salutes, simultaneously hitting a foot pedal which immediately lifts a line of a half dozen toilet seats up in a mock salute. The sergeant jumps back, startled. The audience roars. But there's a message: attitude is just about everything when it comes to cleaning toilets.

The Cedar Point award for motivation went to Jenn Andre, a Park Services area manager, who organized sleep-overs in some of the restrooms in the park just before the season started. The restroom crew brought blankets and pillows and air mattresses and had a party.

When I was a new GM at Cedar Point, only a few weeks on the job, I received a call from Candy Frankowski, who oversaw restrooms (and many other things) at the park. She offered to take me on a tour of every restroom in the park on a weekday in May. I accepted her offer. I admit it felt strange evaluating the cleanliness of female restrooms, even with Candy and crew guarding the entrance. She asked me to give each restroom a cleanliness grade on a 1-10 scale, doing my best to allow for age and equipment. She did the same. Then we compared notes. We were usually close. She took me through the mental checklist she used with each facility. I found the experience to be very educational. I learned things that day I used the rest of my career at Cedar Point.

## Mean Streak

It was still a walk to the Mean Streak, the most remote corner of the park, a solid 20-minute walk from the front gate (assuming no stops). I usually stopped at Maverick first. It had the highest ride platform in the park and offered a magnificent view looking west and southwest out over Sandusky Bay. The mid-summer sunsets were spectacular. The Maverick was a quiet coaster, unlike its next-door neighbor, Mean Streak, which was all about steel wheels on steel track creating on every ride the iconic roar of a big wooden coaster.

Maverick was all about electrical power, mostly hidden under the station, where it was needed to launch the train for the second half of the ride like a bullet fired from a gun.

The crew had to work fast in the Maverick station, especially in five train operation, so I seldom made much small talk with the crew.

On the Mean Streak platform, I saw more sunsets, also at a different angle.

Like the Blue Streak, the trains sat low in the station and the rider stepped down to get in his seat. This made it hard on the operators, who had to bend over and then reach down to do their safety check on the bar and then the belt. It was a job for young flexible men and women. Not me. In a one or two train operation there was enough time between launches that I could talk to the crew. They didn't see many visitors from management; they were off the pathway.

That changed dramatically in 2018 with the transformation of Mean Streak into Steel Vengeance. It has become a new ride. Some riders rank the ride experience equal or superior to Millennium Force.

## Back to the Midway

Then I was back in the flow of the midway. I entered the stream, which flowed in nearly every direction seemingly at will, confusing; but depending on where you were in the park and the time of day and the size of the crowd, there was a current, pulling you and directing you, in a specific way.

Inevitably, I would run into other full-time staff and we'd stop and talk. If I had written something down in my notebook that involved their area, we would talk about it, saving an email or a phone call when I returned to my office. Sometimes they would take me to see something that needed to be changed, like the location of a food cart; sometimes it was something to be added, such as a sign. Sometimes they would ask me questions I could not answer.

I crossed the tracks by the Gemini and headed upstream, toward the front gate, still a long walk away. I did not stop at Gemini as often as I did other coasters. I am not sure why. I had great affection for the ride, in part because of my family connection to it—our twin sons, Mike and Tom, had been born two days after it opened.

I could meander to the right and step into the world of Camp Snoopy and then the world of dinosaurs on Adventure Island. If I had the time, I did both. I liked doing both; children and dinosaurs inhabit the same alternative universe.

I wandered into stores and gift shops. I was not a merchant by training or inclination, but I had learned the basics of display from Don Miears, who headed up Merchandise and Games at Cedar Point for many years. It was a different kind of selling when you can hold in your hand a tangible object. I looked at how the merchandise was displayed, checked the floors for trash of any kind, made sure the glass windows and doors were clean and handprints nowhere to be seen. There was a core group of merchandise items available at any Cedar Point store, a few standard T-shirts, for example, but each store also had some items that were unique to that store.

No one wants to lug bags around all day. In my observation, mom and grandma get stuck carrying the bag with the GateKeeper or Snoopy T-shirts. (They often get stuck paying, too.) A place like Cedar Point is not a mall. People go there to ride rides, not to buy stuff, and I was always amazed at how much our guests managed to buy. The revenue leader each year was the T-shirt category. Hats were good, too.

I listened to the radio . . . constantly, it seemed. I foolishly didn't use an earphone, so I often missed things if I was in a noisy spot. However, if my number, Alpha One, was called, I almost always heard it, even in difficult surroundings. My theory is that your unconscious cuts in and rings the bell in your head. I usually carried my radio in my right hand; I did not like the bulk and the weight of the radio hanging from my belt.

I tended to be a walking contingency plan, especially if it were spring or fall or nighttime during the summer and I had a jacket with pockets: car keys, office key, pocket knife, two pens (always a back-up), sunglasses, lip balm, notebook, laminated cheat cards with radio call signs for managers and supervisors and other information, sanitary wipes or a small bottle of Purell or similar product, sunscreen, cell phone, hat (even on cloudy days), umbrella, breath mints, wallet, cash (at least $50, small bills), a supply (four or five copies) of the Park Guide and the Live Entertainment show schedule for my back pocket, name tag.

## Talking to Guests

I talked to guests. Until the last two seasons of my career (2012 and 2013), I wore a tie, a long-sleeved dress shirt, and dress pants (with a crease). I was easy to pick out, as were my fellow managers and other full-time staff. We might as well have been wearing tuxedos. The tie thing went back to the Roose and Legros days. The bottom line was that senior management believed that the message a tie sends to guests—authority, maturity, rank, power, competency, security—was worth a little discomfort for the male supervisory staff. On hot days I just wore shirts with a loose collar. I never thought wearing a tie was any big deal. Our female supervisory staff did not have to worry about ties but they had their own clothing issues, which I happily referred to the VP of human resources.

Mostly, guests had simple requests: where's the closest restroom? What time is it? How late are you open tonight? Which way to the Magnum? What's wrong with Top Thrill Dragster and when will it reopen? Where can I buy (fill in the blank)? Where can I buy beer? Where do you sell candy apples?

Most of the time I could handle the question. Sometimes I had to refer to the Park Guide or I had to call somewhere to get it. After answering the question, or while waiting for a call back with the information, I almost always asked the guest where he was from. Everyone likes to talk about home. Home was a variety of places: Tempe, Arizona; Mt. Clemens, Michigan; Columbus, Ohio; Philadelphia, New York City, Chicago, even Sandusky, Ohio. I was always curious how long-distance guests knew about the park. After listening to hundreds of guests over many seasons, it came down to three things. First, someone in the group—and it could be anyone: the boyfriend, the girlfriend (less likely), little brother or big brother, mom or dad—was bonkers over roller coasters. Sometimes it was the whole family, though that was rare. A middle-aged guy I knew through the Civil War community, Charles Brintley, a factory engineer for a tobacco company in North Carolina, flew with his wife and adult children to Cedar Point for three days just to ride our roller coasters. We met at the Sarasota Civil War Symposium in Florida one off-season January and exchanged stories about what we did for a living. As I talked to Charles about Millennium Force and the Magnum, there was fire in his eyes. I could tell he was already planning a family trip to Ohio. As it turned out, his rationalization for riding roller coasters for three days would be to celebrate his daughter's college graduation. His daughter approved.

Second was cable TV, which in the 1990s grew rapidly across the country and was responsible for cable channels like the Discovery Chanel or the Travel Channel, which had an insatiable appetite for programming. Roller coasters and amusement parks—fun, popular, exciting, and most of all highly visual—helped feed the programing beast. Cedar Point, with its amazing collection of roller coasters and its unique history, was almost always included in programs on amusement parks and roller coasters. The word was getting out, even in Bend, Oregon.

Third was the internet. A couple of clicks and your 13-year-old son was on Cedar Point's website. Once we got him there, it was all over. As the Eagles sang in "Hotel California:" "We are programed to receive. You can check out any time you like, but you can never leave." We had built an excellent website by the late 1990s which only got better in future seasons. We provided entertainment as well as information. We tracked visits to our website, which exploded from a few thousand when it was launched in the fall of 1996 to millions annually by the time I retired 18 years later. Amusement parks and the online world were a great marriage.

Before having my own grandchildren, I zipped through the kids sections like Camp Snoopy or Planet Snoopy quickly. I recognized the young family demographic as an important market segment, but I didn't really know it on the experiential level. I learned a lot from trade magazines, books, demographic and psychographic articles, industry gossip, etc., but the best learning was spending time in the park with our grandchildren. I had not spent much time in the park with my own children when they were young (though Marie did).

If I had time, I liked to quickly walk through Dinosaurs Alive. It was a big deal when it opened in 2012, but attendance drifted south the next year for a variety of reasons. I felt bad for the employees because often there weren't many guests to talk to. The dinosaurs themselves were impressive, even better than advertised. They were scrunched into a small area, but we let the greenery go wild and it nearly hid many of them but in a way that seemed natural. I thought it worked very well. Dinosaurs Alive was an extra charge attraction inside a bigger attraction, Cedar Point, which at that time charged north of $50 to walk in the door. Extra charge was a tough sell given our history and our market.

Magnum was a daylight station stop. I liked to stand on the platform and watch the trains go up the hill. From the loading platform the view of the first hill was unobstructed and quite powerful. Magnum riders were excited, especially in its early seasons. Lots of fist bumps and high fives when the train came into the station.

It was different at Top Thrill Dragster, just down the midway. The immediate prospect of riding Dragster generated pure and highly visible fear in the station, especially for would-be first riders. Their body language was easy to read. No smiles, no wavy arms. Stoic faces, hands clutched on the bar even before the train moved out of the station. Then suddenly their hands would go to their faces and their heads would shake and they would yell something unintelligible.

I smiled at them and tried to encourage them. I told them I had ridden the ride dozens of times (true enough) and sometimes I exaggerated a little and I said: "At least a hundred times." This claim never failed to impress. I loved walking up and down the platform looking into the faces of guests. On average, they had all waited nearly an hour to ride. Now they were here. It was going to happen. No one ever asked for their money back after riding Dragster—no matter how long a wait.

But the Dragster could be a temperamental beast, especially in its youth.

I was very proud of our practice of keeping the signature coasters operating for a period after park closing if they had experienced significant downtime during the operating day. The practice pre-dated my tenure as GM and I hope it never changes. What I called the Big Three ride experiences—Millennium Force, Top Thrill Dragster, and Maverick—drove a big percentage of park visits, and bragging rights at the office on Monday morning. We had to deliver for those guests. Some extra seasonal labor and delaying third shift ride maintenance was a bargain if it meant giving hundreds of guests the best day of their summer.

I usually walked through the Pagoda Gift Shop on my return to the office or the front gate. I came out the back so I could also checkout

Planet Snoopy—if it was daytime—and Main First Aid. The water was always cold at Main First Aid, the bathrooms were clean, and the staff, nurses and paramedics, were friendly and talkative. Put 50,000 people—and 12,000 cars—together for six to eight hours and you have be ready for as much of everything as you can. We recorded every visit to First Aid and the clear majority were minor, including bee stings, headaches, stubbed toes, sunburn, skinned knees, upset stomach, and slight dehydration. Other nights, we were as active as any metro ER: heart issues, strokes, falls, seizures, insulin shock, and sprained ankles. Cedar Point made ambulance runs and courtesy transports to Sandusky's hospital, Firelands Regional Medical Center, every season on a regular basis.

I always asked the nurse on duty what kind of day or night it had been so far, hoping to hear: "It's quiet, Mr. H."

I made it a point to eat in many different locations. During the operating season I seldom left the park for lunch or dinner. I had many choices in terms of locations. Lunch was often at the Employee Cafeteria. John Taylor, aka Red, ran the kitchen and the commissary. He made great soups, especially a gumbo that was so good we added it as a regular menu item at one of the park restaurants.

Foods was our largest division. In mid-July, with the hotels and water park locations going full speed as well as the park, we had more than 1,500 or more employees working carts, stands, restaurants, and support. The Foods kids had a hard job no matter where they worked. Guest expectations were high, especially given the prices we charged. I believed we provided good value, but that could change quickly if the fountain Pepsi or Coke wasn't mixed right, if the hotdog bun wasn't fresh, if the burger wasn't cooked through, if the fries weren't hot, if the pizza was soggy and the toppings weren't fresh; or, if their experience with the employee was not what it should be. I used to joke that everyone eats and is therefore an expert on food.

In the sit-down restaurants, the cooks worked in their own universe of specialized equipment, tools, computers, raw materials. It was hard, physical work, standing for long periods of time, always in danger of burning fingers, wrists, hands, elbows, face. There is an instant reward for cooks: the food is usually consumed right away, and the feedback happens quickly. That said, at Game Day Grille the cook is usually not invited to the table of four from Lakewood, Ohio, to receive accolades on his perfectly prepared chicken sandwich. He or she never, or rarely, gets direct feedback from guests.

Most of my park walks or tours were done in the day or early evening. Cedar Point is located on the west end of the Eastern Time zone, and at a latitude of 41.482265 and longitude of 82.683510. From the end of June into early July it was not truly dark until nearly 10 p.m., and the park closed at 10 p.m. For most guests, the beauty of the midway at night was not experienced for very long. The nighttime experience was a bit ephemeral.

I loved warm mid-summer nights at the park. The combination of ride lights and the lights from food stands and the games area, plus the special lighting we had added in 2012 under the direction of Matt Ouimet in his first year as CEO, which included some of the midway buildings and structures, would charm the hardest heart. A soft breeze off the lake. The sounds from the midway. The screams off the rides. It was pure America, pure Midwest. Pure Ohio. And pure Michigan, too, as the midway at any given time was one third Michiganders.

## Games

Over my career, most of my time in games was spent in the evenings. I always felt it was their natural environment. Games were about risking money. They were fun to play, but you put down your money to see if your skills could get you a tangible reward, a stuffed animal (plush) of some sort that would make your girlfriend or son or granddaughter flash a full-face smile, jump for joy, and tell you they loved you. Amusement park heaven.

I hung back, watched the kids work their games.

It was in the games and arcades areas that Cedar Point showed its American amusement park roots. The flashing lights. The visual whiff of the county fair or the carnival. The darkness on the edges of your vision. The barking from the game hosts. The clear cling sound when the chain was yanked by the host that announced another player. This was not Disney World. Yeah, it was not Disney.

At Cedar Point games were an important source of revenue. Don Miears was largely responsible for creating the culture and the structure that allowed games to grow. Our success was driven by recruiting the right kind of employee and by a brilliant system of managing costs (both labor and goods), incentives, transactions, and procedures. The greatest skill for a games manager was picking the right plush, figuring out early in the buying cycle what was going to be hot six or nine months in advance.

In the 1970s we still used a lot of professional games agents. A few lasted into the 1990s. They were an interesting crew: street smart, independent, hard-working, worldly. English was their second language; the first was Carny. "He penciled me," described what happened when someone had a dispute with Accounting. Most did not take a day off the entire season, working every day from Memorial Day to Labor Day. From Cedar Point they traveled to Texas for the state fair and then to sports events, where they sold balloons and T-shirts and hats. In winter they rested up someplace warm. Then in the spring they headed back up to Cedar Point.

Bob Stein, a Texan from the Dallas – Ft. Worth area, became a Cedar Point institution, known to everyone in the park. For many years he invested a good part his earnings in Cedar Fair units. (As a public partnership, Cedar Fair issued units instead of shares. There are important differences between owning units versus shares. However, in the context of this book they can be considered essentially the same thing). Bob retired very comfortable.

## CPPD

Most of my park tours ended at the Cedar Point Police Department, located at the opposite side of the Coliseum from Park Operations. Cedar Point operated a full-service police operation. By means of the small print, it meant we were under the jurisdiction of the Sandusky Police Department, but we were chartered as a private police department by the State of Ohio and operated independently. Our 10 full-time officers were professional police officers; they looked and acted the part. They had arrest powers and were bonded (meaning they carried guns). They did not like to be referred to as "Security" or "Security Officers," which they believed conjured up images of overweight mall cops or ancient-looking night watchmen.

The CPPD was a tiny place, carved out of the west side of the Coliseum. There was barely enough room to move around and it was jammed full of equipment and cameras. There was a locker room area at the end of a hall, also a few tiny interview rooms where the detectives worked, and which could have been lifted from the set of any TV cop show. Somehow there was room for the dispatcher and for Lost and Found. The Chief's office was upstairs.

The Chief for most of my GM years was Ray Majoy, a City of Huron (10 miles east of the park) native. His immediate and extended family was large, Italian, and athletically gifted. Many enjoyed careers in law enforcement. The Chief was old school in most things. He referred to his officers, females included, as "my guys." He was well connected locally, statewide, and with the Secret Service and the FBI. He guarded his turf ferociously. He valued confidentiality. He did not seek the limelight. By reputation, he had a fierce temper, which I admit I never saw on display. He was devoted to protecting Cedar Point's good name and reputation.

When I got a call from Ray Majoy, I knew it wasn't about a new roller coaster. His calls often dealt with very serious things, human behavior at its worst.

The Chief was in his 60s when I was a GM. He retired in 2012 and unfortunately passed away not long after.

If I was closing, my last stop for the day was usually the PD. I checked in with the shift commander and got a feel for what was going on in the park. I looked at the cameras which covered the parking lot. We exchanged stories of the day. The goal was always the same: a quiet day, a quiet night.

While I talked with the shift commander, officers—many of them seasonal—brought in CRs (Confidential Report) to get reviewed by a regular officer before going into the system. Most people have no appreciation for how much writing a police officer does daily. When I became a GM and had to start reading them, I was quite surprised at both the volume of written reports and the length of some of the reports. There were, of course, lots of one liners relating to unlocked doors, but most others involved a considerable narrative—they told a story—and it mattered how that story was told. The right word could make a difference in a legal proceeding down the road. The document was going to live forever—that's how you had to look at it. Some of the officers were very good writers. They told very interesting stories very well without losing objectivity. Many were better writers than most of the managers in the park.

Cedar Point in high season was a medium-sized city: 4,500 employees, two thirds of whom lived in company housing; 40,000 or more park guests; a marina with hundreds of boats; about 6,000 overnight guests in hotels and campgrounds. Given the number of people involved, even giving consideration that they were here on vacation and should be in a laid back frame of mind, stuff was going to happen: theft (both employee and guest), public intoxication, line jumping, marijuana use, lost children, vehicular accidents, passing counterfeit bills, inappropriate dress, husband and wife fights, naked swimming in the hotel pools, dogs and cats left in cars, lost or stolen wallets and purses, noisy hotel guests.

An unattended wallet or cell phone had a life span of about 30 seconds on a midway bench, unless fortuitously found by an honest guest. In my 40 years at the park I think I found two or three intact wallets, one of which contained more than $500, and about the same number of sets of car keys and cell phones. Guests routinely turned in hats, sunglasses, stuffed animals, car keys, purses, and cameras to Lost and Found. The ride crews found the same kinds of things under the Raptor or Magnum or other rides. There was a longstanding policy that If we could match owner with object, we offered to mail it to the guest at no charge. In a typical year we mailed back over a thousand cell phones, several hundred wallets and purses, and over one hundred each of hats, glasses, sets of keys and cameras.

At my weekly staff meetings, I was known to read CR's that told stories with happy endings.

## Wrapping Up/Starting Over

When I left the CPPD, I climbed the stairs to the second floor and walked into the Coliseum Ballroom. It was always an impressive space—mid-day, late afternoon, evening, night—and, built in 1907, as locked into the history of the park as much as any other building, even Hotel Breakers and the Grand Pavilion. I never saw, or felt, any ghosts, even though I was the only person in this immense space many times and even though I was there in situations, including late nights and off-season Saturdays, that I felt were very ghost friendly. But, as one of my ghost-believing co-workers once told me: "Just because you don't see them or feel them doesn't mean they aren't there."

Frank Sinatra sang here (supposedly). The Dorsey Brothers played here. So did Guy Lombardo and Louis Armstrong. In the summer of 1965 I watched the The Byrds play Bob Dylan's masterpieces, "Mr. Tambourine Man," and "Turn, Turn, Turn" in this beautiful room.

The wooden floor produced a distinct click when walked on with hard shoes. In the late afternoon and evening the light would shoot through the windows in streaks, creating a soft, honey-like glow in the room. Sometimes I would walk up to the stage just to see what it would look like, and feel like, to address the room. I did get the opportunity a few times, the most memorable being at Dick Kinzel's retirement party in September 2011.

Windows and doors were often left open (there was no AC) so the midway sounds drifted up, including the drive-you-crazy collection of squeaks, beeps, and honks from Kiddy Kingdom. There was midway on all four sides of the building. It was an island, or a castle.

I rarely lingered. I had an agenda, the list of things to do I had written down in my notebook. I could make calls now where privacy and quiet were needed. Emails. Always emails. And voice mails.

In the operating season, and in the off-season as well, in the morning I drove the midway in my car before parking and walking to the office. I often was on a mission to talk to Ed Dangler, our Maintenance VP, or he was on a mission to talk to me. The ride mechanics often discovered things in the darkness. There were always things to talk about. Ed was an optimist, but always hedged his bets. I also talked with Bill Spehn to cover any operational issues. I scrambled to get to the office in time to check the weather forecast and the unofficial attendance for the day before. I read the EOD (Executive on Duty) Report. I checked my meeting schedule for the day. I read the top line on all the CR's from the day before.

On sunny mornings, with the curtains open, my office was slammed with light (which I loved). I could hear the park coming alive.

It was time to do it again. I got myself geared up. Corinne Casali, my assistant, reminded me of meetings later in the day. I descended the spiral staircase in time to watch Marcia Frankart push the Park Op door open. Jimmy Buffett began singing his island-style cover of Van Morrison's "Brown-Eyed Girl." When Jimmy began singing the chorus of "sha lah lah lah lah lah lah t-dah" sometimes the office staff stood up and waved and sang along. The sound filled the midway. The morning light was still soft and fresh as the sun climbed up higher over the lake. The Raptor made fine background music with steel on steel.

I loved it all.

## Chapter 2
# February 5, 1974
### First Coaster, Frontier Lift, and Getting Hired

M y first day at Cedar Point was Monday, February 5, 1974. My new boss, Bruce Burtch, and Bobbi Klaus, who worked in sales, took me to lunch at a Howard Johnson's restaurant on Cleveland Road in Sandusky. It was a cold, scruffy gray day: winter on the Great Lakes. I remember we talked about Detroit market radio stations, one in particular, CKLW, an AM station that owned the area's airwaves at the time. They told me rather excitedly that just about everybody who worked at Cedar Point was young, which turned out to be true.

Several weeks earlier I had answered an ad in the Cleveland Plain Dealer. Cedar Point was looking for a "staff writer," and I had resolved to get the job. At the time I was vain about my writing credentials. I had received a Master of Fine Arts in Creative Writing from the University of North Carolina at Greensboro the previous spring, and I aspired to write at least one of the great American novels. I had never written a line of commercial copy, but I was convinced it was something I could learn to do relatively easily. I believed in my heart that with a little study I could write well about anything. Some guys just know they can hit a curve ball. Other people have that confidence about other things: charming men or women; taking things apart and putting them back together again; doing math; playing the guitar. For me it was words. It was not always easy for me, and I certainly did not see myself as Ernest Hemingway or Walt Whitman, but I always knew I could do it. I could write.

I was living in Cleveland, at my parents' home in Fairview Park, a western suburb. I was 24 years old and had just finished serving for several months on active duty attending the U.S. Army Armor School in Ft. Knox, Kentucky, as part of my college ROTC commitment. I was desperately trying to find a job as an English or writing teacher at a community college somewhere. I thought with a degree from Notre Dame plus a master's degree, I had a shot. I had sent out over 100 letters to community colleges along the east coast, the upper south, and New England (all places I believed would be interesting places to live). I did get some very nice replies, but no job offers.

I was ashamed to be living with my parents. I realize the attitude, and the reality, of living with your parents after college,

has changed dramatically in recent years, but in 1974 you had to be desperate to live with mom and dad. My parents felt likewise. I know they liked having me around through the holidays, but they had started dropping hints that it was time for me to move on.

The Cedar Point job seemed like a godsend—if only I could get it. Writing I knew I could do. And I had spent a lot of time at Cedar Point as a guest over the years and had worked there one summer in college. My parents had a summer house in Sandusky, and I felt like half a native. Working for an amusement park sounded cool. It got me out of my parents' house. At the time, I viewed it strictly as a way point on my journey to a teaching job or a real writing job.

My strategy to get the job was to write a whiz-bang cover letter, detail my knowledge of the park, and put together some writing samples. I was smart enough to know that samples of literary short stories and English papers on the forest imagery in the poems of William Wordsworth were not going to impress anyone at Cedar Point. So, I decided to make up some sample news releases using Cedar Point as the subject. I wrote three or four samples, the best one being about the recent rise in gas prices and the impact on Cedar Point. I took the positive approach and made up quotes from Emile Legros, then president of Cedar Point, stating that higher gas prices could help Cedar Point by attracting more people who would forego long vacation trips to California or Florida that summer and instead stay close to home. It was the time of the first Arab oil embargo. Gas prices were soaring, going from $3 a barrel in October 1973 to $12 a barrel in early 1974.

My interview went well. I was a bit shocked that my potential boss was even younger than I was (he had just turned 23). He was mainly a front of the house guy, someone who could talk to anyone. But he had no real interest in writing, and writing was something he was always being asked to do. He wanted to hire someone who could do the writing. He would be Mr. Outside, courting the news media and escorting them around the park, smiling and laughing, the smooth one. He was looking for a Mr. Inside, someone who could generate story ideas, write news releases and letters, and maybe provide some back-up with the media.

He liked the fact that I was a Notre Dame graduate—he said it would impress his bosses—and he did not seem concerned that I did not have a lot of business writing experience. He liked the fact that I knew something about the park, that I had been a seasonal employee. I got the sense he liked me personally. In the end, I got the job.

My salary was $165 per week or $8,500 per year. I thought it was a fair offer. My parents were overjoyed that I had a job and would be leaving the house. My father was a bit of a skeptic when it came to an amusement park career. Cedar Point was a kissing cousin to carnivals and circuses in some people's minds. After a couple of years, he was totally on board with my working at the park and realized it was a very successful enterprise. He became the park's biggest booster.

## A Cedar Point Family

I did bring with me to work that first day a short lifetime of memories of Cedar Point.

My earliest memories of the park are from family visits in the late 1950s when I was a middle-aged child. Our family—all seven of us—would join several other families from our west side Cleveland neighborhood and visit the park and stay at the Hotel Breakers. I am the oldest of five children, born June 21, 1949.

I remember everything was orange. For whatever reason, perhaps cost and perhaps aesthetic or some combination, management had decided to use a lot orange paint on just about everything. We stayed in a Rotunda Room at Hotel Breakers, larger circular rooms at the end of the wings of the hotel looking out over the beach. I remember the hallways were dark and there was sand everywhere, even inside the rooms. The floors were covered with mat-like area rugs and the rugs and the floors had a sandy grit to them. The furniture was wicker, and it was plain. The hotel smelled of summer: sand, the lake, warmth, dampness, a touch of rot. I have always liked the smell of beach resorts.

The beach was as wide as a child could imagine. My brothers and my sister and I built sand castles on the edge of the water and played football in the sand. We ran into the lake as fast as we could, steadily slowing until the water would press against our legs and hold us back and then we would dive forward into the waves. We splattered ourselves with wet sand. We had sand fights in the water, throwing sand at one another, gooey, drippy, gritty, brown sand. We would dump it on each other's heads, and into our bathing suits. Our mother did not approve.

It was a long walk from the boardwalk to the water and guaranteed to fry your feet if it was a sunny day, so mostly we ran to the water, dodging beach umbrellas and teenage girls sunning themselves on brightly-colored towels. The lake was shallow off the beach. You could walk out quite far before you were in over your head. We used to go out as far as we could until we bounced our toes off the bottom of the lake and took little gasps of air in between waves. You occasionally discovered things: dead fish floating by, a plastic bottle, once a couple of turds which sent everyone running for shore.

The closest I ever came to drowning was an overcast day when I inched out a little too far as the wind was picking up and the waves were building. It was not an undertow or riptide, just a case of not paying attention. Suddenly, the waves were bigger, and my feet were not touching bottom anymore. I panicked a little and swallowed water. Then I panicked a little more and swallowed more water. The waves looked bigger, towering above me like mountains. I was afraid I would never be able to make it back, that the water would grab hold of my feet and drag me out into the lake. Finally, I shook it off and started swimming for shore. I was not a strong swimmer then, but I managed to make it back. I have never forgotten the experience. I never told anyone about it.

At night, our parents and the other parents took us all into the park. We thought it was magical, and a little scary. There was a rocket ship ride on the main midway I used to love to watch. I was too young to ride it, of course, and all the people who did seemed to be teenagers. I can remember the girls screaming as the cabin turned upside down. The fun houses were as advertised: fun. The best one included a giant wooden slide, the culmination of the attraction experience, and really the reason to walk in the door. You were given an old piece of carpet to park your butt on and then off you went down at what seemed like bullet speed. It was pure exhilaration, not fear. We would race around and go through the house again so we could slide down the slide.

## My First Coaster Ride

There was fear, however, on the Wild Mouse. My first roller coaster, a small steel coaster designed and manufactured in Germany, was not intimidating to look at. The ride is an amusement park staple and exists today in modernized versions in amusement parks all over the world. Many pictures of the Cedar Point ride survive. It was located not far from the water tower near the site of the old Crystal Rock Palace. I was probably eight or nine years-old when I rode it. I do not remember who I rode it with, but most likely it was my brother Tom. I was one hundred percent certain the car was going to come off the track and I was going to plunge to my death. It is a unique feeling, the fear of death while engaged in an activity that the rational part of your brain knows is inherently safe. It is a little like approaching a locked window on the 29th floor of a building. The easiest and quickest way for most people to experience this feeling is to ride an amusement park ride, especially a roller coaster. When the car made those sharp turns, I felt I was in space. I remember gripping the bar as tight as I could, and I remember my body tingling (and not in a good way). I was terrified, but I do not remember screaming. Thankfully, it was a quick ride.

The Wild Mouse at Cedar Point, about 1959. My first coaster. It terrified me.
I did not think I would survive the ride. CEDAR POINT ARCHIVES

My maternal grandmother spoke a little of Cedar Point. She was a master storyteller and when I was a child she entertained me with stories of her own childhood. I recall her talking about taking one of the "big boats" from Cleveland to Cedar Point when she was a child and how much fun it was. Born in 1894, she lived during the second half of the great age of lake steamers. I have often imagined her standing high on the deck of the Eastland, or the City of Buffalo looking out onto the lake scanning the horizon for the first glimpse of a roller coaster along the lakeshore.

I know my parents visited Cedar Point when they were young. My father spent parts of many summers at Put-in-Bay and undoubtedly there were visits to Cedar Point, too. In 2010 or so, long after both our parents had died, my brother Greg discovered a picture in an old family album of my father, his twin brother, Joe, and Coletta (then Joe's fiancé) on the midway at Cedar Point. On the back of the picture, in my mother's hand, is written "Cedar Point." There is no date, but my father is in an Army uniform and it is summer and so it must have been taken during the war. I have assumed it was the summer of 1942. My parents were married in the summer of 1942 in Little Rock, Arkansas, where my father was briefly stationed. I'm assuming the picture was taken when he was home on leave before heading out to Chico, California, where they spent much of the war years.

My father, Sergeant Hugo Hildebrandt, on the Cedar Point midway in 1942, with his twin brother, Joe, and Joe's future wife, Coletta. My mother, Ruth Byrne Hildebrandt, took the picture. The fearsome Cyclone roller coaster is in the background. I like to think they had just come from riding it. HILDEBRANDT FAMILY COLLECTION

My father's sleeves are rolled up, and he's wearing his uniform hat. In the background is the Cyclone roller coaster station. I have always assumed they had just ridden it. It was a fearsome ride, probably fiercer in memory than in life, but still a great experience and designed by a genius, the great Harry G. Traver. It lived only 22 years: 1929 – 1951 and died young.

I was excited when Greg told me about finding the picture. It was a tangible connection to my parents when they were young and in love and newly married through the place where I had spent much of my adult life. I had several prints made. I made copies of the back of the picture, too, with my mother's words, and framed them together. I kept the picture on a wall in my office at the park, and one on the wall in my office at home, where it still hangs. I look at it often.

# Sunset Drive

In 1958, my parents built a second home on the Cedar Point Chaussee (a fancy French name for a paved road). It was in an area called Cedar Cove on the bay side of the road. It was a ranch-style one story house (not a cottage, though that is what we called it), about 1,800 square feet, with three bedrooms, a bath and a half, an attached garage, and a million-dollar view looking directly west across East Sandusky Bay toward the Cedar Point Causeway, about a half mile away. From the picture window in the living room or from the backyard dominated by huge cottonwood trees, you could watch the cars come and go to Cedar Point.

My father had spent summers at Put-in-Bay on South Bass Island, where my great-grandfather had built a cottage in 1910. My father loved the lake. His younger brother, Art, had already built a cottage on South Bass. I think for my parents the attractiveness of the Chaussee and the Sandusky area versus South Bass island was the fact that it was about an hour closer to Cleveland. Driving time from our house on the west side to "the cottage" as we called it, was about 75 minutes. To go door to door to a home on Put-in-Bay, with the required ferryboat ride, was more than two hours.

The cottage was, in fact, not a cottage at all, but a substantial home with all the necessary conveniences, including an attached garage, a concrete driveway, and a furnace. When they built it, my parents saw the cottage as a year-round getaway, not just a summer home.

The Chaussee is also known as the Cedar Point Road. It runs the length of the Cedar Point Peninsula, which forms the eastern boundary of Sandusky Bay. It is very narrow for most of its length until the tip, where the park is located. Three quarters of the way the peninsula widens somewhat and that is where a developer created Cedar Cove, where the cottage was located. Most of the homes on the peninsula feature lake to bay lots, but most homes in the Cove had bay views. My parent's house was one of the very first built in the cove, built in part on fill from Sandusky Bay and Biemiller's Cove.

In the summer, we thought it was paradise. My siblings and I quickly made friends with the other neighborhood kids. Some of those friendships have been lifelong. There was usually a house under construction nearby. We'd hang around the workmen and watch them bang away with hammers. When they left for the day, we'd explore the construction sites and gather up scrap wood to form into swords. We had swordfights that would last, with a couple of breaks for some Kool-Aid, for hours. The beach was close by, less than a quarter mile from our house, and we spent endless hours swimming and playing in the lake. We were largely unsupervised, as was the style of the day.

Our mother enrolled us in the Junior Sailing program sponsored by the Sandusky Sailing Club. For six weeks, we spent every morning learning how to sail. I caught the bug more than my siblings. I won the Junior Sailor Championship in 1963, when I was 14. I stuck with it and was a member of the Notre Dame Sailing Club in college.

As we got older, we successfully petitioned our father for a family boat. It was an easy sell. We started with a 16-foot fiberglass Crosby with a 35-horsepower outboard. Next was a 23-foot Lyman, a clinker-built wooden beauty, and then a 21-foot aluminum Starcraft which we called not affectionately the "tin can," and finally a 25-foot John Almand, the best of the lot. These boats covered a period of at least a dozen years. These were the family boats. We also had kid boats.

The first was a flat bottomed old rowboat we named "Bones." A friend of my father's, Art Boehm, gave it to us, hauling it over to the cottage from East Harbor. We put it upside down on two saw horses in the back yard. It was enormously heavy. Under my father's direction, we set about getting it in shape for the water. That meant hours and hours of sanding and caulking—and it still leaked. Later we upgraded to a 15-foot Arkansas Traveler, then to a 13-foot Boston Whaler with an 18 horsepower Johnson outboard motor. Our father was an indulgent parent when it came to boats.

The back of the cottage faced due west, and so we were treated to amazing summer sunsets, and with such a flat horizon we could easily mark the progress of summer as the sun marched inexorably south on the horizon. And storms. Summer thunderstorms and squalls would come at us from the west, starting as a low black line on the horizon and then building to a wall of deep purple behind the causeway over the bay. The light would flash green, and then gray as the wind kicked up and turned the bay to froth and you could watch the line of falling water march right across the bay and into the backyard. The rain would drive against the living room window like a shower of BBs and the wind would roar and sometimes you could not see the dock.

Then it was over, sometimes a rainbow, always so much sky, and the return of yellow light. My mother was sometimes frightened in storms, but my father loved them. He liked to sit in the living room and look out at them and talk about how beautiful they were.

At night, we could clearly hear the steam whistle from the train at Cedar Point. On nights with fireworks, which occurred frequently, we could clearly see the big shells exploding into the sky above the park. Then came the headlights on the cars as they left the park. They were bunched together, hundreds, even thousands, of pinpricks of light above the black water, sometimes moving and sometimes not.

We visited the park many times as kids, but swimming and sword fights, and zipping around the bay in our little boats was sometimes tough competition for the midway. We often attended Mass at Cedar Point. We were a family of practicing Catholics and Hotel Breakers offered both Catholic and Protestant church services every Sunday. My siblings and I were very reluctant church-goers in the summer, but we always went to church.

We all worked at Cedar Point growing up. Robert was the first, at 14, working in the Games department. My brother Tom worked two seasons as a bellman at Hotel Breakers, one of the best, if not the best, seasonal jobs at Cedar Point. Mary Frances worked one summer as a host in a food stand on the beach. Greg was a riverboat captain on the Western Cruise. He was the only one of us who lived in park housing, as he worked at the park in 1976 after our parents had sold the cottage.

I worked much of the summer of 1969 as a ride operator on the Frontier Lift. I turned 20 on June 21.

## Real (Hard) Work

However, the first part of the summer I worked at a foundry in Sandusky, a job arranged in part by my mother through a neighbor whose family had recently sold the plant to a large company, the Vulcan Materials Company of Birmingham, Alabama. It was a remarkable experience for me, certainly the hardest physical work I have ever done. The product made in the Bay Billets plant in Sandusky was a metal that was a blend of magnesium and aluminum. In a foundry operation, things were mixed together and then poured into billets, which when cooled looked like cylindrically-shaped logs. What their ultimate use was I do not know.

I was assigned second shift. I had to buy steel-toed work boots and work gloves. I was given a hard hat and safety glasses. The manager, a chunky guy in his 30s, told me that this workplace was "f------- dangerous" and to pay attention to the safety rules. I was assigned to the cutting operation. My partner was another college student, who had worked there the year before and knew the lay of the land. After the pour, when the logs of aluminum/magnesium had cooled, they were sent down a belt to the cutting operation. Our job was to cut the logs into pre-determined sizes, usually two to three feet in length, and then stack them in a metal cradle.

Then we would bind them up with metal tape. When they were secured, we got onto a tow motor and carefully lifted the batch, which weighed many hundreds of pounds, and even more carefully brought it off the cradle. The last stop in the process was to then move the batch of logs into a drying room and stack them, three batches high.

It was always hot in the foundry. Scary hot. Your hands were always sweating inside your thick gloves and your entire body was constantly soaked. The machine which cut the logs, a huge circular saw the diameter of a bicycle wheel, was scary, too.

It was a manual operation. When the log slid into place, you pushed a button which sent the blade down. The sound when the blade hit the metal was deafening and metal shavings flew everywhere. After the blade popped up, you had to reach down and pick up the log and then turn and carry it to the cradle and stack it. The logs were slippery, coated with lubricant, and it was easy to drop one. It was no fun picking up 30-pound metal logs from the floor. I had immediate appreciation for the steel in my shoes.

When a cradle was full, we wrapped it in two metal bands, pulled the bands tight, and cut off the tips with a wire cutter. Then it was time for the trickiest maneuver: lifting the logs off the cradle on the blades of a tow motor. It was a delicate operation. The risk was that the batch would slide off or fall off the tow motor blades and drop to the floor. When that happened, which was not uncommon, it was a colossal mess as you had to restack all the logs in the cradle, lifting them from the floor. The operation was complicated by the fact that the floor of the foundry was dirt and it was decidedly uneven. It was easy to back up and drop a wheel in a small depression and have the whole batch fall off the tow motor.

When we had a problem, it backed everything up, and quickly. Think Lucy and Ethel except with 30-pound hunks of metal instead of chocolates.

My partner, whose name I cannot remember, was stronger than I was and had better technique. Without him, I wouldn't have survived. Every night I went home sore, dirty, and exhausted from the heat and lifting.

My first injury occurred when several of us were unloading scrap aluminum from a truck. It was all from the Whirlpool plant in Clyde. The truck bed was a pile of long, pointy, scraps of gray metal twisted and jumbled into a scary mess. I pulled too hard on one of the long strips and when it gave way I managed to poke myself in the cheek with the end of it. Lots of blood, but no stitches.

I started work at Bay Billets at the end of May, but I was gone by mid-July. My second injury occurred when I dropped a billet on my foot. It landed high up, almost above my instep, and I was hobbling for several days, badly bruised, though nothing was broken. I decided I had had enough. The Cedar Point midway seemed like a better option.

## Frontier Lift

Cedar Point is always hiring by mid-summer. This was true in 1969 and I'm sure it is true today. By mid to late July, there has been a sufficient exodus of seasonal employees for a variety of reasons that the park, as it approaches the peak attendance period, is always hiring.

As I remember, my interview was cursory. They were happy to have me. It was a cut in pay from my work at the foundry. If memory serves, I was paid $2.35 per hour at the foundry and my new rate was $1.75. However, Cedar Point did have a bonus system. I would earn a portion of my pay—I think it was 35 or 50 cents per hour for every hour I worked, payable in a lump sum after the season. I was sent to Wardrobe to draw a uniform and then got an ID card. The next day I reported for work.

I was assigned to Park Operations, specifically to Rides, and even more specifically to the Frontier Lift. I would have taken any position in the park but restroom attendant, and I expected to be assigned to a food stand or a game. I was pleased to get a ride.

In those years there was no general orientation. Each department or division was on their own hook for training. As I recall, I was directed to the Frontier Lift and told to ask for the foreman. His name was Roger. He was a big guy, dark hair. This was his second year at the park. He attended West Virginia University (WVU).

The Frontier Lift had a relatively short Cedar Point life. It was built in 1968, when Frontier Town was opened, and it closed in 1985. It was a sister ride to the Sky Ride, the cable car ride that was built in 1962 and runs the length of the main midway. It is one of Cedar Point's iconic rides, still going strong. Many rides like the Sky Ride have been removed from American amusement parks over the years because of the difficulty involved in safely removing guests from the gondolas or cabins in the event of a power or mechanical failure. Cedar Point always believed that if properly maintained and operated the rides were safe. We practiced evacuations with the local fire departments.

But the situation was different with the Frontier Lift. The ride extended from the west end of the main midway to the center of Frontier Town, across what was then the lagoons of the Western Cruise and thick woods. Access to the towers was available but inconvenient and access to points in between the towers was extremely difficult. If the ride lost power and the cable stopped moving and the cabins were stuck, it might be a long time before the park could get equipment in place to safely remove quests from cabins. This situation certainly contributed to the decision to take down the ride following the 1985 season. By that time, ridership had declined as well.

But in 1969 the Frontier Lift was the gateway to Frontier Town, the Western-themed area at the far western end of the peninsula. The only way for guest access to the area was the CP&LE or the Frontier Lift. You couldn't walk there until the Frontier Trail opened in 1971.

My fellow crew members were mostly college students, all males as there were very few mixed ride crews in those years. Several were from WVU, a few others were from The Ohio State University, Bowling Green, Michigan State, and other assorted colleges and universities in Ohio, Pennsylvania, Michigan, Indiana, and West Virginia. There was a core group of guys who had been at the park and on this ride since before opening. I had the sense right away that I was a little like the replacement joining the unit because of a casualty. Most were a little wary of me at first. Over the first week I was tested and evaluated, and I managed to be accepted into the crew.

We were on an edge of the park. Our back was to woods and lagoons. Guests lined up in a long queue and then ascended steps to the second floor of the station to board the ride. We had a nice view of the park looking back up the midway from the second floor of the station. We could not see the Frontier Town station. There were too many sight blocks from the trees, but it was pretty much a mirror of our station in terms of functionality. However, the first floor was a large restroom. We communicated with Frontier Town by phone, a communication that was constant and vital to the safe operation of the ride.

Over a period of a few days I was trained on every ride position. As I remember, there were six positions. A catcher, who "caught " the car or cabin when it came into the station; an unloader, who opened the door and helped the guests exit the car; a loader, who helped guests into the car and locked the door; a tripper, who made sure the car was correctly in the trip position and then released it so it could leave the station; an entrance host, who assigned guests to the cabins and checked for strings and stamps or collected tickets; and a breaker.

The hardest job physically was catcher. When the ride was built the station had to be positioned on the midway in such a way that the angle of descent and distance from the last tower to the station was on the steep side. The cabins came in hot and fast and the ride operator had to really lean into the car to catch it and slow it down quickly.

It was a noisy ride: steel on steel as cabins bumped into one another and up against the rail in the station. But as the car ascended on the cable and you were up into the trees the noise went away and it was quite peaceful.

We wore goofy uniforms which we hated. They had a Star Trek look to them. I don't remember what the female uniforms were like, but the males were assigned black pants (early double-knit polyester) and a short-sleeve V-neck top that was mostly yellow but had a border of red around the collar. Again, think Star Trek. The pants were the worst. They were baggy, hot, and did not go well with sneakers. We avoided wearing them whenever we could. Some guys bought their own pants, others wore other pants that were dark and close enough to black to pass. Occasionally, we just wore khaki or even blue pants and hoped we'd get away with it. Most of the time we did. By that time of the summer management needed every warm body they could get, and they didn't push the uniform issue very hard. We all got practiced in telling our foreman, who didn't care what kind of pants we wore, or the occasional supervisor, how our uniform pants were lost, ripped, stained, whatever, but we'd be sure to wear them tomorrow (which we never did).

The right uniform makes a difference in employee morale. I learned that in the summer of 1969.

Our foreman was a standup guy, respected and liked. We all knew he was responsible for all of us, the equipment, the guests, the whole mess, and we wanted him to be successful. Within reason, we wanted to make his life as easy as possible. Our second in command, or assistant foreman, was a wild man. I think he went to Kent State, but I don't recall what he studied. He was a force of nature, much like my college roommate, Frank Mrsnik. He was profane, loud, smart, a good storyteller, aggressive, and high energy. He was a big guy, too, but stronger and stockier than Roger, and had played high school football. He was not conventionally handsome, but he did very well with women. He was the Bad Boy so many girls are attracted to, and he knew it and loved it.

He could work all day and play all night; he had almost super-human energy. Every morning he would entertain us with stories about his exploits the night before. I really don't think he made any of it up.

A Frontier Lift cabin could hold anywhere from one to six guests, depending on size and weight. Most guests came up to the ride platform in twos or fours. If we were at all busy—which was most of the time—we did not allow single riders but would send two or even three other people along with the single. Some guests were not too happy about that, but we were measured by our hourly and daily through-put of guests.

At night especially, the Frontier Lift had a reputation as a great ride on which to make out. We got lots of teenage couples, especially high school kids, coming on to the ride with the obvious intention of lip-locking or worse. The crew enjoyed pairing them with a single rider or, best case, a couple of 10-year-old boys. We really loved doing that.

The guys working the Sky Ride on the main midway were occasionally dealing with spitters and the occasional loose object (pennies mostly). We did not have that problem as riders on the Frontier Lift would be spitting into the woods.

It was nice to work outdoors and to work with guys your own age. The station was open and well ventilated, but we weren't in the sun. As the new guy, I got bounced around from first shift to second, but as we got into August all of us were being asked to work open to close or "OC" as we called it. I didn't really mind.

The Cedar Creek Mine Ride opened that summer in Frontier Town, but I have no memory of riding it in its inaugural year.

I thought a lot about my two jobs that summer, as the contrasting experiences were plain. The Cedar Point work was much less stressful and less physically demanding. In fact, it was mostly fun. Bay Billets was real work. I could not foresee circumstances that would place me in that environment again, at least certainly not for an extended period. My college education would give me opportunities to do something else. I had no idea what it would be, but I knew it wouldn't be sawing aluminum-magnesium logs, and I also knew it wouldn't be catching Frontier Lift cabins.

We heard a lot from the Cedar Point rumor mill that great things were being planned for the park in 1970 to celebrate its Centennial year, even a national TV special. Cedar Point had been transformed during the decade of the 1960s. In 1959, it wasn't much, having just been rescued from transformation into a housing development. In 1969, it was attracting upward of 2 million guests a year and was poised to enter a new golden age.

## It Was the Summer of '69

It was, of course, the summer of 1969, which is now mainly remembered for two historical events: the lunar moon landing on July 20, and Woodstock, just about a month later, August 15-19. I was certainly interested in both events.

The fact that we could watch what was happening in real time on the moon was something I thought was almost as impressive as landing there. I recall the moon walk was later in the evening, around

10 or 11 p.m. It was certainly dark. My family was at the cottage at the time. I can't remember which of my sibling were there or if both our parents were there. We would walk outside and look for the moon and then go back inside and look at our tiny black and white TV. We took pride in the fact that Neil Armstrong was an Ohio guy. Less than 10 years previously Alan Shepherd had first popped into space for 15 minutes, only reaching an altitude of 116 miles. Now we were walking on the damn moon! In my opinion it remains perhaps the greatest human accomplishment of all time. We all thought—I certainly did—that we'd be colonizing the moon within 20 years and landing on Mars by the turn of the century.

Unlike the moon landing, Woodstock hadn't been in the planning cycle for a decade. From the perspective of public interest and awareness, it wasn't planned at all; it just happened. At the time, I knew no one who had attended, though later in life I would meet a couple of people who were there for at least part of the event—and many more who claimed they were there but most certainly were not.

My future wife, home on Long Island from Ohio University for the summer, knew several people who were there. But not me. No, I was working the Frontier Lift at Cedar Point. I wasn't there. You can take it to the bank. The closest I came to Woodstock was seeing an authentic Woodstock music poster, beautifully framed, and hanging behind the desk of the now late Bill Brown, who headed up the media department at Hesselbart & Mitten, Cedar Point's advertising agency of record from 1989 – 1992. Behind the glass the poster showed some signs of distress (it had survived Woodstock), which only added to its power.

I think Woodstock would have been fun for a while, but three days would have been a bit much. We followed it on the nightly news and in the newspapers. My father, I recall, was truly horrified by it all: it was drug and alcohol-fueled debauchery. I did take some pride in the fact that things like Woodstock continued to point out that our generation was indeed different and that we had pretty much taken over. No way Frank Sinatra and Dean Martin were going to draw a half million people for three days.

Imagine Woodstock with Facebook and Twitter. And cell phones. Woodstock, New York would have become New York City. The world as we knew it would have crashed and burned.

Back at Notre Dame that fall, there was a lot of talk about Woodstock. One kid who lived down the hall and who was from New Jersey told us he and three friends had tried to go but left too late and got screwed up in all the traffic and finally just gave up and came home. I think that happened a lot.

Notre Dame didn't start until mid-September in those days, so I worked at Cedar Point through Labor Day and the first of two Bonus Weekends. I remember the last day I worked, a Sunday, attendance was moderate, and the weather was just slightly cool. Summer was gone, and fall was at the door. We were down to a skeleton crew and the crew talk, as it always did at the end of the season, turned to next year and who was coming back and who wasn't.

I was not. I knew the next summer I would be at Fort Riley, Kansas, for ROTC Summer Camp/ Basic Training. Then the next year I would be graduating. I did not see myself coming back to work at Cedar Point. Ever.

## Chapter 3
# Opening Year
### Jumbo Jet, Blue Streak, and Roose and Legros

In 1974, arguably the biggest and best thrill ride at Cedar Point was a steel coaster called the Jumbo Jet. It was located along the beach in the northeast corner of the park in approximately the same location as the late Cyclone roller coaster. The Jumbo Jet trains went up a 50-foot hill, then dropped into a tight spiral that got ever tighter as the train descended until it disappeared into a near vortex. Top speed was about 50 mph. There were no seatbelts or even lap bars on the ride. Riders sat straddling a bench in the middle of the train and usually grabbed the waist or hips of the person in front of them. The sensation of speed was truly incredible and at the base of the vortex at maximum speed the physical force pushed you down into the bench. What made it all work were the laws of physics, bent to the purpose of creating fun for human beings. Riding the Jumbo Jet was not an experience easily duplicated in everyday life, which is one reason amusement parks are still popular. It was a portable ride, as many if not most German and European rides were at that time. It rested on thick wooden blocks.

The problem with the Jumbo Jet was that it didn't work all that well. It was down for maintenance reasons far too often and internally the attitude toward the ride was often negative because of that fact. It was a headache for the ride mechanics, and the butt of many jokes. However, as is sometimes the case with rides that are problematical to take care of, park guests loved the Jumbo Jet. The ride design might not have been up to par, but the ride experience was terrific. There was always a line for the Jumbo Jet.

In 1974, it was still a relatively new ride at Cedar Point, opening in 1972. The story I was told when I started was that in 1971 the then president of Cedar Point, an ex-Disney executive named Truman Woodworth, was sent to Europe with the authority from the board of directors to purchase one major new ride. However, he fell in love with two rides, the Jumbo Jet and the Giant Wheel (a 145-foot high Ferris wheel), and he decided to buy them both, committing Cedar Point to the transactions. According to the stories, he did it for a reason, one which made sense to me then and makes sense to me now. Kings Island was scheduled to open in 1972, just north of Cincinnati, and promised to be a serious competitor for Cedar Point in Columbus and other Ohio markets. Woodworth believed introducing two major new rides at Cedar Point at the same time would create buzz and take some of the focus off the new park. The decision might have contributed to his departure—he left Cedar Point in 1973—but I'm sure there were other factors at work as well.

## Blue Streak

The Jumbo Jet's competitor for king of Cedar Point rides was the Blue Streak, a traditional out and back wooden roller coaster which opened in 1964. The Blue Streak was, and is, a terrific ride, and in its heyday in the 1960s and early 1970s it was the most popular ride in the park. It was named in honor of the Sandusky High School sports teams, called the Blue Streaks. Wooden roller coasters generally fall into two categories: out and back and figure eight. Out and back coasters like the Blue Streak do just that: the track ascends a lift hill, then plummets down and heads straight ahead (over lots of hills and slight curves, of course); then it makes a turn and heads back toward the station (over more hills). The track of a figure eight coaster, like Cedar Point's Steel Vengeance (aka the Mean Streak), folds back over itself. There are many variations of both types. The Shivering Timbers at Michigan's Adventure is an extreme example of an out and back coaster.

So, Cedar Point was hardly the roller coaster capital of the world in 1974. In fact, there were only four: Jumbo Jet, Blue Streak, Cedar Creek Mine Ride, and Wildcat. The phrase "America's Roller Coast" had yet to be dreamed of.

In 1974, more than half of Cedar Point's food outlets were operated by Interstate United, a national food service firm. The park-owned food operation was relatively small and confined to midway stands and a few restaurants, including the Marina Steakhouse. Interstate handled most of the sit-down restaurants and catering. There were still lots of games concessionaires.

## The Dynamic Duo

Although it was about to change in some dramatic new ways, in 1974 Cedar Point was still the world created by Emile Legros, a Cleveland investment banker, and George Roose, a Toledo bond dealer.

I remember meeting Emile Legros and George Roose very briefly, a week or so after I had started at Cedar Point. My boss, Bruce Burtch, took me over to the administration building to introduce me. They each made the obligatory smile and shook my hand and wished me well. I did not have a strong impression of either man at the time.

The Blue Streak, built in 1964 and king of the midway until the opening of the Corkscrew in 1976. CEDAR POINT ARCHIVES.

I would only know Legros briefly. He developed stomach cancer later that year and died on New Year's Day, 1975 (he had been born on Christmas Day, 1905). Mostly, I knew him by reputation, by stories, and by distant observation.

Most employee were afraid of Emile Legros; I remember that very well. One of my new colleagues described for me the appearance of a former marketing director after most senior staff meetings: "His armpits were so wet he had to go home and change shirts."

Legros' wife, Frankie, had the reputation of someone who walked around the place like she owned it, which I guess was at least somewhat true. Legros was a Cleveland guy, a member in good standing of the east side WASP establishment and kept his permanent home in Cleveland. However, he did convert a corner of the old Cedars Hotel, down by the marina, into an apartment for his use when he stayed at the park.

He had a very successful banking and investment career in Cleveland, but he is known today, if at all, as one part of the two-person team who "saved" Cedar Point in the 1960s, along with his partner, George Roose, a Toledo bond dealer and real estate investor. Legros was tall and silver-haired. He looked rich, and I assume he was, and he looked like a serious business person, which he was. He had spent most of his life in board rooms and banks, but he reveled in the fact that he was now in the entertainment industry. His primary interest in the park was the live entertainment offering.

George Roose (R) and Emile Legros, the two men who saved Cedar Point in the 1960s and set the foundation for the park's future growth. CEDAR POINT ARCHIVES

He once said: "We run Cedar Point like its General Motors." He was proud of that quote and the philosophy that supported it. In a 1965 article in Business Week, he stated: "There isn't anything magical about running an amusement park. We just use common sense." In his mind, he and Roose were successful because they had brought modern business practices to the wacky world of amusement parks. There was truth in his claim.

Roose had made his money buying and selling municipal bonds. He was a native of Perrysburg, a Toledo suburb. He was a graduate of Oberlin College and Harvard Law School, and he served in Italy in World War I with the U.S. Army as an ambulance driver, where he had known Ernest Hemingway (or so the story goes). I do not know his motivation. I wish I did. Adventure? Patriotism? He was in his early 20s then. War changes everyone. How did it change him? He did have something of an adventurous spirit as he earned his pilot's license when he was 55 years-old.

Roose and Legros had known each other through work on various other projects, but their acquisition and then revival of Cedar Point made them regionally famous and heroes and saviors within the amusement park industry. Everything else they accomplished in their relatively long lives is long forgotten by the world at large. Their legacy is Cedar Point, more specifically the salvation of Cedar Point. Not a bad epitaph.

As financial or money guys, they were an odd fit to run an amusement park and resort. Neither man to the best of my knowledge ever completely gave up their day jobs in finance and banking, but as the years went on they committed more and more of their time and energy to Cedar Point. I was never able to watch them interact, so I do not know what the chemistry was and if they were friends first and partners second, or if it was the opposite. People who knew them say they were strong business partners, apparently always on the same page ultimately but recognizing each other's strengths and weaknesses. Did they go to each other's Christmas parties, the graduations and the weddings? I don't know. I can't even make a guess. But they were a powerful business team.

Roose was the primary park guy, the creative partner. He pushed for the development of Frontier Town in 1968 and then the Frontier Trail in 1971. He loved railroads and he brought the Cedar Point and Lake Erie Railroad into existence. He was easy-going, smiled a lot; he was soft spoken and polite, almost unassuming. He did not look the part of dynamic business leader. He was below average height, though not short, and slightly built. He was always neatly dressed, usually in coat and tie. In the summer, he wore seersucker suits. He could have passed for a successful owner of a small-town furniture store. He was often described as "a perfect gentleman," which I think he was. I never remember him raising his voice. He inspired great affection. It's an oversimplification, but he ruled through love and Legros ruled through fear. Both strategies can work, in my opinion.

Roose had made the bet on Cedar Point when he was 62. He did not go slip-sliding into retirement.

He was very fastidious about his teeth. He had a good friend who was a dentist and Roose visited the dentist every couple of months. For many years, The Town Hall Museum, an attraction in Frontier Town, featured a large display of antique dental equipment (stuff you can barely stand to look at) mostly obtained by Roose from the dental museum in Bainbridge, Ohio.

He built a house on the beach alongside the Cedar Point parking lot and spent much of his time there, though he also kept his home in Perrysburg, outside Toledo.

I knew him for 10 years. In 1982, when the old administration building was remodeled, and a new executive office was built adjacent to the Marketing office, "Mr." Roose (it was always "Mr. Roose") was moved to a small office in Marketing next door to mine. He was 87 then and certainly slipping.

His vision was deteriorating, and he was a menace driving around the park and in Sandusky. On at least two occasions he drove off in the CEO's black Oldsmobile instead of his own black Cadillac. Everyone got a good laugh about it, but it was also very sad. My secretary, Deb Hessler, had worked for him years before and took good care of him. He had no schedule, occasionally appearing and then disappearing for days. I always wondered what he did in his tiny office. I thought at the time, and I still do think, that the Cedar Point Board of Directors did him a disservice moving him from the executive office. Given his status and contributions to the company, and the industry, he deserved a seat at the table, even if it was emeritus, until the end of his days. But perhaps it was just an issue of his no longer wanting to climb the stairs.

In 1992, he was posthumously elected to the International Association of Amusement Parks & Attractions (IAAPA) Hall of Fame. His partner at Cedar Point, Emile Legros, is still on the outside looking in. They should have gone in together, an oversight that should be corrected.

When he stopped coming into the office, he wrote me a very touching letter, which I still have, thanking me for putting up with him the past few years and wishing me well in my career at Cedar Point.

George Roose died December 16, 1984. He was 89.

## Freshman Year

It was still very much winter and very much the off season when I officially started my Cedar Point career the first week of February. My office was small and windowless, and the walls were covered in dark plywood, but it had a desk and a chair, and two visitor chairs and I considered it home. I had an electric typewriter and a phone. I was ready for business. Marketing then numbered about 15 staff members, roughly divided into two groups: sales and PR/promotions. Our boss

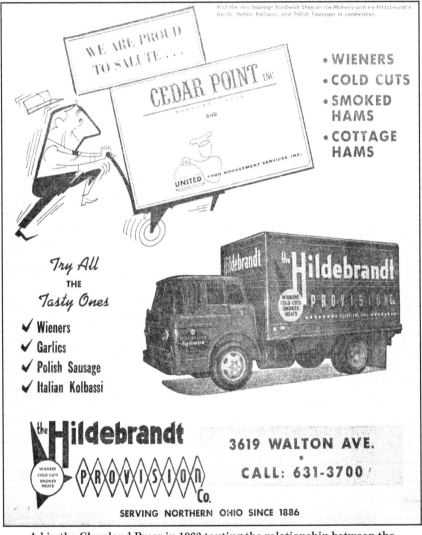

Ad in the Cleveland Press in 1962 touting the relationship between the Hildebrandt Provision Company and Cedar Point. For the 1962 season our family's meat company supplied the hotdogs for the park.

was John Muffly, a former Park Operations manager who had been transferred to Marketing in an organizational change. He was not a marketing guy by inclination, but he did make an honest effort to be one. John was in his late 20s and a proud graduate of West Virginia University. Though the park was run by two old guys, Roose and Legros, it was operated by a very young full-time staff. We all knew it, too, and took pride in it. There was only one person older than 30 in the Marketing department when I started at the park: Bill Manning, our Cleveland area sales representative, who was in his 50s. We considered him ancient, which he certainly was by our standards.

A day or two into the job I was going through old newspaper scrapbooks and came across a full-page ad by the Hildebrandt Provision Company wishing Cedar Point all the best for the 1962 season. Hildebrandt's was a maker of hotdogs, sausage, bologna, and a variety of other processed meats; it was started by my great grandfather, an immigrant from West Prussia, in 1886. The ad included a picture of the newest Hildebrandt delivery truck.

The Hildebrandt Provision Company had won the bid to be the official hotdog supplier to Cedar Point and Interstate United (the food service company which handled catering and sit-down restaurants for the park). It was a mixed blessing, as my father explained when I told him about my discovery. He said the ad ran in a special section of the Cleveland Press and cost the company a lot of money. However, he said they had no choice.

I had the ad framed and kept it in my office all the years I worked at Cedar Point.

## Welcome to the Fourth Estate

I taught myself how to write news releases. I got a book out of the library on business writing and practiced writing news stories. I was asked to write a variety of things: copy for brochures and other kinds of promotional material, scripts for slide shows, news releases, speeches, and letters. I think I did okay, but I know I was guilty on occasion of trying too hard to be clever and just a little bit literary.

My boss' job was to solicit favorable news media coverage of Cedar Point. My job was to help him do it, mainly by generating story ideas and then writing them up so we could send them out to the news media.

Sending out news releases was a very time-consuming affair in 1974 involving a lot of manual labor. There was nothing electronic or digital about it. Envelopes were labeled by hand. News releases were copied and collated and then stuffed into envelopes, again by hand. We all participated in these mass mailings. Newspapers did not use color images then, so anything we submitted had to be an 8 x 10 black & white glossy print. We made a lot of prints.

That winter and spring, I got to know the park from the inside. My boss provided some introductions, but mainly I just wandered from department to department and introduced myself and got to know people, all the time trying to think of an angle to publicize what they contributed to the park experience. It was my job to make them famous, a challenge I came to relish more than I ever thought I would. I used to think how my friends in graduate school would be amazed at what I did now. Some would have been horrified; others would have sympathized. I smiled at the thought. I was having fun.

I learned an amusement park is an amazingly diverse place. We had a huge arcade, one of the largest in the U.S., filled with mechanical machines of all types: Skee-Ball, fortune tellers that spit out cards, kiss meters (supposedly verified by the strength of your grip on the lever), and dozens of versions of pinball. We also had two full-time staff who did nothing but care for all these machines. They were mainly mechanical guys then, but soon enough their world would change to electronic games and the skill set required for their care would change dramatically.

The man who oversaw the merchandise and games operation was Don Miears, a sometimes gruff Texan who spoke in a booming drawl. He was about 40 years-old when I met him. He had worked for AstroWorld in Texas, a Six Flags Park, and for the Astrodome in Houston, so although relatively new to Cedar Point (1971) he was an industry veteran. I quickly learned many employees were afraid of him—he had a reputation for firing a lot of people and he demanded all employees give their best—but I did not feel intimidated by him. Many years later, in 1994, he would become my boss.

I met him when I was assigned by Bruce Burtch to write a story for a trade magazine involving something about our merchandise training program (I can't remember much past that). I sat in his office and played reporter and asked him questions. He was all business, but he was also very helpful, which I appreciated.

The best story I wrote that winter was a feature on Cedar Point's steam-powered railroad, the Cedar Point & Lake Erie Railroad. The story focused on the work that had to be done to these magnificent machines in the winter months to make sure they operated well during the summer season. The man who ran the railroad was a retired sheriff named Mike Hetrick. He was something out of central casting: thick, probably in his late 50s then, broad face, soot and grease-covered overalls, a twangy style of speech that sounded Southern but really wasn't. He had the relaxed and happy way of a person who was comfortable in his position and had no interest in moving up in the organization. The railroad was George Roose's baby, so Mike Hetrick had a straight line to the vice chairman of the board, and he would use it if he had to do it. As a former sheriff, he understood politics very well.

I spent most of a day with him. He told a lot of stories about the railroad and the man who had run it during the 1960s and had built it from scratch: Jack Foster, who had died not long before. He also showed me how they cleaned boilers and fabricated parts and adjusted wheels. Even in 1974, the age of the steam locomotive was long gone and so there was a romance to it. It sucked me in pretty well. The story I wrote strived to communicate some of that romance, the nostalgia, the unique set of skills and the knowledge possessed by a man like Mike Hetrick.

Marie as a young reporter at the
Sandusky Register, 1973.
COURTESY OF SANDUSKY REGISTER

The story had been sold to the Columbus Dispatch by my boss, Bruce Burtch. He convinced the editor of the Dispatch's Sunday Magazine to carry it. I wrote it. The Dispatch sent up a photographer to take some pictures. As these things always are, it was a team effort, but I felt a sense of ownership and always considered it to be my story. The Sunday Magazine was then a staple of most newspapers, the one place for color and length. For a feature writer, it was considered the ultimate placement.

## Opening Day 1974

There was nothing "new" for 1974, at least nothing major, so the year lacked a theme, a mission, an objective, a linchpin. Those nothing-new years were always a challenge for Marketing, and still are. We were reduced to coming up with a gimmick to launch opening day and the start of the season. I do not remember who thought of the 74-foot long hotdog, but it was our job to give it the best shot to open the 1974 season.

About a week before opening day I got a chance to see the 74-foot long hotdog for the first time. It was also the occasion of my first meeting with Dick Kinzel, who was then the number two person in the Cedar Point Food Service department. Bruce took me over to one of the food coolers where we met Kinzel and another food manager. And there it was, coiled up like massive snake. It had no end. And seemingly no beginning, either. Bruce and I were assured it was indeed 74-feet long, and we took their word for it. I knew something about hotdogs, of course, given the fact my father's family had been in the meat business for three generations, and so I viewed it with special interest. It was handcrafted by our hotdog supplier, which I believe was Sugardale, though I am not certain.

**The author as a young PR man, 1975.**
CEDAR POINT ARCHIVES

I asked how they were going to prepare it. Everyone laughed. But somehow they figured out a way.

The big issue was the bun. We may have created a 74-foot long hotdog, but no one could figure out how to create a 74-foot long hotdog bun.

As the winter ended and spring became a real thing, the activity in the park picked up tremendously. I got to experience my first "we've got a park to open" time. My memories of that first run up to opening are vague and mostly impressionistic. I mainly just watched as things flew by me. Opening day was a hard deadline; it was reinforced carbon steel. It was Superman. Everything was a slave to it. You get caught up in it, you sense you are a part of something large and somewhat miraculous and that you have a role to play.

The park is geographically isolated, so all this activity takes place in a confined space and the rest of the world never sees it, which is probably just as well as too much romance would be removed. The vast majority of park visitors never see the park in winter, never see the off season. They only know it as it exists in May or August or

October. With the right frame of mind, Cedar Point is beautiful in any season, including the whitest January days.

In addition to the 74-foot long hotdog, opening day would bring a performance by more than a dozen massed high school bands, a Cedar Point tradition since the mid-1960s and the brainchild of the retired Bill Evans, the publicist for the park during the 1960s and early 1970s. I never had the opportunity to meet Bill Evans, but Bruce Burtch, had known him. In his photographs, he looked a little like George Raft, a 1930s-era actor who often played gangsters.

He had silver hair and always wore large, dark sunglasses. From what I could tell, he was an old-time publicist, which basically means he never let the truth get in the way of a good story. Exaggeration was not a sin, rather a virtue, and when deftly practiced an art form. That's how the Hotel Breakers got to be a thousand rooms and Cedar Point had more than 200 rides and attractions. Rooms, of course, included other rooms besides guest rooms, and attractions included food carts and games.

In truth, I smiled at the hutzpah. We were in show business, after all, and it did no harm. We were the heirs of P.T. Barnum. However, I didn't think we'd keep getting away with it and over time we dropped most of the exaggerated product claims. What we had was damn good. The truth was impressive enough.

Evans' idea with the massed bands was clever and effective. The Cedar Point midway was very large by any standard, so we had the space to do it. Although the performing bands were offered free admission, 15 or more bands (including chaperones and parents) might translate into more than 2,000 admissions. Getting all the bands together in one place with their different sizes and uniforms, made for great spectacle and a visual that easily translated into an AP wire service photo.

The performance itself was short-lived. Typically, the massed bands performed only two to three songs, which was a blessing. Spread out over such a large area, the sound quality was poor at best. The songs were all standards: The National Anthem, then two others. I think "Beautiful Ohio" was one of them in 1974. Each year, there was an honorary Grand Marshall or Chief Conductor, who stood on a ladder in the center of the midway and directed the bands, which covered him on all sides. However, his own band was right in front of him.

Getting all the bands in place by 10 a.m. was a task. The busses dropped the bands off in the back of the park and then the bands lined up along the boardwalk in front of the Hotel Breakers, which in those years did not open until Memorial Day weekend. Cedar Point Police officers helped with the organizing, but essentially it was my responsibility to make sure it got done properly. I really had no idea what I was doing, but fortunately most of the band directors had been doing it for years and they did. I walked up and down the line looking as official as I could. As it got closer to 10 a.m., we really did have a line of bands stretching from the gate by the beach entrance to the park down past the Hotel Breakers. It was impressive to look at.

It was a warm sunny day, already hot, unusual for mid-May along the lake. I wasn't wearing a hat and my forehead, face, and scalp felt like a hotplate. Just before 10 a.m., our Chief of Police, Del Seiler, came up to me with a smile and asked if I was ready to go. He did not say it, but it was understood that it was my call to make. When I gave him the okay, his officers would open the gate and the first band would step out on the midway. There would be no turning back. I remember thinking what I was doing a year ago—scratching out a novel in the Student Center at the University of North Carolina at Greensboro and getting ready to leave Greensboro—and thinking how different my life had become. In front of me stood over a thousand high school kids, proud band geeks all, ready to get this over with so they could ride some rides. I was in charge of this mess.

I nodded to the Chief. "Let's go," I said.

That day, I stepped out onto a live midway as a full-time employee during the operating season for the very first time. Little did I know then that I would walk out on a live midway on opening day for the next 39 consecutive years.

The bands assembled around the center of the midway in front of the western end of the Sky Ride, one of the terminating points of the ride, which stretches the length of the main midway. It is the widest part of the midway in a park which probably has the widest midways of any park in the world. It took longer than the time allotted to get the bands into their assigned positions. It was not exactly Script Ohio. But it worked. The honorary Opening Day Band Director climbed up the ladder, shook out his wand, and wiggled it a few times, and we were ready to go.

From where I stood, near the center of the action, the National Anthem didn't sound too bad. However, at the edges it was barely recognizable. No one cared.

The 74-Foot Long Hot Dog celebration took place immediately after the massed band performance, also on the main midway. There was no practical way to create a 74-foot long bun, so Food Services utilized 74-foot long hotdog buns. It looked a little weird, but it worked. Emile Legros and George Roose took the first sections of the hotdog, proudly holding them up for the world to see, before each took a bite. There was appropriate applause from the crowd, who certainly approved of free hotdogs. It did not take long for the 74-Foot Long Hotdog to dramatically reduce in size.

As fast as our Food Services employees cut off sections of the dog, there were eager hands to receive them. Free food always works, I learned. Always.

There was a cake, too, to celebrate opening day, which also went quickly.

Our photographer took pictures of the ceremony, as did photographers from several local newspapers. One image of the event got picked up by one of the wire service, UPI (United Press International) and ran in dozens of newspapers. The next day, Sunday, there was a photo in the Cleveland Plain Dealer. We pronounced opening day a success, at least from a PR perspective. The sunshine and warm temperatures helped, too. I do not know if attendance was up or down from the prior year—my focus on attendance performance had yet to develop—but I assumed based on the sunshine the comparables were good.

I do not remember anything else about my first opening day. Nothing. It's a blank.

## Irish Hills

In mid-June, still relatively early in the operating season, Cedar Point announced that it had acquired property in the Irish Hills area of southeastern Michigan to build an amusement park. As I understand it, the idea originated with George Roose, who was from nearby Toledo and had spent a lot of time in the area over the years. Only about an hour west of Detroit and a half hour south and west of Ann Arbor, the Irish Hills was known as a vacation area with lakes, campgrounds, and small cottage communities. And a few small hills.

At the time, senior management and the board of directors did not think the Irish Hills park would cannibalize attendance at Cedar Point, at least not to an appreciable degree. The concept was for a much smaller park, nothing like Cedar Point. There would be a Western-theme amusement park and a large campground (Michiganders love to RV camp).

The financial community was generally supportive. However, some questioned the wisdom of creating what in effect would be a wholly-owned competitor only a two-hour drive away.

The amusement park mindset, at least at Cedar Point, in the mid-1970s was that the park's draw was largely confined to northern Ohio and, in recent years, southeastern Michigan. It did not think of itself in truly regional or certainly not national terms. That would change in the years ahead, but in 1974 it thought locally.

In George Roose's vision, the Irish Hills park would be able to capitalize on Cedar Point's brand equity, its reputation—since the early 1960s—for cleanliness, safety, family atmosphere, great rides and live entertainment. I think he saw the Irish Hills park (it was never named) as a junior Cedar Point, drawing its patrons from Toledo and southeast Michigan.

I was very new to all of this, but my instincts told me it was too close to Cedar Point, that for the Irish Hills park to be successful it would have to take visitors away from Cedar Point. Who would replace them? Would all the Irish Hills park visitors also go to Sandusky every year?

No one, including George Roose, expected much if any local opposition to the park. However, the announcement was greeted with less than enthusiasm by a substantial number of residents and property owners who believed a junior Cedar Point would bring traffic, noise, congestion, and too many people to their beloved Irish Hills. They wanted things to remain as they were: quiet, peaceful, scenic, and relatively empty. It was my first experience with the "not in my backyard" mentality. I was quite surprised, and my sympathies were on the side of Cedar Point, and not just because I was an employee of the park. I believed then, and I believe now, that a junior Cedar Point in the Irish Hills would not have compromised the area's character or natural beauty. But it was not a good business proposition.

Cedar Point had purchased the property, about 200 acres, but it needed to get it rezoned to build the park. The opposition to the park quickly organized and began putting pressure on the local politicians who would have to approve the rezoning. It was not going to be a slam dunk.

A group that was pro-park also quickly formed, which was led by the usual cast of characters: construction trade unions, the chamber of commerce, and residents who for whatever reason thought they would financially benefit from having an amusement park, particularly one owned by the famous Cedar Point, right in their backyard.

In the fall, the pro-park group set up several rallies to promote the park. As a PR representative, I accompanied our director of planning and design, Lee Jewett, who was responsible for designing the new park, and several other Cedar Point staff, to one rally. It was held in a high school auditorium and it was jammed with people who enthusiastically supported the proposed park. We were treated as guests of honor. I had never seen anything quite like it. People yelled and cheered after every speaker. I talked with a few members of the media, who were there to cover the event, and with several residents. The residents had self-interest blazing from their eyes, but it was honest and straightforward, without subterfuge of any kind, which I found admirable in an odd way.

Efforts were in vain, however. We were not able to get the 200 acres rezoned. The Irish Hills were "saved." Cedar Point/Cedar Fair continued to own the property for decades, leasing it to local farmers for agricultural use. Corn and soybeans instead of roller coasters and cotton candy. It hindsight, and short sight, it was a blessing. It could be argued forever, of course, since it never came to pass, but I believe building an amusement park in the Irish Hills would have been a bad business move for the company. The company would try two more times to execute its Michigan strategy, first in Grand Rapids in 1977, and then in 2001 with the purchase of Michigan's Adventure near Muskegon. The third time was the charm.

Many full-time employees saw the new park as a career opportunity, either at Cedar Point or at the new park. We all assumed that the Michigan park would be staffed with Cedar Point employees.

## I Love Michigan (the State)

Michigan has an interesting relationship with Cedar Point. Michiganders love the park. During my time at Cedar Point, Michigan attendance represented slightly more than one third of total attendance, usually 33 – 38 percent, nearly one million visits annually. Detroit and SE Michigan represented the biggest piece, but even Grand Rapids, a four to five-hour drive from Cedar Point, generated 175,000 visits a year (comparable to Columbus, which is 50 percent closer and much larger). Michiganders have different perceptions about distance versus most Ohioans. Market research showed Grand Rapids park-goers perceived Cedar Point as "close," while Youngstown park-goers did not. Research showed Michiganders didn't mind driving long distances, even routinely doing day trips to Cedar Point from western Michigan. Perhaps it's the automobile and their relationship with cars?

But put aside all the research data. Michigan has been in love with Cedar Point for 50 years. The famous Detroit radio personality, the late J.P. McCarthy, used to refer to trips to Cedar Point as going to worship at the shrine. There is a mostly good-natured rivalry between the residents of the two states, driven by the well-known football rivalry. Dick Kinzel used to joke that we loved Michigan except for the third Saturday in November (the traditional date of the UM versus OSU football game). I would never say anything bad about the state of Michigan, as Michigan was going to put our kids through college and provide for our retirement.

Thanks, Michigan. I am a fan.

# Marriott Comes Courting

Not long after the Irish Hills announcement, I think in mid-July, there was more big news from above: Cedar Point had signed a tentative agreement to be acquired by the Marriott Corporation.

The 1970s was the decade of theme park construction. Starting with Kings Island in Cincinnati in 1972 and ending with Canada's Wonderland outside Toronto in 1980, more than a dozen parks were built in North America. The Marriot Corporation, successful hotel owners and operators, saw the theme park industry as a good fit with their success in hospitality. They knew hotel operations, they knew employee training, and they knew catering and restaurant operations. Somewhere in the organization, probably at the highest levels, was the itch to get into show business, often a siren song. Their concept was to build three large parks: Washington, D.C. (for the east coast and mid-Atlantic market); Chicago (for the Midwest); and Santa Clara (for California and the West Coast).

The Chicago and Santa Clara parks were already under construction. The land had been acquired outside D.C.

In the summer of 1974, Marriott set its eyes on Cedar Point. Two reasons, I think. First, they knew Cedar Point was extremely profitable and served a large market. It would be a good business to own. Second, acquiring Cedar Point would mean they would acquire its seasoned management team, which was considered the best in the industry based on the extraordinary performance of the park the past 10-12 years.

The man Bill Marriott and his team hired to build and operate their amusement parks was Truman Woodworth, the ex-Disney and ex-Cedar Point executive. He knew Cedar Point very well, especially its people. He had recruited many of the senior managers. He had been with Cedar Point for only three years, 1969 – 1972, but he had left a big footprint. Your impact as a manager or a leader, good or bad, can often be evaluated by the number of stories employees tell about you after you're gone. I heard a lot of Truman Woodworth stories.

The deal was structured as a stock trade. Emile Legros, George Roose, and all other shareholders would receive shares of Marriott stock in exchange for their Cedar Point stock. As I recall, Emile Legros would get a seat on the Marriott board as part of the deal.

Everyone seemed pleased at first. It was not an unfriendly takeover, at least as far as I could determine. There was the obligatory company meeting and memo that said this was good for everybody and to just carry on and it was business as usual. I did not have that much time, money, or heart invested in Cedar Point in July 1974, only six months on the job. In fact, I didn't plan to be there in a year. (I

The author with Gene Puskar, park photpgrapher, both of us brandishing
the tools of our trade. Summer of 1974. Notice the fashionable white belt,
wide tie, and polyester slacks. CEDAR POINT ARCHIVES

didn't know where I'd be, but I didn't think it would be Cedar Point.)
I thought of myself almost as an outsider.

I remember I met one Marriott person, a manager who was sent
to Cedar Point as part of the initial due diligence team. I was with a
group of park people who squired him around the park for a day.

It all ended quickly. Marriott's stock dropped in the summer of
1974. I do not recall the reasons, but I don't think it was driven by the
proposed acquisition of Cedar Point. The stock price dropped below
the price that had made the deal, and that ended the deal. By Labor
Day, it was all over. Looking back from financial adulthood, I can only
guess at the machinations involved in putting the deal together and
then taking it apart. If it had been successful, the future of Cedar
Point would have been quite different. As it turned out, Marriott
exited the theme park business in 1983.

The third Marriott park, designated for Virginia outside
Washington, D.C., was never built (the victim of history lovers and

legions of not-in-my-backyard people and some politicians). Marriott stuck to their core business—hotels—and certainly have been successful at it.

## First Summer

I survived my first season. I endured through Labor Day. I worked every Saturday and every Sunday. I got one day off a week, if I was lucky, and it was always a weekday, usually Wednesdays. I usually got to the park by 8 a.m., and I seldom left before 7 p.m. I had the energy for it.

I lived in a small apartment in Huron, a 15-minute drive from the park. It was the first time I had ever truly lived alone. No family, no roommates. I didn't mind it. For the first time in my life I went to the grocery store as a serious buyer. I ate a lot Shake and Bake pork chops.

I was having fun.

In 1973, Cedar Point had produced a hard cover black and white yearbook for seasonal employees, offered at a nominal charge. Management deemed it a success and ordered a 1974 edition as well. This time it would be soft cover but there would be a limited number of four color pages in the front of the book, including the cover. It was called "Experience '74," certainly not very original. Creating the yearbook was the job of the PR Department. We hired three college students to assist us, one to serve as editor and the other as photographer and a third as an assistant photographer to basically do the photo printing.

The photographer, Gene Puskar, was from Pittsburgh. He was very talented and went on to a very successful career as an AP photographer covering sporting events around the world. He was impish, good looking, charming, and a bit of a rebel. Girls loved him. He became a good friend.

I developed a bit of an unrequited crush on the editor. Jan was from Michigan and had just graduated from college.

We included some cartoons in the book, which by some miracle survived the censor (my boss), which poked fun at guests, employees, and management. Looking back, they are quite politically incorrect, but they were created in a spirit of good fun. They could never exist in a company-sponsored publication today. The back cover was an image of a Sky Ride cabin with guests. The cabin had an obvious dent, where it had probably smacked into another cabin or a part of the station. We loved including it, and we were shocked it got past the censor.

Gene was not the kind of photographer who followed orders, which is one reason he went on to such a successful career. His assignment was to shoot dozens and dozens (probably more than 100), images of ride crews, office staff, food stand crews, games attendants, even the Cash Control staff. Personnel, the precursor of Human Resources, divided the park up into the appropriate groups and scheduled the shoot times. Gene wasn't about to shoot your standard group shot. He did his best to pose each group with a zany twist or inside joke.

I still have two copies of "Experience '74."

That summer, I also had an opportunity to get a taste of the music business. Our promotions manager, Mike Huling, managed to talk himself into the job of managing a local band which featured a singer and songwriter named Larry Keen. He and his bandmates were from West Virginia and I do not remember what they were doing in Sandusky, most likely a Cedar Point connection (the park recruited heavily for summer staff at West Virginia colleges). They mostly played at a lounge in a hotel, called the Greentree, just outside the park.

I would categorize their music as songs John Denver would sing. I enjoyed listening to them. In addition to their own material, they played a lot of covers from artists like John Denver, Johnny Cash, Bob Dylan, and the Band. They were not folkies. They were not rock. They were not country. They were not bluegrass. But I guess a mish-mash of all of it.

Mike was a wheeler-dealer of the first rank, outgoing and blustery and willing to talk to anyone about anything. He was in his early 30s then, married with several young children. He loved to tell stories, party, and find angles in life he could exploit. He decided Larry might be his ticket to a bigger place in the entertainment world. I am sure he was also genuinely convinced of Larry's talent and potential.

As Larry Keen's manager and promoter, one of Mike's responsibilities was to put together a press kit with news releases, bios of the band members, photos, etc. Mike was no writer, so he asked me if I would do the writing. He offered me $200 for the job, which I thought was a lot of money, and I couldn't say yes fast enough. I went to Larry's apartment and interviewed him. He was a nice guy, very friendly, and the bio and news releases were easy enough to write. I had visions of writing the notes for his first album.

Mike spent a lot of Cedar Point time working to promote Larry and his band. After the flurry of a few bookings, my impression is the relationship went south. Mike left Cedar Point in the spring of 1975 to take a job as the general manager of an indoor amusement park in Chicago. After that, we pretty much lost touch.

Karl Moore, another Cedar Point employee, succeeded Mike as Larry's promoter and manager. Larry went on to reasonable fame and fortune as a singer and songwriter, working on both coasts. He has opened for Jimmy Buffett, Bonnie Raitt, and Jay Leno. I have not seen him perform since 1974, which I know is my loss. I am happy for his success.

The midway was smaller then. The main midway ended at Jungle Larry's African Safari, where the Corkscrew is today. There were three routes to Frontier Town: walking Frontier Trail, riding the train, or riding the Frontier Lift. The Hotel Breakers was old and musty and smelled faintly of rot and brown sand. There was much to explore.

I was only vaguely aware of how the park was performing in terms of attendance and revenue. I did not see daily attendance numbers or comparisons to the prior year's attendance. I did not see revenue data. I did get the impression we were doing well, despite the lack of a new attraction, and in fact 1974 was a positive attendance year for Cedar Point with 2.74 million visitors, an increase from the prior year.

Attendance is one of many factors that go into financial performance for an amusement park, but it is almost always the major one. Admissions revenue is the biggest driver of park revenue. As one of our CFO's told me many years later: "An extra hundred thousand in attendance can cover all kinds of mistakes."

During my career, I was almost never taken to task if our admissions per capita (total admission revenue divided total attendance) did not meet plan as long as our overall attendance target was met or exceeded. I would learn later that bragging about your great admissions per capita increase in a down attendance year did not get you much. The irony was that increasing the average ticket price was a result, for the most part, of management actions and decisions. Attendance, however was in large part determined by factors outside of management's control like weather, the general economy, and competition.

In 1974, and until we were well into the computer age, it was the responsibility of Park Operations to call in the hourly attendance to each major department in the park. I learned that first year that management lived and died on those hourly numbers. The amount of time invested in making all those phone calls was something the shareholders would have questioned, but the thirst to know was a powerful thing. The call was expected about eight to 10 minutes after the hour. If there was no call by 15 minutes after people started getting irritated. No call by 30 minutes after, and it was a catastrophe and somebody, somewhere, had to be held accountable. When I retired, 40 years later, I was getting park attendance continually, in real time, on my smart phone.

Labor Day took on new significance for me. Before Cedar Point, it was just a signpost for the end of summer and the start of the school year. Now it was a much bigger deal and would remain so until HalloWeekends was firmly in position and marketed as a true second season. I don't remember much about my first Cedar Point Labor Day as a full-time employee. We closed early, I think at 8 p.m., and it was still light which seemed odd. There was nothing going on in Marketing, just some busy work. It was a slow time for news—the media always had some interest in opening day but not Labor Day. There were almost no company picnics or other large group events, as companies tended to avoid scheduling events around holidays not wanting to interfere with family time.

I learned there were two days in the season when employees used a specific salutation when greeting other employees. One was: "Happy Opening Day," and the other was "Happy Labor Day."

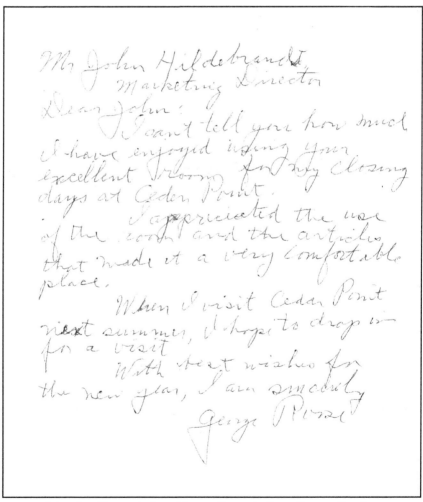

**A handwritten note from George Roose to the author on the day Mr. Roose retired.** AUTHOR'S COLLECTION

## Chapter 4

# The Mentor

### Beer Stories

### First Meeting

Right after Christmas break, only a week or so after the death of the CEO of Cedar Point, Emile Legros, on January 1, 1975, several Cedar Point employees resigned to go to work for the Marriott Corporation to help staff their two new theme parks, both due to open in 1976. The resignation pretty much happened in mass, on the same day. I recall several gathering in the Marketing office in preparation to walk over to the executive office building and turn in their resignations to George Roose. The group included my boss, Bruce Burtch, his boss, John Muffly, and John's boss, Jim Bouy.

There were several others as well, including the director of park operations, Rick Faber.

All were basically recruited by Truman Woodworth, who after his departure from Cedar Point in 1973 took over as CEO of the two parks being planned by the Marriott Corporation. He knew the talent pool at Cedar Point very well and had in fact recruited some of it.

In the space of a week or two, our company had lost its president to cancer and the heart of its executive management to a future competitor. Looking back now, it was a milepost, really the end of the old Cedar Point, the park and the culture that had been reborn and transformed in the 1960s. People create culture, and the people creating the culture at Cedar Point had changed.

The new CEO was Bob Munger, then 46, a member of the Cedar Point, Inc. board of directors. He ran an insurance business in Cleveland but was originally from Connecticut where his father had been a federal judge. Munger had graduated from Yale and came from what my mother would call old WASP money. The family had a summer home in the Canadian Maritimes. He had married women from wealthy families. He belonged to the rich, white, Protestant establishment of Cleveland's East Side, which was culturally and geographically the westernmost extension of the East Coast. He belonged to exclusive Cleveland clubs. He had household servants. He was at bottom a financial guy by trade.

Bob Munger's CFO at Cedar Point was a man named Al Pifer. Before working at Cedar Point, Pifer had been a financial manager

with Carling O'Keefe Brewery in Cleveland. He had worked there with a marketing guy named Don Dittmann. They were friends as well as colleagues. With the mass exodus of marketing talent from Cedar Point, there was a pressing need to hire an experienced marketing person for the park. Pifer recommended Dittmann, who was currently between jobs working part-time as a labor relations consultant and living in Tacoma, Washington.

One day in January, existing in a kind of workplace boss-less limbo, I got a call from the executive office with the information that the company had hired a new marketing vice president, Don Dittmann, and that he would be calling me to introduce himself. I had heard a few rumors, mainly that he was a buddy of Al Pifer (not a good thing, as Pifer had a reputation as a SOB) and that he was really, really old.

Ten minutes later he was sitting in my office.

He was old, no question about that.

I guessed him about my father's age. I was not far off. Don was 54 in 1975 and my father was 56. Unlike my father, he had hair, but it was a weird kind of hair, full of hair cream so it glistened, had that wet look; and in color it was battleship gray with hints of brown. Strange-looking. He was a big man, probably 6' 3" at least, and he filled the chair in my small office, not fat and not lean, and certainly not athletic. Physically, he looked soft but somehow fluid even to the point of being graceful. He walked smoothly and gracefully, I remember that.

He was dressed in a nondescript gray suit, white shirt and tie. The suit seemed slightly big for him but not bad fitting. He wore it loose, which was not the style of the day. The tie was a standard design.

After a few pleasantries, he dug into a side pocket and produced a pipe. He proceeded to tap the bowl once or twice, then put the stem into his mouth. He lit the pipe with a flourish and soon was blowing smoke rings in my office. At the time I smoked cigarettes, so I did not mind the smoke and liked the smell of the pipe tobacco.

We talked for a while, each sizing up the other. He needed to know what he had to work with. I needed to know what he was about.

There were some quickly realized similarities. We both had been English majors in college. He had six children and was robustly Catholic. We had both grown up in the Catholic parish system, and so we shared at least a thousand major and minor cultural touchstones. One of his sons had attended Notre Dame for a while but had not graduated.

He admitted he didn't know anything about amusement parks, but he told me he did know something about selling things.

**Don Dittmann in his mid 40s, about eight
years before coming to Cedar Point.**
DITTMANN FAMILY COLLECTION

He made it clear I was to address him as "Mr. Dittmann." I didn't like it very much, but I did as he requested. A few months later, he casually mentioned that I should start calling him "Don," which I did.

The Cedar Point job was a step back in some ways. He had been very successful in the beer business, both as a general manager of two brewery operations and as the national VP-marketing for Carling O'Keefe Breweries. I was never completely sure what ended his career in the beer business. I heard the story from him in bits and pieces over the years. The beer world and the amusement park world did not intersect, so I had no information except what he told me.

He would often say the best years his life, the time when job and family and personal happiness intersected, was his time in Tacoma and the Northwest. He talked about Washington the way my mother talked about California during the war. He had spent about a decade there, first as the GM of a brewery, and then as a part owner of a furniture company. He said working in the Pacific Time Zone was a great and convenient blessing if your boss worked in the Eastern Time Zone: the window of time when you could get harassed by corporate was relatively small.

He was born in Chicago in 1921, but by the time he was in second grade he had also lived in New Jersey.

We would work together for almost seven years, which does not seem so long now, after a 40-year career. There were three parts to our relationship: January 1975 to October 1979, the period when I was his student in all things marketing; November 1979 to June 1982, the period when Don was recovering from a stroke and brain surgery for an aneurism, though he was still working for Cedar Point; and the period from his retirement in June 1982 until his death in 1990, when he served as my informal consultant on many things but mostly on running the marketing program for Cedar Point. But life, too.

Don taught me about business, about marketing and selling and advertising, about managing other people, about existing and then trying to thrive in the corporate world. I had been an English major, as he had been, and came into the business world by accident. I had prided myself in not taking a single business class in four years at Notre Dame, not even economics (I have lamented my poor judgment many times over the years). Nearly every day there were lessons. He became my mentor by default, but also by choice. We liked each other.

He constantly challenged me. I had to marshal logical, well-reasoned arguments for any idea I proposed. You couldn't glam him.

He dug deep, asking question after question. He didn't care how long it took. I was forced to do my homework before I came to him with anything, large or small.

Shortly after he started, I made pitch to locate a copier in the Marketing office. At the time, there were only two copiers in the company, one in Planning & Design, which was located nearly a half mile from the Marketing office and isolated from all other departments, and one in the executive office. If we needed a copy of anything, our only option was to go to one of these locations. It was a pain in the ass to do this, and a very unproductive use of employee time.

I thought the case was beyond obvious. The cost was minimal. The benefits considerable. In hindsight, I'm sure Don saw this as a teaching opportunity. He told me to do a cost/benefit analysis, commit all the numbers to paper, and make my case in writing. Then I had to tell my story to the feared CFO, Al Pifer. If Pifer approved, I would get my copier.

Pifer made me come in on a Saturday morning to meet with him. Saturdays in the off season, especially in February, are usually a pretty sacred time for people who work in amusement parks. It pissed me off then, and it pisses me off now, but I showed up. Pifer was not unpleasant to me, and really didn't ask too many questions as I went through my proposal.

When I was done, he said: "I have two words for you," and then paused for affect: "Carbon paper." He smiled slyly, then turned serious. "There's nothing wrong with carbon paper. Make sure your staff understands that."

(For those readers who are younger, carbon paper was dark-colored smudgy paper that would allow you to make an ugly-looking copy of the original if placed delicately between two sheets of paper.)

Pifer left me hanging that Saturday morning, but on Monday I got the okay to lease the copier. I was a hero to my staff.

Don liked arguing. He almost never took it personal. We could go at it pretty good for long periods of time, and not dispassionately, but at the end he'd crack a joke or suggest we go have a beer and just move on. Not all bosses could do that, in fact I believe the vast majority cannot do it. I always thought his capacity to argue and fight over issues large and small—and not become truly angry or emotionally invested—was one of Don's greatest strengths.

His office was in the administration building, second floor. It was close to the Marketing office, literally 50 yards, if that, door to door. He had mixed feelings about the location of his office. I think he liked the access it gave him to the CEO, Bob Munger, and the vice-chairman of the board, George Roose. It conferred status as well. But down deep I think he would have preferred being in the Marketing office with his staff.

The fact that my boss, his boss, and his boss had all resigned to work for Marriott was a big opportunity for me—and for others in the company as well, including Dick Kinzel, who went from the assistant food manager for Cedar Point to director of operations when all the post Marriott dust had settled. After a short period of review, a few weeks, as I recall, Don got approval to promote me to communications manager. My responsibilities were a mixed bag, but the chief one was to manage Cedar Point's relationship with the news media, which was a big deal.

I got a nice raise and was put on the management incentive plan. I got approval to hire two staff members. A year before I was a frustrated would-be novelist academic starting a job at an amusement park because I had to make a living. Now, I oversaw public relations and publicity for the best amusement park in the world, Cedar Point. I recognized that Marriott had unwittingly set the stage, but it was Don Dittmann who believed in me and who put me on it.

I really didn't know what I was doing. I had been put in a position for which I was not really qualified by most objective measurements. I was aided immeasurably by Don Dittmann.

Stories about his kids, stories about the beer business, stories about his childhood, stories about his Army service, stories about friends and associates, Don was a master storyteller, aided, I'm sure, by what appeared to me to be a nearly photographic memory. The talk flowed effortlessly, scene by scene, detail by detail. I have always appreciated storytellers, though not everyone does; for some it's all just bloviating and ego.

Don's stories always had a point, a lesson, something that ended it. They didn't just drift off. He told jokes very well, nothing gross, but often slightly ribald. He could do accents well, and he could step outside the story, deliver an aside or a story within a story, and then pick up the main line again without a hitch. (This is not easy to do.)

Some stories were happy, some sad. I felt I knew well many of the people who lived in his world.

The best story he ever told was the story of his military service in World War II. I once asked him as we were leaving the parking garage of the U.S. Steel building in Pittsburgh what he did in the war. I got my answer after listening to a three-and-a-half-hour monologue. It was a remarkable experience. He hated the Army. He thought it was corrupt, inefficient, and wasteful. "You can be a patriot—and still hate the f------- Army," he told me.

Don served as a combat infantryman in France. His feet were frozen during the Battle of the Bulge and he was evacuated back to England.

He told me about the lieutenant in the Sherman tank. The Sherman took a direct hit from a German Tiger and burst into flames. He said he watched the lieutenant struggle to climb out of the turret, screaming and waving his arms, but finally succumb and slide back into the inferno.

Don talked in colors, he talked about the weather, he remembered name after name after name. He recalled huge blocks of conversations with people he hadn't spoken to in 40 years. He remembered what people looked like, what certain places smelled like. He remembered all this in real time.

Countless times over the years he would pop into the Marketing office at or around 5 p.m. and announce he was heading over to the Surf Lounge at the Hotel Breakers and that he would buy the first round. I think the practice was an attempt to replicate his days at Carlings. He always had takers. He liked holding court in a bar, pipe in hand, telling stories and dispensing advice and commentary and opinions on many things.

I was not the only person in Marketing who interacted with Don. He considered himself to be a mentor to us all. Except for our Cleveland sales representative, Bill Manning, who was Don's age, perhaps even older, we were all under 30. There were about 15 of us in the Marketing Department in those years (the number of people working in Marketing averaged about 15-16 over the course of my 40 years with the company). Don was in the role of father-figure, teacher, senior leader to many of us, including Ned Stancliff, Linda Delekta, Jane Duffy, Norm Carter, Preston Taylor, Mark Mills.

Don was always an outsider. His only peer friends in the company were Al Pifer, who of course had got him the job, and Bill Nelson, who succeeded Pifer as CFO in 1977, who was also an outsider.

Don's relationship with our agency, MARC Advertising, was love/hate. He drove them crazy by basically questioning everything they did but at bottom he thought they were very smart people with an outstanding work ethic. Don had great respect for their media planning and buying skills, less so for their creative efforts. If media graded out as an A, creative might be a B+. But there were no C's. Don was notorious for what's called "nit-picking the body copy." He would fight over the use of specific words, even punctuation—which in ad copy tends to be relaxed—and he loved to art direct as well. He did know a lot about graphic arts, which was an alien world to me when I started in business.

He and the agency principal, Jack Goldsmith, had a good relationship, though Jack, who was about eight years younger than Don, was often exasperated by Don's nitpicking. However, I could tell he had great respect and affection for Don.

Jack became a mentor to me. Jack and I kept in contact for 43 years, until he died in 2017 at age 90. He was a remarkable man. I was blessed with two great teachers.

## The Big Climb

I got a call from Bill Nelson on a Sunday evening in late September 1979, with the news that Don had suffered a serious stroke and was now at the Cleveland Clinic. He was 58 years-old. In the short course of his treatment for the stroke, the doctors discovered a previously unknown brain aneurysm. The only option was surgery, so Don had the difficult assignment of trying to recover from a stroke, and brain surgery, at the same time.

I did not have any direct contact with Don for several weeks, though there were updates on his condition frequently through Mary Margaret, and from Bill Nelson. I wrote to Don a few times, but I was not able to talk to him until he was moved to a rehab center in Green Springs, south of Sandusky.

I became the head of marketing by default. Until Don returned, I would report to Bob Munger, our CEO. The park was closed for the season. The intensity of preparation for the 1980 season was not what it would be a decade later. We were still in the off-season rhythm of the 60s and 70s. The fall was a time for rest and a kind of leisurely re-grouping. We compiled stats for the season just finished, scheduled vacation time, started planning for the next season. Group Sales was focused on collections and clearing out accounts.

Typically, Bob Munger spent most of the off-season in Cleveland, coming to Cedar Point usually one or two days a week. I was not put in a position where he would be calling me several times a day wanting to know this or that, which was a blessing. He

I did meet with him several times while Don was out. They were relatively short meetings. I had a list of items that needed action, so I pretty much controlled the agenda, which was fine with him. He

1976 Group Sales Christmas card. Left to right: Bill Manning, Linda Delekta, Jan Guthridge, Norm Carter, Maggie Kurtzweil, Don Dittmann, Mark Mills, Marla Younce, Preston Taylor. Kiddieland Carousel. CEDAR POINT ARCHIVES

tried to put me at ease, sensing my nervousness, I'm sure. I always appreciated that effort. I sensed his interest in marketing was minimal. He understood it was important to every business, but it was not a subject that particularly interested him.

Some in Marketing took Don's absence as an opportunity to try to push through ideas that they didn't think Don would approve. That sort of thing happens in a power vacuum. Some of our sales staff had specific, off the rate card deals, buttressed by a hundred good reasons why they should go forward, that they wanted to get approved in Don's absence. One was to put in place a program of discount cards in more distant markets—something Don was not in favor of doing. I resisted, although there were several ideas I endorsed, knowing it just was the right thing to do.

Don did not like his time in Green Springs. A big part of the rehabilitation progress is to force physical progress, to sometimes push through pain, lots of it. Don didn't like doing that, as he freely admitted, and he developed a deep dislike for some of the people who were doing the pushing. He labeled them sadists, with only half a grin. He likened one nurse to a Gestapo trainer.

Don came back to work in late November. He had been out for about two months. Mary Margaret brought him to work. As it was the off-season, she could drive him almost to the door of the administration building. I met them at the door. I remember it was a cold, dark, and blustery day.

Don's left arm was paralyzed. It was useful only as a paper weight. His left leg was partially paralyzed. He could walk only with the assistance of a crutch and even then walking was very difficult and quite exhausting, He staggered and tottered and shook and always seemed a breath of air close to falling. His office remained on the second floor, up two flights, and that first day it took Don 20 minutes to get to the top. I was on one side of Don and Mary Margaret was on the other. Don grimaced all the way up. I don't think it was so much pain as just frustration that his leg wouldn't work and there was nothing he could do that would make it work. He was sweating and exhausted when we got to the top. When he finally sat down in his chair in his office his whole body slumped into position. He looked defeated, not victorious. It was painful and scary to watch.

For the next two and a half years, until he retired in May 1982, Don attacked those stairs every work day. I still do not understand why the company did not try to accommodate his disability and move him to a first-floor office somewhere in the park. It is one of my Cedar Point mysteries. I suspect that if Don had asked for consideration, it would have been freely given—how could it not have been? Perhaps both Don and the company thought his condition would improve and by next week or next month there would be no need to move offices.

Bob Munger was a kind man and held no grudge against Don. I cannot believe he condemned Don to the torture of climbing those stairs every day. I asked Don about it more than once, but he always blew me off; it was apparent he did not want to talk about it. My conclusion, based on circumstance and observation, not hard evidence, is that Don wanted to stay where he was. Perhaps climbing the stairs was his daily physical therapy, something he felt he needed to do. As time passed, he did get better at climbing the stairs, but it was always difficult for him.

I gave him credit for guts, for just doing it every day. I admired him greatly for it. I also admired Mary Margaret. No husband could have asked for a better caregiver.

He was not the same man, no one ever is. He gradually became more pedantic, more lecturing, a bit more confrontational in style. The verbal flash, the wink and smile, were in retreat. He turned his peers off even more. When Don and I disagreed, there was no longer the opportunity to make things right over a beer at the Surf Lounge. These were difficult years. After several months back, it seemed obvious to all, including Don, that he was not going to get much better. His arm would never come back to the way it was, and his leg would never be whole. If anything, given his age, he would likely continue to decline physically. His ambition, his job, was to hold onto this job as long as he could. He was always on defense.

Don couldn't walk the park. He couldn't drive a car (there was an effort to retrofit his car to allow him to drive but he was never comfortable with it). He couldn't go on sales calls. He couldn't play golf. He couldn't really go anywhere himself. For a man who had been so active and independent, he had to find his condition maddening. I don't think he ever accepted it, and I can't blame him.

In Marketing, we adjusted to his circumstances. Meetings were always held in his office. He typically arrived between 9 a.m. and 10 a.m., and left around 4 p.m. We respected his position and we respected Don and there was no grumbling.

The business kind of took a breather in these years. Attendance declined every year for four years until we had a slight uptick with the Demon Drop in 1983. Some of it was a hangover from 1978, some of it was the 1981-82 recession, and some of it was the lack of a big new thrill ride. In 1980, we built a dolphin stadium on the beach and got into the animal business, a project sponsored strongly by Bob Munger. In 1981 we introduced the Wave Swinger in Frontier Town, a family ride. In 1982, we introduced White Water Landing, a major water ride, replacing the antique Shoot the Rapids.

In 1982, Cedar Point built a new executive office, a one floor extension off the front of the marketing building. The administration building, which had been built in the early 1900s, in the midst of the Boeckling era, was converted to a home for the Finance division. As part of the move, Marketing got a new entrance and more space, including, at long last, a new office for Don. He was not there long, probably less than two months, when he retired.

He seemed quite pleased, relieved too. The company was very fair to him, he told me. I am glad that it was. He deserved it. I got a new boss: Bill Near, who was then vice president of operations.

## Tacoma

Don and Mary Margaret put their house up for sale immediately. Their plan, all along, had been to retire to Washington, to the Tacoma-Seattle area, where two of their children lived, and where they had been most happy as a family. They couldn't get there fast enough. Within a month, their house in Huron had sold and they were living in a home on a golf course in Tacoma. I felt very happy for them.

Don and I started a new chapter in our relationship. The mentorship continued, but now it was by phone and letter (mostly) in the time before email. Over the next eight years, until he died in 1990, Don and I shared an interesting correspondence. Don had learned to type with one hand, or at least he had learned to type anyone as well anyone could with one hand, and that is how we communicated, both of us in love with words and never worried about how many we used.

I kept him informed of general business trends within the park industry, Cedar Point gossip, news about Marie and our boys, Cleveland sports talk, weather trends. Also, lots of business issues. I was learning to be a boss and run a department, and how to get our agency to be more productive. I was also adjusting to a new boss, Bill Near. Don showered me with opinions and advice, all of it well meaning. Some of what he told me I found useful, some of it I ignored. I was thankful for all of it. He was evolving into what he called a curmudgeon, as good a definition as any as to what he had become.

I saw Don once after he left Cedar Point, in 1984 or 1985. My brother Greg and his wife had moved to Seattle from Youngstown a few years before. The marriage did not survive the change in venue, and Greg was living there alone. I went out for a visit in early April, before the start of the Cedar Point season, to see Greg, who organized a camping trip to Olympic National Park. I stayed an extra day so I could visit Don and Mary Margaret.

We spent the better part of a day together, which started with a tour of their house, a ranch with an enclosed atrium in front and a glass-lined back of the house which offered a view of the golf course. Don said one of the things he never tired of watching was golfers making bad shots to the green from the fairway in front of their home. They liked the house very much. It suited them.

We took a long drive, Mary Margaret behind the wheel of the big Chevrolet Impala they had purchased from Cedar Point when he retired. Don was the tour guide. I saw the site of the brewery where he had worked in his glory days, the watery world of Puget Sound, even a glimpse of Mt. Rainer. Don talked constantly. He was very proud of his adopted home town.

We talked Cedar Point, of course, the state of the business and the state of my career. He was sympathetic to my frustrations, counseling patience, which he admitted was not in his nature. He offered opinions on many diverse subjects, mostly sports and politics. His hatred of President Franklin Roosevelt was still intact.

Mary Margaret prepared dinner, which featured salmon, of course, and then I was on my way back to Seattle to my brother's house. In September 1990, I got a call from Mary Margaret with the news that Don had died of a heart attack. We talked for several minutes. She was calm, in charge, accepting, concerned for what I might be feeling. She told me how fond he was of me, and how proud he was of what I had accomplished. After talking to her I took our dog for a long sad walk at Osborn Park.

I kept all our correspondence, both sides of the aisle. When he died I arranged it all chronologically, so it told a story, and had it copied and spiral bound. I made a copy for myself, and one for Don's family, and one just for the hell of it.

I stayed in touch with Mary Margaret, sending her several Cedar Point calendars every year which she loved to give to her grandchildren. One of their daughters and her family continued to live near Kalamazoo, Michigan, and they would visit the park at least once a year and would stop by and say hello. Mary Margaret asked to see pictures of our boys, which we always included with her Christmas card.

In March 1991, less than two years after Don had died, business took me to Seattle. That year we opened our contribution to the wooden coaster wars, Mean Streak. The teaser TV spot featured would-be riders watching logs being turned into coaster planks at a log yard/mill. The agency discovered the perfect lumber mill outside Seattle.

I drove in the rain, at night, from our filming location to Mary Margaret's house in Tacoma. She greeted me with a warm hug, and a salmon dinner, and we talked about Don and many other things. She had her children and grandchildren, almost too numerous to count, which were a great comfort. And she still played golf whenever she could. She volunteered at church. The empty hole was conversation, she said, echoing almost exactly what my mother had said to me after my father had died. She and Don had talked all the time. They had been best friends, co-conspirators, and now the silence in the house was sad and never-ending.

She wanted to know everything about my work at Cedar Point and what Marie and boys were up to these days. She mentioned attending their christening so many years before.

"Don always thought you would leave Cedar Point," she told me. "He said you should see what else was out there." Perhaps I should have. But I did not.

I asked Mary Margaret if there was something of Don's I might have. We settled on a book. It was his copy of "Roosevelt and the Coming of the War, 1941," which is now on my bookshelf.

Despite our best efforts, it was a melancholy evening. Perhaps it was the darkness, the cold weather, the rain.

Mary Margaret died in 2009.

In 2011, I got an email, and then a call, from Julie Dittmann Gole, Don and Mary Margaret's youngest child. Julie had worked for Cedar Point for several seasons as a performer in one of the park's live shows. After college, she had moved to New York and got a job as a publicist. In the course of things, she met a young NYFD firefighter and married him. They had lived in New York, but after his retirement they headed west to Seattle.

Julie told me their oldest son, Greg Gole, was a junior at Washington State University. He was a finance major and interested in applying for one of the audit internships offered by Cedar Point. He had been born in 1991 and had no memory of Don, only stories of Don. As someone who had not known either of his grandfathers, I understood his perspective on his maternal grandfather. He impressed the Internal Audit staff and he got the job, which is one of most competitive seasonal positions in the company. I looked forward to meeting him.

Greg came up to my office a few days after he had arrived at the park. He knew no one. He was tall and handsome, reserved. As we talked, and I shared some of my memories of Don I had to keep reminding myself that he had never known Don, just stories and pictures. It was awkward for me at first. It was plain his interest in working at the park for a summer was mostly driven by Julie, not Don, which I understood.

Julie came out to visit the week of July 4 to see her son and to see the park again. She had remained good friends with John Lyle, our manager of technical services, whom she had known when she worked seasonally at the park. Julie and I had lunch and talked about Don and Mary Margaret and the entire family. I talked with Greg several times over the summer. I gave him a copy of the Hildebrandt/Dittmann correspondence. I do not know how much of it he read, perhaps all of it, perhaps none of it, perhaps some of it (most likely).

I took him over to the old finance building, the first floor now converted to a haunted house, and still shuttered in advance of HalloWeekends. I walked him up the stairs. I told him about how his grandfather had struggled to climb them every workday for more than two years. I walked him down the hall and showed him his grandfather's office, now a storage room filled with Halloween props. He seemed genuinely interested.

We had lunch at Famous Dave's in the marina a few days before he left to go back to Washington. It was a beautiful late summer day, just a light breeze on Sandusky Bay. We talked more about Don. It bothered me that he had never known him, that there was no physical connection, never would be or could be, unless, as Don believed, they would meet in heaven.

*Chapter 5*

# The Corkscrew, Gemini, and 3 million Visitors

## First Steps Toward Roller Coaster Supremacy

I happened to be in New York City on a Sunday in June 1974, the day The New York Times published Robert Cartmell's article on the top 10 roller coasters in the United States. The occasion was my brother Tom's wedding on Long Island. I read the article by accident. Cartmell's article legitimized in mainstream popular culture the coolness of roller coasters.

In the article Cartmell's number one roller coaster was the Thunderbolt at Kennywood Park in Pittsburgh, a coaster and a park I was only dimly if at all aware of in June 1974. What gave the Thunderbolt its uniqueness was that the coaster train went down after it left the station—not up, as is the case with most other coasters—and riders essentially boarded at the top of the highest hill rather than the bottom. Although with the Thunderbolt you sacrificed the tension and anticipation of ascending a coaster hill, the sudden, nearly blind descent almost as soon as you left the station was not a bad trade off.

The Thunderbolt was built in 1924 by the famous coaster designer, John Miller. Its stats are not very impressive by today's standards. It's only 70 feet high with a track length of less than 3,000 feet. However, the first drop is 95 feet and it is all thrill. The track is built into the ravines above the Monongahela River and the rider quickly loses a sense of where he is. The wood screams. The train shakes like a rag doll. It's an incredible coaster experience.

I did not get an opportunity to ride the Thunderbolt until 1975 while on a business trip to our ad agency, which was in Pittsburgh. I knew what to expect—the first drop was not going to be a surprise to me—but being intellectually or professionally prepared is not the same thing as riding the ride. I was surprised by its intensity. I knew I had ridden a great roller coaster. I wished it were at Cedar Point.

The coaster wars began in the mid-1970s and have continued with varying degrees of intensity, until today. In 1974, Cedar Point had four roller coasters: Blue Streak, Cedar Creek Mine Ride, Wildcat and Jumbo Jet. It was the fifth coaster, the Corkscrew, which opened in 1976 that changed everything forever at Cedar Point.

In the mid-1970s the industry was growing and changing. Kings Island opened in 1972. The two Marriott parks opened in 1976. Great Adventure in New Jersey opened in 1975. Theme parks were popping up everywhere. For coaster manufacturers, it was the dawn of a golden age. The 1960s had been good years, the 1970s would be even better.

Steel had begun to supplant wood as the coaster material of choice. Wood was art; steel was science.

## Corkscrew

After the mild disappointment of the IMAX Theatre in 1975, Cedar Point had committed to a thrill ride attraction in 1976. Cedar Point was not the first park to introduce a corkscrew-type roller coaster with inversions. Knott's Berry Farm, near Los Angeles, had opened a similar ride in 1975, as had Opryland, near Nashville. Both were designed and built by Arrow Development Company in Mountain View, California. The chief designer was Ron Toomer, a former NASA engineer, who would go on to design many famous roller coasters. Both the Opryland and Knott's rides had two corkscrew-type inversions, but did not have a vertical loop.

Cedar Point pressed Toomer and Arrow to deliver something bigger and better than what was at Opryland and Knott's Berry Farm.

At the same time, Magic Mountain, in Valencia, California, was constructing a new steel coaster called The Revolution, glamming onto the Bicentennial theme. This ride was designed by a German coaster genius named Werner Stengel and built by Anton Schwarzkopf, a European manufacturer. It would have only one inversion, but it would a first-ever vertical loop.

Cedar Point's Corkscrew would have three inversions: two corkscrews and a vertical loop, a first.

This would be my first experience marketing what has come to be known as "Big Steel."

It started out badly.

Twice in my history with Cedar Point we announced the construction of signature roller coasters and had to backtrack on the name. The first was the Corkscrew. Its original name, which I'm sure would be a great piece of trivia for coaster enthusiasts, was The Great Lake Erie Roller. I cannot remember the other contenders. The name was cleared by senior management, including my boss, Don Dittmann, and our CEO, Bob Munger. We liked the location tie-in with Lake Erie and the action conjured up by the world "roller," not to mention the association with roller coaster. It was also mildly derivative of a coaster name we all thought was the modern gold standard: The Great American Scream Machine at Six Flags over Georgia.

In October 1975, we announced that The Great Lake Erie Roller would debut at Cedar Point in 1976. Press coverage was strong.

Our marketing group had considered Corkscrew as a possible name. No question it was very descriptive visually and tied in directly with the both the look and the action of the ride. It was short, two syllables, easy to say, and was sharp and hard-sounding. But it was also fast becoming a generic name. It was a name we felt we would have trouble legally protecting and making our own. In fact, Geauga Lake (our northeast Ohio competitor) opened a coaster very similar to the Corkscrew in 1977 and called it the Corkscrew. I should add that as it turned out confusion between the two was never really a marketplace issue. In the end, we thought the generic issue was potentially a big problem and went with The Great Lake Erie Roller. It was my name, and I confess I was not above relishing the fact that I had named a roller coaster.

About two weeks after the announcement, Bob Munger started to get phone calls from a few board members, all Cleveland based, that the name should be Corkscrew—not Great Lake Erie Roller. At least one of them—I don't know which one—felt very strongly about it. This was all passed down to me through Don Dittmann. Don sympathized with my (our) predicament. He listened patiently as I uncorked reason after reason as to why we should fight this and stay with The Great Lake Erie Roller.

Then he said we would have to change the name. He told me this was a fight we couldn't win (he was right, of course) and that going with Corkscrew was not a bad thing as the name was at least as good, perhaps better. Yes, he said, the board was interfering with what should be a management prerogative, but that boards do that from time to time. Also, Bob Munger's heart was not in the fight, and he would have to make the case for us. End of story.

We low-balled the name change to Corkscrew. The marketplace had a whole off-season to digest the change. There were never any issues. It would be the same 20 years later, in 1996, when we announced Banshee as the name of our new stand-up coaster but had to pull it back and re-announce the ride as Mantis.

## Location. Location. Location.

The location of the Corkscrew and the way it was designed to provide interplay with the midway and with non-riding guests was a work of genius. The credit goes to Lee Jewett, our director of planning & design for Cedar Point. GateKeeper and Top Thrill Dragster also

The Corkscrew changed Cedar Point forever; in many ways it launched the first round of the coaster wars. Built in 1976, it's still going strong.
CEDAR POINT ARCHIVES

wonderfully involve the midway in the experience of the ride, but Lee Jewett first showed how to do it with the Corkscrew in 1976. The Corkscrew's track, including the two helix elements, flowed right over the midway. It was in the middle of everything. You could sit on the foundation of one of the track columns and eat your ice cream and look up and the train would roar right over your head. And it was a roar, or at least a deep-throated whoosh with a very strong edge.

From many places on the midway you could watch the train crest the hill, then move immediately into the vertical loop. The sound is a kind of distant hum, a steel on steel hum, which grows stronger as it gets closer to you. When it is directly overhead there is a rattle and roar, mixed in with the screams of riders. You can feel the vibration when the train is past you, as the steel relaxes from the weight of the train, as the air comes back together after being cut apart.

The ride stopped guests in their tracks. It was not the height—the Corkscrew's lift hill was only 85 feet high—it was the proximity of the track to the experience of the ride. There is a steel mesh screen about six feet long between the column and the track at the track's lowest point going over the midway. It was added a short time into the 1976 season when Safety realized a tall man could stand on the column support and possibly touch the track.

Guests gawked. They shook their heads. They pointed to the track and the trains. They looked straight up. They smiled and marveled. They caused Corkscrew midway jams all summer. It was a wonderful thing.

The trains were red, white, and blue, in keeping with the 1976 Bicentennial.

The Corkscrew opened to the world on May 15, 1976. It was denied the accolade of being the first modern-day coaster to feature a 360-degree vertical loop by Revolution at Magic Mountain, which had opened on May 8. But it was the first to offer three inversions.

As is often the case with new attractions, construction of the Corkscrew went down to the wire. The ride did not operate with riders until two days before opening day, May 15. George Roose, the 81-year-old vice chairman of the board, was a fan of roller coasters and had planned to be one of the first riders. On the Thursday before opening, he invited a Cleveland TV personality, Del Donahoo, to come out to the park and do a story on the ride. Donahoo was a well-known Channel 3 reporter and show host who specialized in "good" stories, features on interesting people and places. On the local level he mirrored the great Charles Kuralt at CBS, who had the best job in America traveling the country in a motor home hunting down stories about people who lived interesting, albeit unknown lives.

Late in the day, probably after 6 p.m., the word came down that the last bolt had been tightened and it was time to let her rip. I do not recall if our Safety staff rode a first ride to monitor the ride's G-forces with an accelerometer, but I suspect not. This was still the pre-accelerometer age. The first train included several construction workers, Arrow representatives, Dick Kinzel, George Roose, and Del Donahoo. There was lots of yelling and whooping as they climbed into the trains. I was standing on the midway positioned under one of the helixes. It was a beautiful and warm late spring afternoon.

I had a great view of the main hill and the vertical loop. The yelling and the shouting continued as the train ascended the hill. I could see Roose and Del Donahoo sitting together close to the front of the train. Every person in the area had run to the ride as soon as word got out the Corkscrew was going to operate with riders. Employees had poured out of offices. A crowed was quickly building. Cedar Point had not opened a roller coaster since 1972, and never in anyone's memory a ride like the Corkscrew. This was a big deal.

I heard the steel hum for the first time as the train launched into the vertical loop. The sound emptied as the back of the train came out of the loop. The track banked into a curve before heading into the first helix. It was suddenly above me and I recall the screams. I jerked my head up as the train passed over me and into the second helix. Then all I saw was the back of the train as it roared back into the station.

It all worked perfectly, at least as far as I could tell. We all cheered and clapped.

George Roose was pleased, grinning from ear to ear and had shown the world that even an 81-year-old could safely ride the Corkscrew. Del Donahoo was very pleased, as he now had an exclusive story on the first rides on the Corkscrew. It was the lead story on the 11 p.m. news that night, one day before opening. Everyone was a winner.

I got an opportunity to ride the ride the next day. I was not frightened (as I would be on Top Thrill Dragster 27 years later), but I was apprehensive about going through the loop. As it was, it happens so fast it's over before you know it. The dives into the helixes are more thrilling in my opinion. It's a relatively short ride at 2,050 feet, and total ride time station to station is two minutes, 15 seconds. A few weeks later I had the "opportunity" to ride the Corkscrew three consecutive times while we were filming for a publicity video. I wasn't right for three hours afterward. The multiple inversions really got to me, more head than stomach. The Corkscrew and I were good friends for the next 38 years, but mostly from a distance. I didn't ride it much, usually only when I had to (as when our boys reached the magic height of 48 inches and I rode it once with each of them.)

The Corkscrew was a publicity machine. We had TV stations calling us. Our job was to sort through the requests to do stories on the coaster to find a way to accommodate all the requests.

The Morning Exchange on Channel 5 in Cleveland aired weekdays from 8 – 10 a.m. It was a very successful program, a local version of "The Today Show," a ratings killer for the local affiliate. Early in June one of their producers contacted us to see if we could provide a guest who could talk about roller coasters, especially the Corkscrew.

I don't recall how we determined the choice should be Dick Kinzel, but we decided Dick should be the guy to do the story and he agreed to it. I was elected to escort him to the program and be the liaison with the station. We decided to take no chances and drove into Cleveland the night before since we had to be at the station before 8 a.m. We stayed at a downtown hotel, retiring early so Dick could study his notes.

I think it was Dick's first trip to a TV station. He was extremely prepared and had committed to memory every fact available concerning the Corkscrew. In the interview, conducted, as I recall, by Fred Griffith, the co-star of the program, he performed very well. It was a friendly venue.

On the return to the park we decided to take the Chaussee entrance to the park instead of the Causeway. It is the original road into the park, but it had become the back door with the opening of the Cedar Point Causeway. It was a bright and beautiful day. The lake was sparkling blue. Dick was in a good mood and pleased that the interview had gone well. The pressure was off for both of us. When we were at the 1700 block, still about a mile from the park, the traffic came to a standstill. We were backed up. It was a wonderful surprise. Not so much for the families sitting in their cars with a backseat full of kids who were stoked on doughnuts and the view of the lake and the tantalizing closeness of all those wonderful rides.

There were no cell phones then, of course, so even though we were very close to the park we might as well have been on Mars. After a few moments of near giddiness, Dick returned to the matter at hand. He was director of operations, the guy who basically runs the park, and he was desperate to know what was going on. I'm sure a thousand questions roamed through his head: How were we handling the parking lot? How were the rides running? Were we staffed up in restrooms? I had fewer questions in my head. Dick's concerns were immediate, mine long term: How do we get a TV station in Detroit to do a similar kind of story on the Corkscrew.

## Three Million Guests

Cedar Point blew the doors off in 1976. It was the year of the Bicentennial, and the year of the Corkscrew. It was my first experience with marketing a signature roller coaster. The Corkscrew set Cedar Point off as the park with the biggest and fastest and coolest roller coaster. Park attendance hit the 3 million mark for the first time, jumping approximately 500,000 visits or an amazing 20 percent increase. I have not gone back to look, but I'm sure we had, on balance, good weather that season. I also suspect, though it was never quantified, that the national good feelings about the Bicentennial contributed to a consumer mindset that made it easy to justify trips to Cedar Point. The Great Lakes region was still recovering from the gas crisis and recession of 1974-1975, but the economic outlook, while improving was not the explanation for three million visitors. Nor were a few less rainy days. Nor was it the nation's 200th birthday. It was the red, white, and blue sections of steel wedged in behind the Sky Ride West Station and Jungle Larry's African Safari. It was the Corkscrew.

Looking back, it was the success of the Corkscrew that set Cedar Point on its path to be the world's greatest roller coaster park.

## The Coaster Culture

Adding 500,000 new visitors created operational problems. They were good problems, of course, but nevertheless very real. We were not prepared for such success and we scrambled to add more queue for the ride and worked hard with the ride crew to get the coaster to operate at maximum capacity. Per the manufacturer's specs—always a bit suspect when it comes to theoretical ride capacity—the Corkscrew could provide 1,600 rides per hour. It was a three-train operation, which helped immensely. Similar rides at other parks would often be two train operations. But on many days, and every Saturday, the wait time for the Corkscrew was two hours or more.

Our more than 3 million visitors in 1976 were spread over only 102 operating days versus the 140 days the park operated in 2016. Back then, not much happened before Memorial Day or after Labor Day; attendance was jammed into the peak summer vacation time of July and August. There were no HalloWeekends. Cedar Point had its first 50,000 Saturday in 1976; in fact, it had several of them. The park was much smaller then. The Gemini Midway did not exist. Ride capacity was much less: no Raptor, no Millennium Force, no GateKeeper, no Top Thrill Dragster, no Mean Streak, no Maverick, and no Snake River Falls. The list goes on. And on. The bottom line: fewer operating days, less physical space, less ride capacity.

The summer of 1976 the midways were filled with guests. There were lines for rides, lines for food stands, lines for water fountains, lines for restrooms, lines to buy tickets, lines to buy T-shirts. Before guests even walked into the park, they had sat in their cars and crawled up U.S. Highway 250, the Cedar Point Chaussee, and the

Cedar Point Causeway. When the park closed, and it was time to drive home, it could take 45 minutes just to clear the parking lot and the Causeway.

In my opinion, the culture which would drive the organization for the next three decades was solidified in the summer of 1976. As an organization, we did not just sit back and watch it all happen. We worked hard, very hard, to make the guest experience as good as it could be. Yes, we were hierarchical. Yes, we celebrated long hours and OCs. Yes, we valued self-discipline, frugality, and loyalty.

On rides, the focus was on capacity. The Rides staff looked for every technique that would squeeze a few extra rides per hour from every ride. Capacity was celebrated and rewarded. Ride crews were pushed to set records, to compete with crews on other rides. The natural question: did we compromise safety with this focus? The park's safety record speaks for itself; it's the ultimate report card, and Cedar Point got straight A's. Safety was a given, it was always there. We didn't teach or tolerate short cuts.

Ride maintenance was a serious business. It can't be otherwise. In those years—up until he died from cancer in the spring of 1989— the park's maintenance and construction operation was headed up by Harry Bray, a West Virginian who created a ride maintenance system second to none. His lead ride maintenance supervisor was Jack Fletcher, a large, driven, funny, outgoing man who pushed his crews hard and never gave up when it came to solving mechanical problems. Cedar Point ride mechanics ran to ride locations. They worked fast and they worked hard and took great pride in fixing problems quickly and getting rides open for our guests.

We believed in our success. We believed we had created it. We believed we were the best in the world at what we did.

## Gemini

The first week of January 1978, while attending a consumer travel show in South Bend, Indiana, I learned I was going to be the father of twins. "There are two heartbeats," Marie said. I was not afraid; I was thrilled. My father was a twin.

A group of us from Marketing were in South Bend for "Operation Irish," a market blitz designed to increase attendance from the South Bend/Elkhart, Indiana market. I had succeeded in selling Don Dittmann on the program, the first time we had attempted anything like this. South Bend is a three, three-and-a-half-hour drive from Cedar Point, but it's an easy drive, exactly 200 miles from exit to exit on the Indiana and Ohio Turnpikes. It was, and is, mostly an overnight market. I knew from my college days that South Bend tilted to the west, to Chicago, for most things, and that Great America, north of Chicago on the Wisconsin line, considered South Bend part of their market. But I thought there was real potential in South Bend for Cedar Point. The introduction of Gemini was the perfect opportunity: Gemini was going to be worth a long drive.

Operation Irish had a military inspiration; it would be a combined arms approach: corporate sales, PR/publicity, and direct marketing. At the consumer travel show we would have a Cedar Point booth featuring a model of Gemini. We would hand-out brochures and admission coupons (so we could track response) and talk directly to potential guests. During the same period, we would personally visit all the media outlets in the market and talk about Gemini and Cedar Point and the fact we were exhibiting at the show. Our sales team would visit companies and organizations in the market and make our classic pitch of signing up for our Cedar Point consignment ticket program, where organizations would sell discounted park tickets to their employees or members as a benefit program.

Probably half the Marketing staff spent three days in South Bend. Our reception was positive. The hardest sell were the organizations we met with who would handle the ticket consignment program. It was work: promoting the program, selling tickets, handling cash, keeping records, sending in payments, reconciling at the end of the season. Many organizations as a matter of policy could not handle money. The biggest objection to overcome was that many companies just didn't believe there was sufficient demand for the program among their employees or members. We argued Gemini would change that. In all, I think we signed up 12-15 companies, with good leads on several more, and viewed the sales effort as a success.

The local news media were a relatively easy sell. Everybody enjoys reading or viewing or hearing a new roller coaster story. Our PR staff did several impromptu on-air interviews when they visited radio stations. Our goal was always to get the media to commit to doing a first-person story on Gemini or the park when the season opened. We wanted reporters to ride the ride and then talk about it to their audiences.

Over the three days I split my time among the three groups. I went on some sales calls, visited local media, and worked the booth at the show. Working the show was the most fun. The model of Gemini was an instant hook, even for non-riders. It scooped people off the show floor and deposited them in front of our booth. When you can say: "Gemini will be the highest, steepest, and fastest roller coaster in the world" you have about said it all. The kids would gawk at the model. Adults would smile and shake their heads. Nearly all eagerly accepted the brochures and the coupons. Most show visitors had heard of Cedar Point, and quite a few had thought about coming in the past. "It's on the list for this summer" was a frequent comment. An hour into the show, the marketing power of Gemini was obvious. It even had appeal for non-riders.

I took the opportunity to drive around campus. I had been an undergraduate at Notre Dame only seven years before. Now I was married and working and soon to be a father. My Notre Dame days seemed like distant history.

At night our group did a little partying. We were all young, everyone under 30, and most still unmarried. Disco was king then. One night we all visited a local South Bend dance club and bar. It was my introduction to the disco craze. One of our sales reps, Mark Mills, put on quite a show. Mark was short, thin, and very athletic—he had played shortstop for the University of Michigan and though only about 140 pounds could hit a golf ball into the next county—and he was an amazing dancer. Handsome, too, and he spent the night dancing with one good-looking woman after another. His experience with women had never been my experience, but I appreciated his gifts and really felt no envy: I would be driving home to Marie, and I was going to be a father twice over.

We viewed—I certainly viewed—Operation Irish as an outstanding success, at least the first phase. The proof would be measured by how many people from the market visited the park in the summer of 1978—and beyond.

We drove home to Sandusky in a snow storm, at least in Indiana. South Bend is in the lee of Lake Michigan and a northwest wind piles up snow with amazing speed. I drove the van which contained the Gemini model and the show booth. The wind blew the van all over the road and at times we could hardly see 100 yards. My navigator and companion was Nancy Diem (then Steinmuller), a PR staffer and the first person I hired when I became Communications Manager at Cedar Point. Nancy loved music and crooned the words to Billy Joel's "Piano Man," as we drove into the growing darkness on the road to Ohio.

The winter bad winter had a major impact on the construction of Gemini. The Cedar Point Peninsula is a very difficult construction site even in a relatively mild winter. The wind howls off the lake and across Sandusky Bay. It is damp, in the bones, face-peeling cold. If you work around the edges of the peninsula, the wind is even more vicious, slamming into the shore from the lake and the bay. The carpenters and ironworkers who toiled on the rides dressed for conditions, but efficiency drops markedly in extreme cold and wind, no matter how thick your Carhart's are.

After the Blizzard of '78, there was white everywhere and piled into drifts of snow and sand that often exceeded eight feet in height. The impact of the storm and the continuing severe weather slowed construction on Gemini. Internally, by the first of March, we knew we would never make opening day. However, as an organization we put on the expected happy face: we expect to open the ride on May 6, opening day for the 1978 season.

Gemini had competition. It was far away, on the West Coast, and the competition was largely overlooked by the local and regional media, but we were very conscious of it: Colossus at Magic Mountain, just north of Los Angeles. It also was scheduled to open in 1978 and would boast similar stats to Gemini.

Gemini is a hybrid, part steel and part wood. The structure was wood, treated southern yellow pine, but its track was tubular steel, like the Corkscrew or the Mine Ride or a hundred other steel coasters. It was designed by Ron Toomer of Arrow Development. It was not the first of its kind—the Mine Ride at Cedar Point, built in 1969, is a wood/steel hybrid—but it was the first hybrid built to such a grand scale. I do not know the origin of the concept, whether it was driven by the park or by Ron Toomer, but somewhere in the mix of Ron Toomer, Dick Kinzel, and Lee Jewett the Gemini came to life.

The tubular steel track was well within Arrow's comfort zone. They had pioneered the technology and had confidence it would provide a smooth ride. The relatively light tubular steel track meant the wood supporting structure could be much lighter than on a traditional wood coaster. But the wood provided mass, a traditional profile, and aesthetic appeal.

The biggest sell on Gemini, once past its amazing stats, was the fact that it was a racing coaster. There would be two sets of trains operating on parallel tracks, so riders could combine the thrill of the ride itself while competing to be the first train back into the station.

Gemini was designed to provide monster capacity, with six 32-passenger trains, and it delivered. Theoretical capacity was an amazing 3,300 per hour.

## How Gemini Got Its Name

The naming process for Gemini involved input from several different constituencies: senior management, the board of directors, middle management, the advertising agency (MARC & Company), the Marketing, Planning & Design, and probably some others as well. There was nothing objective about the process. It was completely subjective. In the end, we knew the decision would be made by Bob Munger, the CEO.

As a group of groups, we came up with at least 100 names. Some of the names that were not chosen: ThunderFlash, The Screaming Banshee, Double Trouble, Fun's Run, Twin Spirits, Thunder and Lightning, High Roller, Tandemonium, Double Dare, Lakeshore Drive,

Demon Duo. The name Gemini was suggested by our advertising agency, specifically Ron Schnurr, who headed up the market research department and was not considered part of the creative team. Once the name surfaced, it achieved a rapid consensus and Bob Munger gave it his imprimatur. Gemini it would be. It fit, of course, communicating the singular attraction of the ride: it was a racing coaster with twin tracks. Gemini is Latin for twins. It's the third astrological sign in the Zodiac, originating from the constellation of Gemini. The constellation is associated with the twins Castor and Pollux in Greek mythology. Castor and Pollux are associated with St. Elmo's fire and were protectors of sailors. When Castor died, as he was mortal, Pollux implored his father, Zeus, to give his twin brother immortality, which he did, uniting them forever in the night sky.

The ride's station design, signage, and advertising all borrowed from the space theme.

The building of Gemini and Marie's pregnancy were parallel events. We were teased a lot about it, and at the park there was even a betting pool as to whether the twins would be born before, after, or at the same time as the coaster's first ride. Marie didn't think it was very funny.

There were two parts to the sell: the fact that Gemini would be the highest, steepest, and fastest roller coaster in the world; and the fact that it was a racing coaster with twin tracks. It was advertised at 125 feet high (in actuality it was closer to 126 feet) with a 118-foot first drop. The angle of descent was 55 degrees. The ride was 3,935 feet long. Top speed was an amazing 60 mph. Within a decade, these stats would be less impressive, but in 1978 they were the leading edge of the roller coaster frontier.

In January, in a brainstorming session, our PR group came up with the idea of hosting a conference on roller coasters. We decided to host it the July 4 weekend, when we were certain the new ride would be open and any bugs worked out. We saw it as a strategy to promote Gemini, but also Cedar Point and its growing position as the roller coaster capital of the world. To give the conference legitimacy, and a solid news hook, we decided to approach the Department of Popular Culture at Bowling Green State University, located just 60 miles west of Cedar Point in Bowling Green, just south of Toledo, to see if they would be interested in sponsoring the event or participating in it in some way.

Coasters were a growing phenomenon in popular culture. New coasters were being built all over the U.S. They were beginning to create their own sub-culture of enthusiasts who wanted to know everything there was to know about coasters and who would travel the country, and even the world, to ride roller coasters. Their spiritual leader was Robert Cartmell, who had written the seminal article on roller coasters as a worthwhile obsession in The New York Times in 1974. Coaster enthusiasts would officially organize in early June 1978, as the American Coaster Enthusiasts (ACE) at Kings Dominion, an amusement park outside Richmond, Virginia.

The meeting at Bowling Green went very well. The director of the program, Dr. Ray Browne, was also its creator. The program was still young then, only five years old, and still searching for legitimacy in the academic world. Dr. Browne was tall and outgoing, self-assured, and eager to hear more about what he termed "those crazy coaster riders." Instinctively, he saw the coaster phenomenon as legitimate popular culture, and he also saw the association with Cedar Point as a great way to publicize his program. It was a perfect fit: Gemini meets PhD.

Working with two associate professors, Mike Marsden and John Nachbar, Dr. Browne and his staff agreed to put together the program for the event, setting up speakers and presenters. The program would feature non-academics as well as academics. Dr. Browne convinced Bowling Green State University to allow the department to offer a two credit course on roller coasters, which included attendance at the event, which we had named "Coastermania." There was a lot of academic backlash once the course was announced. I don't think Dr. Browne cared, in fact I think he reveled in it. The announcement generated a lot of news coverage, including The New York Times. He loved the limelight.

Robert Cartmell, the rock star of the coaster culture, agreed to give a presentation at the event, giving it instant credibility with coaster enthusiasts.

We invited Gary Kyriazi, who also had a national reputation as a coaster expert. He was the author of "The Great American Amusement Parks," published in 1976. Kyriazi was working on his TV documentary, "America Screams," starring horror film star Vincent Price. Coastermania was the perfect event to include in the film.

Gary and I bonded. We were both in our late 20s and had been English majors in college (Gary at UCLA and me at Notre Dame). I envied him his success with his book. Gary would come to Cedar Point many times over the years working on a variety of projects. His love of coasters, and amusement parks, has always been a constant.

The severe winter had crippled construction on the ride for two months. Finally, in late March the weather broke and the race to opening day began. It is difficult for the layman to look at a building or even a roller coaster at a given point in the construction and have an informed opinion on how much longer it would take to complete. The party line was that it would be ready for opening day, but as opening day got closer it became obvious to everyone that it was not going to happen. We all pretended—to group sales clients, news media, general public—that everything was on schedule, but we were whistling past the roller coaster when we said it. In Marketing, we all knew there would be a time, very soon, when we would have to deal with reality.

## When is Gemini Going to Open?

Reality for me came a few weeks before opening day, in late April. My boss, Don Dittmann, was in Tacoma, Washington on personal business. A Cleveland television crew (I think from Channel 3) showed up at the front gate unannounced (they were in the area doing another story) and asked to do a piece on the new roller coaster. We welcomed them with open arms. I assigned one of our young PR reps, Lynn Dugas, to work with the crew.

Before she went to meet them at the front gate and escort them to the ride, she asked me what to say when they asked the inevitable question of when Gemini was going to open.

I thought about it and decided we couldn't say it would open when we knew it wouldn't. "Tell them it's doubtful for opening day but we are shooting for Memorial Day weekend."

It's a no-win situation. Do you somehow dance around it now and deal with the bad news in a few weeks, or do you tell the truth and risk guests delaying their visits until later in the summer, after the coaster had opened? In a season of only 110 operating days, every day mattered. Anyone looking at the half-built structure would know it wasn't going to open in a few weeks.

I didn't have the opportunity to talk it over with Don Dittmann. He was 2,500 miles away and in a different time zone. I had no idea how to reach him.

Lynn reported back that the interview went well. They shot lots of footage of the carpenters and ironworkers on the ride. She thought the story would focus on the construction.

I didn't think much more about it.

However, I did watch the 6 p.m. news on Channel 3. They led with the Gemini story. And the Gemini story led with the reporter standing in front of some construction equipment announcing that park officials confirmed that Cedar Point's big new roller coaster would not be ready for opening day. My stomach started churning immediately. The story was no coaster on opening day, not coaster doubtful for opening day.

In hindsight, and based on subsequent experience, I should have immediately recognized the delicacy of the situation and handled the story myself. I should have dodged and weaved like a good White House spokesperson and said something like we are planning or "hoping" to open the ride on opening day. I also should have tried to contact Bob Munger, who was at Cedar Point, to get direction.

I got a call at home about 7:30 p.m. Marie and I were having dinner. It was Don Dittmann. He was calm but concerned. He asked me what happened. I told him. According to Don, Bob Munger, our CEO, had seen the news story. Munger was furious.

"I've just finished speaking with Bob Munger. I told him he needed to talk with you because obviously I wasn't there, and you were." Don said. I couldn't argue with his logic.

"Listen," he said, "You are going to have to talk to a very angry man. I can't sugarcoat it. I told him you would tell him the truth about what happened."

Don's voice was serious—he needed to communicate to me that this was serious, that he couldn't be there to help me, and that I was on my own. He wasn't trying to make light of it; he was concerned. He didn't say it, but I knew he didn't know how Munger was going to react when I talked with him. He gave me a number where I could reach him to report back after I had talked to Munger.

I hung up the phone—a wall phone in our kitchen—and looked at Marie across the table, who was almost eight months pregnant with twins, and thought about what might happen. I did not think I would be fired, though I couldn't rule it out, but I was certain I was at risk for demotion or a cut in my bonus rate or worse.

"Get it over with," she said. "Call him." My wife is a person of action.

We both knew she was right.

I called the Cedar Point Police and asked to be put through to Munger's apartment (when he was at the park he lived in an apartment attached to the Cedars dormitory). The officer commented that Munger was expecting my call.

I remember it rang only once and he picked up.

"This is John Hildebrandt, Mr. Munger," I said.

"Tell me what the hell happened!" he shouted.

I did, best as I could. I did take responsibility. I was smart enough not to argue my case with him.

He gave it to me pretty good. He closed by telling me it was his call as to when the coaster would open. He had to be concerned about overtime, the cost of the ride. It was a big decision. I admit the issue of how much construction labor to invest in the ride versus the potential of lost revenue due to a later opening was something I had not considered.

Then his rant was suddenly over. He started to mellow.

I called Don right away and replayed my conversation with Bob Munger. I thought I could detect in his voice some relief that I wasn't summarily fired. Bob Munger had a temper. You couldn't predict what he would do.

The next morning, I got a call to go see Bob Munger. I was frightened walking up the steps to the second floor of the administration building. I didn't see anything good coming out of this meeting. I had called Marie at the paper before going out the door. She was endearingly blunt and told me using some good four-letter words that we would be fine no matter what happened.

The rage had passed. Bob Munger was smiling. He told me to take this as a teaching lesson, as an experience to build on. He pretty much apologized for losing control—yet he reiterated that I had screwed up. It was a short meeting. As I left, I felt much better. I believed then, as I do now, that Bob Munger was a good man.

## Countdown

The season opened with the ride still under construction. The midway wasn't empty, but it wasn't full, either. Overall, it was a slow attendance start to the season, as we all had pretty much expected. The pressure to open the ride was intense and kept building. The media called, guests called, group sales clients called, the financial community called. Tempers were short in the administration building and it permeated the entire organization. Everyone was on edge.

Out at the ride site, everything was at a fever pitch. The first hill was capped, and we got lots of coverage from a picture of Jim Colvin from maintenance, the project manager on the job, holding a huge tape measure over the track showing the top height at more than 125 feet. (We also had an independent survey done to confirm the height. We took no chances.)

Our agency had to keep re-doing the announcement campaign. This went on week after week. There was a division of opinion within management whether to open the ride the moment it was ready or to announce a specific date when we were sure the ride was ready and give ourselves a three to five-day cushion to start to get the word out and give the media a few days to do stories on the ride. In the end, we opted for the second plan. Early in the week of June 12, Maintenance, Operations, and Arrow signed off that they believed the ride would be ready for the public by Saturday, June 17. Advertising started mid-week.

Like the Corkscrew, I cannot claim that I rode on the first train on Gemini. But I was on one of the first. The view up the first hill was spectacular, looking east, the Hotel Breakers and Lake Erie clearly visible. I was in the front seat. I do not remember who I rode with. I remember how cool it was to be so close to the second train. We talked and laughed on the ride up. The chain lift was loud but not overbearing.

There are, in my opinion, three distinct thrill points in riding Gemini. The first, and most impressive, is the first drop. It is 118 feet from the top to the bottom of the track. It is not so fearsome now compared to Magnum and Millennium Force, but it is still impressive and in June 1978, it was quite scary. I remember thinking I would be carried into the ground, like I was riding a bomb. It was an amazing thrill and the best experience on the ride.

The second thrill point is in the second half of the ride, when the track goes under a steel support beam. Although the clearance is more than adequate, the action of the ride—the track lifts as it passes under the beam—the rider is 100 percent certain he or she is going to be decapitated on the spot. The first time through it's terrifying. I do not know if this near-death experience was designed into the ride or not—I suspect not; it was actually an unintended, but positive consequence of the design of the structure and the track—but it quickly became one of the signature experiences of the ride. From the midway, it's fun to watch all the hands in the air suddenly go down to the bar as the train flies under the beam. I have ridden Gemini a hundred times. I still duck.

The third thrill point is the spiral at the very end of the ride. It's a hard, fast, and unexpected spiral which brings the trains back up to station level. I've never particularly liked it. I never look forward to the experience. But it is a thrill. No other ride at Cedar Point has a comparable finish.

The racing experience on Gemini adds to the fun, but in practice most of the time the trains are not that close together. The ride operators work hard to dispatch the trains in a way that they will stay together, but it's more art than science and subject to many variables.

The weakest part of the ride experience are the tops of the figure eight where the trains transition to the next drop. The speed of the trains drop dramatically. You can catch your breath, you can look around, you can talk to your riding partner or the riders in the other train; these are not experiences that make for a great roller coaster ride. A great ride is unrelenting and takes hold of you and owns you, body and soul, until the train is in the station and the restraint pops open.

## Gemini is Alive

We were ready on June 17. Or so we thought. I was pleased that it didn't appear that our children would be born on the day the ride opened, though Marie said it was going to be a very close thing. It was a sunny Saturday, cool and clear, a big Canadian high pressure system had rolled down over the Great Lakes. The night before was jacket weather.

Our plan was to open Gemini at 11 a.m., two hours after the park opened and an hour after the rides began running. The midway was

First ride on Gemini, June, 1978. Bob Munger, then the company's CEO, is in the first row with Harry Bray, VP maintenance and construction. Munger is wearing a tie, and, if you look closely, holding a cigar in his right hand. CEDAR POINT ARCHIVES.

Gemini for the generations: Our son, Tom, and his eight-year-old daughter, Hadley, celebrate her first ride on Gemini (August 27, 2018). Tom and his twin brother, Mike, were born only two days after the coaster opened on June 17, 1978.

blocked by queue railing by the Witches Wheel on one side and by the train tracks at the entrance to Frontier Town. We had seasonal staff at both ends of the midway for crowd control.

Enter George Roose. Our 83-year-old vice chairman was a member of an exclusive organization of Ohio boosters called the Ohio Commodores. Very loosely patterned after the famous Kentucky Colonels and named for Commodore Oliver Hazard Perry, the victor in the 1813 Battle of Lake Erie, the Commodores were made up of people—mostly but not exclusively male—who in theory had done great things for the State of Ohio. The organization had been formed in the 1960s and was an unofficial part of the governor's family.

George Roose had arranged for the Ohio Commodores to hold their summer meeting at Cedar Point in 1978 and had invited Governor James Rhodes to attend the meeting and officially open the new coaster. The Governor had accepted the invitation, so we were not completely unprepared, but the schedules of governors are always subject to change and many of us doubted he would show up. But we were ready for him. It was an election year and it would be great publicity to open a new coaster at Cedar Point and tout Ohio's tourism industry. He had everything to gain by accepting Roose's invitation.

The Commodores had a breakfast scheduled for the Coral Dining Room at 9 a.m. The Governor was scheduled to attend and make a few remarks. At about 10 a.m., the Governor, George Roose, and any Commodore who wished to ride would walk down to Gemini. The Governor would cut a ribbon, and all would ride the ride. When the Commodores were off the ride platform, the midway would open and guests could enter the Gemini queue.

My assignment was to stick with George Roose and the Commodores and lead them up to the ride. I told the Park Operations staff, specifically Dick Kinzel, that I would call from the Coral Dining Room as the breakfast was ending so they would have a heads up. We estimated it would take at least 10 minutes to get to the ride, possibly more with the inevitable stragglers.

There were about 150 Commodores at breakfast, couples mostly, all old (from my perspective) and wealthy.

The breakfast went quickly, too quickly. The Governor didn't talk long. I stood in the back of the room with one of our sales reps and watched it all unfold. At the conclusion of his remarks, Governor Rhodes thanked George Roose for the opportunity to visit the park on such an important day. At 9 a.m. or so, approximately one hour ahead of schedule, the Governor shouted: "Let's all go ride a roller coaster!" Within seconds, he was headed for the door with Mr. Roose scrambling to catch up with him.

The Governor had no intention of riding Gemini. Riding roller coasters was not in his playbook. He was ahead of schedule by design. We found out later he had a golf date that had been moved up an hour.

I ran to the closest phone. I called the ride station and asked to speak to Dick Kinzel.

"The Governor, George Roose, and the Commodores are all headed for the ride," I said. "Get ready."

Dick was not too happy. "We aren't ready. Slow them down. Talk to Mr. Roose."

I told him I would do my best.

Then I called Don Dittmann. He had the same counsel: "Talk to Mr. Roose."

I told the sales rep to alert the PR Department and headed to the door. I had to run to catch up with the Governor and Roose. They were leading the parade. I knew no one would walk ahead of them, but I had to dodge and weave through the crowd to catch up. Roose walked down the boardwalk in front of the Breakers, then turned and led them through the Rotunda, the lobby, and the long hallway which led to the hotel entrance. I caught up to Mr. Roose and the Governor in the lobby. They were talking, but I knew I had to find a way to interrupt. I started walking alongside Mr. Roose and looked for an opening. I was amazed at how fast they were walking. There was a short pause in their conversation. I pounced.

"Mr. Roose," I said, "they're not ready for you at the ride. They won't be ready for an hour. We need to slow things down."

There was no response. He didn't even look at me. I might as well have been talking to a penguin.

The group never broke stride, but by now it had spread to a long thin line.

From the hotel entrance Mr. Roose led them along the edge of the parking lot to the hotel entrance to the park. I could see the Park Admissions staff scrambling. They weren't ready, either.

I tried talking to Mr. Roose again. He didn't acknowledge me. As Don Dittmann said later that day, "What were you supposed to do? You had God on one side and Jesus Christ on the other."

We flew through the admission gates. The manager on duty, I think it was Candy Frankowski, was smart enough to tell her staff just to open the gates and smile. There was temporary queue across the entrance to the new Gemini midway. The ride rose impressively behind it. It was a beautiful early summer morning, clear and blue Canadian high pressure.

We passed through the queue, the last barrier to the ride, and Mr. Roose led the group down the midway. I could see the mad scramble in the station, people flying around everywhere. There was an Ohio

Highway Patrol car and a black Lincoln parked by the entrance to the ride: The Governor's getaway convoy.

I found Dick Kinzel on the ride platform. As director of park operations, he was the ranking Cedar Point official present. I told him he would have to represent the company. (Bob Munger, our CEO, was of course thinking the ride would not open for another hour and was nowhere around.)

The Governor and George Roose were anxious to get things moving. However, there was—and is—a safety protocol on all Cedar Point rides which requires that all rides be operated empty at least once before operating with riders. Dick Kinzel rightly pointed out to Mr. Roose that we would have to do this before anyone could ride Gemini. There was no argument from Mr. Roose. He understood.

The crew went through their checks and the first two Gemini trains left the station to cheers and applause. Two went out, but only one came back.

About halfway through the ride, the blue train failed to make it up one of the hills and rolled backward or "valleyed" in industry talk. The train went up and down a bit and then settled at the low point between the two hills, approximately 25 feet above the ground.

However, Gemini is a racing coaster. There is a second train. We piled the Ohio Commodores into the red train. They were loud and boisterous, very happy to be there, even though they hardly fit the coaster rider profile, as nearly all of them were over 40 and the average age was probably late 50s – early 60s.

The Governor was introduced. He spoke briefly, thanked George Roose, and then cut the ribbon. He was whisked off the platform as soon as the red train arrived back in the station. I'm sure he was playing golf by noon.

It took at least two trains to give all the Commodores a ride. By now the midway was swarming with guests eager to ride the world's highest, steepest, and fastest roller coaster.

What caused the blue train to valley were several factors which combined to slow the speed and momentum of the ride. There was not enough weight in the train to generate enough speed to make it over all the hills. A complicating factor was that the lubrication on the wheels was not designed for cool weather.

Harry Bray, our vice president of maintenance, was quickly on the scene to evaluate the situation. Given where the train had stopped, winching it up to the top of the hill and then filling it with employees and letting gravity take over just wasn't going to work. It would not generate enough speed. The train would just valley at the bottom of the next hill. The only solution was to take the train apart where it was and lift the pieces off the track. Then reassemble it. He told Dick Kinzel his guys would work like hell, but it would take most of the day.

While all this was going on, I caught the image of Bob Munger walking up the exit steps to the station platform. He was by himself and even though I was a fair distance away I could see that his face was as red as the bright red train just entering the station. He was loaded for bear. He had one of his ever-present cigars in his hand, although I'm not sure if it was lit. He waved it around as he spoke to Kinzel and others. Some who were on the Gemini platform that morning say they saw him put the cigar in his mouth and bite it cleanly in half. I did not see that happen, but he was very pissed off, mostly, I think, out of simple frustration and embarrassment.

The ride was opening six weeks late, and now when it finally does open only half of it is running. He's thinking it's a beautiful Saturday, the park is full of people, and many will leave frustrated because they didn't get to ride Gemini. The fact that the blue train valleyed was no one's fault. It was part of the learning process of the ride. If he had to take anyone to the woodshed it was George Roose and the Governor, and they were untouchable.

Guests seemed to like the ride. The midways were filled with guests. By early afternoon, the temperature was in the upper 70s and the lake and bay were a sparkling blue. It was all going to work out.

I worked Sunday morning. Gemini was back to being a racing coaster, and it was already demonstrating amazing capacity.

## Mike and Tom Check In

I was home by early afternoon. In those years, Sunday was my normal day off during the operating season. Marie was due in a week, so I was in a hurry to get home. I recall that in the evening, probably around seven or eight, in the soft light part of the day, well before sunset, we were standing outside on the driveway in front of the garage. I was sweeping up grass cuttings. Marie said it wouldn't be long. I recall how happy I was, and how apprehensive, too. I was glad to be who I was and where I was and who I was with.

Early the next morning, in the gray time, Marie nudged me awake and said it was time to go to the hospital. We were not in panic mode, but we dressed very quickly and got in the car and headed to Firelands Hospital.

It was Monday, June 19, 1978.

Marie was in labor until late afternoon. I spent the day going in and out of her room, offering what support I could. We would talk for a while—we talked about names some because we still didn't know whether we'd be parents of a boy and a girl, two girls, or two boys—then Marie would kick me out and I would wander the halls. I was going to be in the delivery room when the time came—it was an order, not a request—but one I had happily agreed to many months previously. It was a sunny day, I remember that, though I spent the whole day indoors.

The boys were born at 4:30 and 4:33 p.m. The delivering physician was Doctor Vermeeren. One of the nurses asked me if I wanted to touch my sons. I remember touching each of their cheeks with my forefinger. That was my first physical contact with Mike and with Tom. Mike was 5.4 lbs. and Tom was 5.9 lbs. Good-sized for twins. Marie had gone almost to term.

Tom was named in honor of Uncle Tommy, Marie's favorite uncle, Tom Candreva, her mother's baby brother. Mike was named Michael simply because I had always liked the name. At the time we named him we did not know that Michael was the name of his paternal great great great grandfather. Michael was a middle name; his given name was Hugo, as is mine, as was my father's, and my grandfather's. I knew firsthand such an odd name was problematical—and someday he might curse me for it—but it was honoring a connection with my father and his family that I thought was important. He would go by Michael, we assumed, as I went by John. But it was also cool to have a special name, as I rationalized it all. He might live his whole life and outside his family and know no other man named Hugo.

I used the pay phone in the lobby to call my parents, who were ecstatic to be grandparents. They passed the word to my brothers and my sister. Marie talked with her parents, Tessie and Ben Martilotta.

I held the boys in Marie's hospital room, one at a time; a week later I could easily hold them both at the same time. I was kicked out and sent home around 8 p.m. I had a list of things to bring back to the hospital with me the next day.

I was ravenously hungry. I went to the Ponderosa Steak House at the Sandusky Mall. I thought about a lot of things as I ate. I knew, as all parents know, that my life had irrevocably changed. Life was very serious now, no more fun and games. I was all grown up.

Marie stayed in the hospital until Friday morning. In those days, especially with twins, caution prevailed. Every night I ate at the Ponderosa Steak House; it became my new home. On Wednesday night, I brought my parents and Aunt Margaret there for dinner. For whatever reason, I have never been to a Ponderosa since.

I have no memory of work for that week. I know Don and Mary Margaret Dittmann were happy for us. As Don had said to me a few weeks back while sitting in the Surf Lounge after work, "Children are what life is all about."

The boys came home on Friday morning. I believe Marie held them both in her arms as we drove through Sandusky and then out Perkins Avenue to Fairway Lane. Today, we'd have been arrested for child endangerment. We laid them together in the crib in what would become their bedroom. They fell asleep quickly.

## Coastermania

Gemini was open, and attendance was starting to recover. Our next biggest challenge was hosting Coastermania on the July 4 Weekend. We had picked the date to give ourselves some breathing room in case the coaster had opened late; also, there was a gathering of coaster enthusiasts at Busch Gardens in Williamsburg in mid-June we didn't want to step on.

In all, our event attracted about 300 enthusiasts from literally all over the country. They were an odd conclave: coaster fans, academics, industry types, coaster manufacturer representatives. BGSU and the Department of Popular Culture (Ray Brown) had put together the program and they had given it a decidedly academic bent. I think many of the coaster enthusiasts were surprised. They were at the event to ride coasters and meet other coaster fanatics; they weren't there for an academic discussion about why some people are so stoked up on coasters.

One presenter talked about the sociology, demography, and psychology of coaster fans. Another talked about their architectural significance.

The sociologist hit on an obvious but true observation: coaster enthusiasts are not daredevils and not risk takers, which goes against the popular conception. There is no correlation between riding coasters and sky diving or mountain climbing. In part, coaster enthusiasts are attracted to coasters because in fact there is so little risk. It is a very safe thing to do. The numbers don't lie: the Gemini has given, to date approximately 55 million rides without a major injury. However, coasters don't feel safe. They don't look safe. They are scream machines. They are a way to get very safely scared.

The coaster culture was just emerging in 1978. The just concluded gathering at Busch Gardens was the event which gave birth to the organization now known as the American Coaster Enthusiasts or ACE, which now has more than 5,000 members, an international footprint, and publishes a color magazine on a quarterly basis.

Coastermania had been created to generate media attention for Gemini and for Cedar Point. It succeeded very well. The event was covered bay lots of regional media outlets, especially in Detroit and Cleveland, but also some national outlets, including The New York Times. The article hit a nerve. They talked with Robert Cartmell, who danced around it but basically said Gemini was a good coaster

Gemini: The world's highest, fastest, and steepest roller coaster in the world when it opened on June 17, 1978. CEDAR POINT ARCHIVES

but not a great one. I said it was a great coaster for nearly all the guests who would ride it.

The truth was, as all of us at Cedar Point knew, for coaster enthusiasts Gemini's ride experience did not live up to expectations as being the highest, steepest, and fastest in the world. A lot of the coaster fans who came to Coastermania were at least somewhat disappointed in the ride experience; it just did not meet their lofty expectations. Everyone loved the first drop, but the rest of the ride not so much. It was too slow, the big sweeping turns were boring, the beam that appeared ready to take off your head was a cheap trick, and it was too quiet; they wanted the rattle and roar of a steel tracked wooden coaster.

To my knowledge there is only one other coaster that is like Gemini, the smaller Excalibur at Valleyfair, which is of course within the Cedar Fair family. Gemini did not, like the Corkscrew, get replicated around the country and the world. The lack of thrill versus the cost hurt its marketability.

Gemini would go on to become the signature ride at Cedar Point for more than a decade, really until the opening of Magnum XL-200 in 1989. The Demon Drop in 1983 and the Iron Dragon in 1987 were good rides—and the Demon Drop became arguably the scariest ride at Cedar Point when it opened—but Gemini was still king.

Its capacity was legendary. With all six trains in operation and with an experienced crew working the ride, Gemini could give nearly

4,000 rides per hour. No other coaster came close. The line would move so fast there was virtually no standing and waiting for guests. Even when the line spilled out onto the midway at peak times on Saturdays, the line moved so fast it seemed to vanish in minutes.

For a park like Cedar Point, which drew on average three million guests each season, it was a huge advantage to have a big popular ride that could generate that kind of capacity. It was King of Capacity at a park where capacity mattered and was highly valued. For most guests, Gemini was plenty of coaster. For most Cedar Point guests, it was their first serious coaster experience, a rite of passage, a step up to real coaster-riding. Many times in conversations with guests over the years they would talk about their first Gemini ride with pride. It was a ride for the great mass of Cedar Point guests. Guests of a certain age have great affection for Gemini.

Gemini is amusement park art.

Gemini has since been eclipsed by many larger and more thrilling coasters, both at Cedar Point and in the coaster world in general. It hasn't run in six train operation in many years, and many operating days it operates with only two trains. Ridership is less because guests choose to invest their time in rides like Millennium Force and Maverick—understandably. The search for the ultimate thrill has moved on past Gemini.

I visited Gemini many times when I was GM of Cedar Point. It was one of my twilight or evening stops. I would walk up the exit and then cut over through the path in the bushes and then up the spiral stair to the platform, right next to the red (blue) train operator. Sometimes I would surprise the operator, sometimes not. Many times, another crew member would spot me coming up the exit and put the word out. The Gemini platform is comparatively high and the view up the midway is impressive. If you look down the midway you have a clear view of the CP&LE Railroad crossing and the midway which leads into Frontier Town. The train whistle and the clanging of the bell easily carry over to Gemini platform. I would always walk to the end of the platform and watch the trains fly through the spirals before coming into the station.

The weather the weekend of Coastermania was terrible. We were assaulted with a strong northeaster which meant three days of wind, rain, and cold. A lot of the Coastermania attendees grumbled because opportunities to ride were reduced. Park attendance was dismal, and I think we gave up all the attendance gains the park had garnered since June 17. On Sunday afternoon, with the conference over and staring out at an empty midway, several of us met in Nancy Steinmuller's office to do a post mortem. Nancy, who had been our lead person dealing with Dr. Brown, the coaster enthusiasts, and the overall event, was exhausted. She had done a great job, but none of us were in a self-congratulating mood, probably influenced by the weather.

Nancy had just come in from the midway. Her dark hair was wet and matted. When the meeting was over she looked at all of us and said, without smiling, "I'm going to go home and make love to my boyfriend." She said it with great determination.

Her boyfriend, Jim (a year later, her husband), was a seasonal craftsman, a potter, on the Frontier Trail. After the meeting, one of the male members of our group thought one of us should give the guy a call with a heads up. However, we decided to let him enjoy the surprise.

The sun was out on July 6, and then the avalanche of attendance began. Every day it seemed like we had a new record day. I remember running into Don Dittmann once as he was leaving the office and asking him what kind of attendance day it was: he just jerked his thumb up. Then he paused. Then he quickly jerked his thumb up twice in succession. Then he repeated the gesture again. All was right within the Cedar Point world. The terrible winter, the construction agony, the cluster on June 17, the cold and rainy July 4 weekend, all were forgotten. We knew a few weeks into July that barring a weather catastrophe we were going to have a record year, even beating the Corkscrew year of 1976. We would end the year with just over 3.1 million visitors in 130 operating days. It would be 1986 before we hit three million visitors again.

Cedar Point was invited to make a presentation on Gemini as part of the "What's New Theater" at the IAAPA trade show in Atlanta in November. I was asked to make the presentation. It was my first IAAPA show. I had no idea I would be presenting in such a large venue and to so many people (400-500). But I had a great story to tell and lots of great pictures to tell it with (thanks to Dan Feicht). In doing research for this book I came across the 40-year-old script for my presentation. A couple of sentences at the end of the presentation say it all, "Gemini gave 1.6 million rides in only 83 operating days. That translates into 19,277 rides per day." In terms of capacity, it is a coaster like no other.

Perhaps because of its proximity to the births of our boys, I started sending out reminders on the park-wide computer system whenever June 17 came about. I would write something like, "What great event in Cedar Point history occurred 20 years ago today?" Answer: Gemini opened.

On the 25th, 30th, and 35th anniversaries of the opening of Gemini I organized a group photo of all current full-time employees who had been employed at Cedar Point back on June 17, 1978. We put up a large banner on the ride platform. On the 30th anniversary, we invited guests who had just ridden the ride the opportunity to sign a banner, which we later displayed in the Town Hall Museum. What many of them wrote were love letters.

Gemini is not shock and awe. Perhaps it never was. But it has always been loved.

I chose Gemini to be my last ride of the day on October 27, 2013, the last operating day before my retirement.

## Valleyfair!

The other big news in 1978 was Cedar Point's acquisition of Valleyfair, a small amusement park in Shakopee, Minnesota, located on the Minnesota River just southwest of the Twin Cities. After two rounds of blanks—the failed efforts to build new parks in Michigan (Irish Hills in 1974 and Kalamazoo in 1976), Cedar Point hit the mark.

I do not know who first talked to whom, but in September Cedar Point's acquisition of Valleyfair was official. Dick Kinzel was named as general manager, a surprise choice at the time.

Valleyfair had opened only two years prior, in 1976, taking advantage of the Bicentennial hoopla. It was built and owned by a small group of local men, one of whom, Walt Wittmer, had supervised the construction. Walt stayed with Cedar Fair (the new name of the parent company, combining the names of the parks) and would ultimately become general manager, succeeding Dick Kinzel and retiring in 2002.

Valleyfair was no Cedar Point, but it was no kiddie park, either. When it opened it had a good base of rides and attractions including a nice wooden roller coaster.

Kinzel left in a few days for Minnesota.

Dick was on his own, but as Dick has said many times over the years Bob Munger always had his back; he was a great mentor. Dick thrived in independent command, and nine years later he got his reward when he was named chief executive officer of the company.

There is nothing like record attendance and a short run to Labor Day to bring out animal spirits. The movie "Animal House" opened in Sandusky that August. A few co-workers—I can't remember who they were now—organized an impromptu gathering to go see the movie. Word spread quickly around the park and practically every full timer under 35 got the word to meet at a local bar to have a beer before we headed to the movie. Somehow, I got a pass from Marie to join the group. (Frankly, I did not belong anywhere but home with two-month old twins at home). The beer was cold. We were primed, happy almost giddy when we got to the theater. We went to the late showing, so the theater was nearly empty except for us. Our group was mostly guys, but there were a few girls, in all probably two dozen of us.

When we sat down in the theater we noticed a couple sitting in front of us. Their backs were to us but in a few seconds—the house lights were still blazing—most of us realized we were looking at the back of the neck of a fellow full-time staffer. Next to him was a big bunch of red hair. Our colleague was a notoriously private person. Several people in our group worked for him. I think I saw his and his date's heads starting to slide down further in their seats, but I knew it was not going to work.

Someone yelled, "Look, it's ------! With a woman!" It was full bore from that moment on. I felt sorry for the guy—as guys get emboldened in groups, especially after a few beers—but he was saved because a few moments later the lights went down. Most of us never really got a good look at his date. .

The movie was perfect. If there was ever a movie made for a bunch of guys, it was "Animal House." It could never be made today for many reasons, but it was a winner then, and that night more fun than a roller coaster. I was no particular fan of fraternities. I had no experience with them. There were no frats at Notre Dame. But the Deltas were okay with me.

The season was a grind. No matter how much you loved the park, the season was a grind. By early August, we were counting the days until Labor Day. The seasonal staff shrunk every day. Down in front of the Cedars Dorm on warm August nights seasonal employees said goodbye with bone-crushing hugs and passionate kisses, headed back home or to college or wherever they were obligated to go. Cedar Point was stripped down to its bare essentials, all of it held together by procedures and rules, the fear of losing a bonus, pride, self-discipline, camaraderie, loyalty to crew and co-workers, doing right by all those people who had paid their money to ride Gemini.

# Chapter 6
# The Jungle Man
## Lions and Tigers and Me, Oh My

It was the end of a long day, and there was the prospect of a three-hour drive back to Sandusky to think about. It was high summer, stinging hot, mid-July, and the blacktop in the parking hot had the look of lava. Don Ingle parked the Cedar Point van close to the front door. He had just arrived at one of the Dayton, Ohio TV stations. It was outside of town, in the transition zone from city to country.

His companion was Larry Tetzlaff, better known as Jungle Larry. He and his wife, Safari Jane, operated Jungle Larry's African Safari at Cedar Point, a combination zoo and performance venue. Their menagerie included a lot of serious animals, including lions, tigers, and snakes.

This was the last stop on a publicity swing to Dayton media outlets. Don and Jungle Larry had already been to the Dayton Daily News and several radio stations.

Larry was an indefatigable promoter, of both himself and his business. He was always on, a natural performer, and he looked the part of great white hunter. He stood 6' 6" tall, well-muscled for his age, a big shock of black hair, and he always wore a complete safari outfit: boots, khaki pants, safari-style shirt with at least a dozen colorful patches, big leather belt, and an enormous, wide brimmed hat complete with a snakeskin band. He was an impressive-looking man.

The deal with the station was that Don would bring Larry by around 4 p.m. and they would interview him for a short story for the evening news, assuming they weren't called away for breaking news, of course.

Larry charmed the receptionist right away: big smile, a big sweep when he removed his hat, and a twinkle in his eye. Don told her they were from Cedar Point and were here to see the producer of the evening news.

The producer arrived a few minutes later. She was pleasant enough, but you could tell she thought this was a minor story, a bit of fluff, and something to get through as quickly as possible. She did say she was a Cedar Point fan and loved roller coasters. She was young, probably thirtyish. She led Don and Larry past the reception area

into the station proper and past the set for the evening news. The reporter assigned to do the story met them by the producer's office.

The reporter was even less interested than the producer, as were the cameraman and the sound guy. They didn't even try to hide it. You could tell they thought Larry was a joke. Larry, to his credit, picked up on their attitudes immediately—but he hid it well.

"Well, what should we talk about?" the reporter asked them. He was in his late 20s and you could tell he wanted to work in a bigger market.

"What about if I find a few snakes around your building," Larry said.

"What do you mean?" the reporter fired back.

"Snakes. You know: Adam and Eve. Slithery things. I'll bet you have lots of them around here."

It was plain from the look on his face the reporter was afraid of snakes.

"Let's go out back," Larry suggested.

Somewhat reluctantly, the reporter agreed. A minute later they were out the back door. It was a snake paradise: tall grass, brush, piles of old concrete, old equipment, various collections of junk. The cameraman started shooting Larry and the reporter walking along inspecting various locations. After the dark and the coolness inside the studio, the heat and light outdoors was jarring. They were already sweating. Then Larry found the grail: a pile of rusted corrugated metal. He quickly swooped down with one of his huge arms and lifted one of the metal sheets. Underneath was a scene from a horror movie: a mass of slithering black snakes. The reporter jumped back in horror. The scene would probably haunt his dreams for months, perhaps years.

Don jumped back, too.

Larry was smiling. He knew the script from here.

The cameraman knew he had some great TV. If he was afraid, he didn't show it. The sound guy hung back as far as he could.

Next Larry bent down and then reached into the pile of snakes with his huge right hand and grabbed one right behind the head. Then he stood up, pivoted, and looked right into the camera, holding the snake carefully but firmly. The snake's tail began to wrap around Larry's arm.

At this point, the reporter, too, was starting to recognize that this was great television.

Larry waited until the sound guy got his mike boom in place. Then Larry proceeded to look directly into the camera and deliver his practiced sound bite on the great benefits of snakes, especially their effectiveness in keeping down the rodent population. He finished with a classic Larry bit. He noted that most snakes are not poisonous, including this one, and to prove it he would let it bite him.

At this point, the reporter and the cameraman were thinking a local Emmy Award.

Larry held the snake with his left hand and with his right hand he slowly moved toward the mouth of the snake. Then he stuck out his thumb. The snake grabbed the tip, bit his thumb, and then backed off. There were a few drops of blood. Larry put the snake back down with his brothers and sisters, pulled out a handkerchief and wiped off his finger. Looking back into the camera, he finished his comments with an appeal for all of us to respect God's creatures.

Jungle Larry's feature aired at both 6 and 11 p.m. and was the longest segment in both news shows.

Don never tired of telling the story.

This is not my story to tell, but I tell it anyway because it is so good and because it's the best story of Larry in the field. Don Ingle, our public relations manager at the time of the story, tells it better than I do. But then he was there.

## Jungle Larry

I worked with Larry from the time I started at Cedar Point until his death from heart disease in 1984. He was a very interesting man and I am glad I got to know him and work with him.

I first saw Jungle Larry when I was a very young child, perhaps five or six. Our parents had rented a cottage for a week near Vermilion (25 miles east of Sandusky) and one night they took the family to Crystal Beach Amusement Park located on the east side of town. Larry and his first wife, Safari Jane, operated a small animal attraction at the park. What I remember is a large pit, filled with snakes, and my peaking over the top of the fence and seeing Larry handling the snakes one by one and talking to the people. I thought: wow.

Larry came by his interest in herpetology while growing up in Kalamazoo, Michigan. He was a snake guy before anything else. He caught the interest of Frank "Bring Them Back Alive" Buck and worked for Buck as a teenager in the 1930s. He later milked venomous snakes for the U.S. Army during World War II.

Jungle Larry was well known in Cleveland and Northeast Ohio because of his regular appearances on the children's TV Show, "Captain Penny" on WEWS-TV. As a child, I was an avid viewer. During this period, he also operated small zoo operations at Puritas Springs Park on Cleveland's west side and later at Chippewa Lake Park, just south of Cleveland. He came to Cedar Point in 1964. It was a good marriage. He brought his well-known name and brand to a park just starting to pick itself back up, and Larry got his foot in the door at a larger park with aspirations to become a very large park. The marriage survived for a long time: 30 years, until 1994.

Today, the effort to teach animals tricks and have them "perform" for humans is not viewed favorably by many in our society. In the '60s and '70s, it was much less of an issue. Larry's operation was part zoo and part circus. He and his family believed strongly that many animals, including big cats, lived better lives in captivity if they were trained to perform. We had an occasional complaint from PETA-like groups, but it was never a real PR issue for either Jungle Larry or the park. Also, Larry was a committed conservationist and worked tirelessly on behalf of wildlife populations. He had lobbied the state of Florida to toughen regulations on zoos and animal attractions.

He really was a master showman, the most natural show person I've ever known. He lived for the limelight and never shrank from it. He was always on. Always. He was a publicist's dream because he would always make time to talk to the media. It didn't matter if it was the Cleveland Plain Dealer or some tiny weekly up in the Upper Peninsula of Michigan. He was good at it, too. He had a good physical presence for TV and a good voice for radio. He spoke slowly and clearly. He was a good storyteller, and like all good storytellers the story

**Jungle Larry and friend, a Tiglon (half lion, half tiger), about 1977.**
CEDAR POINT ARCHIVES

occasionally fell short of the truth, the whole truth, and nothing but the truth. We all knew he exaggerated a bit, but that was his charm.

There was a good motivation for his self-promotion: his earnings from Cedar Point were largely determined by the attendance at his attraction. He had good reason to blow his own horn.

Yet, in the end, I don't think it mattered. It was just his nature to be on stage.

He was, of course, like similar people who love to perform, somewhat self-centered. I don't think he could help himself and I did not hold it against him. His world was his world. He was not particularly interested in yours. I knew Larry for 10 years, and I doubt if he ever knew if I was married or not, or if I had kids, or where I went to college. It wasn't that he didn't like me. We got along well. A cynic might say he had every reason to get along with me because I was able to publicize what he did. But it was more than that.

Larry neither smoked nor drank. He had indulged in both vices as a young man, as he would tell anyone who was curious, but he gave them up for health reasons. It had happened years before the time when I knew him. He liked to talk about the "pearl oysters" he used to cough up every morning as a smoker and how much better he felt since giving up tobacco. Larry made up for his vices in eating. Even for a big man, he had an enormous appetite. I did not travel with him frequently, but the few times I did I marveled at how he put it away.

I remember one media swing to Pittsburgh. After doing the round of morning TV talk shows and an appearance on the market's big AM station, KDKA, we had a late lunch at a restaurant on the top floor of the U.S. Steel Building. We were guests of our agency. Dressed in full jungle regalia, Larry made quite a sight in the restaurant, which was mostly filled with business people. Several people recognized him and stopped at the table to talk. He was in his glory. It must have fueled his appetite. I remember he had a fruit drink, an appetizer, a full entree, and then finished it off with two desserts after the server recommended both the cherry pie with ice cream and something else I've forgotten.

Larry often ate lunch in the Employee Cafeteria at Cedar Point. He never missed lunch. It was a short walk from Safari Island. He would hold court in the cafeteria, always full of stories.

Most media reps took Larry at his word. He was a feature, not hard news, and their interest in what he had to say was usually at least somewhat feigned. I do recall an exception, a young reporter from a Michigan newspaper, I think the Lansing State Journal, who was probably put off by Larry's promotional style and decided to investigate a few of his claims, including the fact that he could run the 100 yard dash in around 10 seconds and that he had a doctorate from the University of Michigan or Michigan State University in one of the biological sciences. The reporter pointed out in his story the near impossibility of someone Larry's age running anything close to 10 seconds in the 100 yard dash and living to tell about it, and as hard as he tried he could find no record of a Lawrence Tetzlaff being awarded a doctorate from any Michigan college or university in any field of endeavor.

Every day, Larry walked into a ring with three or four lions and got them to do what he wanted them to do. It never failed to impress me. He didn't use a whip, or a gun, or a chair, unlike the circus lion tamers of my childhood. Larry only used two broomsticks. He didn't carry a weapon, and there was no one kneeling outside with a rifle. He got the lions to do amazing things, and he never forgot the audience as he put the lions through their paces. It was a show. To anyone who did not take him seriously, I would point out the moment of truth when the gate is lifted, and you make eye contact with the first of four adult lions as it bounds into the arena. Not for the weak of heart, at least in my opinion. Lions, and especially tigers (some seasons Larry brought tigers to Cedar Point instead of lions), occasionally prey on people. They do, in fact, eat people given the right opportunity.

I considered it a great perk of the job that for about half the year I could take a break from my office and in about five minutes or less be looking at a male African lion or an enormous Bengal tiger. Plus assorted other wildlife, from young elephants to monkeys, birds, zebras, and snakes.

The business brain behind all this was Larry's wife, Nancy. She was personable but at the same time coolly logical, careful, contained. Her ego was always under control. She was Larry's second wife. The first wife, whom I never knew, was named Jane and used Jungle Jane as her stage name. When Nancy married Larry she agreed to take Jungle Jane as her stage name, eventually becoming Safari Jane. Not many women would do that. She was the perfect partner for Larry, and together they made a great team. They had two children, Tim and David, both of whom worked in the business.

Nancy worked with the big cats, too, a rarity for a woman, certainly at the time. She got in the arena and put on a great show.

When Larry retired from the ring in 1982, David took over his role of working with the big cats.

In the U.S. certainly, and in much of the world as well, public attitudes toward performing animal shows have changed considerably. Cedar Point could never host an attraction similar to Jungle Larry's African Safari today. The park would be overrun with protesters.

The proximity of large, potentially dangerous animals to families from Grand Rapids required serious attention to detail. Larry and Nancy Jane knew what they were doing in terms of guest and animal safety. The worst guest experiences I can recall were the occasional blast of lion or tiger urine which reached an unsuspecting guest. You learned if the tail went up, you backed away. One reporter caught a splatter of lion piss in his face once. He was surprisingly good about it.

## The Great Escape

There is a story that one of Larry's monkeys, a squirrel monkey to be specific, escaped from the compound in the summer of 1966 and showed up at the U.S. Coast Guard station located at the tip of the peninsula, were he was promptly adopted.

However, to my knowledge there was only one significant animal escape in 30 years. This happened in 1977, in the middle of the summer. One of Larry's workers accidentally left open a door on one of the monkey cages. The monkey was off like a rocket. As I recall, this happened early in the day before the park opened. It was a good-sized monkey—not chimp size but not an organ-grinder monkey, either. Larry's deal with the park was that any animal that escaped was fair game. Cedar Point was not going to take chances with guest safety.

At the time, the lagoon area in the center of the park was thickly wooded. It was a large area, probably 10 acres, connected by a series of service paths to the animation scenes on the Western Cruise. It was full of bugs and snakes and numerous mean-spirited raccoons.

The monkey took off for the woods. Perhaps it reminded him of home. The staff at Jungle Larry's lost sight of him almost immediately. According to my boss, Don Dittmann, Larry assured the Cedar Point staff that the monkey would be back any time, as he will get hungry and we are his source of food. However, any time, turned into lunch time and still no monkey. Meanwhile, the director of safety, Dick Coulter, had closed the Western Cruise as a precaution—what would happen if the monkey decided to attack the guests in the boats? He also closed the Frontier Lift, since the ride traversed the wooded area. What would happen if the frightened and disoriented monkey decided to somehow climb one of the 80-foot-high towers and jump into the cabin with guests and start biting and clawing them? I thought it was a bit much.

Our only responsibility in this mess would be handling the media inquiries that we expected at any time. We drafted a brief statement, which we had at the ready, but the calls never came. We couldn't understand it.

The whole park knew what was going on, but no one called the Sandusky Register or, worse, WKYC-TV in Cleveland. It is true there were no cell phones, no internet in 1977. As a guest you would have had to search out a pay phone (there were many scattered around the park), but as an employee it would not have been hard at all to get an outside line.

Later in the afternoon, Larry organized an expedition into the woods to find and hopefully capture the monkey. The plan was to locate him, then bait him with some of his favorite foods, then throw a net around him. The option of a tranquilizer gun was not seriously considered. The expedition consisted of Larry and a few of his men, several Cedar Point Police officers, and a few Park Services guys. They roamed the woods for at least two hours. They spotted the monkey several times, but waving bananas didn't draw him in. Word came down that the senior suite was getting upset about the whole thing, especially with two popular rides closed because of it. Our safety administrator, Dick Coulter, was also losing patience. He was an avid hunter and believed he knew something of the monkey's state of mind: frightened, hungry, isolated, and confused—and therefore dangerous.

Still, no call from the media. Don Ingle and I were flabbergasted. Any news outlet would have loved this story.

I left for home about 7 p.m. Don Dittmann said he would call me with any updates. A part of him was clearly enjoying all the drama. He always thought Larry was too much the showman, and he described the "monkey expedition" in Keystone Kops language. The visual of the six-foot six-inch giant in safari regalia followed by a guy with a huge net followed by three cops followed by a couple of seasonal employees in Park Services uniforms, all eyes focused on the trees above was a bit comical in his mind.

We heard one of the cops stepped on a fox snake. The bugs were bad. The raccoons kept out of sight.

They continued to search into the evening. There are several accounts of what happened that night, but the monkey never returned to his cage. Legend has it he rests underneath one of the Iron Dragon footers.

Still, no calls from the news media. The story had changed now: no happy ending. I thought for sure there would be a call at some point, but I'm still waiting more than 40 years later.

The showbiz side of Larry was on full display with his efforts to breed what he called a "Super Cat." Tigers and lions will occasionally breed. They are quite unlikely to date in the wild, as the wild populations of both cats are separated by thousands of miles, at least in recent times. However, it can happen in zoos and wild animal farms. The offspring of a male tiger and a female lion is called a tiglon. The converse is a liger. Both are rather strange-looking—tawny in color, like lions, but with a muted, faded stripes. They are usually sterile, but there have been a few successful attempts to breed tiglons and ligers with other lions or tigers.

Larry had three tiglons, one on display at Cedar Point and two at his operation in Naples. As I recall, the Cedar Point tiglon did little performing. But it was surrounded by signage and commentary about Jungle Larry's plans to breed it with a jaguar and ultimately with a leopard (highly unlikely) to produce a new breed of animal, a true "Super Cat."

Between shows Larry loved to hang out near the Tiglon cage and engage guests in conversation about his plan. He made it sound entirely plausible. Larry was good, really good.

Larry and Nancy, and their animals, spent the off-season at their property in Naples, Florida, which they leased from the Julius Fleischmann estate. In 1994, 10 years after Larry's death, Nancy and the boys decided to concentrate full time on their growing operation in Naples, and Jungle Larry's African Safari ended its three decade run at Cedar Point.

An amusement park archeologist coming to Cedar Point would have a hard time finding evidence of Jungle Larry's African Safari. The original island in the dark and wooded lagoons is long gone, melded into new land for first, the Corkscrew, in 1976, then the Power Tower in 1998, and finally Top Trill Dragster in 2003. All the structures are gone. A few of the props, including an old safari jeep, have been integrated into the props used in HalloWeekends displays. Each season, fewer people are aware of their provenance. The gift shop across the narrow midway from the Top Thrill Dragster station, called Speed Zone, is a circular building for a reason: it was built to resemble an African jungle hut and was originally called Jungle Gifts; and for 30 years it was the perfect place to sell rubber snakes.

## Chapter 7
# Selling Tickets

*"There isn't a problem that can't be solved by selling 100,000 more tickets."* – Bruce Jackson, Cedar Fair CFO 1988 – 2005

F or 30 years, from my first day on the job on February 4, 1974, until I was named general manager of Dorney Park in May 2004, it was my job to sell tickets to Cedar Point. Blow all the fancy words and phrases away—market share, yield pricing, per capita spending, revenue enhancement, whatever—I knew I would ultimately be measured by how many admission tickets were sold on my watch.

Selling tickets is influenced by a great number of variables. No one has yet figured out the chemistry to guarantee success, but we do know a lot of the ingredients. Selling tickets is both art and science; it is a mystery, a sometimes maddening mystery.

Everything we did as a marketing group was designed to help sell tickets to the park, to produce what we termed clicks of the turnstile (now scans on a bar code reader) or, in the case of the resorts, heads in beds. The goal was always very simple, really.

## Pay One Price (POP)

Up until the 1970s, most amusement parks charged on an a la carte basis. You paid for what you did. You didn't pay for what you didn't do. Attractions such as roller coasters charged by the ride. You bought a ticket for the Leap the Dips, the way you paid for a hotdog or some cotton candy. It was basically that way for over 75 years, from the birth of the industry in the decades following the Civil War, to the late 1960s and early 1970s, when the new pricing system, called POP or Pay-One-Price, took hold. With POP, a guest paid one price and had access to all, or nearly all, rides and attractions.

The individual pricing model was easily understood by consumers as it mirrored many existing pricing models for consumer products. POP took a little more thinking—for those on both sides of the transaction.

For the parks, a one price system was very attractive. There were lots of savings in labor—no more ticket sellers scattered all over the park—and in infrastructure, as there would be no ticket booths, either. Administratively, it was the way to go. Parks also saw

marketing benefits, if they were successful in communicating to park-goers that a one price system was a great value.

Guests instinctively liked the POP option, too. Paying only once was faster and easier. It took less time, and time was a critical component of the park experience. I think most guests figured they could beat the system, that they would get more than their money's worth. The marketing proposition was very simple: with POP you get more rides. POP did, of course, make everything the same price: a ride on the Blue Streak (the Millennium Force or Gemini of the 1960s and early 1970s) theoretically cost the same as a ride on the Super Jets or the Bayern Curve. Guests did the math: "This means I can ride the Blue Streak 10 times and only pay for it once."

Most park-goers had a gut feel that POP was a better value. Selling something which enjoys a positive gut feel is always an advantage.

With POP, parks did give up the option of premium pricing for their signature attractions. However, it was a good trade off. Parks would not really figure out how to maintain POP pricing and still charge a premium for signature attractions—getting park-goers to pay twice—until the successful introduction of Fast Lane and similar programs nearly 40 years later.

The flip side is that the basic rationale for POP is that everything is available, and you get to pick and choose and nobody does everything, especially grandma. However, the rub is that grandma still must pay. The POP strategy presupposes you are at the park to ride rides, which is true for most but certainly not all guests. When parks began eliminating so-called General Admission and requiring everyone to pay the same price, there were howls of protest from some groups, particularly older adults.

Most parks, including Cedar Point, dipped their toes in the water of POP before jumping in. Both an individual ticket option and a POP option were available for several years. Cedar Point promoted "One Price Days" on Monday, Wednesday, and Friday for $4.95. The season I worked on the Frontier Lift as a ride operator, in 1969, both options were available. Within a few seasons, it became clear that POP was the winning option for both park-goer and park.

I think the summer I started full-time at Cedar Point was also the first summer of a strictly POP option. I know in those years I answered a great many guest comments—or had to address them in person on the midway—from guests who felt they were being ripped off by the park because they didn't ride any of the rides (well, maybe just a few they would admit if pressed, like the train and the paddlewheel boats) and still had to pay the same as someone who rode 20 rides (like their daughter and her friends). Also, I was told we were missing lots of attendance from people who just wanted to walk around and look at the flowers and eat candy apples and ice cream and watch people. Some guests would tell you in detail how much they spent in the park and claim that they spent most of their time eating.

The complaints continued throughout the 1970s, but gradually weakened until there was near universal acceptance of POP.

As I write this, toward the end of the second decade of the Millennium, the POP pricing model is still mainly in place. However, the Season Pass model—one price for a season versus a single day—has become the preferred admission pricing model, especially over the past 15 years. For many parks, season pass admissions make up half or even more of their attendance.

When POP started, in the late 1960s, there was only one or two prices: adult and child (excluding group prices). However, that began to change for a number of reasons until by the 1990s there were dozens of single price options at Cedar Point and most other parks as well. When I started in Marketing, about 30-40 percent of ticket buyers purchased regular, retail-priced one day tickets. The rest purchased tickets as part of a one day group event. When I retired, 40 years later, about two percent of guests purchased the advertised one day price. The so-called Gate Price was $54.99 in 2013, but the average admission price was far lower after allowing for Season Pass and a variety of group and promotional admissions.

Over the years, by design, we added all these ticket programs to segment the market and attract more visitors. Thanks to increasingly sophisticated computer and IT support, we were able to do this without confusing the marketplace—and ourselves—to the point we lost control.

The regular adult single day admission price, the retail price, was the keystone price, the public price, the price that answered the question: What does it cost to go to Cedar Point? All other ticket prices were geared off this price, which at Cedar Point was called the Funday ticket. Season Pass, Starlight (evening), Two Day, Student, Junior, Senior, Resort, Promotional, Groups Sales, Consignment, all keyed off the Funday price. The typical airline flight is filled with passengers who have paid an array of different prices for essentially the same service. Hotels as well are typically filled with guests who have paid different prices for the same or similar room. If you took a random sample of Cedar Point guests walking down the Frontier Trail, you would find the same dynamic at work.

Guests who purchased full price retail got nothing extra for it. The guest who came into the park using a ticket purchased in advance from his local credit union—saving 20 percent off retail—or with a coupon he picked up at McDonald's, got the same use of the park as the guest who paid full retail price. However, no one stands in the Raptor line and compares ticket prices with other guests—even when it's an hour wait.

We used to joke within Marketing that only a crazy person pays full price for a Cedar Point ticket.

## Group Sales

Groups certainly did not. The company or organizational picnic has been around since the 19th century. Group picnics, whether family or company sponsored, were a very big deal in this era. They were often elaborate affairs, involving more than one meal, and lasting most of the day.

In collections of vintage Cedar Point images in the Sandusky Library, the Rutherford B. Hayes Presidential Center, and the Cedar Point Archives there are many images of guests at company picnics at the park. When John Albino was the director of food operations he had several vintage Cedar Point images decorating his office walls. One large image showed a number of men in uniform, almost certainly band or orchestra uniforms, sitting around a long table piled high with food. There was barely enough space on the table to put down a quarter. In the background are lots of trees, tables, and people. The image was taken in the old Cedar Point picnic area, probably circa 1900, now the site of Planet Snoopy, a young family attraction.

The diners are packed tight around the table and looking at the camera. Most are smiling, including one man at the far end of table, as he holds a giant chicken or turkey drumstick up to the side of his face. Every time I was in John's office, which was frequently, I looked at that picture and suddenly felt hungry and imagined myself eating that drumstick. I wanted to grab it out of his hand.

The market for company picnics was diverse—manufacturing facilities to hospitals and even retailers—but it was also constrained by geography: the closer the better. Most company picnic clients were from Cleveland and Toledo. Far fewer were from Detroit or Columbus. Companies were uneasy in asking employees to drive two hours to attend a company event. I could understand that uneasiness, but it was our job to overcome it.

Some companies bought tickets for the park for their employees and their families; some bought tickets and included a prize drawing; some bought tickets and did ice cream and pop; and some bought tickets, a full catered meal, parking, and provided T-shirts and drawings for very nice prizes.

When a company was on hard times but still wanted to host a picnic, they offered what we termed a partial subsidy, where the company split the cost of the event with the employee. There were exceptions, but the general rule was that the bigger the subsidy the higher the employee attendance at the event.

We reserved our most aggressive group pricing for picnics and one day outings, what we called Scheduled Events, primarily because we believed they represented a significant amount of incremental ticket sales. For us, it was an article of faith, since there was no easy way to really verify the assumption. If a sales representative booked a new company picnic for 3,000, especially to include a catered meal (catering is a high margin business), it was cause for significant celebration. If a sales representative booked a new consignment GAD (good any day) client, it was nice but no big deal. We viewed the picnic as representing new, incremental admissions. We viewed the consignment client as a new distribution outlet which primarily serviced existing customers. Tickets sold by our GAD clients were valid for admission any day of the operating season, giving the buyer great flexibility.

Over the years I had the opportunity to participate in many picnic presentations in the field. Some companies preferred their representative collect all the information and present to an internal group of decision-makers. Others liked to convene the picnic or event committee and have parks make presentations to the whole group. We greatly preferred the latter and lobbied hard to have the opportunity to do it. We always wanted the chance to ask for the business directly and to hopefully close the sale.

We learned picnic committees had their own dynamics and properly navigating the politics of the group could be critical to getting the business. Our best sales reps understood this and worked it to their advantage. Unions were known for the size of their committees, reflecting their inherently political organization. Understanding negotiation, they were always looking for a better deal.

The other issue with company picnics was the picnic or event itself, executing it at the park. It was our longstanding policy that sales reps had to be present at the park for all their events. It was not always possible, but the excuse had to be world class. Clients always felt better if the person they had been dealing with since January was there the third Saturday in June. I agreed.

In the 1970s and 1980s, Cedar Point became increasingly committed to a marketing strategy that pushed advance ticket purchase as a key driver of attendance. The core of this strategy was the Good-Any-Day or GAD consignment ticket program. Cedar Point sales representatives called on companies and organizations in our marketing area with a simple proposition: take Cedar Point tickets on consignment (no money upfront) and make them available to your employees at a discount (savings of 15 or 20 percent depending on quantity sold). Every month, remit to us the money for the tickets sold the previous month, and at the end of the season return to us any unsold tickets. What you owe: tickets shipped minus tickets returned.

We presented to potential clients the opportunity to add a nice employee benefit—the chance to buy discounted Cedar Point tickets—at no cost to the company or organization.

It met the challenge of being a good elevator pitch.

The GAD program was geared to a single location organization: factories, hospitals, government offices, places where the bulk of the organization's workforce was on site. Tickets were usually sold through the Human Resources office or the company credit union. We looked at the client as a co-marketer, providing brochures, posters, stuffers, and other promotional material to aid in getting the word out to their employees or members. We found that our point of contact with the organization was critical to selling tickets. HR managers who believed in Cedar Point, who came to the park themselves, who cherished childhood memories of the midway, were always the best clients. We trained our sales reps to find these people in each organization.

The program was not designed for small organizations or businesses. We expected our clients to sell at least 100 tickets.

Two key assumptions were at work in the GAD consignment strategy. First, we believed that once an employee purchased a ticket—versus picking up a few coupons at McDonald's—he would be more likely to visit the park (most clients did not offer refunds). Second, we believed that if a guest had already purchased a ticket (in some cases a month or more in advance), they would be likely to spend more in the park during their visit. Both assumptions carried the weight of holy writ when I started at Cedar Point. They were based on common sense, but have never, to my knowledge, been truly validated. It would be hard to do so, especially the assumption that GAD buyers spent more in the park.

We also believed that for park-goers the opportunity to split their purchase by buying in advance was an important motivator and a way to rationalize the whole park experience.

The two biggest obstacles to overcome for our sales staff were organizations that had many locations, such as retail stores or fast food restaurants, and organizations that had a policy against handling cash. Over the years we struggled with designing an advance sale ticket program for multi-location organizations. We never really succeeded. No HR Department was going to manage dozens of ticket programs spread across the land. Every McDonald's restaurant is its own HR department. However, we learned it was a different deal if there was a significant financial incentive for the ticket seller.

I also do not recall any success in convincing an organization to make an exception to their no handling cash policy for Cedar Point. I can understand why companies have these policies. Cash is messy.

Cash sometimes disappears never to reappear. Accounting for cash is stressful. Some of our clients wanted to get out of handling cash but couldn't because of the fear of employee push back if the program were eliminated. Most companies would have preferred handing out a card or a coupon that carried an admission discount. I know my own company, Cedar Point, would never have been a GAD account if it included the responsibility for handling cash—and we were an organization with sophisticated systems for handling cash.

Over the years we did have situations where the employees of a client misappropriated Cedar Point ticket money to help fund a new RV or a trip to Vegas, but it was rare.

The consignment agreement—tickets shipped versus tickets returned—also meant Cedar Point got the money for tickets purchased but never used. The amount of what we called "breakage" varied every year, but every year it was a substantial number of tickets. We budgeted for it every year but always took a conservative approach. It always amazed me that every season thousands and thousands of tickets were purchased but never thru-gated. Why? Sickness, family issues, business issues. We all had our own theories.

Initially, and through the late '70s, the GAD was sold strictly as an employee benefit program. We actively discouraged clients from marking up the ticket to their members or employees. We turned down offers from retailers and others who thought selling Cedar Point tickets would build traffic and add new revenue. For many years, the only place a member of the public could buy a ticket in advance to the park was at a Sears store, which offered Cedar Point tickets at full retail price (Sears in turn earned a small commission). As the GAD program grew in the '70s and '80s and the opportunity to buy discounted tickets became more common, Sears's ticket volume dropped dramatically.

We did sell GAD tickets to some accounts that were borderline. When I joined the company in 1974 the largest consignment account was the Michigan Parks and Recreation Association (MRPA), an umbrella trade organization representing municipal recreation departments across the state. Through MRPA, we were able to offer Cedar Point tickets for sale at city recreational departments all over Michigan. There were two mark-ups, one for the individual department or locality and one for MRPA. In theory, you had to be a legal resident of the city where you were buying the ticket (tickets were usually offered at the city's administrative offices), but in practice it didn't matter a wit; you could be from Mars, or even Moscow.

We had levels of GAD pricing, usually three, all based on ticket volume. The best price was offered to groups that sold 10,000 or more tickets. The middle range was 1,500 up to 9,999. The first category was 100. Most clients were in the middle category. However, the highest ticket volume, by far, was in the 10,000 plus category, probably 75 percent of all GAD tickets.

There was incentive for organizations to find ways to associate with other organizations to garner the best price, especially to get to the 10,000 or more level. In the 1970s and through the 1980s Cedar Point's largest GAD clients were regional Human Resource organizations. Most large metro areas had organizations representing the HR managers of local companies which shared best practices and negotiated with providers of recreational services—among other services—to get the best price or access. In Toledo, we worked with TIRES (Toledo Industrial Recreational Services); in Cleveland it was CESA (Cleveland Employee Services Association); in Detroit it was MESRA (Michigan Employee Services Recreation Association).

Utilizing these organizations, Cedar Point could easily develop presold ticket relationships with hundreds of different companies. We got access, and sponsorship, and the member companies got the best Cedar Point pricing for their members. Win-Win, as they say. Working together we sold millions of Cedar Point tickets over the years.

The ideal GAD ticket outlet was an organization that viewed the opportunity to sell discounted tickets as an employee benefit and pushed it accordingly. They made sure their members knew about it, utilizing internal marketing tools like bulletin boards, in-house TV, paycheck stuffers, newsletters, and website access (starting in the mid to late 1990s). We provided posters, park brochures, stuffers. We were always under pressure to provide more support, especially paid advertising in company publications. We maintained a pretty consistent "No" to these requests. We had to take this position, otherwise we could easily spend half the park's ad budget on these requests. The largest clients pushed us hard to utilize some of our regular park advertising to drive sales to their outlets.

In the 1980s and 1990s we switched increasingly to what I called the for-profit strategy. While we still dealt with our traditional client base, we found ourselves in relationships with large for-profit organizations who wanted to sell Cedar Point tickets primarily to make money. It started with the Michigan AAA, the second largest AAA region in the country, which included offices in the Chicago area as well as the entire state of Michigan. They demanded a better price than our best GAD price, and after the smoke had cleared they got what they wanted. However, so did we: a strong marketing partner, new and better sales outlets, a single source for administering the ticket program, professional ticket/cash management, control of who bought the ticket (theoretically, only Michigan AAA members could buy tickets). Within two years, Michigan AAA became Cedar Point's largest ticket seller.

In Ohio and in neighboring states we worked with other AAA partners, but none had the power or the number of outlets enjoyed by the Michigan group.

Of course, AAA as an outlet was not perfect. Your average AAA office is usually not fighting with McDonald's for retail locations; its foot traffic is relatively weak compared to some other outlets. Also, the demographic of AAA members and Cedar Point park-goers is not a heavenly match. AAA members definitely skew old, while the core Cedar Point buyer skews young.

## Mejier

Enter Meijer, a regional mass merchandiser (it had its origins as a grocery store) with about 80 stores. Headquartered in Grand Rapids, Meijer owned the Michigan market and also had stores in western Ohio, Columbus and Cincinnati, northern Indiana and Indianapolis, and a minor presence in Chicago. Fred Meijer, the founder, had enjoyed a reputation not unlike Sam Walton at Walmart. The demographics of the Meijer customer was solidly middle class and certainly skewed younger than AAA.

Plus, they had a brand new store in Sandusky.

In 1995, we made a deal with Meijer to sell Cedar Point tickets. The folks at Meijer were good negotiators. The final agreement included very specific responsibilities for both parties in terms of advertising support, point of sale materials, ticket incentives, sponsorship, etc. It was all business. We both benefitted. Meijer got a new retail item with essentially no cost of sales. Meijer also got association with a popular, well-known brand that fit their family image. Cedar Point got great sales distribution in key markets with a partner that generated high and frequent foot traffic.

I accompanied our sales team, usually Jan Guthridge and the lead sales representative, to the Meijer headquarters outside Grand Rapids once or twice a year, usually in late winter or early spring to set up the program and then in October-November to wrap things up. We always did it in one day, a long one since it was a four and a half hour car trip one way, but it gave us time to discuss our selling strategy.

The lobby of the headquarters building was huge to accommodate the dozens of vendors waiting patiently to visit their buyer and make a deal. There was lots of Meijer information on the walls and stacked on tables. Meijer represented a huge opportunity for most suppliers with its 80 stores and growing. The flip side was that a failure to get into Meijer could be a black eye for any salesperson. There was outward calm in the lobby, but a great deal of business was being done in the building. Meijer wanted the product at the lowest possible price and with lots of extras like co-op advertising, special packaging, etc. The vendor wanted to sell the product to Meijer at the highest price possible and with favorable terms and conditions.

Cedar Point didn't fit the standard Meijer versus Vendor playbook.

Our senior Meijer contact would always delay her arrival at the meeting until all the regular agenda items had been agreed to. She was always very charming and talked about what a great relationship we had (certainly true) and how it benefitted both Meijer and Cedar Point. Then we each played a little hardball, but with a smile.

She reminded us that handling the CP ticket program is a nightmare administratively; we need more advertising support from Cedar Point; we need more courtesy tickets from Cedar Point to make this thing work; we are barely making any money on this program.

I countered that the opportunity to buy discounted Cedar Point tickets drove traffic into their amazing stores; I reminded her that Meijer had essentially no cost of sales with this program; I reminded her this was a consignment ticket program and they only owed us for the tickets they sold.

In the end, we always reached a fair deal. We always shook hands and smiled.

Cedar Point and Meijer have been ticket-selling partners since 1995, so both parties continue to benefit from the association.

With partners like Meijer, Michigan AAA, several Ohio-based AAA's, employee benefit associations like TIRES and COESRA, numerous credit unions and individual companies, the Cedar Point GAD consignment ticket program reached its peak in the mid and late 1990s, generating more than a million admissions every season. We liked to think no other regional amusement park had a comparable program.

## Good-Any-Day (GAD) Tickets

There was very little turnover in GAD accounts. Sales representatives rarely got the call ending the relationship. There was a message in that fact, but I really don't know what it is.

We did struggle to establish GAD accounts in more distant markets, such as Pittsburgh, Dayton-Cincinnati, Chicago, Indianapolis, all markets where we faced significant local competition and relatively low awareness. It is a more difficult sell when the HR manager you're talking to in Indianapolis has never been to Cedar

Point and really questions how much demand there will be for Cedar Point tickets within his or her workforce.

It was the job of the park's advertising and publicity programs to generate awareness and demand for the park. It was the job of the presold GAD program to close the sale by making it easy, convenient, and "a deal," for park-goers to buy locally in advance of their trip to the park. It was a beautiful thing.

Our competitors thought the GAD program was a beautiful thing, too. In most markets, Cedar Point was the leader. A Geauga Lake, Sea World, or Kings Island salesperson's best shot was the argument that you are already selling Cedar Point tickets why not just carry our tickets too and offer your employees more choices. The argument often worked.

There were tensions, of course. Our GAD accounts resented the promotional programs we ran with fast food chains and others to distribute coupons. They believed such programs undercut their offering that it was easier and more convenient to grab a handful of coupons with your double cheeseburger or chicken nuggets than make the effort to go to the credit union or the local Meijer store and buy the tickets in advance. They had a good argument. It forced us to build in restrictions and limitations to our promotional offerings that made the GAD ticket a better option. The GAD ticket you bought at Meijer or Michigan AAA or the UAW Local 890 was exactly that: good any day of the season. The promotional Pepsi or Coke can you picked up at the local convenience store might be restricted to weekdays only and have a date range.

From the park's perspective, we needed both kinds of marketing programs. We had to work hard to keep everyone happy.

Our GAD clients loved free tickets, as did the grocery store managers who had to be encouraged by courtesy tickets to put up endcap displays of special point of sale material and stacks of Pepsi or Coke cans in their stores. Our courtesy ticket policy with clients was conservative, at least from our point of view. Did the HR manager of Apex Manufacturing in Parma, Ohio (Cleveland area), who managed the Cedar Point ticket program for the company, keeping track of 450 ticket sales (a value of approximately $15,000 in 2006), deserve four courtesy tickets to the park? Yes. We trained our sales representatives on how to handle courtesy ticket requests—and how and when to make the offer themselves. For Cedar Point sales reps, there were no elaborate dinners, golf outings, or concert tickets for clients. We substituted Cedar Point courtesy tickets for Billy Joel tickets. The system worked for all involved.

Some clients, as well as some media representatives, did not see the value of a courtesy ticket the way we did, buying into the "It doesn't cost you anything to give me a free ticket, plus I'll spend money when I'm there" way of thinking. True, we did not put a cap on daily attendance and there were no assigned seats like most sporting and entertainment events, but anyone who sells tickets for a living knows the ticket is the product, the key to everything; it's what you sell.

At the start of the season we assigned a number of courtesy tickets to each sales representative and instructed them to manage their territories accordingly. We reminded them they were responsible for managing a significant company asset. The sales representative was expected to manage to that number; he or she knew it would be hard to get more.

We also had the advantage of being able to offer in-park benefits that were truly no cost to us but had high perceived value to the client, the biggest one being immediate boarding on our world class coasters. To walk a client up the exit or through the back area to the ride platform of Millennium Force and then be welcomed into the first seat—saving up to two hours of time on a busy Saturday—has very high perceived value. The client understands this is something special, true VIP treatment. Our cost, our risk, was that we might irritate or offend the other guests waiting their two hours. However, if you were smart about it—doing it infrequently and limiting it to small groups—the risk of offending other guests was low. When I was GM, the rule was that I had to approve any courtesy boarding in advance.

Cedar Point managed the presold program, both GAD distribution and Scheduled Event, through the Group Sales department. For more than 20 years, starting in the early 1980s, the department was run by Jan Guthridge, a very capable and intelligent manager who understood the business side of the business of sales. He managed the balance of power among competing ticket programs very well.

When I started at Cedar Point in 1974 our sales representatives were older, ranging from mid-20s to mid-50s. As these folks left for whatever reason they were replaced by younger people, many just out of college and many with park experience as seasonal employees. A starting sales representative position paid at a competitive rate, but if you wanted to make significantly more money—and the sales field allows for upward mobility in terms of compensation—you needed to sell something else; for example, TV commercial time, real estate, jet airplanes, medical equipment, pharmaceuticals, financial products—it's a long list.

The least favorite activity for our sales team was collecting money from clients. One of the biggest risks in both the Scheduled Event and GAD programs, but especially the latter, was the amount of financial exposure incurred by hundreds of thousands of tickets on consignment in hundreds and hundreds of outlets.

The basic GAD agreement called for clients to remit to us the money for tickets sold the previous month by the 15th of the current month. Relatively few clients met this requirement. They always had an excuse or excuses, especially for the July 15, August 15, and September payments. Thanks to working in the computer age, we knew exactly how many tickets had been thru-gated. Mostly, the clients blamed people downstream, individual ticket outlets. Our best weapon to get their attention was the re-order demand which occurred every summer in late July. Many clients ran out of tickets. They needed more—and right away to avoid ticking off their employees or members or customers. We sometimes tied approving the re-order to picking up a check.

Clients, and their internal financial management, loved all that cash flow. Complicating the issue was the fact that our chief competitors in the '70s, '80s, and '90s—Geauga Lake, Sea World, Kings Island—were much less concerned with in-season ticket payments than we were. We were told by clients that our competitors were only concerned with payment and reconciliation after the park had closed for the season. However, that wasn't Cedar Point's style.

Our sales management philosophy was that the individual sales representative was responsible for everything that involved the client, including collecting money if it were required. In many organizations that is not the case—as some sales representatives pointed out to us—preferring a good cop (sales) versus bad cop (finance) approach. But again, that was not Cedar Point.

Jan Guthridge deserves much of the credit for managing the collection program for Cedar Point. Starting in mid-July, he reviewed the status of ticket payments with every sales representative every week. In the fall, each sales rep knew he or she had to have their accounts cleaned and closed before they received their bonus.

Our overall performance in terms of collections was stellar. My old boss and mentor, Don Dittmann, who had come to the park from the beer business, was astounded at the low number of write-offs every season, especially given the exposure involved.

The sales world mostly existed outside the park. Like advertising, and to some degree PR/publicity, the critical activity took place away from the midway. The same was true in other areas of the park as well, for example, some financial activities, but for the sales rep whose territory included Detroit, for example, the reality of his world was handing the pen to the president of UAW Local 880 in a dark union hall on a cold and snowy February afternoon in Dearborn, Michigan, and hoping he will take the pen and sign the consignment agreement. The midway was a long way away.

I spent as much time as I could in the field with our sales team, starting in the summer of 1982, when I became director of marketing, right through to my retirement 32 years later. I felt it was important to go into the field, to understand how it worked and to evaluate our staff. Plus, I just enjoyed doing it. I especially enjoyed seeing the different work environments our clients did business in, from shiny new office buildings with views of interstates gleaming in the sun to a beat-up metal desk in a side room off the factory floor where you could smell some strange chemical. In any given day, a Cedar Point sales rep would visit five to seven unique work environments. I considered it a perk of the job. Not sure our sales reps would agree. It gave me an opportunity to learn about different businesses, see how they were organized and operated. Our clients loved to talk about what they did, their product, what made them great. For the most part I was an eager listener.

Mary Moran, a Detroit rep, and I once had to step around dead rats, quite frozen, on the sidewalk in downtown Detroit on a cold January day on our way to the Detroit News to try to sell them on a GAD program. I can also remember the interiors of law firms that had been created to impress clients: glass, gold, and sky.

We usually got a good reception. We represented playtime. Initial small talk was almost always about the park. We were often a break in the day, a meeting they looked forward to having. Bill Manning, our Cleveland sales rep in the '70s and definitely old school (he kept track of his business life using the back of letter-sized envelopes which he stuffed in the pockets of some the most bizarre-looking sport jackets imaginable) had a unique method of breaking the ice with clients: he opened up one of the souvenir poster maps of the park and with a flourish he laid it down on the client's desk, covering most of the desk—and whatever the client was working on. Then he would launch into his presentation of all the wondrous new things at Cedar Point this year.

Most of the full-time staff had no clue as to what went on in their name outside the park, especially what went on in the off-season. It wasn't their fault, it was just the way it was. Occasionally I would invite a senior manager to go along for a day in the field so they could see what goes on, but it seldom actually happened; something always seemed to derail it at the last minute.

Clients loved to tell you about their visits to the park and their experiences on Magnum or Raptor. Their business faces changed into little kid faces. It was fun to witness, one of those times when you realized you were indeed part of the entertainment industry. And a Cedar Point sales rep always had something new to talk about. It made the presentation more effective—and it certainly helped when it came time to deliver the news that the ticket price was increasing.

Some of our reps became quite good at delivering the elevator pitch for the new ride or attraction; they were at least as good as our PR staff.

Of course, some clients weren't park-goers. Almost half the adult population of the country has little or no interest in going to amusement parks. Some of them end up as HR directors or AAA office managers or union representatives. It can't be avoided. They dealt with Cedar Point because it was part of the job and really didn't care for small talk about roller coasters.

I never considered myself a good salesperson, but I learned to be a successful manager of good salespeople. I respected what they did. I knew it wasn't easy. They were measured objectively (selling tickets) in a way that most others in the company were not.

## Online Ticket Sales

In December 1995, Cedar Point launched its website, which looking back marked the high water mark for the presold GAD ticket program. We did recognize very early on that the e-commerce capabilities of our website, and the internet in general, were going to be powerful. I recall sitting and talking with Jan Guthridge and Lee Alexakos in those early digital years about the benefits of online ticket sales. It was just a question of how and when, not should we. We all foresaw a gradual movement away from buying your park tickets at the company credit union or the HR office to pulling out the credit card and then hitting the print button on your computer. It was our version of the retailers' quandary: bricks and mortar stores versus online sales.

We decided there would be room for both for a long time.

There were many advantages to online sales through our website. It was easier and more convenient for the guest. Administratively, it was easier for the park: the middleman, the broker, the distributor were gone. You didn't have to collect money; it was in your bank a second or two after the ticket buyer hit "Confirm Purchase." We could see a time when the entire presold structure would go away. Media advertising would set the hook and direct the potential buyer to the website.

Not so fast. You also gave up certain benefits, a key one being the exposure and awareness provided by those thousands of ticket outlets across the marketplace. But never bet against convenience. One of the things I learned in business is that even small, incremental improvements in convenience, in making things easier to do—whatever you are doing—are usually rewarded handsomely by the marketplace. The gradual switch to digital ticket selling was inexorable. The purchase of Cedar Point tickets at Meijer, along with toothpaste, mac and cheese, hotdog buns and a new hoody for Jerry, gradually moved to your computer or your phone.

## The Season Pass

In 1974, when I started at Cedar Point, the park sold well less than a thousand season passes. My last season at the park, 2013, we sold well north of 100,000. Therein, lies a tale.

Like POP for one day tickets, the season pass concept is easily understood: you pay one price up front, you get admission to the park every day of the season. In 1974, there was so little demand that passes were sold only at the HR office, outside the park near the marina. I do not remember the price of a pass then, but I believe it was nearly $100. The price of a Funday ticket was $6.25. To break even required 15-16 park visits. No one was buying, and that was fine with management. The attitude was that the season pass was being provided almost as a service to guests who really, really wanted one, which mostly meant guests who kept their boats in the Cedar Point Marina, and the occasional true-believing park fan. Season Pass holders were perceived as a very peripheral market. The working assumption was that as individuals they carried a ham and cheese sandwich from home in their back pocket, asked for a cup of water at food stands and bought one keychain a year as a souvenir.

Unlike nearly all other major amusement parks, Cedar Point is not located in a significant-sized metro area. Cleveland is 60 miles east and most of the Cleveland DMA's population is east and south to include Akron and Canton. Toledo is 60 miles west. South it is 120 miles to the center of the Columbus DMA. To the north the population was in the millions but they all lived underwater. The acronym DMA refers to a designated market area, which is basically the geographic areas served by the major broadcast TV stations and measured by Nielsen.

For most Cedar Point visitors, the drive to the park is at least 60-90 minutes; it is not something done on a whim, at least not for the most part. However, for most visitors to other theme and amusement parks, the drive is 15 – 45 minutes, much more manageable and something that met the "done on a whim" threshold.

Our main competitors fell into that 15-45 time frame: Kings Island, in Cincinnati/Dayton; Geauga Lake, Cleveland/Akron; Kennywood, Pittsburgh; Carowinds, Charlotte; Valleyfair, Minneapolis/St. Paul; Worlds of Fun, Kansas City; Six Flags Over Georgia, Atlanta; and Canada's Wonderland, near Toronto. The list goes on.

In the late 1970s and early 1980s parks in metro areas—which meant most parks—began testing new strategies for selling season passes. Those new strategies mostly involved slashing the price, sometimes dramatically, but also included significant advertising investment to help sell passes. Cedar Point was not impacted much competitively by the new season pass strategies, so we tended to shake our heads collectively and feel our one day ticket strategy was superior. We used to ask ourselves: Why are they doing this? How can they offer a season pass for essentially the same price as the retail walk-up price?

The answer was they were committing to a volume strategy: get more people in the park and good things happen.

Given our geographic situation, Cedar Point was never going to have a majority of guests who were season pass holders. However, I thought there were possibilities for Cedar Point to increase attendance with a lower season pass price. I really didn't see a downside, assuming we didn't make a big pricing error. We put together a proposal in the fall of 1983 to introduce a value-priced season pass for the next year. After some negotiation, we arrived at a retail price of $39.95, a savings of $40 from the prior year price. It was not an easy sell to management, but we persevered and finally got the green light. I considered it a personal victory. It was a group effort, and as usual Alexakos had done the number crunching and the financial analysis, but it was something I could point to that wouldn't have happened without me.

It worked. We went from selling about 2,000 passes to selling about 20,000 passes, which generated about 80,000 park visits in 1984, which it turned out we needed as 1984 was, for Cedar Point, a poor attendance year.

I remember thinking at the time that if conditions were right and we were smart about how we marketed the program, we might sell 100,000 plus passes someday. Years later we did pass that mark, and the growth continues. We asked ourselves: who is our best customer? Wouldn't it be ideal if every one of our guests was a pass holder? In theory, yes.

As market research demonstrated conclusively, season pass holders were Cedar Point's best guests. They loved the park and were ambassadors for us in the marketplace. They were knowledgeable, loyal, and, over the course of the season, spent plenty of money at the park.

In the 1980s and 1990s the Six Flags and Paramount Parks went all-in on the season pass strategy. It certainly worked for them. Every year each of their parks sold several hundred thousand passes. They evolved a marketing and operational infrastructure to accommodate that kind of volume. Richard Zimmerman, GM of Kings Dominion when we acquired Paramount Parks from Viacom, and who 13 years later would become CEO of Cedar Fair, was a strong advocate of the season pass strategy. When he came to Cedar Fair, he often referred to what he called Paramount's "Season Pass Playbook," the advertising, segmenting and pricing wisdom accumulated over a decade or more of positioning the season pass as the best way to enjoy the park.

Cedar Point grew its season pass infrastructure, too, but on a smaller scale. We added perks programs, special pricing, parking, special events like ride nights and early entry to the park. The most important decision we made was not to offer a separate pass for our Soak City water park. If you wanted Soak City on an any-day option you had to buy what we called a Combo Pass, which included both Cedar Point and Soak City, and was priced accordingly. Most Six Flags and Paramount parks included admission to their water park with the ride park.

On a per capita basis, Cedar Point's average season pass revenue was extremely high, easily the highest of any seasonal amusement park.

When Cedar Fair acquired Paramount, we attempted to sprinkle the Cedar Fair way of doing things—mainly more aggressive (higher) pricing and a few reduced perks—on the Paramount Season Pass Playbook. The changes didn't take, and we took a short term hit in pass sales at several former Paramount properties. We learned a painful but valuable lesson: The Kings Island or Kings Dominion season pass holder was his or her own park-goer, didn't give a rip about what went on at Cedar Point, and was used to being catered to (and liked it).

Cedar Point 125th Anniversary Commemorative Ticket.
In the background is the Cyclone roller coaster.
CEDAR POINT ARCHIVES

## Chapter 8
# Proud to be a Flack
### My New Hero: P.T. Barnum

There is a great history of publicists, starting with P.T. Barnum and Buffalo Bill Cody in the 19th century, men who believed a little exaggeration for a good cause (their particular enterprise), did not require ceding the high ground.

What we largely practiced at Cedar Point was product publicity, not public relations. The job of the PR Department was to get positive media exposure for Cedar Point. In many ways, it was a simple assignment and clearly understood. Our job as marketers was to sell tickets to Cedar Point. Advertising sold tickets. Direct selling to groups sold tickets. Promotions sold tickets. So did articles in the Cleveland Plain Dealer about Cedar Point's new roller coaster. Our job was to keep Cedar Point in the news—in a favorable way, of course—and to get the word out about our product, the world's greatest amusement park.

Not all products and not all companies are set up to use product publicity as a major marketing tool. However, Cedar Point was well positioned to use it effectively. We were a consumer product enjoyed by millions, an institution, or brand, more than a century old. We were very visual, which gave us an advantage in dealing with television but also with most print media.

### "Jaws"

The summer of 1975 was the summer of the movie "Jaws."

It was my second summer as a full-time employee. I was newly married and found myself, thanks to the departure to the Marriott parks of my boss, Bruce Burtch, and several other Cedar Point managers, now responsible for the publicity effort at Cedar Point. Not much more than a year previously I had been looking for an academic job teaching English and writing. I was now a flack, the somewhat pejorative term for people who do and say just about anything to get their clients positive coverage in the news media.

I did have a staff. Don Ingle, who I had recruited from the Sandusky Register (Don had decided after covering a shocking murder of a local high school girl that he would be far happier dealing

with good news than bad news); and Nancy Steinmuller, a former copywriter for a sewing machine manufacturer in Cleveland.

Our collective average age was 24 or 25, but we certainly did not consider that to be a liability. By my current perspective, we were just kids.

Don was a Chicago native, very bright, a graduate of a prestigious journalism school (University of Missouri). In truth, he did have a natural gift for the communications business. He left Cedar Point in 1982 to work for Burson-Marsteller, a national PR firm. He later worked for several other agencies and companies in senior management positions and is currently a professor on the faculty of Chicago's DePaul University, where he teaches communications. He has won several teaching awards.

Don made the transition from journalist to publicist in about a week. He never looked back. He understood newspaper writing requirements and could pound out news releases, cut lines, and pitch letters quickly, a significant skillset for a publicist. He also had an outgoing personality. He prided himself on his ability to charm whoever he needed to charm to get coverage for Cedar Point. He was average height, had brown hair and a moustache, and was a good athlete.

We became friends as well as co-workers. Don had, after all, worked at getting Marie and I together for the first time. We were briefly housemates before I got married. We all still tell Don stories: the constant condition of the back seat of his car, a mountain of used napkins, McDonald's bags, Wendy's bags, Burger King bags, empty (mostly) soda cans, candy wrappers, old newspapers, dry cleaning, stained coffee mugs, ketchup and mustard packets, baseball caps; Don's proclivity for wearing what our mutual friend Kevin Terrell referred to as flood pants, which meant Don usually showed a lot of sock (I mean he showed a lot of sock); Don's hosting of legendary parties with Don as emcee, at the piano belting out ribald songs about life at Cedar Point while chain-smoking Marlboro's and one hand around a beer or a blonde.

Nancy was also very smart and a very versatile writer. Also, a very resilient person. She was the first person I hired in my business career. She was also a west side native and had gone to high school at St. Augustine Academy, the female equivalent of my high school, St. Edward. She was outgoing as well, but not in an aggressive manner and never offended. She was an immensely likable person, which was one of the keys to her effectiveness. She had a very soothing voice. She could have done voice-overs professionally.

Nancy would leave Cedar Point in 1979, after four years, to take a PR job with the Henry Ford Museum and Greenfield Village in Dearborn, Michigan. Her brother-in-law owned a weekly newspaper in Newberry, Michigan, in the Upper Peninsula or UP as it is called. He tried for years to convince Nancy and her family to move to Newberry. He offered her the job of publisher of his newspaper and part ownership. Eventually, she accepted. She has been there ever since.

Turns out, Cedar Point also had sharks in 1975. In the late 1960s, Cedar Point had added Sealand as a family attraction, something to balance the appeal of rides. Located on the public beach next to the bathhouse, on the future site of the Oceana Stadium, Sealand featured several indoor aquarium-type exhibits, the two major ones being a shark tank and a penguin tank. The aquarium was operated by a full-time staff of two, Steve Trott, the manager, and an assistant, Mike Marcus. In addition to Sealand, they also managed the Pet Farm on the Frontier Trail. They were an interesting combination. Steve was older, well into his 30s, and had an interesting sense of humor. He would often speculate half-seriously how much fun it would be to turn the poor penguins out on the Lake Erie ice in winter to see how much fun they'd have. He used to joke with people that he had started feeding them Lake Erie perch to get them ready. Steve did not see his ultimate job as being a fish guy. In fact, he would leave the park a few years later and move to the IT industry, eventually working for a bank in Richmond, Virginia.

Mike was very much a fish person. He fit the word nerd like Babe Ruth fit the word slugger. He was younger than Steve by 10 years, short and thin with unkempt hair. We became good friends, and he helped me with winter storage for Marie's small sailboat. He married a former employee, who worked at the Pet Farm. She was probably ten years younger than Mike, and quite beautiful. They did not look like a couple. Mike had a serious heart condition—he had been a "blue baby" at birth—and he died before he was 40. I frequently pass the house where Mike lived when I first knew him, on Camp Road in Huron Township, just across the tracks from Barnes Nursery. I think of him often.

## Sharks in the Park

Sharks were everywhere the summer of 1975. "Jaws" opened Memorial Day weekend and ruled the box office for most of the summer. It was the first movie to be termed a "Summer Blockbuster." Marie and I went to see the movie with Keith and Pat Monroe, friends from graduate school who had moved back to the Cleveland area. We miscalculated on when to arrive at the theater and ended up having to sit in the first or second row. The opening scene is one of the most terrifying things I've ever see on a movie screen, made more intense by the fact we were sitting so close to the action. I felt like I was in the ocean with that first victim. Marie wanted to leave, but we persevered.

Sometime in June, as I recall, we got the idea of trying to capitalize on the lemon sharks we had on display at Sealand, especially the biggest one, which was nearly eight feet long and looked quite menacing as it swam the never-ending circle of the tank. In fact, its jaw got a little cockeyed from the constant right-hand turns.

I asked Steve if there had been much action around the shark tank since the movie came out. He replied instantly that attendance at Sealand was way up so far this year. He said it was hard to get a position along the glass in front of the shark tank.

"Let's do a story on this, I said. "We'll put out a news release saying attendance at Sealand is way up because of the movie."

I think Don Ingle wrote the story. It was short and punchy and included some quotes we put together for Steve. We didn't have an image to go with it, but we felt the story was strong enough to run without it. Plus, we knew most newspapers and TV stations had access to plenty of stock shark images.

The story was picked up immediately by both wire services, AP (Associated Press) and UPI (United Press International). It ran everywhere, big metros like Cleveland and Detroit, and small towns like Archbold, Ohio and Traverse City, Michigan, and in towns across the country. The lead was that an Ohio amusement park was seeing an increase in attendance due to the popularity of the movie "Jaws."

Not strictly true, but we were happy to let things go without correction.

Calls poured in for more information about our sharks. We set Steve up with interviews with dozens of radio stations. The interviews were short, but effective. It helped that Steve was not a PR guy; he was a scientist, a tech guy, and he came off as a legitimate expert, which for our purposes he really was. At bottom we spoke the truth: attendance at Sealand (not Cedar Point, which many stories got backwards, but we didn't care) was up, and in a year of mild recession where overall park attendance was slightly down.

In addition to the radio news stories and interviews, and the newspaper stories, several TV stations came out to do stories. I think they were a bit underwhelmed with Sealand and the relative size of our lemon sharks but they had come this far to do the story and so they made the best of it. The stories opened with a shot of the park, then cut to the line at the entrance to Sealand, then to the shark tank, then to a brief sound bite from Steve, then a few comments from random guests, and ended with a brief clip from the movie.

In those days, we utilized a clipping service to measure our success generating print coverage of the park. In the weeks following our "Jaws" coverage we got bags stuffed full of clippings. We converted the space used by the stories into column inches, so we had a somewhat objective measurement of our success, and success it was.

One of the sweetest aspects of the endeavor was that we had stolen a march on Sea World, then a major competitor, especially in the Cleveland area. Sea World, of course, was a marine-life park and had a lot more sharks on display than we did.

One spark had generated a big flame. Recognizing the right set of circumstances and then creating a story out of bits and pieces is very, very satisfying. I was always proud of the PR and publicity work we did to help launch Cedar Point's coaster galaxy, but the coasters themselves provided a lot of the flame. More fun in many ways were the stories we created and sold ourselves.

The "Jaws" story did not have legs. In a few days it was old news, which is the natural life of most news, and quite expected. We went back to trying to generate stories about our new IMAX theater and the movie "Man Belongs to the Earth."

And we kept looking for the next "Jaws."

## Power Boat Racing on Lake Erie

We settled for the Stroh's Grand National, an offshore power boat race sponsored by Stroh's beer and hosted by Cedar Point.

Cedar Point hosted the event for three seasons, 1975 – 1977. The Grand National was the only race on the circuit that was held on freshwater. In addition to the big ocean racers the event drew smaller race boats as well, perhaps 60 boats in all.

How it came to Cedar Point is a long story, a combination of events, people, and beer. Norm Schultz, director of the Lake Erie Marine Trades Association (LEMTA), the sponsor of the Cedar Point Boat Show, was a friend of Dean Palmer. Dean and Norm were both active in the Mentor Yacht Club. Dean was well connected within the local powerboat community and president of the Great Lakes Power Boat Racing Association (GLOPRA). Norm and Dean came up with the idea of approaching Cedar Point. With its beautiful wide beach for spectators, one of the largest marinas on the Great Lakes, hundreds of hotel rooms, restaurants, and a service infrastructure, Cedar Point was an ideal location. I do not recall who approached whom, but the local Stroh's distributor, Jerry Linton, was on board right away as a partial sponsor.

At the time, Stroh's Brewery was going strong. Headquarters were in Detroit, where it brewed its signature beer, a "fire-brewed" pilsner called Stroh's. Stroh's was ubiquitous in Cleveland when I was growing up. It was a workingman's beer, an everyday beer. Among my high school and college friends, there were many jokes about

Stroh's Grand National Offshore Powerboat Race souvenir program.
The park hosted this event for three years, 1975-1977. AUTHOR'S COLLECTION

how you were "fire-brewed" the next morning after having a certain number of Stroh's beers the evening before. Stroh's was well known in Detroit, Toledo, Cleveland, and other parts of Ohio, Michigan, and northern Indiana.

It was priced as a "popular beer," which meant it was priced lower than Budweiser or Miller or Schlitz, the brands which ruled the beer business. Back then there was no real option for other beer brands. Miller Lite was not in the market until 1975. Imported beers were rare, expensive, and snobbish. Craft beers had not been invented yet. If offered a truly local beer in the mid-1970s, you were quick to change the subject.

Stroh's had their reasons for liking the sponsorship opportunity. Association with Cedar Point was always a good thing. Cedar Point had a great brand image—and, in fact, sold a lot of Stroh's beer in the park. Cedar Point's geographic market was a very good fit for Stroh's. Sports of almost any kind was a good match for a beer—that had been demonstrated in lots of markets by lots of beers. If Budweiser did a lot of sports tie-ins, it must be a good idea. They were smart people, the General Motors of beer. Admittedly, not many Stroh's drinkers were power boat racers or identified with the drivers, but those problems could be overcome.

Stroh's was in.

For Cedar Point, it was not as simple. We sold a lot of beer at the park, but we did not promote the availability of beer. We all wondered a bit if an open association with a beer brand was the right thing for squeaky clean Cedar Point. Part of my rationalization was that baseball seemed to make a relationship with beer work; in fact, they were a good model. The event would certainly generate revenue for the marina and some of our restaurants. The Hotel Breakers (our only hotel at the time) would fill up regardless, so that was a push. Would it sell park tickets? I was skeptical, but others—mostly people associated with the race and/or power boats—were sure spectators would arrive by the tens of thousands. We could use the event to generate publicity about the park.

In the end, we decided to jump in.

The American Power Boat Racing Association (APBRA) sanctioned a series of offshore power boat races each year, nearly all held in exotic locales like Key West, Marina Del Ray, the Bahamas and San Diego. Sandusky, Ohio, was not a natural fit. Race courses were up to 200 miles long and took several hours to complete. A race was designed to test navigational and boat-handling skills as well as speed. The race course for the Stroh's Grand National started and ended off the beach at Cedar Point but included 187 miles of Lake Erie in and around the Lake Erie Islands.

The boats were enormous but elegant, all shaped roughly like a torpedo, most 38-40 feet long. They were the ultimate "cigarette" boats. They sported huge temperamental engines which could generate 1,000 horsepower and drive boat speeds up to 70 mph, even in rough seas.

As expected, the drivers were a colorful lot. In most cases, the drivers were also owners, or at least crew members. Most boats had a crew of three: driver/wheelman, navigator, and mechanic/engineer.

It took a lot of money to play in this game. The cost to own and campaign a boat was not for the faint of heart or for someone who had to worry about replacing extremely expensive engines.

The sport attracted entrepreneur types, usually a little older but still in the game. They aspired to the lifestyle and glamour of the European Grand Prix circuit. One major difference, of course, was the skill level required to handle a race car versus an offshore power boat. Offshore power boat racing was not without considerable risk, and it was physically grueling, requiring the crew to stand and for more than two hours while continually being bounced and pounded by ocean waves, but I don't think it compares to handling a 200 mph Formula One race car.

Don Ingle was a natural to manage the publicity plan for the race. He loved sports and was attracted to the glamour of the event. It was a chance to work with different people in the media—the sports desk—and he was very successful in getting both pre-race and post-race coverage. He arranged radio interviews for the drivers and crew members and went into Cleveland, Detroit, and Toledo to meet with the TV sports producers. Most were agreeable to coverage and understood this was a unique event for Lake Erie.

Cedar Point hosted a media reception the night before the race in the Convention Center, the second floor of the old Grand Pavilion, the oldest building at the park. Thousands of shrimp gave their lives for the success of the event. In my experience, shrimp—especially large, well prepared and well displayed shrimp—are utterly irresistible to anyone who works in news or advertising for a newspaper, TV station, radio station, or magazine. (Today I would add online news organizations as well). They lose control. The shrimp are vacuumed off the serving displays and onto plates and then into mouths at an amazing rate of speed. And they come back for more.

There were a few questions internally about focusing so much effort on what was at best a secondary activity versus roller coasters. We certainly underestimated how much staff work was involved to host the event. I ended up writing the worksheet which detailed all the internal responsibilities for the event. Lots of pages. Two weeks before the event I spent a Sunday at home in the dining room of our Sandusky apartment writing everything out.

The offshore crew did spread the money around Cedar Point. The stories of $100 tips in the bars and restaurants were probably exaggerated, but not by much, and there were two documented cases of female employees who left town with new friends to head to the next race.

As spectator events, all three races failed miserably. Even in the best conditions, offshore racing is not, by definition, viewer friendly unless you are viewing the race from a helicopter. There were no masses of people on the Cedar Point beach to watch the race. The starting line was about a half mile out (U.S.C.G. requirements). There just wasn't much to see. Afterward, several people, including driver/owner Sandy Satullo, questioned the lowball crowd estimates—but they were accurate.

We used one of the Cedar Point ferryboats as a press boat for the race. It was anchored near one end of the starting line and filled with sports reporters, assorted VIP's, Stroh's representatives, and various other folks—and of course refreshments (including shrimp). I did not go on the press boat for any of the three races. My responsibilities were ashore, and I didn't want to be stuck on the boat for three or four hours, shrimp notwithstanding. The Press Boat was in perfect position to offer those on board a great view of the start of the race—and the finish—but in between it was in perfect position to offer a great view of Lake Erie and not much else.

We did have access to a small boat to run people back in to the marina if they got seasick (every year a few did get sick).

Each year, the race attracted a fair number of spectator boats, most of which anchored near the start/finish line. We never did a hard count, but I would estimate at least 200 boats, at least for the start of the race. It was an impressive sight.

The race ended by mid to late afternoon. The ferryboat blew its horn as the first boat crossed the line and the spectator boats picked up the cue and began to blow their horns well. The winning boat headed quickly to the Marina. There was celebrating to do.

## Assessing the Event

The Marketing group was responsible for running the event as well as publicizing it. Don Dittmann challenged us to demonstrate that the Stroh's Grand National was a good business investment for Cedar Point. It was a tough sell in many ways. The event generated little or no incremental attendance. The Hotel Breakers would have filled regardless of the race (especially in early August). The marina ended up providing lots of free dockage to boats working the race. The main beneficiaries of the event were the bars and restaurants frequented by the racing crowd. Was it worth the cost? Was it worth the staff investment?

We were successful in generating publicity about the race. Even though our name wasn't on it, we were identified as the host of the event in every story about the race. It got us in a different section of the paper or the newscast: sports. It was fun. Exciting even. A break from roller coasters.

In the end, Stroh's passed on sponsoring a fourth race and without a title sponsor (with a required minimum investment of $50K or $100K), the event went to a different location in 1978.

## The Birdman Returns to Cedar Point

Another successful publicity event we generated a few years later was the re-creation of the first long distance flight over water, a historical event which took place on August 31, 1910, when pioneer aviator Glenn Curtiss flew non-stop from the beach at Euclid Beach Park just east of Cleveland to the beach at Cedar Point, a distance of 70 miles. The flight eclipsed the record held by a French aviator Louis Bleriot, set the year before, in 1909, by flying 26 miles across the English Channel.

The flight itself was a promotional event for both Euclid Beach and Cedar Point—and Glenn Curtiss, of course. It was sponsored by the Cleveland Press. George Boeckling, the owner of Cedar Point, reportedly offered a $15,000 prize to Curtiss if he successfully landed at Cedar Point. (In 1912, $15,000 was a lot of money.)

The flight was a success. Flying in an open bi-plane with an inflated bicycle tire as a life jacket and wearing goggles and a cap, Curtiss covered the 70 miles in less than 90 minutes and an average speed of 46 mph. By today's standards, he didn't fly very high, probably no higher than 300-400 feet above the lake. Technically, he flew above water the entire trip, but he was never much more than one quarter mile offshore.

He landed without a hitch to a huge crowd, which included George Boeckling, on the Cedar Point Beach. Some estimated the crowd size as high as 8,000 to 10,000. Fortunately, a lot of images taken of the landing, including several that seem to validate the crowd size estimates, exist in the Hayes Presidential Center in Fremont, the Sandusky Library Archival Research Center, and the Cedar Point Archives.

There was a marker on the southeast side of the Coliseum commemorating the flight erected by a group of early aviators, but outside of aviation history buffs the flight had largely been forgotten. (The marker was moved in recent years to a more appropriate location along the beach.)

Now it's the late 1970s and approaching the 70th anniversary of the flight. Amateur hang gliding is becoming very popular. So are minimalist airplanes called ultra-light aircraft, basically just a

**Glenn Curtiss on the Cedar Point Beach, August 31, 1910.**
Note the bicycle (or automobile) tube life preserver. CEDAR POINT ARCHIVES

seat, a wing, and a small engine. I think all are open-air. The biggest difference between Curtiss' plane and a 1970s ultra-light was the quality and the dependability of the materials. The physics of flight certainly hadn't changed. Flying an ultra-light airplane, especially in the early years, required nerve.

Lots of hang gliding groups and aviation buffs hung out at Edgewater Beach on Cleveland's west side. The bluff above the beach was high enough to allow hang gliders to soar out over the beach and the lake. One of the hang gliders, Chuck Slusarczyk, had graduated to ultra-light aircraft, and in fact was one the leaders of the ultra-light community and well known to the Cleveland news media.

In late July, Slusarczyk contacted our PR Department and offered to reenact the 1910 Curtiss flight on Labor Day weekend. He dubbed it "Curtiss Flight II," and said he had already gotten the Cleveland Press to sponsor him (the newspaper had sponsored the original Curtiss flight) and it could be billed as a preview event for the Cleveland National Air Show. Chuck was full of self-confidence. He made it seem easy. He gave us a short lesson on the physics of flight and asked for the order. We hesitated. This guy was unknown to us and what he was proposing was by definition at least a little dangerous. At the same time, we saw the obvious promotional benefit. It would be something we could talk about with the news media at a time of year when amusement parks were kind of old news (this was certainly true in the pre-Halloween era). It fit the definition of the classic publicity stunt: an out-of-the-ordinary activity created to generate media coverage. It would play well in Cleveland, our biggest market.

Don Ingle and I were both for it. We pitched it to Don Dittmann, who in turn pitched it to Bob Munger, then the CEO. Munger was a pilot himself, though he hadn't flown much in a number of years. In his youth he had flown bush planes in Canada, so he knew something about airplane risk. The word was passed down that before we gave the okay for the flight he wanted our vice president, maintenance, Harry Bray (also a pilot), and our safety administrator, Dick Coulter, to check out the plane—and the pilot. You couldn't argue that request. Don Dittmann asked me to set it up.

Slusarczyk had a kind of workshop/factory/office on the near west side of Cleveland, actually not far from Edgewater Park and my mother's childhood neighborhood. We agreed to meet there.

I drove the three of us from Sandusky. I knew Dick Coulter well, but it was really the first time, and the only time, in my career that I spent extended time with Harry Bray. The plan was to make a day of it. We left for Cleveland after the park opened, and at Harry and Dick's suggestion we had lunch at the Iron Gate in Westlake, then one of the best restaurants on the west side. It was a fine meal, and I remember eating about 10 times what I would normally eat for lunch, which included dessert. I got the impression that the Iron Gate was a mainstay for both when doing business in Cleveland.

We almost exclusively talked about guns and hunting. They each knew a lot about both subjects and loved to talk about them. I had never hunted anything in my life, and my experience with guns was limited to my training in the U.S. Army. I mostly listened but asked the occasional question because I was interested in what they had to say. I got quite an education.

It was a long and leisurely lunch, but then it was time to meet with Chuck. His office or workshop was in a small building on the near west side. We found it easily enough. Chuck was on his best behavior, as well he should be, and built a quick rapport with Harry. Chuck and Harry talked aviation for nearly two hours as Slusarczyk gave a detailed review of the plane and reviewed his flights to date on ultra-light aircraft. Dick asked a few questions, but his focus was on the event at the Cedar Point Beach and how best to prepare for it.

After two hours, Harry gave a thumbs up and said he was satisfied. How that translated was that he could look Bob Munger in the eye and tell him the pilot was not an idiot and knew what he was doing and the plane itself would likely perform as advertised.

On the drive home, the talk was more hunting and guns. I found it interesting, but it did not create in me an urge to hunt. I knew I would continue to hunt my meat at the grocery store.

We cranked up the publicity machine in preparation for the event, sending out news releases and, more importantly, making phone calls to radio and TV stations to line-up interviews and/or stories about the upcoming event. Response was good, though not Evel Knievel good. Don and his team pitched it more as a re-creation of an historical event, not as a daredevil story. We weren't selling possible death and destruction, just guaranteed excitement.

## Flight Time

The day of the event, Sunday, August 26, was bright and clear, lots of blue overhead and only a light late summer breeze. Weather had been a critical issue in the planning as the acceptable flight conditions for ultra-light airplanes were limited. In fact, Saturday had been the original target date but had to be moved to Sunday because of weather. Chuck Slusarczyk, or "Birdman II," as the Sandusky Register dubbed him, took off from Euclid Beach about 5 p.m., and without incident. He was dressed for the occasion in a near-as-possible re-creation of the Glenn Curtiss look, including hat, scarf and gloves. His crew tracked the plane along the Lake Erie shore. An observer would call in from the nearest phone to the Cedar Point switchboard with an update. In theory, the flight would last about 90 minutes. Average altitude would be about 300 feet and he would fly about 400 feet offshore and fly at about 35 mph.

The flight went perfectly. We had a nice-sized crowd (perhaps 750 – 1,000) building on the beach, a good portion of which had been zoned off for the landing. Our lifeguards had positioned a large "X" on the beach as a target. The plane needed to land on hard packed sand, just like Curtiss' plane 70 years earlier, so the "X" was close to the water's edge in an area of beach we had prepared for the landing. Dick Coulter had positioned an emergency medical team on the beach. The Cedar Point Police were there in force as well.

Slusarczyk's wife and children, all in period dress (a nice touch) were present to greet their hero.

All eyes looked east along the lake. Lots of folks had binoculars. Then people started shouting, "There he is! There he is!" and pointed to a speck in the sky just past the 315-foot-high Space Spiral. Slusarczyk had no plans to buzz the crowd. He was headed straight for the beach. No one was allowed into the landing area. CP Police and lifeguards monitored the line. We all watched the plane descend toward the beach. People in the crowd started yelling as it got closer. Then it was on the beach and a huge roar from the crowd. However, a few seconds later, as the tires bit into some soft sand, the plane pitched forward into a vertical position and Slusarczyk was shot forward face first into the beach. There was the predictable huge gasp from the crowd. I think for a moment or two we were all seriously concerned. I know his wife was because she started to scream. But in a second or two, Slusarczyk jumped up waving his arms that he was okay.

The crowd rushed the plane, led by his wife. I can still remember her running past me with her big sun hat in her hands.

Chuck hugged his wife and spun her around in the best Hollywood tradition, then reached down for his kids. It was quite a scene. Chuck had some P.T. Barnum in him. You had to love it.

I remember looking down at his tiny airplane and thinking it must have been a hell of a view from up there.

Media coverage was spotty, not as good as we had initially hoped. Sunday is the toughest news day for publicists. Unless you could guarantee the Pope, a Great White shark attack, or physical evidence of an alien encounter, most TV stations, operating with a reduced staff, passed on requests to cover Sunday events at Cedar Point. The Cleveland media gave the event good coverage, which we expected, but we had limited success in Toledo and Detroit.

## Walleye

We weren't done with water events. For two years in the early 1980s Cedar Point hosted the LEMTA Lake Erie Walleye Championship at the Mar ina. This event was the brainchild of Norm Schultz, general manager of the Lake Erie Marine Trades Association. Norm knew the park well as his trade association sponsored a huge in-water boat show at the Cedar Point Marina in September, an event that had started in 1973.

In his earlier life, Norm had been a PR man for a marine products company. He was smart and a good communicator.

The walleye fishery had come back to Lake Erie, especially western Lake Erie in the late 1970s. Within a few years it had become a national story and the increase in fishing and related activity had become a significant boon to the regional economy. Norm's job, and LEMTA's, was to build on that boon, celebrate it, ultimately selling more fishing boats.

We agreed to be the host site, and to help publicize the event. Don Ingle and his team had a new publicity target: outdoor writers. The tournament was certainly a long way from promoting roller coasters, but in part we justified our involvement to promote our marina and Lake Erie location. We were, in truth, more than an amusement park.

# The Craft

I had never worked in a newsroom. I had never taken a course in journalism or PR or communications. I had a lot to learn in those early years. Don Ingle was a big help on the print side. Don Dittmann understood the business side of communications.

However, my greatest asset was Marie. As veteran reporter and columnist, she knew how a newsroom worked, what made it tick, and the process involved in turning story ideas into actual stories. She was more at home on the hard news side. Although she was required to write some puff pieces, as she called feature stories, she had been put on this earth to be a reporter and an opinion writer and that was why she walked into the building every morning. She stayed away from Cedar Point stories, as was appropriate, but she didn't hold back when it came to advice, such as don't try calling on editors of afternoon papers before noon because they are going nuts trying to get the paper out. Over the years, I used her as a back-door consultant whenever I had to write or deliver sensitive information. She was indispensable.

As a PR group, we were committed to a strategy of personal contact with the news media. We would be proactive, not reactive. What that meant in actual practice was that as an organization we worked the phones and got in the car and drove to Detroit or Dayton or Youngstown and met with reporters and editors and producers in person. We developed relationships. We pitched stories. We bought lunches. Don Ingle and Nancy Steinmuller, and in later years Robin Innes, Lynn Dugas, Melinda Huntley, Joan Van Offeren, Laurie Kinnamon, Lydia Sullivan, Jennifer Link, Barb Colnar, Bryan Edwards, and Janice Lifke Witherow were the people in the field and they did a great job. Not every visit resulted in a story, but you knew it eventually would. They mostly called on travel editors, assignment editors, news directors, state editors, broadcast producers, on-air personalities—an interesting conglomeration of journalists and entertainers. Most were good with a 15-30 minute meeting, but there were some exceptions. One was the news director of a major radio station in Detroit who invited Don Ingle to go with him to the raunchiest strip club in the city for the lunch special and a lap dance.

The challenge was to pitch a story idea that ideally had a local twist. The news media always lights up when they can take a regional or national story and make it their own. It was our job to give it to them. If the team leader of the Millennium Force was from Grand Rapids, it made for a nice feature (broadcast or print) about how a local Grand Rapids college student was in charge of running the big new roller coaster at Cedar Point. Easy sell. And in our experience the reporter appreciated the fact that we were making his job easier.

I did have the benefit of some formal training. My first off-season, my then boss, Bruce Burch, arranged for the two of us to attend a two-day seminar sponsored by the Publicity Club of New York on writing and placing news releases. I remember that most of the other attendees were very envious of our product: roller coasters. It was my first business trip to New York City. Bruce bought me a drink in the Oak Room of the Waldorf Astoria, which I thought was a very big deal, then we walked through the lobby and some of the public rooms, which I thought was even a bigger deal, especially since it was early December and the hotel was decorated for Christmas. He demonstrated what he called a trick of the trade: If you are in a hurry or dealing with bad weather and cabs are in short supply, go to a hotel and enter at a side entrance, then march out the front door and act like a guest. If asked, the doorman will whistle up a cab for you—assuming you are a guest of the hotel—and you'll be on your way. Tipping the doorman was optional, he said, but recommended. Over the years, when the circumstances favored it, I've used this strategy in big cities like New York and Chicago. It works.

Back in the day of the 1970s and 1980s, distribution of news releases and photographs was very much a manual operation, involving a long table and numerous people sorting, labeling, stuffing, sealing and stacking. One of the presenters (and a sponsor) of the seminar, was a company that provided all these services—as well as writing services—for companies that wanted to outsource news release production and distribution. They also customized the mailing list given the parameters set by the client. Reporters, columnists, producers, on-air personalities, and editors changed often. Ultimately, you were only as good as your mailing list.

Outsourcing our news releases was not something we could afford to do, but it was an option, even in 1974.

I learned to know what I didn't know a year later in a return visit to New York to attend a two-day course on financial public relations. Cedar Point, Inc. was a client of Edward Howard, a Cleveland-based PR firm. Cedar Point used Edward Howard exclusively for financial communications, including the production of the annual report, issuing news releases on quarterly earnings, and courting the financial press. Edward Howard was full service, however, and I believed would have loved selling roller coasters as well as earnings statements. I viewed them as competitors to some extent. I felt I was in a race to become competent enough in public relations that my superiors, Don Dittmann, Al Pifer (the CFO) and Bob Munger, would feel confident that all publicity functions, apart from financial communications, belonged in-house.

The account person from Edward Howard was Stan Ulchaker. He smoked a pipe, wore good-looking suits, was average height and weight with a broad and friendly face. He was probably 10-12 years my senior when I first met him in 1975. We enjoyed a good relationship from the beginning, I think bonding as fellow scribes. He was also from the West Side of Cleveland and a big Indians fan. I recognized right away he was a very talented professional.

I used to wince inwardly when we were in situations where we were being introduced and he always mentioned that he was "Cedar Point's public relations counsel." That certainly was how he thought of himself. To Stan, his role as PR counsel went beyond publicist. I assumed he wanted to be the guy who managed the client's crisis communications program, who got a favorable article on the client company in Forbes, who drafted the speech the CEO gave at the Harvard Business School Club, who advised the client on how to handle problem situations. In those years in the '70s, he did function as PR counsel and my team functioned more as publicists. That changed over time, as our internal capabilities grew.

Don Dittmann suggested I learn a little more about financial communications—part of my education in business—and encouraged me to sign up for a four day course in financial public relations offered by the Publicity Club of New York. I didn't know what to expect. I was a little intimidated as I knew nothing about finance at that point of my career. It was a significant learning experience for me. I came away with increased respect for Stan and the world he lived in.

## New York City

I stayed with my in-laws in Cedarhurst, which was conveniently located to JFK Airport. It was the first, and only time, I stayed with them without Marie with me. Both were soon to retire. Ben in less than a year, in 1976, and Tessie a year later in 1977. I went into the City with Ben each morning. What that meant was going to bed early, as the alarm clock went off at 5 a.m. Tessie made breakfast, promptly served at 5:30 a.m. Ben and I then drove a short distance to the Long Island Rail Road station in Cedarhurst. (Tessie, a non-driver, was part of a car pool of teachers).

I remember standing in the station with Ben in the darkness and the cold waiting for the train. There were others there, mostly men, standing in shadows. Ben bought me a New York Times. The train arrived sometime around 7:15 a.m. A lot of the people had been riding for a while, joining the train further out on the Island. Their coats were off. Many were talking and joking; they were obviously friends who traveled into the city together every day. We were fortunate to get a seat. Ben nodded to a few folks. I saw two groups that were playing cards, and with gusto, something I had heard went on regularly on New York commuter trains. Ben showed me how to fold the Times in a way that allowed you to read the paper in tight quarters without reaching out to turn pages and sticking it in your neighbor's face. There was a definite trick to it.

The LIRR took us somewhere in Brooklyn. We hustled off—it was closing in on 8 a.m. now—and Ben led me through the multitudes to a subway entrance. This was a different experience, more like a traditional subway ride. The train rolled and jerked. And smelled. Riders were squeezed in like bullets in a clip. Our destination was downtown, but where I wasn't sure. We changed trains again in Manhattan. I stayed on board, headed to a hotel in Midtown. Ben took a train south to the financial district. When he got to his stop, he walked up to the street and then several blocks to his building. He took an elevator up to the seventh floor. He sat down to his desk. It was about 8:45 a.m.

My commute back home in Sandusky was a bit different. From our second floor apartment on Perry Street, it was about 10 minutes to my parking space at the park. Only one stoplight. And I got to enjoy the beauty of Sandusky Bay and the skyline of Cedar Point on the journey.

When the course ended around 4 p.m., I took a subway train downtown and followed the directions Ben gave me to his building. That was an adventure, too. He gave me a full tour of the Smith Barney offices and introduced me to a number of his co-workers. He was obviously showing me off and I was happy he thought that much of me. He took me into one of the big computer rooms and we stared at the crazy whirling machine. He looked at it with fear, pride, and envy. He knew it was going to very shortly take his job away, send him home for good a few years before he was ready.

Then we headed back to Cedarhurst. Ben bought me a Daily News in the subway station.

I remember being nervous for my first few radio interviews, but I found I enjoyed doing them. They were mostly "good news" interviews, not follow-ups on ride downtime or accidents or poor financial performance. The key was being conversational in your delivery and being short and crisp. Listeners can spot a frown or a bad attitude through the airwaves—they don't need to see your face. We did have information to get out: key stats about a new ride; the date for opening day; details on a new promotion. If the interviewer wasn't going to set you up for it, for whatever the reason, you had to learn how to do it yourself, how to "bridge," as the consultants and the textbooks said, to get to the information you wanted to get out.

TV was different, and more difficult. We are visual creatures and we make instant decisions about people based on how they look. The combination of audio and visual tells us all we need to know. You don't have to be physically attractive to be a successful flack (though it can help) if you come across as concerned, honest, outgoing, knowledgeable, interesting, friendly... likeable and believable.

Live TV or radio was different than something being recorded for airing at a later date. Live was a more stressful situation, unavoidably so. I empathized with our staff when they had to go live in a hard news situation at the park. I did not have to do it that often in my career for a variety of reasons, but I recall it was always stressful. You are "the tip of the spear," to use a military metaphor. You represent the entire company, all employees, the Cedar Point brand, all of it, as you wait all by yourself, alone, making small talk with the TV reporter as the tech in the satellite truck shouts out the time remaining until they go live with the Cedar Point segment. You have some idea what the reporter is going to ask you about but he or she can always pull a surprise (they often do). You rehearse in your head what you are going to say. You understand that in some situations a single wrong word can doom you, and the park.

Several times in my career, the company brought in a communications consultant—usually a former news reporter or sometimes a person from the business side—to do crisis communications management for park management. I thought it was a good investment. Also, it was smart that in each case the company involved a wide range of managers, from GMs to department heads. Most of the people in the room would never be asked to go one-on-one with a news anchor, but they came away with a greater appreciation of what's involved for those who would be. A common training technique was for the consultant to role play with individual managers, setting up a situation—always a bad situation (fire, drowning, ride accident, storm damage, etc.) where the manager had to act as the park spokesperson. The audience was his or her fellow managers.

The managers felt the stress. The questions were tough. Most did not perform well. Afterward, more than one said they'd rather do anything than have to do it for real. They were genuinely horrified at the prospect. I thought what my colleagues did—maintaining and operating the world's biggest and fastest roller coasters—could be stressful, too.

Brevity is a key ability. Unless it's National Public Radio (NPR), all interviews are short, bursts of questions and quick answers. With experience, comes a clock in your head, a sensor that warns you when you've talked too long. My wife and I are heavy consumers of news,

Receiving the 1978 Photo Department of the Year, Public Relations Division, Award from the Professional Photographers of America and Eastman Kodak Company. Left to right: Nancy Roth, Nancy Steinmuller, Mary Schroeder, John Hildebrandt, Jamie Jo Berry Todor, Lynn Dugas, Don Ingle, Jane Heyman, Presenter. Our star photographer, Dan Feicht, is the man behind the lens.
CEDAR POINT ARCHIVES

including broadcast and cable news. We are amazed at the number of people who appear on news shows regularly who have to be cut-off, sometimes aggressively, because they've gone on too long. It's embarrassing to watch. I do appreciate these guests are thrown unfair questions that in truth require longer and more measured responses, but the hosts are bound by the laws of commerce, which are as fixed and unforgiving as the need for an occasional bathroom break.

Talking in sound bites, which sounds somehow fake or disingenuous, is really an accomplished skill, rare and highly valued in the world of publicists and PR practitioners. A very few are naturals, most have to learn the skill over a period of time. Some never do.

Most of our work was driven by product publicity and classic PR, which my mentor Don Dittmann beautifully described as "Do good. Then tell people about it." Crisis communications is a different animal, requiring some different and additional skill sets. The best PR people can both pitch and hit, and in my opinion they are the real stars of the communications business.

When it came to responding to a media request involving a hard news (bad news) story, such as a power outage, fire, weather emergency, ride incident, we always had to create what we called "The Statement," a brief (usually) written news release or statement on behalf of the park and in response to the basic question: what happened?

Crafting a media statement was an ugly but interesting exercise. Drafting it was the responsibility of the PR Department, but approving it might require several levels of management, including the CEO, depending on the situation. It was statement by committee, with numerous managers weighing in on this word or that. Sometimes, we'd go through five or six iterations before we had it set. The writers were generally on the side of perhaps offering too much information, the approvers on the side of occasionally offering too little.

The purpose of the media statement was to give the park's or the company's point of view about what had happened. We didn't speculate. We didn't volunteer information. Even within our PR group, there would be arguments over the use of a single word. Most of the time, we had to go to one of our in-house managers to explain one or more technical issues so our PR spokesperson could then render it in plain English in the statement. There was always a time issue, too, especially as cell phones became more and more common on the midway. It seemed at times the media had advance knowledge the electrical power in the park would malfunction at exactly 7 p.m. There was increasing pressure to respond as quickly as possible and no sympathy when you could not.

Before cell phones, news media would physically have to be on site to get pictures or video, which usually meant at least an hour's drive from Cleveland or Toledo, which meant you had at least a little bit of prep time. The digital age settled all that. When an incident occurs now, the media are bombarded with amateur video and photography almost instantly. For a great variety of reasons, coaster trains are sometimes stopped partially up the lift hill. It's a great visual, of course, because it's man bites dog. I have watched as throngs of guests reach for their phones and go into a frenzy of picture-taking to post on social media or email to their favorite TV station.

## Courtesy Tickets

The tradition of offering free admission to your attraction for the Fourth Estate with the hope—or in some cases the expectation—of favorable coverage is a tradition as old as P.T. Barnum. In my experience at the park it worked both ways. We invited media representatives and their families to visit the park because we wanted them to be familiar with our product.

We were open in our invitation, and never expected or even hinted at a quid pro quo. Media representatives also invited themselves to the park. Some he-hawed around it as though they were ashamed to have to ask—but they had two or three amusement park age kids at home and park tickets cost real money, so they did. Some phone calls were painful. I felt bad for them.

Over the years, we worked out a set of internal protocols regarding the news media and courtesy tickets. First, tickets were for working press—reporters, editors, photographers, anchors, etc.—not the security officer in the newspaper's parking lot. We limited ticket requests to four tickets. We made some exceptions, of course. If the news anchor from one of the TV stations in Cleveland or Detroit asked for six tickets, we couldn't say "no problem" fast enough. We avoided if possible sending tickets in the mail. Instead, we required media representatives to pick up tickets at the park and to show ID (all courtesy ticket recipients were required to do this). We kept a record of every ticket we issued.

Part of the courtesy ticket issue was that some media representatives, and others from vendors to government officials to the public, viewed courtesy tickets as a no-cost item. What's the difference if I come into the park free—it costs you nothing? Not so. The ticket was our product. It represented the roller coasters, the shows, Frontier Trail, everything.

Once I got a call from a local businessman, a vendor who sold product to the park. I knew him from a local civic organization, not through the park. However, his regular Cedar Point contact had recently left the company—so he decided to call me. After exchanging pleasantries, he got down to business. Would it be possible to get six tickets, so he could visit the park this weekend?

No, I said—though I dressed up my response beyond a simple no.

He was quite upset, and told me he had gotten free tickets in the past. I wouldn't relent. It made me mad that he had sold us product—we were the customer—yet he expected Cedar Point to give him free tickets. If he were smart, he would have made a fuss about buying four tickets. Then he uttered the worst possible response: the tickets didn't cost us anything.

I was tempted to transfer him to Dick Kinzel.

## Chapter 9

# Who's in Charge of the Weather?
God

The only weather that really mattered at Cedar Point was the weather that occurred six months of the year, May through October, when the park was in operation and we were busy trying to make a living.

Cedar Point had lots of interesting weather the other six months of the year, November through April; the south shore of Lake Erie has as much weather variety as any place in the country. But for those of us at the park it was weather for polite conversation, weather to read about or view at your leisure, weather in the abstract, weather that was somehow unserious—unless it was a tornado, or a blizzard, or a horrendous line of thunderstorms that struck in the middle of the night—since it didn't impact attendance.

One of the best things about the off season (and retirement) was not having to worry about either the weather forecast or the actual weather. You could enjoy the weather, even when it was bad. Yeah, weather was still important, I guess, but not in comparison to weather that impacted your livelihood. I have always felt a bond with others whose economic wellbeing is directly impacted by the weather: farmers, commercial fishermen, ski resort operators, manufacturers of snow removal equipment, golf course owners. I know almost any business can argue they are impacted by weather, but for most it is damn subtle.

Not for amusement parks, which almost by definition are outdoor entertainment. When it rains, the midways are empty. Worry is Monday or Tuesday in late July or early August and the local weather reporter is predicting that a big low pressure area approaching from the southwest will hit either Saturday (very, very bad) or Sunday (bad). It does depend on the park's geographic location, of course. There are some parks, like those located in southern California, where on an annual basis weather is a minor concern. But for most of us, weather during the operating season was a constant worry, an anxiety that never left you.

My very good friend, Bud Greene, a native of North Carolina, often says Sandusky is a fit place to live from about June 15 to

September 15; the rest of the year it's just crap: cold, wet, windy, sometimes snowy. In retirement, Bud went back to North Carolina. Bud lacks the bad weather gene.

The Great Lakes are known for their beautiful summers. As one of our local Cleveland weathermen pointed out many times, Cleveland enjoys quite a few more sunny days in June, July and August than does Atlanta. Unlike areas in the South or the Atlantic coast, the Great Lakes rarely must battle extreme heat (90 plus) or high humidity for weeks at a time. Usually after a day or two of the hot stuff we get a beautiful high pressure system from Canada that blows off the stink and shows off a blue sky that sparkles like new money.

## The Lake Erie Chill

The Great Lakes downside is the spring: April, May, and the first and sometimes second week of June. The Cedar Point microclimate is dominated by Lake Erie. Cedar Point is surrounded by water, water that even coming out of a mild winter or an early spring is still around 50 degrees when the park opens in mid-May. It only takes a whisper of wind to pull the chill off the lake and onto the shoreline. On bright, beautiful days in May it might be 52 degrees at Cedar Point and 72 degrees 18 miles inland in Norwalk. Guests who came from what we called the interior (10 miles or more from the lake) rarely accounted for the Great Lake Erie Chill in their travel plans. In truth, the chill was not a major impact on attendance, but it could impact the quality of the guest visit. Many guests were not dressed for the weather. They wore sandals and shorts and a T-shirt, and 52 degrees or even 60 degrees might as well be 42 degrees. We sold lots of sweatshirts on days like that. Lots of sweatshirts. Our Merchandise staff rubbed their hands with glee when the chill arrived in the evening of a big attendance day. Many early season days it would be warm in the morning and most of the afternoon, and then a lake breeze would spring up (caused by the difference in temperature between the water and the land) and send guests looking for sweatshirts.

Most of the guests who were candidates for sweatshirts were junior high and high school kids, mostly girls, who wanted to show the world it was summer, and they were cool with it. I used to get cold just looking at them. I felt bad for the ones who didn't have cash or access to a credit card and who had to endure the chill for the next six or seven hours. Occasionally on the midway you'd see a whole family walking together all wearing their brand-new Cedar Point sweatshirts. Our Merchandise staff was smart and offered an "entry level" sweatshirt for under $40.

The chill affected our employees, too. The first year kids, despite the advanced warnings from veterans, often didn't bring warmer clothes with them to work and suffered the consequences. Even if you are moving around a lot, it feels cold on the Raptor platform when you are wearing shorts, didn't bring your jacket, and the Lake Erie chill arrives.

Every year, usually sometime in early to mid-July, the Lake Erie water temperature and the average air temperature crossed over, and Lake Erie became a welcome air conditioner on hot summer days, keeping the park several degrees cooler than areas inland, especially if a lake breeze sprung up in the late afternoon or evening. The chill was gone until next May.

Lake Erie was generally a temperature friend in the fall, though I always felt its attendance impact was overrated. It was true Lake Erie cooled slowly; some years the water temperature was still in the 70s into mid-September. I can remember swimming with my sons once on September 15. Autumn nights away from the lake might be cooler by 10 degrees or more. Most of our guests lived in areas which experienced frost weeks earlier than Cedar Point. There were years when Cedar Point did not experience a hard frost or a freeze until Thanksgiving. Erie County has the second longest growing season of any county in Ohio, comparable to Hamilton County (Cincinnati) along the Ohio River. The fall climate along the lake is excellent for growing grapes, but I never felt it made much difference for the park. I don't think many people were even aware of the difference between lakeshore and inland temperatures. I doubt the TV weather forecasters in Columbus or Pittsburgh or Lansing spent much time pointing out how different things might be at Cedar Point that night.

We recorded weather, of course, and looked for patterns in search of expectations and explanations. Park Operations oversaw the record-keeping. Every day the temperature was recorded at noon and at 6 p.m., and the weather for the day was accorded one of the following designations: sunny, cloudy, showers, or rain. The difference between sunny and cloudy was, pardon the pun, cloudy. It was very subjective. It depended on which staffer made the call; it depended on the length and depth of the overcast, e.g. days with filtered sunshine were usually designated sunny. The designation showers meant it had rained during some portion of the operating day, which covered a lot of territory, 10 minutes up to several hours. The attendance impact depended greatly on when the showers occurred: morning and midday showers were the worst. The dreaded rain designation was accorded to days where it had rained at least four hours of the operating day. All the designations were art as much as science.

All this weather data was compiled in an annual compendium called Summaries and Comparisons, which counted, measured, and compared a true host of things, from weather to voluminous attendance and admission statistics going back many years.

Given Cedar Point's geographic location in North America, its weather mainly comes from the west, riding the big west-to-east jet stream. Weather systems come to us from the northwest (Canada and the Pacific Northwest), the west, and the southwest. The prevailing wind is west to southwest. Yet some of our worst storms were three-day Nor'easter's that moved untold millions of gallons of water from the east end of Lake Erie to the west end, causing beach erosion and flooding. We were impacted to a much lesser degree from the weather systems that clawed up the east coast. We were hurricane proof—except for some peripheral rain and wind—unlike our sister Cedar Fair parks like Dorney Park in Allentown, Pennsylvania or Kings Dominion located outside Richmond, Virginia.

## Tornados and Waterspouts

But not tornado proof. In my 40 years at Cedar Point we experienced one confirmed tornado touch down in 1977, and one waterspout in 1998. The 1977 tornado hit in early evening—Marie and I were having dinner at a restaurant in Sandusky—and wiped out many trees in Frontier Town and overturned campers in Camper Village. Fortunately, there were no serious injuries. I remember touring the area the next morning and being shocked at the damage. I thought it would take a week to recover. I was wrong. Frontier Town opened the next day. A group of men and women who know what they are doing, and with the right tools and equipment, and who are properly motivated, can accomplish a great deal in a short period of time. Our Maintenance division, assisted by some good contractors, made it happen.

The second tornado was technically a waterspout. Of all the weather events I have seen firsthand in my life, the waterspout that hit Cedar Point on June 30, 1998, is king. Waterspouts are basically marine tornados; when they come ashore they become true tornados, though fortunately they usually dissipate as soon once they hit land. Waterspouts were forecast as a possibility on June 30. Conditions were favorable: unstable air, cool water temperature. I remember in the morning it was cool and wet with low clouds.

I had gone into town for lunch. As I drove back over the causeway I am sure I glanced to my left, to the west, but I didn't note anything out of the ordinary. I drove along Perimeter Road past the marina and drove through the curve by the Wildcat and the CP&LE station house. Perimeter Road then straightens out and heads due west with Sandusky Bay on the left side and the woods and Frontier Trail on the other. Suddenly I was staring at a huge waterspout heading directly for the park, and also heading directly for me. It had just come to life in Sandusky Bay. It looked to be no more than a mile away, off the southern tip of Johnson's Island, and wound like a snake up into the sky. It swirled and sparkled. I could clearly see the water sparkling in the funnel. I slowed the car.

I picked up my radio and called it in (dozens of employees in the marina and in Frontier Town were doing the same) to the CPPD. I decided to try to beat the waterspout around the tip of the peninsula rather than turn around—probably not a good decision—but there was not enough room to turn safely. As I drove past the Mean Streak, the waterspout was behind me. My goal was to get back to the Marketing office and into the center of the park.

The waterspout behaved as it was supposed to behave. It dissipated as soon as it hit land, right in front of our flume ride, White Water Landing, in Frontier Town. It did travel across the peninsula scattering tables and chairs and bending and breaking some small tree limbs, but no injuries and no real damage. There was some consternation on the midway. Most guests, and employees, did not differentiate between tornados and waterspouts, and what they saw in the sky was damn scary. Guests gravitated toward buildings and cover. Many made a dash for the arcade on the ground floor of the Coliseum.

At the coaster stations, employees encouraged guests to stand underneath the stations. Guests flooded indoor restaurants and stores. In Marketing, we encouraged guests to come into the office, some even went into the photo darkroom (interior of the building, no windows, and concrete block walls). We had a good-sized crowd in the park that day, probably 30,000 guests.

Reports came in that there were more waterspouts. But the immediate danger seemed to have passed in a few minutes, and we had not lost power, a huge plus.

We all felt lucky, very lucky. The waterspouts had been photographed and appeared in newspapers across the country the next day. The images were quite dramatic. The cover shot on the Sandusky Register, taken by Tim Fleck, showed the waterspout just as it hit Cedar Point.

In 2012-2013, when Cedar Point went through the process to become officially designated a "Storm Ready" facility by the National Weather Service, many of us thought back to that afternoon in 1998. All the Storm Ready work was done by Ken Berryhill, our director of safety; in fact, Ken had pushed hard to get the designation. Most of the work involved employee training for weather emergencies, communication protocols, and designating and appropriately signing buildings at the park which could be used for shelter in an emergency.

Cedar Point was one of the first parks in the country to achieve the Storm Ready designation. I was proud it came on my watch.

The "when" of precipitation was critical in its impact on attendance. Rain in the morning was almost always the worst possible situation. Rain later in the day was never to be welcomed but always less impactful on attendance. There was a revenue hit in-park as some guests bailed early, but those who stayed tended to spend more. Rain drove guests into our arcades and stores and restaurants. On rainy days the main arcade in the Coliseum was jammed, even on light attendance days. You could spend a lot of money very fast keeping your kids entertained playing video games and other games of "skill."

Don Miears, who for many years headed up our Merchandise and Games division, used to remark how much he liked a nice hard, but brief rain in the late afternoon. He loved seeing all the ponchos on the midway.

## Toledo Versus Cleveland

Though located midway between Toledo and Cleveland, Sandusky and Erie County tilt east to Cleveland in terms of economic and cultural orientation. Sandusky is definitely part of the Cleveland media market. Sanduskians listen to Cleveland news, go out to dinner in Cleveland restaurants, take shopping trips to Cleveland, and follow Cleveland sports teams. They also watch Cleveland weather news. Toledo, Ohio might as well be Toledo, Spain. However, in truth Sandusky's weather is more like Toledo's than Cleveland's. The western end of Lake Erie, where Toledo is located, gets more sunshine than the eastern end, for example, where Cleveland is located, and far less snow.

Most of the interesting weather in Cleveland occurs east of the city, including the infamous Snow Belt (there is a primary belt and several secondary belts). Cleveland and points east and south are also affected more by Atlantic coast storms, including the occasional hurricane.

Most of Sandusky's weather comes from the west, more specifically Toledo, and if you want an accurate gauge on the weather, look at what's happening in Toledo.

For much of my amusement park career there were no cell phones, smart or otherwise, and no internet service. We relied on the National Weather Service (NWS), part of the National Oceanic and Atmospheric Administration (NOAA). There was no easy access to radar. TV and radio could give you the broad brush, but not what was happening in real time. Certainly, the tens of thousands of guests in the park had no way of knowing what was going on. Mainly they just looked at the sky. Cedar Point had a PA system for the park but there were several shadow areas where audio did not reach.

Over the years, Park Operations and Safety discovered park locations where they had a good view to the west and could watch storms as they headed for the park. One was the Raptor ride platform, and another was the Mean Streak platform. When the Maverick opened in 2007, its ride platform became an excellent vantage point. When I was GM I watched numerous storms arrive at Cedar Point from the Maverick platform. Sometimes I thought about my father who used to sit, transfixed, in our living room on Sunset Drive and watch summer thunderstorms roll in across Sandusky Bay. He listened to the thunder and the sound of rain pelting the glass window. I listened to my park radio, as the office called out to managers and supervisors in the park the latest radar updates. There was constant, serious chatter. It was my job to listen, and I did.

Park Operations, Safety, and the CPPD all believed in what we called the Sandusky Bay factor. Sandusky Bay covers a large area. It extends west of Cedar Point approximately 15 miles and is at least two miles wide for most of its length. Storms coming in a solid line from Toledo would sometimes break into two parts when they hit Sandusky Bay: one part would veer south over land and miss us; the other part would veer north and head out over the lake. Cedar Point would be spared a direct hit or sometimes any hit at all. It was a bit of a mystery. You could never count on the phenomenon occurring every time, but it happened enough to be noticeable.

In the mid-1970s, Cedar Point contracted with a private weather forecasting service in Pittsburgh to provide two forecasts per operating day, one in the morning and one in early evening. Their focus was the weather for the Cedar Point Peninsula, not Cleveland, not Toledo. They had access to multiple weather radars. The forecast came into Park Operations and then circulated around the park. The company also provided alerts for severe weather. That was perhaps their greatest service. Both the CPPD and Park Operations monitored the NWS broadcasts. Our greatest in-park weather risk was from thunderstorms accompanied by lightning. Tornados were always a possibility, but thunderstorms were much more common. The summer I worked seasonally at Cedar Point, in 1969, a guest was killed in a thunderstorm by a falling tree near the hotel. In the 1980s another guest was killed in a storm by a large tree limb in the marina. We also had a guest killed by a lightning strike near the Raptor in the 1990s.

# Wind

Wind is also an issue at Cedar Point. It can significantly impact the guest experience because wind velocity and direction opens and closes some of Cedar Point's most popular rides, including Magnum, Top Thrill Dragster, Millennium Force, and GateKeeper. The threshold varies by ride, but we learned that a northwest wind of 25-30 mph would shut down Magnum (we learned that the hard way when in its first year of operation in 1989 a Magnum train could not get through the bow tie element in the back of the ride on a windy day and riders were stuck for more than an hour until we got the right equipment to get them down).

One of the worst wind situations I can ever remember occurred the second day of operation in 2012. It was a Sunday, probably Mother's Day. Attendance was light, probably around 5,000. It was cool and partly cloudy but dry. However, we had a raging northwest wind ahead of a big cold front; the wind was a steady 25 – 30 mph with gusts to 40 mph. Nearly every major ride was down for wind the entire operating day. Guests were obviously disappointed and frustrated. They did not understand why or how wind could shut down a mountain of steel like Millennium Force or Magnum.

In some cases, it was a judgment call, in others it was adherence to the protocols established by the ride's manufacturer. Sometimes the call was not so clear cut. Do you risk opening a ride like Millennium Force when you know there is a 50 percent chance the wind will stop it from making it up the fourth hill on the test run (even if loaded with water dummies), and that if it doesn't make it up the fourth hill you will lose the entire next day to taking the train apart and off the track and then reassembling it again in the station?

I remember that day very well because as a favor to a ride manufacturer we had agreed to give a group of Chinese amusement park operators a tour of Cedar Point. There were eight or nine in the group, including two translators, and it was my job to escort them around the park. They were quite disappointed they couldn't ride many of our best rides, but I think they still enjoyed the opportunity to visit what I confidently told them was the best amusement park in the world. They took lots of pictures, asked lots of questions. With one or two exceptions, they were young, most in their late 20s or 30s. China, I learned, has many amusement parks and water parks.

I remember the faces of the other guests in the park that day. They just didn't understand about the wind. It was an issue of wind direction, too. Northwest winds were the worst because they affected the most rides.

We gave several student groups the opportunity to return to the park at a later date. It was our policy to handle guest comments on an individual basis. For those who made the effort to contact us, we were generous.

Ed Dangler, who headed up the Maintenance division during most of my time as GM, was an industry veteran and had worked at several parks across the country. When he came to Cedar Point in 2007 he said a big part of his learning curve was adjusting to the wind factor in operating rides.

Cold was less of an issue. If it was dry, cold temperatures didn't keep guests away from the park. Cold temperatures in spring and fall could significantly impact ride maintenance and delay the opening of certain rides, but no father ever looked his 10-year-old son in eye and said it was too cold to go to Cedar Point today. During HalloWeekends guests dressed for the weather, including hats and gloves.

By the time I was a general manager (2005), Cedar Point had taken responsibility for its own weather forecasting. Any guest or employee with access to a TV or a smartphone could access weather information, but the official weather central for Cedar Point was the Park Operations office. The office staff had at least one, but sometimes two computer screens locked into what they considered the best weather sites for our area. Some of the staff became quite skilled at reading radar and projecting the speed and direction of approaching weather, especially lines of thunderstorms. Marcia Frankhart was a star at reading radar. I relied on her judgment and her skill, as did the managers and supervisors out in the park. There were established protocols for opening, operating, and closing rides in various weather situations, but ultimately it often came down to a judgment call.

Guests did not always understand. Our approach was conservative. We always erred on the side of caution. The rain would stop. The sky would start to lighten. Guests would start scrambling for the entrances to coasters. But nothing happened. The coaster trains didn't move. Some guests would get frustrated, some even angry. But they did not know what we knew: there were still lightning strikes west of the park and a good chance we'd get clipped by a second line of storms within 15 or 20 minutes. We had great respect for lightning. Some of our higher rides like Millennium Force or Top Thrill Dragster were struck by lightning several times a season.

I felt badly for our guests on rainy days. There were guests who joked about coming on rainy days because they'd have the park to themselves, but a lot of what they had spent their money and time to experience was not available to them. The best course of action was patience and a positive attitude. In reality, there were very few days when it rained constantly for the entire operating day. Many rides could operate in light rain with reduced capacity. Weather of course was beyond our control and guests knew that on a rational level, if not an emotional one. We had consistently, starting in the 1960s, communicated to guests that there were no rainchecks or refunds once you chose to enter the park. However, that didn't stop guests from lining up outside Guest Services demanding refunds and rainchecks every time we had a serious rain day.

Weather did impact staffing. There were no hard and fast rules to follow, but at some point you reduced staffing in the park given the current and projected weather. When I was GM, I learned to trust the judgment of my senior managers on managing labor on rainy days. They knew what to do.

## Local TV Weather Forecasters

We all had a love versus hate relationship with the local weather forecasters, especially those based in Cleveland. Everyone at the park had a favorite, and some had a favorite enemy as well. Weather broadcasting, as opposed to weather forecasting, is an even trickier business, a never-ending conflict between partly sunny and partly cloudy. And the natural human instinct is to want to hedge your bet and cover your ass, so even though you knew probably it wasn't going to rain you still put up the 10 percent or 20 percent or 30 percent chance I'm covered. Also, weather is about conflict: cold versus warm, dry versus wet, light versus dark. Viewers and listeners naturally increase when there is weather conflict. Thunderstorm lines get hyped. Hot, muggy weather is sometimes treated like there is arsenic in the water supply.

Park-goers made decisions to visit, or not to visit, based on what their local weatherman had to say. We used to joke that many times we'd keep checking different weather sources until we found the most positive one and then we'd clutch it to our chests and not let go—no matter what developed. We believed that bad forecasts were almost as bad as bad weather itself. The worst situation was a bad weather forecast for the weekend—but delivered early in the week. We knew that all over our market area weekend plans to visit Cedar Point were being put on hold, or even cancelled.

I was born and raised in Cleveland, so my bias was clearly to the east. I watched far more Cleveland TV weather than Toledo in my years at the park, even when I learned that our weather was more Toledo-like than Cleveland-like. I used to watch Cleveland weather but, in my mind, make what I called a Toledo adjustment.

The gold standard for Cleveland weather was Dick Goddard, the chief meteorologist for Channel 8 for an amazing 55 years, retiring at age 83 in November 2016. He holds the Guinness Book of World Records for the longest career as a weather forecaster. I had the opportunity to meet Dick Goddard a few times when he visited Cedar Point, a classy guy and a very good weatherman. He was a fan of the park—and owned our stock, as I recall. My mother was a longtime fan; he was certainly her favorite local TV personality. When my mother was in a nursing home and all her possessions were reduced to a small bookcase and some family pictures, the ever-smiling face of Dick Goddard with his signature and some kind words greeted her each day.

For most of the time I was GM, my go-to weather person was Betsy Kling, the chief meteorologist for WKYC-TV - 3 in Cleveland, the NBC affiliate. An excellent weatherperson, Betsy also loved roller coasters. It was not a put-on, she really loved roller coasters. I discovered that fact when she appeared as a courtesy of Channel 3 at Cedar Point's Science Day event in 2009. I made sure I got a chance to meet her, and included some of my colleagues as well, who were also anxious to meet her.

I asked if she wanted to ride a couple of roller coasters while she was here. She jumped at the chance and so we went to Millennium Force and Top Thrill Dragster. I offered Betsy the opportunity to ride in the front seat of both coasters, which she was all over, and I took the seat next to her. I have ridden these coasters dozens and dozens of times, but they are always a thrill, they always generate trepidation, excitement, and fear. Betsy loved the experience and thanked me, and the park, for giving her the opportunity to ride.

Each season, when Betsy was at the park for Math and Science Day, I arranged for her to ride a few coasters of her choice.

Betsy attended my retirement party, driving out from Cleveland to Sandusky in-between the 6 and 11 p.m. news. This really impressed my guests.

What weather all came down to was worry, a constant background to your day or night. For some in the park—Park Operations, Safety, Cedar Point Police, for example—weather was real, and serious, and challenged your decision-making skills such as when to close (or reopen) rides and attractions. For others it was relatively immaterial, such as the Cash Control Office, where they might have to count a lot of wet bills. In my Marketing life, I mainly worried about its impact on attendance. For the Park Operations staff, it was weather's impact on ride safety.

The park staff all complained about weather. We talked about weather constantly. If affected our moods, our temperament, our attitude toward the future. I knew some senior management who went into a total funk on rainy days, as if a powerful vacuum were attached to their emotional center and then turned on to suck every

Getting ready to ride the best roller coaster in the world, Millennium Force, with Betsy Kling, Chief Meteorologist, WKYC-TV, Cleveland. HILDEBRANDT COLLECTION

drop of positive attitude right out of them. It was painful to be around people like that, but we all understood it because even the most positive among us had experienced it. Things compounded when one rain day turned into two or three (or more; it happened). Looking back, I feel sorry for the spouses and families who had to put up with all wailing and complaining. I was guilty of inflicting a very negative attitude on my wife, Marie, due to meteorological events at the park, on more than one occasion.

Marie: I apologize.

Rain days were tolerated well in the early season because we believed, by our Cedar Point logic, that the visits lost to rain in May or June could be made up with sunshine in July and August. In my earlier seasons especially, I lived in dread of a rainy August, especially the first three weeks. August is the driest month of the summer in Sandusky, averaging only 2.74 inches of precipitation, and is the least windy, but I knew that once every five or six years Sandusky has a wet August. In the 1970s and into the 1980s and 1990s, August would generate more than a million visits, most of those visits in the first three weeks. Rain in that period was disastrous, as schools started the fourth week. There were no opportunities to get those visits back. Three or four rainy days in mid-August could cost the park 100,000 visits.

At the corporate level, we liked having it both ways. Weather was always a convenient and rational excuse for attendance underperformance. And it spoke to the truth: rain days equal poor attendance days, simple cause and effect. The news media, and the investment community, certainly understood and accepted it. However, the flip was certainly true: warm sunny days equal good attendance. But hold it. Not so fast. Sometimes it does and sometimes it doesn't. Rain always means lower attendance, but sunshine doesn't always mean stronger attendance (but often it does). Go figure.

Senior management didn't like using weather to explain attendance trends. They preferred the "weather usually evens out over 140 operating days" line when pushed—and in most situations and most seasons they were correct. However, three rainy Saturdays in October will kill you. It will.

We used heat sometimes as a weather excuse, blaming heat waves for lower attendance. In truth, it was hard to make a firm case that heat and humidity impacted attendance in a meaningful way. In my opinion, there just wasn't data to support it, even though there was plenty of anecdotal evidence. There were plenty of 90 plus degree days that were clear attendance winners, but some that weren't.

# Cedar Point's Weather Wish

I have been often asked: what is the ideal weather from the park's point of view?

If you are a guest at Hotel Breakers, it's when the early morning air is cool but not cold and you can get your coffee in the Rotunda and walk the Boardwalk in shorts and a T-shirt without need for a windbreaker or a sweater. The sky is clear, deep blue, and the water sparkles.

Mid-morning on the midway you can feel a warm sun on your face and arms. You have left the raincoat, the sweater, the sweatshirt, the jacket, the long sleeve shirt in the car or the room. There is no risk in exposing as much skin as you want: you are not going to get cold.

But it's warm—not hot. No stickies. No sweaty wet skin. No damp clothes. The air is thin, not thick. You lazily drink water, you swig. You don't gulp it and then pour some on your head.

At the water park and at the beach the towel is for drying off, not getting warm. You don't need a T-shirt after swimming.

There is a very light breeze, perhaps 10-12 mph, enough to make the lake and the bay interesting to look at but not enough to sideline any rides—even the Sky Ride—and not enough to complicate wearing a hat or losing cups and napkins off the picnic table.

In the evening, there is a magnificent Lake Erie sunset, casting streaks of beautiful light onto the midway, into the lattice-like structure of Magnum and the dark wood cabins on the Frontier Trail. The air cools slightly, enough that you notice it and welcome it. But at 11 p.m., as you exit the park, you feel as comfortable as you did when you entered.

In more technical terms, as Dick or Betsy might forecast: Clear skies; high 80-82 degrees, low in the high 60s; light southwest winds on the lake 15 mph or less; relative humidity low, zero percent chance of precipitation. Forecast for tomorrow: more of the same.

In any given season, we might experience 10 days like this.

## Chapter 10
# Closed for the Season

*"The lack of manmade sound is striking. The park is asleep. And it doesn't snore."* – Unknown

## A Different World

Sweet November I called it, the three weeks between Halloween and Thanksgiving, when the off season is fresh and new and the past year is still closer than the next. The darkness creeps in early, a soft cloud that sometimes moves in from the lake in late afternoon, touching the mostly naked trees and wrapping itself, like a blanket over the shoulders, around the dark buildings that line the midway. Daylight Saving Time is gone, welcome to the dark world. You stare at your PC screen and forget the time and it is 5 p.m. and it is only five minutes to sunset. The vehicles still moving in the park have their lights on.

There are days of soft November sunlight which retreats gradually and grudgingly all afternoon. The lake goes still, flat as a backyard fish pond. The sun is often blood red in a ball with dazzling streaks out over the water. There is no wind. Along the beach there is that beautiful crinkling sound of the lake making contact with the shore. No crashing surf but a short quick kiss.

There is still a bit of color in the trees, but peak is two to three weeks past.

The animals are more visible now. There is often a fox sighting, occasionally a deer that has worked its way down the beach from Sheldon's Marsh. A feral cat or two appears from underneath the Cedars Dorm. The gulls work the edges of the peninsula for food, but gather by the hundreds on the main parking lot. Geese fly overhead and honk themselves into proper position. The eagles return and perch, sometimes half a dozen of them, on the big cottonwood at the very tip of the peninsula in front of the cottages at Lighthouse Point.

Instead of 50,000 or more people moving around within 400 acres you have 250 or so, and most of them are inside buildings. The place is essentially empty.

The park is quiet, still, even amid building a new ride. The park music is gone, except for a week or two before Christmas, some years, when the Tech Services guys play Christmas music on the midway

sound system. The sound carries into the buildings; we are all tired of it after a few days.

It is November and the lake and bay are all water: no boats. The water is getting colder, you no longer think of it as a place you might swim; in another month it will look like the Arctic.

When you drive onto the Causeway in the morning there is often no car in front of you. You tend to drive faster, yet it is easier to take in the water and the sky. Without the green background provided by the trees, the park skyline has changed, now thinner, looking vulnerable.

And it is different inside your head, too. The year is over now. Nothing can be changed or done over or re-invented or re-priced. I'm sure some athletes feel a similar thing right after the end of the season: you can't take back that weak fastball you threw to Calavito. The organization's focus will switch to next year very soon but for a while—in Cedar Point's case until after the Thanksgiving and Christmas breaks—the old season lingers in the heart and in the mind.

Guests know Cedar Point only when it's open which is on average about 140 days a year. Employees know Cedar Point as a great, sleeping, benevolent beast for, on average, 225 days a year. The park sleeps more than it is awake. It has a long hibernation. We know this world well.

For 40 years I worked in a seasonal business. I have no other experience. But I know I like it. I like the clarity and simplicity. I like the cycle. I like a beginning, a middle, an end. I like a fresh start ever year. In my mind, and I suspect in many others, the Cedar Point seasons never run together. Each is a unique set of circumstances that will never be repeated. For any given year I remember what was new, what the attendance was, the broad theme of the weather, the seasonal employee base rate, myriad other details. In this, I was like a farmer or a baseball player, or like many others who make a living by a business that turns on and turns off by design, or by nature's law.

When I was GM, both at Dorney Park and Cedar Point, I loved to drive the park just at dusk. The last thing I did on my last day at Cedar Point before I retired was to take a tour of the midways and all the spots where you could navigate with a vehicle. It was a dark, overcast day in mid-December, a Thursday as I recall. It was right around 5 p.m. and the park was empty. I really had it to myself for the last time.

I have been in sports stadiums when they are empty of people and drama. It is an interesting experience. Your mind inevitably is drawn to the contrast. You stand in the spot in center field where the center fielder most often positions himself—you can see the wear and tear on the grass from his spikes—and you look in toward home plate, very far away, and imagine the tens of thousands of fans all around you. It is the same with amusement parks. One day, the midway is thousands of bobbing heads and sneakers and sandals slapping the concrete; the next day there is no one except a couple of maintenance guys who wave at you from their truck and two ladies from Accounting who are walking after lunch.

In my experience, people loved seeing the park when it was closed. At Cedar Point, administrative offices were scattered across the peninsula; inevitably, business guests had to walk or drive through some part of the park to meet with park staff. The first-timers always commented on the experience, how disconcerting, but fascinating, it was. "I can't believe I'm driving down the Cedar Point midway," was a common statement. They said it in a way that you knew they'd be sharing it with friends and family, especially with their kids, the instant they had a chance. Many times, while giving an off season tour of the park my guest or guests would ask to have their picture taken on the midway.

## Labor Day

The hint of the off season begins the day after Labor Day. Historically, Labor Day has always held great significance for seasonal amusement parks like Cedar Point. For most of its existence, up until the last 15 years or so, Labor Day marked the end of the operating season, even if the park was open a few more weekends. At Cedar Point, daily operation began mid-May, so Labor Day came after an unbroken run of 110-115 operating days. The advent of HalloWeekends changed the significance of Labor Day. Now it is more the marker of the end of the regular season, and signals the switch-over to Halloween, which now lasts up to eight weekends, depending on the calendar, really a second season.

In the day, Labor Day was the opportunity to celebrate, to blow off a season-long accumulation of stress, which often involved loud music, copious amounts of alcohol, and both boys and girls acting badly.

I remember once in a corporate planning meeting during the time I was general manager—I was the only operating person at the table, everyone else was staff—Dick Kinzel looked at me and in response to a comment someone made about the season said:

"John knows there is an end. John knows Labor Day will come."

What he was saying is that I was in the brotherhood, that I understood what a grind the summer could be, especially the last weeks, that I would have to live through it, that I was a front line soldier. I'll admit I appreciated what he was saying.

I did have a Labor Day song, "Come Monday," by Jimmy Buffett. Starting a week or so before Labor Day I used to pop it in the music player in my car and start singing along with Jimmy as my car cruised past Maintenance and the Hotel Breakers parking lot on my way to Perimeter Road.

My actual Labor Day rituals were tame. Of my 40 Cedar Point Labor Day nights, nearly all were spent at home, usually with a few beers in front of the TV (especially if there was a sporting event to watch) and talking to my wife. My first year as GM of Cedar Point I was invited to a Labor Day party after the park closed. The kids from Park Operations took over one of the local bars in Sandusky. A couple of full-time managers and a few seasonal supervisors tried to get me to come. Reluctantly, I agreed. I felt awkward, and I could tell my presence at the party put some employees on edge. I felt like I was the chaperone at the high school prom. I had one beer and left.

The park was quiet on weekdays during Halloween season, especially Monday-Thursday, but it was still in fighting trim. You had to drive the midways carefully to avoid hitting trash cans. There were Halloween decorations everywhere. Many days in September and October are warm and sunny, very summer-like, and it felt odd on those days not to be open. It was a strange feeling to walk out the door into a warm afternoon sun to a quiet and empty midway.

The time between Halloween and Thanksgiving has its own rhythm, and its own pressures. Winterizing the park starts as soon as the park closes on the last Sunday night. The very first thing that happens is that the trash cans disappear. They are all checked and emptied and cleaned and then staged in groups, awaiting transfer to winter storage underneath Point Pavilion, the group picnic shelter at the front of the park. There are 2,000 trash cans to put away for the winter.

All the food stands need to cleaned, the food prep equipment scrubbed. In Merchandise and Games, they were busy doing inventories and organizing the merchandise that would winter in the stores. Maintenance was busy taking coaster trains off the rides, so they could begin winter overhaul. The plumbers began the long process of draining pipes in Hotel Breakers and other locations.

When I was GM, my rule was that the midways had to be clear of all Halloween decorations and related material by Thanksgiving. As the event grew bigger and bigger, that came to be a more difficult objective, but I felt to give in at all would have meant Halloween in April all over the park.

Pressure came from the top, too. Dick Kinzel was on a mission every off season to maintain the park using the fewest number of part-time workers possible. Starting the week after Thanksgiving, each GM in the company had to turn over to Dick a weekly list which detailed every part-time employee still on the payroll, how many hours they had worked, and at what rate, and why they were still working. It was not a report that gathered dust or got deleted after a quick scan. Dick studied each report and if he had a question about anything he didn't hesitate to call you. All the GMs hated doing these reports, of course, and felt that many of Dick's guidelines were unreasonable, but for Dick it was about the principle of always controlling costs, especially in a period when revenue was pretty much non-existent. It was okay to be a little unreasonable if it helped teach his GMs, and their staffs, that controlling costs was all-important. I complained to my peers as much as any GM—especially since Cedar Point was Dick's home base and I was always under his eye—but I will admit, grudgingly perhaps, that doing the damn reports every week made me more focused on the cost side of the business.

Cost control did not come naturally to me. I was not a spendthrift, either, but I was more apt to daydream about ways to grow revenue than ways to cut costs.

Dick Kinzel wasn't much for lights in the off-season, either. Cedar Point was one of Ohio Edison's biggest clients. The cost of electricity was the single biggest line item in the budget. We were electrical hogs; we sucked it down during the operating season like no one else: roller coasters powered by linear induction motors; wave pools; 1,500 hundred hotel rooms and campsites; restaurants, parking lot lights, midway lights, and ride lights. But after the park closed for the season, it all pretty much went away.

Maintenance had a well-thought-out plan for eliminating all but essential lighting for the nighttime hours during the off-season. However, it did take a few weeks to implement. There were a lot of light systems to coordinate. You couldn't just flip a switch and go from in-season to off-season. As the years passed and the cost of electricity became dearer, we eliminated more and more lights until by the time I retired the park in the off-season might as well have been London during the Blitz.

Invariably, someone would leave a light on at a ride location or food stand or merchandise shop where they had been working during the day. Invariably, Dick Kinzel or Jack Falfas would leave work after dark and drive down the midway and see the ride location or the food stand lit up like a Christmas tree, a spot of bright light surrounded by blackness. Invariably, I would get a call from Dick or Jack pointing out to me that the fill-in-the-blank had a light on. Invariably, Ed Dangler, our vice president of maintenance, would then get a call from me passing along the information about the f----- light that some idiot had left on.

# Ghosts? Or No Ghosts?

It was creepy at night in the off-season, especially on cold nights when the wind would blow and make lots of interesting noises. I was very fortunate that throughout my time at Cedar Point my off-season parking spot was very close to my office. Walking any distance on a dark January midway was no fun. The most chilling nighttime sound came from the Space Spiral, an observation ride with a gondola that rose 285 feet in the air. There were two sets of steel cables on the ride. If there was any kind of wind at all, the cables would beat against each other and the steel frame of the ride. The sound could fill the front half of the park on some nights. Driven by the vagaries of the wind and the fact that the cables were in constant flux, the sound was never predictable in volume or pitch. You listened and were surprised.

My office in the Coliseum was less than 100 yards from the Space Spiral. Most nights, I was usually the last person out of the office. When I flipped off the light in the lobby and stepped outside, it was very dark. I would put my briefcase down, put my back to the midway and Kiddy Kingdom and attempt to lock the door. It was never easy, especially in cold weather. Inevitably, the Sky Ride cables would suddenly clang, and I would elevate several feet in the air. I hurried to my car, always feeling better when I had shut the door and turned on the headlights and the radio and I could hear Mike Trivisonno on WTAM groaning about one of the Cleveland sports teams.

I have often been asked about Cedar Point and the supernatural, specifically ghost sightings. I can say I never experienced one, even when walking through the Ballroom alone late at night. I considered the Ballroom and the Hotel Breakers to be the two most likely places to be haunted on the peninsula.

In my time at the park, I was in plenty of positions where a ghost sighting might even have been expected. But, nada. However, I had colleagues who saw them, or felt them, and there are persistent legends of specific ghosts. For example, the old section of the Hotel Breakers is supposedly inhabited by at least two ghosts, both female, and by style of dress from about circa 1910. The Cedars Hotel, built in the same period, but long an employee dormitory, also has more than one ghost, a male and a female.

I have been to many other places that are ostensibly filled with ghosts, including many Civil War battlefields. I have walked the entire ground of Pickett's Charge at Gettysburg, and was moved by doing so, but no Confederate infantryman appeared suddenly by my side. I have even been to the Gettysburg battlefield at night, and once on Halloween night, but no ghosts.

When I was GM of Dorney Park and living in Allentown our Rotary Club had a speaker a few weeks before Halloween, an attractive female college professor who investigated supernatural phenomena. She was blonde, looked about 40 and as I remember had a very strong speaking voice. She had visited the Gettysburg battlefield many times. One story she told us involved an audio recording supposedly from July 3, 1863. She said sounds are sometimes captured, or recorded, on rusty metal, in this case a nail that was dug up on the battlefield near Devil's Den. It was a natural phenomenon, she said, but little known and rarely observed. One of our Rotarians in the audience, an engineer of some kind, commented that what she said was true—in theory, perhaps. Using special equipment, the sounds can sometimes be recovered. In this case, she said, you could clearly hear (in very Southern speech) a man calling out names and soldiers responding by shouting "Present!" The professor was a good storyteller. She had us all.

At Cedar Point, the nail would have recorded laughter, children's voices, coaster screams. Not so bad.

For a couple of off seasons in the early 1980s, Jungle Larry over-wintered his pack of wolves at Cedar Point. He hired a local man to care for them. There were two or three wolves in the pack. Sometimes at night they would howl. It was quite unnerving, even for the CP Police officers who worked second or third shift. I heard the wolves a few times when I worked late. I felt bad for the wolves, confined to a pen, unable to live any kind of natural life, but the howling certainly got your attention.

It was easy to turn into a hermit in the off season. You might go months without seeing someone. In bad weather, it was always easier to pick up the phone or send an email. Most of our other parks had a main administration building which housed most of the full-time staff. From a communications perspective, it was a better way to go.

## Christmas

It was true I worked every Memorial Day, Independence Day, and Labor Day weekend for 40 years. However, the flip side was that Cedar Point closed for Thanksgiving at noon on the day before and depending on the calendar we were off eight to 10 days at Christmas. The shutdown at Christmas amounted to an extra week of paid vacation for the non-union staff. It was a significant employee benefit and recognized as such. Many of my non-Cedar Point friends were aghast that I had to work on those summer weekends; in turn, I was aghast that they had to work Christmas Eve and the days between Christmas and New Year's.

Christmas was the end of the year; it was time to put the past season away for good. The money had all been counted, good or bad. While budgeting was done for the upcoming year in November and initially reviewed by management in December, your head was still disentangling from the prior year, certainly emotionally. Most of us saved at least a few days of vacation to take just before Christmas so we were usually off work two weeks. It was hard to get anything done at Cedar Point between Thanksgiving and Christmas. We had a lot of staff who took off nearly the whole month of December.

The Christmas break gave you a clean separation between seasons. I had my rituals. I always came into the office at least one day during the break and cleaned house. I dumped old financial reports, trade magazines, various operational reports, whatever I could find that I didn't think I'd need anymore. I tried to be ruthless, but in hindsight I kept too much. I re-organized my files and created new ones. I went through all my drawers and got rid of all the detritus common to someone who works out of an office. It always felt good to do this. I was usually there alone.

As the end to my holiday drew close, I would grow increasingly wistful as it came closer to the day to go back to work. The night before returning, after Marie and the boys were in bed, I would sit in front of the Christmas tree and turn out all the other lights in the room. I would pour myself some Scotch or a glass of wine and stare at the tree and think of many things: my parents, my brothers and my sister, Aunt Arlene, my Grandmother Byrne, all the past Christmases I had experienced in my life, a quick shuffle of my memory deck. Then I'd switch to the New Year. I was always optimistic in a general way, but you never knew what was going to happen in any given season. They were all crap shoots. My last acts were to offer a toast to past and present and future and then unplug the tree for the last time.

## Two Blizzards

We had two severe snowstorms, technically blizzards, during my years with the park. The first occurred in January 1977, and the second only a year later in January 1978. There were many snowstorms over the years that required closing the park early, but these two storms were nasty and dangerous.

I did not get to experience the 1977 storm first hand. Don Dittmann and I were at an agency meeting in Pittsburgh. We heard reports all afternoon about the deteriorating conditions at the park. The causeway was closed because of whiteout conditions; some employees got out in time, but many others did not and were trapped at the park. I talked to Marie numerous times. She was home alone but our downstairs neighbors, Ruth and Ben Stevens, kept checking on her. Fortunately, Marie never lost power at the apartment. The Register kept her busy making phone calls to get updates on the impact of the storm in Sandusky.

There was no Weather Channel in 1977 and 1978, and certainly no internet. There was little access to weather radar. The lack of information, both before and during major weather events was amazing by today's standards.

The Cedar Point Causeway (renamed the Richard L. Kinzel Causeway in 2011) can be truly treacherous in snowstorms, especially if the wind is strong from the southwest, west, or even northwest. There is nothing to brake the wind between Edison Bridge and the causeway, eight to 10 miles. The snow is blown in great swaths across Sandusky Bay and when it hits the causeway it staggers and much of its energy is dropped on the road and the three bridges. The snow piles up quickly; the lack of visibility can be total.

One employee, a secretary in the executive office, stalled in a drift trying to leave work. Although quickly picked up by CP Police she suffered frostbite on one of her ears.

The storm continued into the night. The remaining employees all gathered in one of the executive apartments in the marina. At some point, the wind and snow subsided enough that the director of safety, Dick Coulter, decided it was time to get the hell out. He and the CP Police organized a caravan of cars and led everyone out of the park and across the causeway and into Sandusky.

In Pittsburgh, everyone panicked. The agency closed early even though no snow was in sight. The city was enveloped in a late afternoon traffic mob as residents tried to get home, or get to the store and then home, before the storm hit. Reports out of Ohio were dramatic; we heard the National Guard had been called out in some communities. Don and I were not scheduled to spend the night but ended up doing so. I was extremely disappointed I had missed all the excitement. Pittsburgh only got two to three inches of snow.

We drove home in bright sunshine and blue skies. The storm was gone. It was very cold but that was nothing new in the winter of 1977.

The Blizzard of 1978 was a much bigger event, one of the great winter storms of the past century. It has entered the realm of mythology, but it was no myth; it was real. The epicenter of the storm was northwest and north central Ohio. The storm hit on a Wednesday night as rain, but quickly turned to snow and continued in Ohio until Friday afternoon.

This storm killed people: 51 in Ohio, the most of any state; one elderly woman froze to death in Erie County.

I remember getting home Wednesday night in the rain and slush from a racquetball game. I didn't leave again until late Friday afternoon. We ended up with over 30 inches of snow. Temperatures dropped to near zero. The wind was steady at 40 mph for hours and hours. White hell, as one person described it. Drifts were the size of houses.

Because of the timing of the storm, there were no employees at Cedar Point to evacuate. No one could get into the park on Thursday. Cedar Point offices did not reopen until Monday.

Marie and I lost power sometime Wednesday night. When we woke Thursday, the house was already getting cold. Our first house was a small ranch, built in the 1950s, and aside from some token insulation in the roof it was ill-equipped to deal with winter. The windows leaked. There was no fireplace, wood or gas. Worst of all was the fact that the outside walls were not insulated. They were freezing to the touch. Whatever heat remained in the house was getting sucked out very quickly. The house seemed to rattle on its foundation when a big blast of wind hit.

Surprisingly, the phone worked, so we were able to talk to friends and family, but connections were spotty. We also had a portable radio, so we were able to follow the weather news. The local station, WLEC-AM, somehow stayed on the air with a skeleton crew.

Marie was five months pregnant; in fact, we had found out a few weeks previously that she was going to have twins.

We layered on the clothes. That was about all you could do to try to stay warm. We took inventory of what we had to manufacture light, which was basically candles and two flashlights. We were light on battery backup. We did have several cans of sterno, left over from one our camping trips, which was a salvation. Using the sterno, we were able to heat canned soup, which we augmented with crackers, bread, and some refrigerated leftovers. At least the beer stayed cold.

All day the temperature in the house kept dropping. I did not completely trust the thermostat reading so I also checked with an LL Bean temperature clip I wore on my winter jacket. By mid-day, it was in the 50s inside the house.

Later in the afternoon, but well before dark, I decided to go outside and see what it was like for myself, the sort of thing you do when you're 28 years-old. Marie did her best to dissuade me, but I was determined. Visibility had improved; I would dress appropriately. I tromped around the house and yard a bit. Our house was back off the street and protected by several other houses, so drifting was not an issue. One car was in the garage, the other was entombed in snow. I guessed the snow depth at close to two feet in the driveway. I walked down to Galloway Road and followed it up to the intersection of Hull and Galloway, at most a quarter mile away. I saw no cars, no people. There was a massive drift across

**Cedar Point is beautiful in winter, too: Blacksmith Shop on Frontier Trail on a snowy December afternoon.** CEDAR POINT ARCHIVES

the intersection, one of the biggest I had ever seen, at least six feet in height. I marveled at it, but it also scared me. It was time to go home.

We dined by candlelight and the blue flame of sterno. Marie and I talked a lot—there wasn't much else to do—mostly about our family to be. We talked about names. We didn't know the sex of our children, and wouldn't until they were born, so we had to prepare three sets of names.

We went to bed early and piled on every blanket we owned. The interior temperature was now in the low 40s (it was nine degrees outside). We wore long underwear and flannel pajamas and snuggled. At that stage of my life I did not have to get up during the night to pee, so I was spared that experience. It was very cold in the morning. We used the last of our sterno to heat water for coffee.

Then, a little before noon, we suddenly had light.

Paul Hohler, the father of Marie's good friend, Karen Greene, used his influence with the future family of his youngest son to get our driveway plowed on Saturday morning. It was quite a task; it would have been impossible to shovel. Our driveway was long with a hedge on one side. The only way to plow the snow was one long continuous push the length of the driveway. The snow pile was enormous and would not be gone until mid-April.

It stayed cold for six weeks. Every day was the same—highs in the mid-20s—but fortunately we did not get much more snow. One young man rode his horse across Lake Erie to Canada. On St. Patrick's Day a small plane crashed in Sandusky Bay after taking off from nearby Griffing Airport in a sudden snow squall. The plane put a hole in the ice but did not break through and sink. The first responders arrived on snowmobiles. On March 17, the ice on the bay was still almost a foot thick.

It took a week or more for Maintenance to clear the midways and parking lots at the park. Snow plowing was, and is, a big deal at Cedar Point. We were responsible for taking care of the seven-mile-long chaussee as well as the causeway. The park covers 400 acres, the buildings and rides are scattered everywhere, and we were required to maintain clear access to everything in the event of fire.

All that inconvenience aside, the park could be stunningly beautiful in winter. There were certain areas—Ft. Sandusky and the cabins on the Frontier Trail—which in the softly falling snow near twilight looked like what was in the poet Robert Frost's mind when he wrote" Stopping by Woods on a Snowy Evening." The coasters look very serene draped in snow, impervious to it, certain of themselves. On bright sunny days the white is dazzling, especially if the lake and bay are ice and snow covered looking like an enormous white blanket. Along the beach, looking out to the lake, you can imagine yourself

Robert Peary or Ronald Amundsen staring into the blue and white horizon. If there has been sufficient wind from one of the northern quadrants, the ice is bunched up into huge hedgerows, almost little mountains of white.

Dan Feicht, the Cedar Point photographer and videographer for many years, captured the beauty of the off season better than anyone. His rival is Scott Fais, a former local resident who became a TV journalist in Florida and is currently managing editor of IAAPA's Funworld magazine. He has always dreamed of doing a photo book on Cedar Point in the off-season.

## Getting Ready to Go Again

I used to describe the period from January 1 to opening day as a big snowball rolling down a hill. It is quiet the first week of January, but by the week before opening it's craziness and the snowball is the size of Pennsylvania.

Starting just after Thanksgiving but kicking into high gear in January, the ride overhaul program is the monster in the room for the Maintenance staff. People outside the business, and many inside it as well, do not understand or appreciate the effort required to overhaul as many as 30 coaster trains in essentially 140-150 days. Each train is broken down to its essential parts and inspected for wear. New parts are installed, per the manufacturer's requirements. When I was a GM and used to tour the ride shops in the off-season I was always amazed by the work. One piece, a Millennium Force train, was now in several hundred pieces, and two mechanics stood over those pieces and were responsible for checking every one of them and then carefully putting it all back together. Our mechanics had great attitudes, and they knew they were doing important work. Ride mechanics were by far the largest single group in Maintenance, representing more than a third of the Maintenance workforce.

It was all Mongolian to me. I have never had any skills in this area. A lot of kids, mostly boys, learn about basic carpentry, plumbing, painting, electrical and mechanics from fathers or older brothers. I had no older brother. My father knew a little electrical, but in his spare time he read history books, not shop manuals, and he was fortunate enough to be able to pay someone to do handyman work around the house. When I was a child, we used to get occasional Saturday visits from two employees of the Hildebrandt Provision Company to do work around the house. My siblings and I knew them as George and Stanley. George was a WWII veteran, but he had fought for the other side: he was one of the lucky 30 percent who survived service in the German U-Boat fleet. Stanley was Polish by birth and had fought the

Germans during the war. But in Cleveland, Ohio, in the 1950s, they had become good friends.

All my life I have had great respect for people who have technical skills. Two of my dearest friends, Bud Greene and Art Mirtes, both graduates of the General Motors Institute (GMI), and professional engineers, helped me take care of our succession of homes in Sandusky. There was nothing they couldn't fix: lawnmowers, snow blowers, cars, furnaces, clogged sinks, roof repairs, windows, household appliances. And they could build stuff, too: desk tops, work benches, bird feeders, shelving. All I could offer in return was beer, which was always gladly accepted, and very unskilled labor, which was also gladly accepted.

There were firm deadlines to meet if we were going to have all rides operational and licensed by the state by opening day, always the goal. Every week or so I met with Ed Dangler and our ride maintenance manager and reviewed where we stood on each ride. We were at the mercy of the ride manufacturers and suppliers in terms of parts. In my years as a GM, getting parts on time became more and more of an issue with lead times for some parts approaching a full year. The mark up on parts was very high, unconscionably so in our opinion, but we had few options. All manufacturers stipulated they would back off liability if we used any parts not blessed by them. Understandably, we were reluctant to use generic parts, even if they met or exceeded manufacturer specifications.

Ed had seen it all in his career, and I considered myself blessed that he was my vice president of maintenance for my last eight years as GM. A New Jersey native, Ed was an electrical engineer by training and had worked at several parks in both the Six Flags and Paramount systems. He had transferred to Cedar Point from Kings Island in 2006. He was an excellent communicator. He had the skills to explain technical subject matter to non-technical people like me.

Ride maintenance started working overtime in January, usually going from eight hour shifts to 10 hour shifts four days a week. Some years Saturday work started in late January. It was a race. The finish line was very very specific: opening day.

Starting around St. Patrick's Day, there began a gradual shift to outdoor work as all the refurbished trains were moved to their specific ride and staged for installation. Inside the shops the work increased as the deadline got closer. More overtime, more pressure. In management, we were always trying to find the right balance between overtime and staffing. Do you hire more mechanics, or do you increase overtime? Most of our ride mechanics looked forward to a certain amount of overtime and the extra dollars it brought, but we also did not want our ride mechanics exhausted and burnt-out before the season began.

Each department or division had its own procedures for preparing for the season, its own deadlines, its own rhythms, its own benchmarks. The effort to launch a new season is truly herculean in many respects. I was always in awe of it, especially as I came from an essentially staff department where just about the only physical preparation involved was cleaning up the Group Sales Booth. We didn't have more than 60 ride units to get ready, or dozens of food locations to stock, or 2,000 trash cans to carefully place in the park. We weren't going from 14 or 15 employees to more than 1,000 in a few weeks. We weren't getting almost 1,500 hotel rooms ready for guests. We weren't trying to train hundreds of seasonal employees, almost half of whom were first-time employees, to operate rides, make beds, make change, stock shelves, display merchandise, and operate a fryer (safely).

Lois Ann Lawrence, the admin in Planning & Design, for many years, coined the phrase: "Don't you know we've got a park to open?" every time there was even a whiff of something not getting done on time. It was never delivered with a smile. This was serious business.

Much of this work had become institutionalized. There were records. There were written procedures. There were full-time employees with many years of service who knew how to close the park down and then reopen it again. But it was still not easy. It was always a close thing.

## Stay Out of the Way

Richard Zimmerman, the regional vice president who was my boss for three of the nine years I was GM of Cedar Point, once told me that the best thing a GM could do the three weeks leading up to opening day was to stay out of the way. It was good advice. In my marketing days, much of my get-ready time was spent outside the park, in studios producing radio spots or negotiating a promotion with a fast food company or other partner. In my GM days, it was very different. My job was to be at the park and to be visible. I usually did not offer advice, but I felt it was important to be involved. I was aware that the thing all operating managers feared the most in the weeks and days just before opening was a new project—no matter how small—and I did my best not to add unanticipated work, though sometimes I had no choice.

The snowball that started slowly down the hill in January was at avalanche speed in the days and weeks before opening. I did not enjoy March and most of April so much, but the last three weeks were something special, especially in seasons where we were going to open a big new attraction. The midway was a wild place: Maintenance vehicles everywhere, including pick-up trucks, scooters, front end loaders, lifts, dump trucks, cement trucks, small cranes, golf carts, and just about every vehicle imaginable; all driven by people in a hurry. There were cars, vans, box trucks— also all driven by either people in a hurry or people gawking at the strange new world of a huge amusement park and resort 10 days from live action.

In our safety meetings, we all stressed to one another the importance of driving slowly, of watching out for pedestrians who weren't paying any attention to where they were going. We urged people walking to look both ways, to be careful walking around the corners of buildings, to avoid blind spots (the park was full of blind spots).

The landscapers are out in force and the earth is being turned over and you can smell it and you like it, even the pungent smell of mulch. The lake air moves inland when the breeze is from the north and carries with it a smell that is a mixture of sand, water, peat, fish. It sounds unappealing, and some days it is, but other days it smells and tastes of spring.

The sound was wonderful, almost titillating: the first time you hear Raptor drop off the lift and then feel the big whoosh as it climbs up the second hill; the big click that follows the Blue Streak train engaging with the chain and then seconds later the purest, most nostalgic, most historical sound in the wide wide world of amusement parks, the sound of a train ascending the lift hill on a wooden roller coaster; and the most welcome sound to me, the steam whistle on the George R, as the locomotive made the turn and headed for the Frontier Town train station.

We were alive again.

# Chapter 11

# Things Natural

## Battle for the Planet of the Gulls

It was not a pretty sight. It belonged on a cable TV nature show. I once watched a big herring gull swoop down and take a duckling in the marina. I was walking along the walkway between the Bay Harbor and the Marina Store. It was early in the season. The ducklings were very small, and the gull had come up behind the mother and her brood and swooped down and grabbed the one who was bringing up the rear. The gull flew off toward the parking lot with her dinner.

Herring gulls are a big, aggressive birds and will eat just about anything. The area around Cedar Point, including Sandusky Bay, is one of the largest seagull rookeries on the Great Lakes and home to five species of gulls. In truth, western Lake Erie and Sandusky Bay is teeming with fish, from baitfish to bass, perch and walleye. If you're a gull, you have the added benefit of Cedar Point as a good place to rest and roost and an even better place to discover delicacies such as Cedar Point fries, hotdog buns, and funnel cakes.

## Defending the Gulls

Gulls have their defenders, including the U.S. government, which offers them protection from hunters or other groups who do not much like them for various reasons, but to many others they are a nuisance of the first rank. "Rats with wings" is a common pejorative, and there are others not suitable to print.

The screech of gulls, constant it seems, is part of life in and on the water. For some, a few, it is bird poetry. However, gulls perching on the steel columns of a roller coaster means streaks of what looks like white paint on the columns. The roofs of buildings have lots of white splotches. Our beautiful concrete midways are sprayed white in spots. Gulls attack open dumpsters. They like to roost in the Sports Stadium along the beach. They particularly like to sit on the seats— maybe they pretend they are seeing a show. They do not excuse themselves when they need a bathroom break.

Cedar Point management has been fighting gulls for a long time, certainly all my career, and with little success. In truth, it is a war we cannot win, only lament, and then fight the good fight. The

park has always taken full advantage of whatever legal resources are available—which aren't much, from our point of view—to control the population. Maintenance has dutifully applied for every permit available. We can shake the eggs of a specific number of gull nests each year before the chicks are due to be hatched. For nearly all my time at the park, Tim Smith, a Maintenance supervisor, was the appointed executioner. Tim was the go-to person for all animal issues at Cedar Point.

Many, too many, of our guests liked feeding our resident gulls fries and assorted other delicacies on the midway, on the beach, or at food locations. By mid-season, the gulls became very aggressive— much to the delight of some of our guests. I'm not aware of any guest ever being bitten by a gull, but it's probably just a matter of time before it happens.

Bill Spehn, our VP-park operations for many years, discovered a potential solution on a website: blast the sound of gulls in distress and that would keep other birds away. We tried it. We plugged in a CD of gulls-in-distress sounds into our midway music system and played it for two hours every morning before the park opened. The sound was excruciating to the human ear. It drove our ride mechanics and others doing pre-opening work nuts. I was often in the park myself before opening and it drove me nuts, too.

Did it keep the gulls away? There was no scientific evaluation. Bill thought it did but even he had to admit the effectiveness was marginal at best and impossible to measure. There were still plenty of gulls around. Most of them anyway, were on to us. We declared defeat and moved on.

We took heat from some guests over the cleanliness issues the gulls created. It was frustrating because the only way to keep the park clean of gull droppings was to manage the gull population, something we really couldn't do very effectively. Many of the places they liked to perch were impossible to access for cleaning.

Sooner or later every full-time employee and many seasonal employees had the misfortune to get smacked with some gull droppings. There was never any warning. Suddenly you felt a light plop on your head or shoulder, or perhaps your hand or arm. You were initiated into the club. In my career it happened to me three or four times. Never fun.

On July Fourth we got a little payback. We shot fireworks from the section of the beach alongside the main parking lot. The area was a prime gull hangout. Hundreds hung out in the general area. An hour before the show, it was protocol to test the system by shooting a test shot. It's a very loud noise—you can hear it in Frontier Town— and it comes without a calling card. The gulls freak out. I think they think it's Tim Smith with a surprise weapon. The birds start screeching and carrying on and flying around crazily. The group of us at the test shot (Safety, Sandusky Fire Department, CP Police, and Park Operations) enjoyed watching the gull hysteria very much. It took a half hour before the gulls figured out they weren't going to die after-all and calmed down enough to return to the area. Then, a short time later, the main show started and in seconds there wasn't a gull within a mile of the park. We loved it.

A magnificent bald eagle soars over the track of the new
Steel Vengeance roller coaster. CEDAR POINT ARCHIVES

## "The Eagles Are Coming!" (The Hobbit)

Sea Gulls and Bald Eagles share a taste for Lake Erie fish, but share little else. While gulls are pretty much universally hated by park employees, eagles are loved. The Cedar Point Peninsula and Sandusky Bay and the adjoining wetlands and woodlands are excellent bald eagle habitat. When the eagle population began to recover in the 1990s, they found our area to their liking. Bald eagle sightings are very common, even in the summer months. Most park guests are not thinking about eagles when they come to Cedar Point, but they are around. Marie and I see them often in our neighborhood, which is only about half a mile from East Sandusky Bay and bordered by open fields and wood lots.

The best time to see eagles at Cedar Point is winter, when the park is quiet and empty, and the leaves are gone from the trees.

Eagles like to perch in large trees along the edge of the park or the Causeway and scan the lake and bay. Sometimes they like to gather in groups. It's not unusual to see two or three in the same tree, though they keep a respectable distance from one another. One day in January I drove back to Camper Village after lunch to show a business guest the campground and we saw eight eagles perched in a large cottonwood tree. We were both just amazed, and thrilled. We kept what we thought was a safe distance away and got out our cell phones and took pictures. Park employees often sent an email or a text to others in the park to let them know about eagle sightings.

To the best of my knowledge, there hasn't been an eagle nest at the park, and I can understand why—though eagles nest in late winter or early spring and the chicks are gone by early summer.

In winter, when the bay and lake are mostly frozen, you will often see eagles on the ice bordering open areas by the Causeway bridges. They share the space with gulls and geese, but they are given a wide berth.

## Muffleheads

The most famous insect at Cedar Point is the mufflehead, part of the chironomidae family of insects. They look very much like mosquitos (think identical twins) to most of us, which is why they are hated and feared by park guests and even many employees. Unlike mosquitos, muffleheads don't bite. That's the main thing you need to know: they don't bite. It's not an arbitrary decision on the mufflehead's part; they don't have the necessary physical equipment.

Muffleheads emerge in the uncountable millions from Lake Erie in late spring and early summer, generally mid-May to mid-June. They live short lives, only a matter of days; they mate and die. They are at their worst when the wind is off the lake; great clouds of muffle heads are blown onshore, including places like Cedar Point. Drive two to three miles inland, and muffle heads might as well be an endangered species. They attach themselves to anything and everything. They are attracted to light and warmth, like most flying insects, also to doors and windows, windshields, lawn chairs, roller coaster ride platforms, lights in queues, beaches and boardwalks, waterslides, food stands. Some nights, when conditions are right—low winds—they gather in huge balls ascending into the sky until they disappear into the blackness. I admit it's unnerving to witness this phenomenon.

They are food for swallows and martins, who eat them with real enthusiasm, dive bombing into the clouds of muffleheads and then zooming in and out licking their beaks. Out in the lake, the fish get fat.

They are work to clean up. They stain with little green dots everywhere they stop. They need to be swept from doorways and window sills, washed away from sidewalks, scrubbed off windows.

Their bodies blanket the nose cones of coaster trains. Ride crews spend lots of time with hoses, spray bottles, and rags wiping away all evidence of their presence; but it is a losing game.

We eat our share, too. At dusk, or at night, when the coaster train slams into a ball of muffleheads, more than a few get swallowed by riders; at the very least we come away with stained clothing, faces, and teeth. Again, they don't bite, and they don't carry Lyme disease.

## Snakes in a Park

There are no longer any venomous snakes at Cedar Point, but there are snakes living at the park, notably fox snakes and northern water snakes. The fox snakes are usually found in the wooded area in the center of the park in and around the lagoons. There are water snakes there as well, but they are mostly seen in and around the marina, where they give the occasional fright.

The northern water snake looks superficially like a copperhead or a cottonmouth, with dark bands across a brown to grayish body. They average just under three feet in length. They eat small fish, worms, frogs, mice, and small birds. In turn, they are eaten by snapping turtles, other snakes, fox, raccoons, opossums, and larger birds.

As snakes go, they are not known for their aggressiveness, but they will fight back hard if they feel threatened. They will bite.

These snakes are often seen on the rocks around the marina break wall. They occasionally sun themselves on the sidewalks, even in front of the marina office and store or the restaurant, where they always draw a crowd. The floats where jet skis and personal watercraft are stored is a favorite spot for water snake sunbathing. It's rare, but it does happen, that a snake will go up one of the intake valves on an inboard/outboard (I/O) motor and get inside a boat. We had a couple of instances when I was GM where a dock holder found a water snake in his boat. In one of those situations, his wife had nearly stepped on it. She was not bitten but her screams could be heard over a very wide area.

Most guests do not see the annual duck migrations. The ducks straggle in during the fall months, scattering around the peninsula in floating and bobbing groups. Some groups seem to number in the thousands, certainly the hundreds. They are most visible from the Causeway or from Perimeter Road. In the spring, when the ice breaks up, they return on their way north to the Canadian lakes

Cedar Point is a barrier island, pointed northwest, and for seven miles forms the eastern boundary of Sandusky Bay. It is mostly sand, except for pebbles on the beach side; any rock on the peninsula was brought there by homo sapiens. It is very young geologically. Lake Erie in its present form is only 4,000 years old. At its narrowest spots, the peninsula is only a hundred yards wide. It is widest at the tip, where the park is located.

# Big Trees

For most of its existence the peninsula has been covered with brush and cottonwood and cedar trees, which thrive in its sandy soil. Some of the cottonwoods are enormous, including several at the park. For most of my career, the landscape supervisor was a man named Tom Roberts, whose job it was, in part, to watch over the big cottonwoods. Their beauty and shade aside, his concern was the ultimate problem for all big trees: big wind. At some point Tom had to make the call to remove big trees for no other reason than they might get blown down in a summer thunderstorm and hurt people. It was something he was always thinking about.

When the emerald ash borer reached Cedar Point about 2009, it devastated our ash trees, killing more than a hundred. I remember Tom walking me down Frontier Trail and pointing out tree after tree that was living on borrowed time, doomed due to a little green insect native to China that viewed all ash trees as filet mignon.

Cedar Point's sandy soil was good and bad. It was good at construction sites because it drained so well. There were no quagmires of mud common to most construction areas. It was bad in that the soil drained so quickly plants didn't always get a full shot when it rained.

Tom was responsible for making more than 400 acres look good. Not an easy job. Our guests had high expectations for Cedar Point.

Tom retired a year before I did. He wrote the best retirement letter I've ever read:

> *January 11, 2013*
> *Mr. Edward Dangler and those concerned,*
> *Time takes no prisoners. One day you are 22 and the next you are 62. I wish to express my gratitude for all those in between. I've always thought my job here was to provide the wrapping paper for the biggest box of toys in the world. This would not have been possible without the help and support of hundreds throughout the years at every level... It has been my honor and privilege to work beside these people and be the caretaker of this grand old place. All 365 acres of her! She is a living breathing thing that has provided for us all. Thank you for the opportunity the park and the people here have given me to live a career like no other, build a home, raise my family... and feel good about myself. I feel part of this ground and will miss it every day from now on. I have recognized that it is time, after 40 years, to take my leave... I only hope it will be as satisfying as my years at Cedar Point. I wish you all good fortune and may the Force be with us all.*
> *P.S. Keep 'em off my grass!*
> *Thomas O. Roberts*

# Chapter 12
# LBO

**Demon Drop, Avalanche Run, Thunder Canyon, and Iron Dragon Meet Wall Street**

In the fall of 1978, I think in mid to late October, after both amusement parks had closed for the season, the employees of Cedar Point and Kings Island met for a touch football game at the high school field in Wapakoneta, Ohio, about 60 miles north of Dayton along I-75.

The HR Departments of both parks had organized the event and secured the field. We also negotiated a special rate at the Holiday Inn in Wapakoneta. The town was supposedly a neutral site, though closer to Kings Island than to Cedar Point. It was a near three hour trip down the interstate so many of us planned to spend the night. Wapakoneta is mostly known as the hometown of astronaut Neil Armstrong, the first man to walk on the moon.

At Cedar Point we had a loosely organized touch football league. I don't know that Kings Island had anything similar.

At Cedar Point, we were flying high. We had just finished a record attendance year. We operated the world's highest, steepest, and fastest roller coaster. We believed, as fervently as any true-believer anywhere and at any time, that we worked at the world's greatest amusement park. We were clearly the best park in Ohio.

We probably had 20-25 players on the team, enough to platoon and freely substitute. We had two good quarterbacks, Steve Mills, who was the QB on our undefeated Cedar Point Bulldogs team, and a young man from Maintenance, whose name I've forgotten, who had been a high school QB. We were jazzed. We had uniforms made up. We had actual practices. Some of the female employees organized themselves into a cheerleading group.

I played guard, a blocking position, in fact ineligible to catch passes. Most likely a good thing.

Marie and I drove down early Saturday morning. My parents watched the boys, who were only four months old. We were on a lark. It was going to be one big party. There was no question we would win the game.

And we did. I think the score was 28-14. It was never close. Kings Island did not have cheerleaders and their uniforms were second rate. They had decidedly fewer fans, even though Kings Island was closer to Wapakoneta. More importantly, they only had about 10-12 players

so most of their guys had to go both ways the entire game. I remember they did have an excellent QB who was faster than anyone on our team. We found out after the game he had been a high school star in the Cincinnati area. It was a clean game, no fights, fun for both sides, although I could tell they did not like losing to us.

We were good victors. We invited them all to the Holiday Inn after the game to join the party. We pretty much took over the place, including a big suite on one of the upper floors. It was wild, and it was fun. Kevin Terrell, a good friend and our cash control manager, was sitting on the edge of a Murphy bed drinking an Old Grand Dad, smoking a cigarette, and flirting with a girl when Jack Falfas decided it would be fun to put the bed up. Kevin and the girl suddenly disappeared into the wall. A few moments later Jack pulled the bed down and Kevin was all smiles, the drink and the cigarette still in place. The girl was smiling, too. It was that kind of night.

Many of us drank too much, including some of the Kings Island guys. I remember talking to one of them, a marketing guy but I do not remember his name. In between long swills of Budweiser, he told me they were building a ride that was going to kick Gemini's ass.

## Beast (The Ride)

That ride was the Beast, the best wooden roller coaster I've ever ridden. It was the coaster Robert Cartmell and the coaster enthusiast community had expected to ride at Cedar Point when Gemini opened—at least in terms of thrill level. The two coasters were not brothers, they were more like two different species. Gemini was the capacity king, but the Beast was the thrill king. Ultimately, if you are a roller coaster, the thrill king is what you want to be.

The Beast opened in April 1979, and instantly became a fan favorite. It opened as the highest, steepest, fastest, and longest wooden roller coaster in the world. (In 2018, it is still the longest wooden coaster in the world.) It was 110 feet high with a 141-foot first drop. It had a top speed of 65 mph and was more than a mile long at 7,359 feet. When it opened, it had four tunnels. Ride capacity was approximately 1,200 riders per hour. Unlike Gemini and other Cedar Point coasters (past and future) most of the ride was not visible from the midway. The ride disappeared into wooded ravines, adding to its mystery. Riding it at night was a special experience. It had been designed to take advantage of the local terrain. The Beast was largely designed internally by Charles Dinn, Al Collins, and Jeff Gramke—with a little outside assistance from John Allen.

The ride experience is spectacular. The first drop into a below grade tunnel with the wild roar of metal, the staccato bursts of light, and the incredible feeling of pure speed is one of the great amusement park experiences in the world. It compares favorably to much longer first drops on other coasters. The second lift is a surprise the first time you ride it. The ride seems to go on forever. I was envious as soon as I had ridden it. As I often told people, the Beast deserved to be at Cedar Point. We did not talk about it that much at the park, but we all knew King's Island had done us one better with the Beast. In terms of ride experience, we had nothing that was comparable. We would not match it until Magnum opened in 1989, a decade later.

The marketing campaign for the Beast drew envy as well. It was brilliant, starting with the name. I do not know how the ride came to be named the Beast, so I can't assign credit, but it is one of the best coaster names ever created. It's short. It's easy to pronounce. It's immediately understandable. It associates the ride with all the right things: wildness, fear, unpredictability, ferocity, size, strength.

We did several focus groups in Columbus that year to test our advertising messages and get a feel for Kings Island compared to Cedar Point on a number of issues. The Beast was very popular among both teens and young adults and families. It had a 48-inch height requirement which mean most eight-year-olds could ride it, if they were so inclined. The teens went wild for the Beast. One after another talked about how great it was. Some in fact did compare it favorably to Gemini; there was no question they considered the Beast the better ride. The capacity of Gemini was not something you built a 30-second TV spot around. It was fun—and the first drop was always great—but Gemini did not deliver a Beast-like experience.

The Beast was Kings Island's signature ride for a very long time, some would argue it is still the best ride in the park. Heading into the 1980s, Cedar Point and Kings Island had similar thrill ride offerings. It would take until 1989 with the introduction of Magnum XL-200 that Cedar Point offered a ride experience that would equal or exceed the Beast. Cedar Point added several big rides in the 1980s, including White Water Landing (1982), Demon Drop (1983), Thunder Canyon (1986) and Iron Dragon (1987). Kings Island added the Bat in 1981, a prototype ride, the industry's first suspended coaster, designed by Arrow Development Company; but it was plagued by both design and mechanical problems and was closed and removed from the park after only three seasons. In 1987, the same year Cedar Point introduced Iron Dragon, Kings Island added the Vortex, a big inverted coaster.

We expected to at least hold serve in Gemini's second season, but attendance dropped, though not significantly.

# Oceana

In 1980, the plan was to get it all back with performing dolphins and sea lions. This new attraction was sponsored by Bob Munger. He pushed for it, believing it would broaden the park's appeal to families and poke a competitive stick in the eye to Sea World. With the addition of performing dolphins, Cedar Point now offered an aquarium, Sealand; Jungle Larry's African Safari; and a petting zoo, the Pet Farm. We were in the animal business.

What to call our new dolphin stadium? Oceana was my suggestion and I admit I was very pleased that Bob Munger chose my name. The only other Cedar Point attraction I've named is Luminosity, the nighttime show on the midway which debuted in 2012 and ran for six seasons. It was Matt Ouimet's (who succeeded Dick Kinzel as CEO) first Cedar Point attraction.

For its time and place, Oceana was an impressive structure. It seated 1,600 and its main tank was designed to hold four dolphins. A secondary tank was designed for two sea lions, Brandy and Skipper. About a third of the structure was open to the lake and the beach. The lake was a beautiful backdrop and never failed to impress. About the only negative to the structure was the fact it blocked access and view of the beach and lake from what became known as the Oceana Midway. However, at the time that was a very minor concern.

We hired two trainers, Cheryl Miller Young and Craig Vajda, both with academic backgrounds in biology. Their training included participating in the capture of four Atlantic bottlenose dolphins off the coast of Florida.

Oceana was designed for year-round living. The water could be heated, and an inflatable roof was put in place for the winter months.

Coco, Misty, Striker, and Breeze would perform at Oceana for 17 years. Cheryl and Craig remained their trainers for all the time they were at Cedar Point. Striker performed until he passed away from a respiratory infection in 1996. The others developed medical problems as well. Breeze was moved to the Dolphin Research Center in the Florida Keys to live out her days, which as I recall passed quickly. Rather than start over with new dolphins, the park decided to end the shows. In 1999, Oceana was renamed the Cedar Point Aquatic Stadium and reconfigured for a high dive act.

The dolphins had a great run. For dolphins, they lived relatively long lives. They had a single set of trainers. They had friends and companions. For years they were among the best trained performing dolphins in the world. But they lived in a tank 15 feet deep with a small surface area for almost 20 years. It was hard for me to get past that. I used to sit in the stands and watch the shows and think dangerously anthropomorphic thoughts. There was Lake Erie, less than 100 yards away. The ice in winter would be a bummer, but think of all that water, all that beautiful water. No sharks. No killer whales. You'd be on the top of the food chain. Lots of perch, millions of walleyes. Yum.

The end of the act was a sad time at the park. A lot of employees were emotionally attached to the dolphins. Craig became a high school science teacher in a local school district. Cheryl became active in the Erie County Master Gardener program. Her husband Mark continued to work as a ride mechanic at the park.

In 1980, Oceana failed to reinvigorate the attendance effort. It was a nice new asset for the park—but it wasn't a roller coaster. While in-park revenue continued to grow, attendance dropped for the second year in a row.

## Rocking the Boat

In 1981, Cedar Point debuted Ocean Motion, a mid-level (at best) ride and located it between Oceana and the Coral Courtyard adjacent to the Beach Gate entrance to the park. It was a simple concept: rocking boat. The boat was pirate themed. The rocking was forward and then backward simulating a boat moving forward going up and down as it navigated the waves. One staff member joked that if the Navy wanted to test seasickness preventatives they should send people to Cedar Point to ride Ocean Motion. I rode it once, which I barely survived. I was moments away from puking when the ride ended. Marie was dragged onto the ride by our sons and a good friend, Kate Terrell. Our boys loved it. Marie had a panic attack.

I'm convinced there is a gene for riding circular and spinning rides. I don't have it. It's true that younger people, mostly under 18 or so, seem to take more joy than discomfort in spinning rides. Our grandchildren, all under 10, are not bothered in the least. But for most of us the first signs of intolerance begin in your late teens or early 20s and only accelerate with age. As I walked the park over the years and watched people exit rides—the Scrambler, for example—I saw few older people. But there always were a few, the ones with the gene, I suppose. They were all smiles.

Attendance in 1981 was disappointing, a drop from 1980, which was a drop from 1979, which was a drop from 1978. Three years of declining ticket sales, even if revenue is on the rise, is cause for concern. You know in your gut something is missing, something in the marketplace has changed.

# White Water Landing

In 1982, management invested in a major new ride to change the trend: White Water Landing, a Western/Appalachian themed flume ride we marketed as the longest flume ride ever built. It was in Frontier Town on the site of the original Shoot the Rapids, which was built the same year Frontier Town opened in 1968.

White Water Landing had a relatively long and successful life. It operated for 23 seasons, closing after the 2005 season. It was dismantled to build a new coaster, Maverick, which opened in 2007. It had fulfilled its product life cycle, going from star attraction to major ride to average ride. I remember how barren the ride site looked in 1982 when we were building White Water Landing. It would look the same way again in 2006 when we were building Maverick.

In many ways, White Water Landing was the most themed ride Cedar Point has ever built, especially from a visual perspective. It was relatively bare the first few years but in time the landscaping in and around the ride was thick and green with lots of white pine and large shrubs. It felt woodsy; it felt right. Tom Roberts and his assistant, Martha Beverick, did a superb job dressing up White Water Landing for the midway.

White Water Landing was a popular ride, as most water rides are, but it did not break through to superstar status. In hindsight, management probably had unrealistic expectations in terms of its ability to increase attendance. In 1982, for the fourth straight year, park attendance declined, though modestly. Management was concerned with the trend. I remember attending an American Management Association sponsored marketing seminar and explaining to the instructor our situation. We were having a beer in the hotel bar. A few other attendees were there, including two FedEx managers who were giddy (and smug) when talking about the growth of their company. The instructor told me we were right to be concerned, that we had to figure it out while we still were on top.

Of course, 1982 was a recession year, especially in the industrial Midwest and the Great Lakes Region. Factories were closing everywhere. The Japanese were beginning to devour Detroit. Blue collar and working class—actually every class—folks were abandoning places like Youngstown, Ohio, and Flint, Michigan, and moving to Houston and Atlanta and other Sun Belt (a relatively new word in 1982) cities.

Cedar Point felt the impact most directly in the decline in company-sponsored picnics and outings, both large and small. The first thing to get cut when business goes south is the company picnic followed by the company Christmas party. Some companies choose to cut back the event rather than eliminate it, requiring the employee to pay for a portion of the ticket cost or cutting back on the meal (no more ribs and chicken, bring on the hotdogs) or even eliminating it.

The summer of 1982 was my first as marketing director. I remember going on sales visits with Jan Guthridge, our group sales manager, and one of our sales representatives, and listening to HR managers explain how it's tough to green light a day at Cedar Point when business is off 20 percent and you just laid off 30 people. I got it.

We always considered this business segment, which we called Scheduled Event, to be gravy business. We knew if the company was footing the bill, many people would attend the event even if they had no interest in amusement parks to show they were loyal and appreciative employees. How many? There was no hard data, of course, but our collective guts, combined with anecdotal evidence, suggested as many as 20 percent would not otherwise be there. We also believed that regular park-goers would be more likely to visit the park again on their own, if the first visit was subsidized. Also, the catering business was very profitable.

We lost a lot of Scheduled Event business in the early 1980s. Much of it was a long time coming back. I cannot blame the loss of attendance during this period just on the loss of corporate events. What role did the Beast play, if any? What about the general slowdown in the economy? What impact did the lack of a major new coaster have on park attendance?

I remember having a conversation with our treasurer, Tom Salamone, who was also a good friend, about attendance, in 1982 or 1983, and telling him that there was no way Cedar Point would ever reach the three million attendance level again. The 1970s were gone, I said. The market was shrinking, not expanding. Fortunately, I turned out to be dead wrong. But in the early 1980s, growth seemed like a dream.

## The LBO

Through the late 1970s and early 1980s, Cedar Point was an object of interest for several large companies, including MCA/Universal, then headed by Lou Wasserman. Cedar Point, Inc. had low debt and lots and lots of cash. It operated a business that should continue to throw off lots of cash for the foreseeable future. Universal made a low-ball offer to acquire Cedar Point, Inc., a decidedly unfriendly takeover attempt. It did not win approval from shareholders, but management and the board knew there would be more attempts by other companies and eventually one would succeed, and we would lose control of the company. Better to invite in a strategic partner and investor who could help bolster our defenses.

Our CEO, Bob Munger, and the board wanted to control their own destiny. In 1980, Cedar Point invited a diversified British company, Pearson PLC, owners of Madame Tussauds Wax Museum and Royal Daulton China among other enterprises, to partner with the company in a friendly association. I do not recall how big a stake they acquired, but I believe it was close to 30 percent. Pearson got two seats on the board, David Veit, who ran all their U.S. interests, and Michael Herbert, who ran Madame Tussauds Wax Museum in London. We had added to our board talent.

In 1983, the board decided to convert Cedar Point, Inc. into a private partnership using an LBO (Leveraged Buy-Out) strategy. LBO's were very popular in the 1980s. Basically, a group of senior management forms a partnership with outside investors and borrows enough money to buy out (usually at a premium price) all the existing shareholders of a company. When the smoke clears, you have a new organization which is highly leveraged but controlled by senior management. You also have a private company. Management operates the business efficiently and knowledgably and when the time is right—usually in three to five years—the company goes public at a good stock price and everyone makes money and is happy.

I was certainly not privy to the LBO discussion, but I believe the idea of doing it came from Roger Vandenberg, a representative of Narragansett Capital, a company well known to Pearson. The New York investment bank, Lazard Freres & Company, which had close ties to David Veit, became our investment bank and was charged with raising the cash to do the deal.

I once heard our then CFO, Bill Nelson, comment to a group of Cedar Point managers: "This is how wealth is created." In this case, he was right.

That's how it's supposed to work, and that's how it worked for Cedar Point. Of course, no one knew in the summer of 1983 how things would work out in the spring of 1987, when the partnership went public as Cedar Fair, L.P., a master limited partnership, at $10 per unit. Some LBO's bomb terribly and cripple the company because the debt is too much to handle. Some are destroyed by changing economic conditions in their marketplaces. Some work out just as they are drawn up. Cedar Fair was one of those companies.

The internal management group that was invited to join the partnership in 1983 included Bob Munger, of course, and about eight other individuals. It did not include me. I think it was a case of close but no cigar. I thought I was deserving, of course, and I thought marketing as a core business function should be represented at the partnership level. Yet, I realized they had to cut if off somewhere and I had been in my current position only a year. I also knew I wasn't the only one who felt they he should have been included. At the time, many of us in management wondered why the partnership had not included more members, ideally all middle management. However, I can appreciate now the complexity of trying to manage all that administrative work. I also think the model for most LBO's was based on cutting in only the most senior managers. Still, as time passed, and more employees began to understand what the LBO was all about there was resentment among the supervisory and middle management ranks. It did not hinder the performance of the company, and it did not become a major issue among employees, but it never really went away, either.

The managers invited to join the partnership had to have skin in the game, which meant they had to invest some of their own money into the partnership or borrow money to invest.

Nearly all the LBO drama took place in New York City and in boardrooms and banks and similar places. It was all off stage. It did not exist on the midway. "Business as usual" was a phrase we all heard a lot. It was the management mantra. My link to the LBO world was my friend, Tom Salamone, the Cedar Point treasurer, whose job it was to swap financial projections, cash flow analyses, and other financial information with the board and potential investors in the LB0. He did not breach any confidential issues with me, but he did explain to me what was going on and why, which I appreciated knowing. Early in the process Tom was overwhelmed with the amount of work involved, and he was pretty much a one-man band, especially in doing financial projections under incredibly tight deadlines.

Turns out the guys in New York were using PC's and Excel spreadsheets. Such resources did not exist in Sandusky, Ohio. Tom had to do everything by hand tab or with the minimal assistance of our AS400 mainframe. Tom asked Bob Munger to get him a PC and Munger approved the request. Tom got a PC and taught himself how to do spreadsheets. His was the first PC at Cedar Point. It cost $6,000. It was the summer of 1983.

## Demon Drop

"Business as usual" meant for Cedar Point a new ride introduction. In 1983, it was the Demon Drop, which became one of Cedar Point's best thrill ride investments. Like many if not most rides, it was a very simple concept: riders sit four abreast in a gondola; the gondola is then lifted vertically up a tower structure 131 feet in the air; it holds its position for a few seconds—the anticipation of the drop is a big part of the thrill—then drops 90 feet straight down at over 50 mph; the ride ends with a run out, then drops below the track and reverses back to the station.

The ride was designed and built by Intamin. Its generic name was Free Fall. Cedar Point's ride was the first generation of the ride,

The Demon Drop was rated the scariest ride at Cedar Point for six seasons, until Magnum opened in 1989. CEDAR POINT ARCHIVES

which became very popular and sold well for Intamin for several years, appearing at parks across the world.

Was it a coaster? Some parks claimed it as such. Cedar Point and later Cedar Fair never did, and we looked down on parks which did.

The name was somewhat controversial. We did receive a few letters and phone calls from religious groups that did not like what they felt was a glorification of the devil. Bob Munger was a little concerned by this feedback. In truth, we saw "demon" in a very generic sense and in all our marketing materials for the ride we avoided any kind of depiction of a (or the) devil. Demon Drop was an amusement park ride, a means to have fun.

But it was a scary ride experience for most of our guests. In our guest surveys, it was consistently rated the scariest ride at Cedar Point, starting in 1983 and not eclipsed until the opening of Magnum in 1989, when it dropped to number two. I confess I found the ride experience a little unnerving but not particularly scary. I was certainly in the minority, as demonstrated by the constant screams when the ride was in operation.

Demon Drop was well located, just inside the Main Gate on the lake or north side of the midway. It delivered a lot of excitement to the entrance area, announcing to the world this is a great amusement park and here's a first bite. Kudos to Lee Jewett for great placement.

Demon Drop had a 26 year run at Cedar Point and was eventually moved to Dorney Park in 2010.

The ride logo was one of the best we ever created. Using colors associated with the dark side—black background, yellow and orange lettering—we created a logo that worked wonderfully in all mediums. Demon Drop hats and other merchandise had record sales. It was the first ride introduction at Cedar Point where the ride impact was matched on the merchandise side.

Demon Drop had a smallish footprint and the structure itself was straightforward steel supported by concrete footers. However, it broke new ground with its controls and electrical systems. In many ways, it was our first high tech ride. The strength of our Maintenance division was mechanical, not electrical systems. The Demon Drop learning curve was steep, aggravated by the fact the manufacturer was European so there were built-in issues such as language and time zones. Our head electrician, Ed Naufel, lived at the ride all summer. The impact on guests: too much down time. Demon Drop's capacity was about 700 per hour, which was average at best and certainly couldn't compare with Gemini or Corkscrew.

We sold it well. We didn't hold back. We were hungry for long lines.

Ed Fine, the creative director at MARC Advertising, put together an agency team that created one of our most successful campaigns ever. The focus would be on the ride experience with the core 30-second TV spot shot in and on the ride, and the campaign would integrate into all media.

## Scrooge McDuck Meets Demon Drop

Ed pushed hard to use Paul Frees as the voice-over for both the radio and TV spots. Frees was a famous voice, though few people outside the industry knew who he was. He was the voice of the Pillsbury Doughboy and Scrooge McDuck, among others. In short, he didn't work for scale. And he only worked in a studio in San Francisco, near his home in Marin County. He wouldn't do phone patches. If you wanted to work with him, you had to do it on his terms. In the pitch for Frees, Ed played several of his voices. What we wanted was someone who could communicate fear, seriousness, and excitement. We wanted Darth Vader, not Scrooge McDuck. No question Frees was who we were looking for. His price tag, as I recall, was $10,000 or $15,000, far more than we had ever spent for comparable work.

My boss, Bill Near, supported the recommendation, and we made the deal. The three of us made the trip to San Francisco in March 1983. It was my first-ever time in California, the heaven my mother had talked about so much. Bill and I flew in on Sunday morning. We met Ed at the Hyatt Hotel downtown. We had a late lunch in a restaurant at the top of the hotel. The day was overcast, windy, and cool, but there were still some boats out on the bay.

The plan was to record everything in one day, a morning and an afternoon session. There was enough time, but we would have to work very efficiently. Ed was scheduled to fly back to Pittsburgh on the red eye Monday night. Bill and I were going to fly home Tuesday morning. The studio was small and non-descript, which is usually the case, but it was the place where Frees liked to work so that was why we were there.

Paul Frees arrived right on time, driven by his wife, a fortyish blonde woman. He was 63 at the time, destined to live only three more years. He was wearing a white suit and had a whitish beard. I had images of Burl Ives, Colonel Saunders, and even Tom Wolfe. He was a bit overweight, but far from obese, and his voice was deep but in the range of ordinary. I thought he looked old, but then I was only 33. Frees was two years younger than my father. We made small talk to break the ice. I could tell quickly enough that he was used to being the center of attention and reveled in it, but he was not a braggart. Ed worked him well, playing to his ego. Ed's job was to get him to give us his very best effort.

I described the ride to him. He joked he would never ride such a thing. He asked me if I planned to ride it. I said: "Of course." He gave me a look like I was a Martian and told me I had picked an interesting way to make a living.

We got down to work.

Our job was to record all the voice-overs for all the Demon Drop advertising, which meant pre-opening and post-opening 60-second radio spots, 30-second TV spots, plus a variety of TV and radio tags.

Frees read through the copy and asked some specific questions about pronunciation and emphasis. He seemed to get it right away. The engineer said he was ready to go and Ed said, "Let's do it" and we started on the first read.

The best voice over talent seem to have a clock in their heads and certainly Frees had one. His first read was two seconds too long. He knew it without being told.

Ed coached him with just the right amount of flattery and specific direction. Frees' voice was no longer ordinary. He had switched to the scary, mysterious voice we wanted. It was a performance, not a reading. He worked it hard, adding emphasis in specific locations of the script. He commented several times that this was good copy, fun to perform. In fact, he worked himself into a visible sweat by early afternoon. It was hard work for him, but he was having fun.

Occasionally, just to break the routine, he would start reading in one of his character voices, his favorite being Scrooge McDuck. In-between takes he would tell a few Walt Disney stories. As the day wore on he became more relaxed. Ed knew we had nailed it. We looked at one another and knew we were making some great advertising.

My job was to bless what we did when we did it. My trust level for Ed Fine was very high, but ultimately the advertising product belonged to Cedar Point, and protecting the Cedar Point brand in our public communications was an important part of my job. I ended up requesting a few minor changes in the script, but I was smart enough to stand back and let something great happen.

Ed flew home on a red eye back to Pittsburgh. Bill and I spent the night in San Francisco and had dinner at a seafood restaurant near Fisherman's Wharf. Bill knew food and knew restaurants and this place did not disappoint.

Creating the TV spot we would use to sell the ride was also a memorable experience. The spot was filmed at night, a first for a Cedar Point TV commercial, and went against the tradition of filling our TV spots with sunshine and blue skies and smiling faces.

The idea was to mirror the radio campaign: make it dark, scary, mysterious. Visually, we'd show a young man inside the gondola. The gondola moves backward into the tower. There are close-ups of the young man's face, fearful and wide-eyed. Shots of the tower, looking up. Quick cuts of the gondola moving up the tower. The payoff is a close-up of the young man screaming in fear.

We had to plan to film the ride commercial in the context of the ride's construction schedule, which meant dealing with a moving target. The line in the sand, of course, was opening day, May 7. We needed to shoot the spot as early as possible so we could get it on the air in advance of opening day; at the same time we knew the construction of the ride would be extremely tight (they all were tight). The construction crew, both internal and contracted, viewed the Marketing staff requests for access to the ride as a monumental pain in the ass.

It did not help our cause that senior management favored the construction group. Making a TV commercial, while certainly important, was second to getting the ride open on time.

It was my job to broker an arrangement which preserved the core interests of both groups. In the case of the Demon Drop, after much back and forth, I got two nights of lighting prep and one night of filming.

Ed Fine and MARC recommended a director, Jim McCartney, who had directed several of our spots from the prior year. He was good, and a known quantity. Jim felt strongly we needed to bring in two specialists, an experienced lighting director who could create the nighttime experience, and a director of photography who had experience with night shooting. Both guys were expensive but, in the end, a good investment.

### Demon Drop Dummy

All our advance planning assumed that the ride would be operating when we filmed the TV spot. We shot in late April, about three weeks out from opening, and the ride site was still a construction site (which we expected). Turns out things were more complicated— as we found out a few days before shooting—as the manufacturer had decreed that the ride was not yet ready for riders. At first despair and much grumbling, but then a solution. Cedar Point had a talented animation department. Let's create a dummy stand-in for the actor. If we cut quickly and from an appropriate distance and given the fog and other lighting effects . . . no one will ever know.

No one ever did.

The guys in Animation, led by Terry Williams and George Richmond, did a great job creating our stand-in. The weather was not our friend the night of the shoot. It was dry, which was the most important thing, but it was bitterly cold with temperatures in the 30s and a stiff breeze (which made creating fog a challenge). I was not dressed for it and suffered accordingly. The night we spent filming the Demon Drop TV spot was the coldest night I ever spent in the park, and that included some cold and damp HalloWeekends nights in late October.

I was very impressed with what the lighting director had created, mixing and matching streaks of white, gold, and red within the structure. The director, Jim McCartney, invited me to look through the lens just before we began shooting the sequence of shots with the actor sitting in the gondola. It was quite a look, very movie-like. There were many takes, in part because the wind and the fog machines did not want to play well together. We were not recording sound, which made it simpler, but the actor was challenged to make his face work in extremes without the benefit of words or sound. Thanks to his stand-in, he never did ride the ride.

We were in a race to get done before daylight. The director of photography was a perfectionist (they all are) and to me it seemed we squandered too much time on things no one would notice but us (actually no one but him). Shortly before dawn, as we were starting to shoot the shots of the actual drop, we developed a mechanical problem with the ride. The gondola would move backward into the tower, and then would ascend to the top of the tower and move out to the drop position.

But it wouldn't drop. It was stuck. The only way to get it to release was to send someone to the top of the tower (133 feet or 10 stories) and release it manually. One of the techs from the manufacturer, Intamin, walked up to the top and released the gondola. He stayed up there until we thought we had all our shots covered. There was a crack of light in the eastern sky out over the lake now. The agency and the production company, after considering everything, announced we needed a few more shots of the gondola (with our stand-in) in free fall.

There was only one Intamin tech left on site. He asked Jack Falfas and me if we would go with him to the top of the tower to help release the gondola. We didn't hesitate, especially Jack. I was so cold I was shaking, and I was bone-tired, but I started up the stairs, which ran alongside the exterior of one side of the tower, behind the Intamin tech and Jack.

The first couple flights were not a problem. There was a railing and there was enough natural light now to make the stairs very visible. My problem occurred about halfway up the tower, probably the 60-70 foot level. I looked out at the lake and the parking lot (the cars were tiny). I looked up at all the stairs still to climb. I looked down at the shiny steel steps. I looked at the huge open spaces between the steps. Suddenly, I froze. I couldn't move. My gloved hand grabbed the rail. I couldn't go any further. Not for $10,000 bucks. Not for $20,000 bucks. For the first time in my life I experienced extreme acrophobia. I hesitated a moment, then yelled up to Jack that I couldn't make it. He turned back to me and gave me a sign that it was okay. He yelled back that he and the Intamin guy had it covered, which they did.

Within 15 minutes, the shoot was done.

You never know until you see everything in a studio, but we all felt we had all the pieces we needed to make a great TV commercial. The spot became one of our best new ride introduction spots ever. Every component clicked: sound, lighting, voice over, acting.

For most of the 1983 season park attendance was up and down, trending more up than down, but it was clear that Demon Drop was not a Corkscrew or a Gemini. It had impact—it stoked buzz in the marketplace—but we knew by July it was not going to replicate Gemini-type numbers and in truth it had not been expected to crash the turnstiles. But we all hoped, as the pro football coach hopes, that the fourth-round pick will be rookie of the year.

All of this played out as Tom Salamone and David Veit and the Cedar Point directors and Lazard and an army of money men put together the LBO.

## Snow in August

The 1983 season was memorable for another TV commercial, a spot we officially called, "Summer's Going Fast" but unofficially became known as the "Snow" commercial. The idea originated within MARC Advertising, but I do not recall who really gave birth to it. However, Ed Fine led the agency team that presented it. The concept was simple. Create a sense of urgency to visit the park before it closes for the season by showing viewers images of the park in winter.

Without clearly understanding it at first, or at least not fully appreciating the emotional cord we hit, we created a very powerful call to action and without any financial inducement, no coupon, and no special price. It was advertising at its purest: strike hard at the heart.

It all came together wonderfully. The spot opened with general images of families enjoying the park, midway shots, and soft cuts to various rides, all to a music track that was soft, nostalgic, and almost lyrical. The voice over was provided by the great Norman Rose. He spoke slowly and delicately in his rich baritone about the fact that summer was going fast and that soon winter would be here. Visually, and this is where the viewer really got hooked emotionally, the visual of the Corkscrew train approaching the helix dissolved into an almost identical visual of the same scene covered in snow. The camera lingered for a moment on the winter image (an image our photographer, Dan Feicht, had shot the previous off season), as Norman Rose gently urged viewers to get to Cedar Point before all the magic went away.

In 1983, the park season effectively ended with Labor Day. The park was open two weekends after Labor Day, but attendance was light and mostly made up of groups. This was also a time when very few schools started classes before Labor Day. The whole of August was still a vacation period.

We liked what we saw when we were done editing the spot. It started running the first week of August. It was going to have a short window, so we bought heavy for the first week. The spot mostly ran in Cleveland, Detroit, and Toledo, our core markets.

I remember the first Sunday in August we had a 34,000 attendance day, quite unexpected. Although it had only been running three or four days, at least one Cedar Point manager, John Albino, was ready to assign complete credit to the new spot for generating Sunday's attendance.

"The people are here because of the 'snow' commercial," he announced on Monday, in a tone that was definitive.

What followed was a surge in attendance over the last three weeks of the season. The weather cooperated but it was not a weather-induced attendance surge. We knew it was more than that. The snow commercial generated lots of buzz. The net positive was influenced by several factors, including the Demon Drop, good weather, and a new sense of urgency to visit the park before Labor Day, which was created by a killer TV spot. Advertising had done what it was supposed to do: make a difference. The 1983 season ended with a slight increase versus the 1982 season, our first year over year (YOY) increase since Gemini in 1978.

Interestingly, when we talked to park-goers in focus groups in the off season they often remarked that the spot made them feel sad—not happy—because it reminded them that summer was ending and winter was coming. But they also remarked that it spurred them to come to the park.

We ran the same spot in 1984. Again, it helped build our late season attendance, although the year-end attendance numbers were down. Over the next several years we tried different executions of "Summer's Going Fast" including an animated version. In 1995, we created our next-best effort, a spot called "Sled." It was the creation of Sara Venizelos, Dave Derby, and Tom Millman at Meldrum & Fewsmith and shot in March on a patch of snow-covered ground in a park in Chicago. The spot shows a young boy going from riding a roller coaster to riding a sled. It was a very successful TV spot and won numerous awards, including the Brass Ring as the best amusement park spot of the year at the IAAPA Convention. However, I believe our first execution was our best. When park-goers saw "Sled," they smiled. When park-goers saw "Summer's Going Fast," they cried. The 1983 spot hit harder emotionally.

## Avalanche Run Bobsleds

In 1984, nothing much happened in the park. It was the first full year of the LBO and management had decided not to add anything major in terms of capital investment. So, no new ride. At the same time, we jacked up the admission price by a dollar, a significant percentage increase at the time. The combination of no new attraction and a steep admission price increase had a negative impact on attendance and we dropped 124,000 visits from 1983 to 2,544, 600 in 1984. My focus was always on attendance, because that was what I believed my performance was ultimately measured against. However, attendance is only part of the battle. Revenue from in-park spending and hotel rooms is also a significant portion of total revenue. In 1984, a combination of cost control and raising prices largely offset the disappointing attendance.

At the end of the 1984 season, David Veit, the Pearson executive who with Bob Munger essentially ran the company, suddenly appeared in my office one afternoon. He was a short man with thinning unkempt white hair. He was probably in his early to mid-40s. I was surprised and a bit nervous. We exchanged pleasantries for a few minutes, and then he asked me how I thought the season had gone. I wasn't sure where he was going with this, but I answered truthfully that except for the revamping of the season pass program (we dropped the price substantially and went for a volume strategy, which worked) I was disappointed in the year.

"I disagree," he said. "We had a good year under the circumstances. And we'll do better next year."

I like to think he knew even then that the LBO was going to work out as planned.

I know it felt very, very good to hear his words.

In 1985, we didn't hesitate to play the coaster card. Our new ride was an Intamin-designed bobsled ride we called Avalanche Run. We located it on the beach adjacent to the Space Spiral on the site where the Jumbo Jet once stood.

I was part of a group that was sent to Opryland in Nashville in June of the previous year to ride the ride and evaluate it as a possible ride for Cedar Point. The Opryland ride had a bayou theme coupled with swamp monster branding. The cars or more accurately the "sleds" were six passenger units. The sleds ascended the main lift hill in conventional fashion but instead of continuing along the track they dropped off into a steel trough or flume and then followed it through various gyrations until it reached the station.

I remember I rode the ride with Jim Colvin, one of our Maintenance supervisors, and Lee Jewett.

Our consensus was that it was a good, if not great ride. It certainly wasn't going to dethrone Gemini or give the Beast at Kings Island a scare, but it was a novel coaster experience.

While we were at Opryland, we also had an opportunity to ride their new river rapids ride, which they called Grizzly River Rampage. I was impressed. It was big, bad, and beautiful and deserved to be at Cedar Point. My colleagues felt the same way. The 10-passenger rafts were big and the action on the water was terrific, including tunnels and waterfalls. The rockwork and wilderness theming tied it all together. I was convinced it would be a winner for Cedar Point. I was not alone.

Back to Avalanche Run. We did have capacity concerns with the ride. We were a big park with attendance that averaged nearly three million visitors. Cedar Point, and I really do not remember who drove this, pushed Intamin to re-design the ride to accommodate 10-passenger sleds. Intamin agreed to do so. Theoretical capacity increased to about 1,800 per hour, very respectable. However, we traded up from a sports car to a SUV.

The Avalanche Run sleds were big and hulking and just did not deliver the thrill and fun of the smaller sleds. Of course, very few Cedar Point guests ever rode the six passenger version of the ride so they had nothing to compare it to. Avalanche Run was impressive to look at. The sound of steel wheels on a steel track, surrounded by a steel flume, got your attention. It was a genuine roar. It also had a 46 inch height requirement (versus 48 inches for most coasters), so it could almost be termed a "family coaster," a description that would be welcomed by many park-going families but damning to thrill riders.

We were aware the ride experience was more Mine Ride or Wildcat than Gemini or Corkscrew. I was cautioned by senior management not to oversell the Avalanche Run ride experience. It created a dilemma for the Marketing group and the agency, a kind of Catch 22. Overselling was what we were all about. Given the investment in the ride and the attendance expectations built into it, we knew it had to be the lead story. How do you lead with a family coaster? You don't, at least in my opinion. We had to thread the needle in our communications about the ride, both advertising and publicity and PR. I think we did so effectively. I knew if I was going down I was going down on the side of selling too much thrill rather than too little.

Our pre-opening TV spot featured animation of the ride (and an avalanche). It was our only option. There were no existing rides we could plausibly use as stand-ins and Avalanche Run itself was a construction site. The animation was done by a firm in Albuquerque and the editing was done by a LA firm, which required a quick whirlwind trip to New Mexico and then to California. We flew to Albuquerque first, arriving in the late afternoon. We immediately went to the studio. After reviewing the work, we requested several changes, which they worked on overnight. It was my first visit to the Southwest and I remember the clarity of the sky, all the shades of brown surrounding us on the ground and on the buildings and in the hills and mountains.

Attendance in 1985 took a nice jump. Avalanche Run got much of the credit, as did a growing economy.

## Thunder Canyon

In 1986, Cedar Point unveiled Thunder Canyon, our version of the Intamin 10-passenger river raft ride. It was built on land at the end of the Frontier Trail, most of which was thickly wooded. Nearly all the trees and vegetation on the site had to be removed during the construction of the ride. When it opened it had an intentional Western feel and look, especially with all the manufactured rock work which was a sand color. However, within a few years so much vegetation had grown in and around the ride that it had much more of an Appalachian look. (Ditto for White Water Landing.) No matter, both looks worked. The interior of the ride rapidly became a mini-wilderness.

There were thin paths that led to observation points for remote cameras and water elements (mostly waterfalls), but the rest of the area was thick vegetation. It was—and is—the most remote place at Cedar Point, especially after the closing of Paddlewheel Excursions and the development of Dinosaurs Alive; it is a dense green and buggy place home to numerous fox snakes and raccoons and thick vines of poison ivy. For the past 20 years or so Thunder Canyon has closed by Labor Day for HalloWeekends preparation (it was the location for Werewolf Canyon and now Cornstalkers). One of my Labor Day rituals when I was GM was to go to Thunder Canyon and access the interior of the ride. I would walk along the path that led to the ride position just ahead of the big waterfall. I would sit on the stool and look down into the now empty flume. It was always quiet, and I was always alone. I liked it that way. I didn't stay very long.

When they pitched us their big idea for the new ride TV commercial, our agency, MARC Advertising, recommended that to give the ride an authentic western look and feel we needed to shoot in the Mojave Desert of California. Bill Near, my boss at the time, smiled at me during the presentation. It was a smile that said these guys must be crazy.

We found another way to get the job done.

We made a great effort in all our communications about the ride to establish Thunder Canyon as a river raft ride, not in any way a traditional flume ride like White Water Landing. We wanted to make sure our guests understood and appreciated the difference, that Thunder Canyon was a much bigger deal.

One of the biggest decisions in the construction of the ride was whether to get the water from Sandusky Bay and Lake Erie or direct from the City of Sandusky. As the marketing director, I was not a direct participant in these discussions; however, I was aware of what was going on. There were, of course plusses and minuses with each approach. Water from the city would be clean, potable water, but it would require a serious investment in infrastructure—pipes mostly. Thunder Canyon did not meet the Ohio Ride Safety Division's definition of a pool or waterslide, which described and assumed an immersive guest experience. Rather, in the Thunder Canyon experience water was accidental or arbitrary—not guaranteed—and in fact some riders on each raft would stay nearly completely dry.

Lake water was authentic, it was argued, part of making the experience as real as possible. Yes, it would usually be colder and darker, but it was the real thing. It was also free. We could build a pump and suck in as much as we needed as often as we needed it.

In the end, the park decided to go with lake water.

The ride was designed to accommodate the natural water temperature. We did not want to freeze our guests. The ride could be ridden with all the waterfalls and geysers turned off, which is what we did in early season or on extremely cold days at any time during the season. And it was not all or nothing. We could ratchet the water effects up and down in increments.

However, for the TV commercial shoot in early May we had all the water effects at 100 percent. It was very uncomfortable for our riders, who were mostly seasonal employees, and who after their first dunking were seriously questioning their decision to be a part of this undertaking. This wasn't glamorous in the least. They couldn't wear ponchos; they had to dress in park clothes—shorts and T-shirts. There were a couple of places on the ride where if conditions were optimal at least two and as many as three riders passed directly under waterfalls. You couldn't avoid it: you were sitting in a specific seat and wearing a lap belt; getting up and moving was not an option.

Thunder Canyon was a home run. Everyone loved it. We built an observation deck at a spot easily accessible from the Frontier Trail, so spectators could have fun watching the boats go by and watch as the riders screamed in anticipation as they saw they were headed directly for the largest waterfall on the river.

Another plus was a 46 inch height requirement which allowed us to market the ride as a family ride. A water ride can be a family ride and keep its edge (unlike a coaster).

Thunder Canyon powered Cedar Point to a record attendance year: 3,133,600 versus the previous record of 3,105,500, set eight years previously in 1978 with Gemini. No one saw it coming, which made it all the sweeter. It was a 417,000 or 15.3 percent increase versus 1985 with Avalanche Run.

Two other factors were part of the mix. The Reagan economy was kicking in big time, and that helped our cause, giving us a below the surface current that flowed in our direction every day that we were open. We also had re-introduced a junior ticket priced considerably lower than our regular ticket, making Cedar Point more affordable to younger families.

That fall, I think when he was here for a Cedar Fair partnership meeting in September, David Veit again stopped by my office unannounced.

He was beaming. "The marketing, the advertising, the attendance, were all very fine, very good this year," he said in his clipped English accent.

I am sure that the 1986 season with its record-breaking financial performance sealed the deal in terms of the LBO. I'm sure the partners all felt vindicated to a degree, now that the pressure was off. They had something to sell. The process of going public again and how to maximize it was the issue, not how do we survive.

## Dick Kinzel Becomes CEO

At the end of the year, there was a lot of gossip, lots of whispers that Bob Munger's time running Cedar Point and Valleyfair was at an end. He had been ill and missing in action much of 1986. The business on the midway continued to operate very well, really a credit to his leadership over a period of 11 years, and the systems and protocols established by Roose and Legros, which he had largely left in place. Bob Munger was not a culture warrior. The rumor was that David Veit was pushing for a strong CEO or COO to work under Munger.

Over Christmas break, I ran into Jack Aldrich at the Sandusky Mall.

"It's going to be Dick Kinzel," he said, not revealing his source. He was right. The day we returned from break, Bob Munger called a meeting of all the full-time staff (a very rare event) and announced that he would be stepping up to a more corporate role and that Dick Kinzel would be running the parks. Dick addressed the group. He did fine, but he was visibly and understandably nervous. He grew into a good speaker, especially if he liked the subject matter and was comfortable with it. He had plenty of time to hone his skills. Dick Kinzel would run Cedar Fair for the next 24 years. Only George Boeckling, who ran Cedar Point from 1897 – 1931 (34 years) would have a longer run.

I don't know the board's rationale for the decision to go with Dick Kinzel. Perhaps one of the biggest considerations was that Dick Kinzel was the only senior executive who had run a whole park (Valleyfair), not just pieces of one, and had done so successfully for a long period of time—eight years.

Jack Aldrich and Dick were friends. Jack met with Dick on Dick's first day as CEO. According to Jack, they mostly talked baseball, a favorite subject for both men. After his conversation with Dick, Jack stopped by my office.

"I'll tell you one thing," Jack said. "There's no lack of confidence next door." Then he gestured with his arm toward the executive office. "He told me he knows he can do the job. He doesn't have any self-doubt."

## Iron Dragon

Our new ride for 1987 was a coaster, a suspended coaster, where the car hangs below the track, like a ride at Busch Gardens: The Old Country called The Big Bad Wolf. I was part of a group that went to ride the ride. This was an official visit, not a spy mission. I met with their marketing chief and he walked me through the campaign they had put together. They were quite proud of it, and in fact it was well executed, starting with the name, which worked well with their European themes—the wolf being a symbol for fear, terror, etc. for centuries. I remember riding it and thinking the ride experience was pretty good but not great.

Lee Jewett did his standard outstanding job in locating the ride, with the station across from the entrance to the CP&LE Railroad, most of the track in and out of the trees on the island, and a big finish over water near the Corkscrew helix.

We named our ride Iron Dragon, one of our better ride names. Dragons are always cool, even when they are spitting fire. They are inherently scary. They are universal, not tied to any specific tradition. There are European dragons and Chinese dragons and they are stars in HBO series like "Game of Thrones" and in books like "The Hobbit." They are used to top billing. And they fly, mimicking to some extent the action of the ride. Visually, I think we nailed it, creating a logo that was bold and effective, a dragon in the European tradition. We used the logo as the main visual in our 1987 poster calendar, which we distributed to schools, the news media, coaster enthusiasts, and group clients.

The pre-sell TV spot was shot in March in a residential neighborhood in New Orleans. We needed a place that looked like summer: leaves on trees, a few flowers, and green grass. The plot is simple enough: suburban town is terrorized by a dragon, which means cop cars coming to a screeching halt, small children whisked away at the last minute, a menacing shadow of a dragon crossing over streets, yards, and houses, then a final confrontation as a teen couple comes face to face with the shadow of the dragon as they cower against a wall. It was the inexpensive approach, no need to create an elaborate model of a dragon, the shadow would do well enough. And I think it did.

The regular season TV spot featured cuts to live action of the ride.

Iron Dragon was the first coaster to open on Dick Kinzel's watch, though the decision to build it had been made a year before when he was still at Valleyfair. I never really considered Iron Dragon a Kinzel coaster. His first coaster was Magnum in 1989, two years later.

Iron Dragon had a little Avalanche Run in it. It had a 46-inch height requirement, which meant it was a family coaster. It was fun to ride, but not particularly thrilling—notwithstanding the comments of our then CFO, Bill Nelson, who after riding it for the first time pronounced it "a balls-out thrill ride." Clearly, Bill hadn't ridden many roller coasters.

As the season wore on other employees, and some guests, began to refer to Iron Dragon as "Dragging Iron."

Attendance in 1987 dropped off the record set in 1986 with Thunder Canyon but still exceeded three million, the first time in its history the park had had consecutive three million plus attendance years. The 1987 season was perceived as successful.

Cedar Fair, LP went public in May 1987 at $10 per unit. The units performed well, and the LBO was very successful for all concerned. We were a public partnership, trading in units versus shares, an unusual business model then, and now, but it has worked very well for Cedar Fair.

# Bob Munger

Early in the fall the word got out that Bob Munger had throat cancer and his prognosis was not good. That summer he was rarely at the park and really didn't need to be as Dick Kinzel was functioning well as CEO. The last time I saw him was late October when he was in Sandusky to support the park's purchase of the old U.S. Coast Guard property at the tip of the peninsula.

We took our sons to Washington, D.C. for Thanksgiving week. When we got back to the hotel from visiting one of the Smithsonian museums, there was a message that Bob Munger had died. He was only 59.

He was "to the manor born," as my mentor, Don Dittmann, used to say. He was the son of a federal judge, grew up in Connecticut, summered in the Canadian Maritimes, graduated from Yale, married affluent women, lived in a mansion, had a butler and a housekeeper, belonged to all the best clubs in Cleveland, flew bush planes in Canada, hunted ducks and geese, favored white shirts and blue blazers and gray slacks and loafers (no socks).

He was really not a midway guy. He was a businessman who ran amusement parks. That said, I believe he loved the park and cared for its employees.

I believe he was an introvert by nature, content to spend time alone. Many park employees were afraid of him and believed he was unapproachable, but in truth I think he was just shy.

I always thought he had a good heart. I had experienced it directly.

His legacy is Corkscrew and Gemini (the IMAX Theater, White Water Landing, and Oceana are no more); the acquisition of Valleyfair; the LBO; the mentoring of Dick Kinzel. Not so bad.

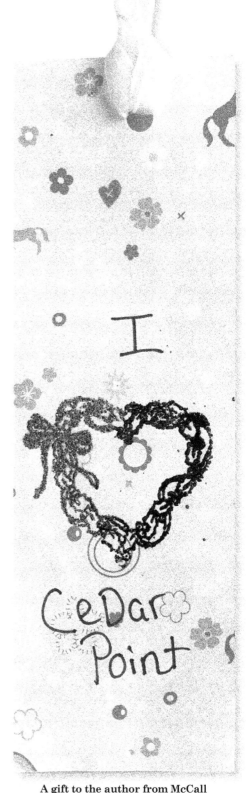

A gift to the author from McCall
Faukenberg, a real Cedar Point fan.

## Chapter 13

# Glory Road – Part 1
*"Even when you see it, you won't believe it."*
– Newspaper Ad for Magnum

Cedar Point had an incredible run for a period of about 15 years, from 1989 through 2003, roughly the era of the '90s, a time bookended by the opening of Magnum in 1989 and the opening of Top Thrill Dragster in 2003. In between were Mean Streak, Disaster Transport, Snake River Falls, Raptor, Mantis, Power Tower, Millennium Force, and Wicked Twister. These 10 rides, assisted by a generally strong economy, the growth of Cedar Point as a vacation destination, and a stable competitive environment, gave Cedar Point a terrific attendance ride. Attendance never dropped below three million visitors during the period, even in years like 1992, 1995, 1997, 1999, and 2001, when the new attraction was not a big new ride.

I turned 40 the summer Magnum XL-200 opened, and I turned 54 the summer Top Thrill Dragster opened. Ditto for Marie. Our boys were 11 for the Magnum opening and 25 when Dragster opened.

Attendance peaked in 1994, the year of the Raptor, at 3.6 million visitors. It's a record that will likely stand for a very long time. In 1995, the year of Cedar Point's 125th anniversary and the debut of the Summer Spectacular laser show, but without a major new ride, attendance also exceeded 3.5 million.

The 1988 season had been a major disappointment. It was the year of the drought, for starters, the hottest and driest summer in anyone's memory (certainly mine). On June 25, 1988, the temperature hit 105 degrees at Cedar Point, a new record. We did not have a new ride to market. It was the year we introduced Soak City. The heat helped usage, of course, but Soak City was really not a water park, only a few water slides. It was located outside the park and was an extra-charge attraction. It did not drive attendance to Cedar Point. The 1988 season was an endurance contest. We all knew what was waiting in the wings—a world class coaster—and there was no despair, though always disappointment, in the low attendance numbers. We knew why: no major ride, poor weather. We were not losing guests to a flaw in our business model, a point of view shared, I think, by everyone in management.

One unquestionably good thing that happened in 1988, at least from my point of view, was the fact that Notre Dame went undefeated

and won the 1988 NCAA National Championship. The Fighting Irish football team, led by quarterback Tony Rice, beat previously undefeated West Virginia University 34-21 in the Fiesta Bowl.

Jack Falfas, perhaps the most competitive person I've ever known, was a proud graduate of WVU; in fact, he had played football for the Mountaineers his freshman year. Jack and I decided we should have a wager on the game, but not something routine. After much negotiation, we agreed that the loser of the wager would be required to:

1. Make a $50 contribution to the winner's university.
2. Wear a T-shirt of the winner's university at the Cedar Point Golf Outing in September 1989.
3. Wear a cap of the winner's university at the Cedar Point Golf Outing in September 1989.
4. Shout the name of the winner's university on the first tee, either GO IRISH! Or GO MOUNTAINEERS!
5. Purchase a suitable mat and frame of the cover of Sports Illustrated showcasing the winner of the game (assuming Sports Illustrated uses the cover of the magazine for this purpose).

The terms were converted to a multi-page written agreement which defined terms, reviewed contingencies, and covered other details. We had the agreement, titled 1989 Fiesta Bowl, notarized by Deb Hessler. I still have it. I also still have on display in my home a beautiful framed Sports Illustrated cover showing Tony Rice in action against the Mountaineers.

An honorable man, Jack wore the shirt and cap at the golf outing and shouted "Go Irish!" with gusto.

When Jack was promoted and transferred to Knott's Berry Farm as GM in 1997, I implored him not to become a USC fan (hated rival of ND). He agreed, which meant a lot to me. Jack has come to dislike the USC Trojans even more than I do.

## First Agency Review

We also conducted an agency review in the summer of 1988. The result was that MARC Advertising, our partner for 16 years, was let go and Hesselbart & Mitten, a smallish agency in Akron, Ohio, became the new agency of record for Cedar Point.

From a marketing point of view, the agency review was the birth of the Magnum campaign.

The review was ordered by Dick Kinzel. Bill Near and I were happy with MARC and had no plans to conduct a review. This was

Magnum XL-200 set a new standard for roller coasters the day it opened in May, 1989. It was so popular additional queue had to be added to the ride. The first coaster to top 200 feet, its success spawned Steel Force at Dorney Park, Mamba at Worlds of Fun, and Wild Thing at Valleyfair. CEDAR POINT ARCHIVES

Dick's second season as CEO. I think he wanted to shake things up a little. He bore no animosity toward MARC that I was aware of, but MARC had been our ad agency for more than 15 years, a lifetime in the advertising business, and he believed it was time to take a new look at how we advertised the park.

Dick knew that in 1989 we would be marketing a big new roller coaster. If not a slam dunk for a successful season, it was the next closest thing. Although he never said it, I think he felt whatever new agency was chosen would have a relatively easy time of it in 1989. They would have the opportunity to learn the first year and prove their mettle after that, when they didn't have a world class roller coaster to promote.

Dick charged Bill Near and me with conducting the review and getting the field down to three options. He wanted in on the final presentations, but how we got to that point was up to us. As I recall, the decision to do the review was made the day July 5. There was not a lot of time.

It fell on me to manage the review process. I didn't think MARC had done anything to deserve the review, which essentially was a no confidence vote by the client, but I also knew nothing lasts forever, especially in business and most especially in the advertising business. MARC knew it was going to be an uphill battle to keep Cedar Point. The percentage of agencies holding onto the business after a review is very low, perhaps 15 percent. A review is commonly the kiss of death. Sometimes incumbent agencies decide not to compete in reviews because they sense the inevitable result and decide to cut their losses and move on. But most do not. They stay and fight. They are hyper competitive by nature and believe, in their hearts, that they can and should win.

I know Tony Bucci of MARC talked to Dick Kinzel and was assured MARC had a chance. A slim one, probably, but a chance. MARC decided to stay in the game.

I had never been involved in an agency review, much less conducted one, and I knew this was an opportunity for me, a chance to learn how to do something which is a necessary skill set for anyone in marketing or advertising management. I had thought about it, of course, and read about it as the trade press was always talking about agency reviews. I was determined the review would be comprehensive, fair, and well managed.

I started with geography. I felt that within two to three hours of Cedar Point, an easy drive for meetings, there was a good agency fit. There had to be. With the automotive business there were lots of agencies in Detroit. Cleveland had a number of good full service shops. After lots of phone calls—there were no websites to visit in 1988—I came up with a list of 12 agencies that included shops in Columbus, Cleveland, Detroit, Pittsburgh and Toledo. I thought it was important to meet with them on their own turf, not at Cedar Point. I wanted to see their work environments, how their staffs related to each other at home versus the road. I wanted to learn about them and what made them tick. Bill and I visited all 12 agencies within a three week period, sometimes visiting two in one day. All visits were worthwhile. I learned a great deal. They all worked hard to try to find out if MARC was still involved. We told them the truth: yes. We didn't ask them to do any work on our behalf, or to prepare any presentations.

Cedar Point was an extremely desirable client. Any mid-size or larger agency in our market would kill to have us as a client. We were a leading brand, really an icon, and perceived as very successful, both financially and aesthetically. We were a sexy, high visibility product. We were show business, the entertainment industry. We also paid our bills. Cedar Point would be drawing power for creative talent; who wouldn't want to work on the Cedar Point account? Cedar Point would help attract new business, too. When I made each of the 12 calls, I could feel the surprise and excitement on the other end of the line.

## Death by Tech

After our 12 visits, we cut the number to six semi-finalists. We invited these agencies to prepare a presentation. We again visited each agency to hear their pitch. I will always remember the presentation of one of the Columbus agencies. For their presentation they had invested in what was then high tech presentation equipment and software. Ten seconds into the presentation, three slides into it, the slides started going backward. Then they froze; they may as well have been enveloped in concrete. It happens. The senior agency rep made a joke, while his second in command disappeared into the back room. After a minute or two, he reappeared with a smile and said everything was okay.

The presentation started again, from the top, and this time the slides didn't start going backwards until we were about 20 seconds into the presentation. The second in command was up in a heartbeat and disappeared into the back room. He reappeared a minute later with more assurances, but nervous assurances. The senior guy made another joke. I felt bad for all of them. It was fast becoming a nightmare.

The third time was unfortunately not the charm. The presentation worked a little longer, which was perhaps the worst possible scenario because we were just about ready to believe the problem had been fixed for good. It wasn't solved at all. This time the senior guy got up and disappeared into the back room. We could hear yelling and screaming. It was not good.

When the senior guy reappeared, red-faced, he said they had given up. He apologized, keeping it light with the comment that the two guys in the back room, both free-lancers, "will never work in this town again." Probably true.

The air had gone out of the balloon. There was no blowing it up a second time. We struggled to go through the presentation manually. The edge, the attitude, the message was weak. They had no chance. It is sad but true that sometimes you are only as good as your equipment. It is nearly impossible to recover from a serious equipment failure or technical screw-up, no matter how undeserved or explainable. If you choose to live by the sword, you choose to die by it, too.

We cut the six semi-finalists to three finalists plus MARC.

There were three agencies, plus MARC, in the finals: Hesselbart & Mitten (H&M), Meldrum & Fewsmith (M&F), and Liggett Stashower

(LS), all from the Cleveland-Akron area. The final presentations were held in the Executive Conference Room at Cedar Point. We allocated two to three hours for each presentation and spread them over several days. We gave them each the same assignment: introduce the world's highest, steepest, and fastest roller coaster. We provided them with basic information about the coaster and required each agency to sign a confidentiality statement. As it was, and I believe still is, customary, we gave MARC the opportunity to go last, if they preferred to do so, which they did.

H&M was the dark horse in the competition, as they were the smallest and youngest agency. However, they had a significant weapon – John Ragsdale. John was the creative director and then at the peak of his ability. He drove the machine.

My heart was with MARC. They were the only agency I had ever known and many of their staffers were friends as well as business associates. Their presentation had been excellent. The extra bit of bussing the much of the agency up to Cedar Point, and then appearing with posters and shout-outs outside the conference room, hit the heart hard, as it was calculated to do.

The next day, however, H&M got the business. Dick had made the final call. He wanted fresh ideas, and he liked the connection

**Magnum's layout cut right through what would become Soak City water park creating a visual unique to amusement parks. Can you see Canada from the top of Magnum? Yes! The Magnum layout is one of Lee Jewett's finest creations.**
CEDAR POINT ARCHIVES

H&M had made with our guests. He liked the passion they brought to Cedar Point. And he liked John Ragsdale's enthusiasm and self-confidence. Dick was never afraid to go with his gut, and his gut said H&M.

Bill Near gave me a call and we took a walk around the park and talked about it. I was very upset at the time. I just didn't feel MARC deserved to be fired. Bill was understanding and allowed me to vent. It was one of the best conversations we ever had. He played the role of big brother and did it well.

It was my job to call MARC with the bad news. Tony Bucci was unavailable, so I gave the bad news to Michelle Fabrizi. We had worked closely together for six years and I had great respect for her. It was a short, difficult conversation. She was professional.

The Liggett folks were professional, too. I don't think they expected to win. I felt badly for Lynn Lilly because I felt she had made a real connection with our guests, that she was one of them, and knew how to talk to them.

I don't recall many specifics of my conversation with John Ragsdale. He was very happy, of course, and I sensed that he knew they would win. John was the kind of guy who always sensed he would win.

The Magnum XL–200 had its sales team.

## Magnum XL-200

The name Magnum was not without controversy. The two most common definitions of magnum are a large bottle of wine (twice the normal size) and a firearm (most commonly a 357 magnum pistol). Neither fit the Cedar Point brand. But magnum also means something of unusually great power or size. The word derives from the Latin word "magnus," which means large. And that's the context of the name of the roller coaster. The "XL-200" was added to reinforce the message of size and the world record-breaking height of the ride. It was Lee Jewett's idea, and it was a good one. The ride is most commonly referred to as Magnum, without reference to the subtitle, but especially in the early years the "XL-200" was a good hook to have.

Much has been written and said about Magnum as the ride that launched the coaster wars in the amusement park industry. I think it's an accurate statement. It was the first coaster to pass the 200-foot barrier and the first so-called hyper coaster (200 feet plus). It was also a coaster without inversions, a steel counterpart to the great wooden coasters. Guests loved the fact that it had no inversions. So did Dick Kinzel. So did I.

Magnum would be the signature ride at Cedar Point for 11 seasons, until the opening of Millennium Force in 2000. It succeeded Gemini, which had enjoyed a signature ride run from 1978 through 1988.

Magnum was not originally designed to be 205 feet high. An extra 20 feet was added at the suggestion of a board member, which proved to be one of the best marketing decisions in the history of Cedar Point. The lesson: sometimes it's okay to have too much of a good thing. The cost to add the extra 20 feet was paid for quickly; in fact, some said it was paid for the first week of the season.

It is a very beautiful ride, perhaps the handsomest at Cedar Point, even after nearly 30 years. The red track and silver columns work beautifully together. The silver blends easily into the sky and the lattice-like bracing looks fragile, spidery. Many park guests consider it the most elegant coaster in the park.

"Highest, Steepest, and Fastest roller coaster in the world" is not a bad calling card. In the park business, it's hard to think of one better. It's like getting the number one draft pick—and the number one draft pick's name is LeBron James. I had the challenge of working with a new agency and I had the best marketing tool imaginable. I knew it was a perfectly good storm.

The building of the ride went well, at least from my perspective. It was not Gemini, an experience none of us wanted to go through again. We had faith in the manufacturer, Arrow Dynamics, in particular the principal designer, Ron Toomer, who enjoyed a great personal relationship with both Lee Jewett and Dick Kinzel. They liked him and trusted him.

H&M went to work on selling the ride. John Ragsdale was a good fit for Magnum, and I enjoyed working with him. We had the Notre Dame connection, of course (accidentally discovered during our first meeting), but I was impressed with his intensity and his commitment to work. It could be all-encompassing, and I did not envy his wife and family in that regard. He would not settle. There was always one more tweak to a TV or radio spot edit, one more camera angle to consider. I loved it that his passion and talent was being devoted to our park, our coaster.

John's eyesight was failing, though he was only in his early 40s, and rarely drove a car. He depended on his colleagues to get him from place to place.

The advertising we did for Magnum has, in my opinion, stood the test of time better than any other campaign we ever did for any other coaster or any other attraction. You could sell the ride today with the same advertising. The teaser spot was brilliant. It began with then state of the art computer generated imagery (CGI) around the ride logo and a deep, electronic voice intoning "Magnum," then cut to various high intensity images (surfing, heavy metal guitar-playing, sky-diving, car racing, fighter jet flying, among others, as the voice-over asked: "So what's it like to ride the Magnum?" It ended with the "highest, steepest, fastest" claim. The cutting was fast, the sound track intense and the sound effects perfectly placed. And not a roller coaster image in it. The imagery used for the "So what's it like to ride the Magnum" section was all stock footage.

The voice of Magnum was a Californian who had done work for Levi jeans and beer and soft drink companies. He was a great choice: young-sounding, hip, smart without being a smart-ass, confident. Not easy to pull off. He lived in Santa Monica, California, and had an in-house studio. He didn't travel to the client, the client traveled to him. It was my first visit to Santa Monica, a beautiful place. The house was in typical suburban-feeling street. Houses were large, but not Beverly Hills large, and packed tightly together. The session went very well. He liked us, and he liked the idea of doing a voice over for a roller coaster commercial.

The radio spot introducing the ride was written by Sarah Venizelos, a brilliant copywriter who would go on to run her own agency 15 years later. The best line was "See that little yellow spot? That's your mother."

As soon as the ride opened, we did a film shoot to capture images of the actual Magnum. John Ragsdale used 8mm film rather than the standard 16mm to give the images grit and a blurry, fast-paced look. We edited the spot in a Chicago studio. I remember going indoors out of the bright late spring light and into the cool and dark studio and seeing the images of the ride on the big screen and knowing we had an absolute winner. The spot was cool. It was just a touch irreverent. It was intense. Our advertising target, the 12-24 year-old market would eat it up. They would see the spot and make a commitment to themselves that they were going to ride Magnum before the summer was gone.

## The Best Radio Spot Ever

The radio spot we used for most of the summer was called "Magnum Testimonial." Nothing fancy, but a killer application. A few days after the ride opened, H&M stationed two broadcast producers and a copywriter at the bottom of the exit ramp and interviewed guests as they came off the ride. Most of their questions were basic. They could all be summed up: So, what's it like to ride the Magnum? Our guests did not hold back. They loved it. I stood off to the side and mostly just watched. I remember thinking that we had really created something special, that this coaster was going to change our business and challenge the whole industry. Over the course of the day, we interviewed more than a hundred guests, and all variety of guests: kids, grandparents, couples, men, women, black, white, Asian, groups of teen boys, groups of teen girls. They gushed. They screamed. They yelled. They talked over themselves and their friends. It was a logistical challenge separating the guest comments, getting them to sign agreements, paying them each a dollar. All they wanted to do was talk about the ride experience.

It was a challenge editing the comments to fit the requirements of a 60 second radio spot. Our Magnum voice started the spot with the words: "So what's it like to ride the Magnum?" From that point on the spot was non-stop guest comments over an exciting music track and some live coaster sounds. Some comments were one word or two, some told mini-stories, but the Magnum was the hero of every comment. The spot ended with a father from Detroit. "I know one thing. If my 12-year-old son rides the Magnum he'll come off a grown man."

It was one of the most effective radio spots I was ever involved with in my 40-year career at Cedar Point, perhaps the most effective of all.

Of course, we beat it to death. We used the same technique with the launch of other big coasters, including Mean Streak, but it wasn't the same. Nothing matched the energy and enthusiasm of the Magnum testimonial.

The Magnum advertising did what it was supposed to do: create awareness of the ride and tease the ride experience. It was up to the ride itself to seal the deal and get word of mouth going in the marketplace.

Magnum did not disappoint. The jump in ride experience from the Gemini—the coaster thrill standard most of our guests had been accustomed to since 1978—to the Magnum XL¬-200 was like going from a minivan to a Corvette. Many of our guests simply did not appreciate what a great coaster could do until they rode the Magnum. The jump in ride experience from the Magnum to the Millennium Force 11 years later was real enough (mostly speed), but nothing like the jump from Gemini to Magnum. Millennium is Magnum's big brother. Magnum and Gemini are different species.

## Are You Ready to Ride?

So, what's it like to ride the Magnum?

The queue and station experience is underwhelming if you approach the ride entrance from the Corkscrew midway. The station is painted white and blends into the trees and landscaping. You cannot see much of the ride, even the first hill, from the queue. Once on the platform it is more of the same. The ceiling is low. The ride retains its mystery. Most of the time, Magnum is in three-train operation and things happen fast. When you finally get into your seat you look ahead and to your right and the first hill is right there, spidery and silver with a bright red track. When I was GM, the Magnum station was one of my favorite tour stops. The view of the Magnum hill was spectacular. It was easy to observe the ride crew. You had a clear view to the northwest, so it was a good spot for weather watching. There is nothing but sky behind the Magnum first hill; it stands alone.

When the train leaves the station, it crosses over the midway. Then there is a sharp turn to the right and the train engages the chain at the base of the lift hill. The sound is unmistakable and can be heard back in the station, a deep metallic clunk. There is a brief pause, then the rattling of the chain takes over as the train heads up the hill. It's a long, slow climb. Plenty of time for the rider to take in the view. Only a few riders look down to the right or the left through the open space by your knees; it can be a bit terrifying. Some guests will only ride the Magnum at night, so they don't have to look down as they ascend the hill. If you are seated on the left side the open space just leads to air; if you are seated on the right the open space by your knees leads to steps and a railing. For those with height issues, the right side of the train is a much better option.

The open-style steps have a purpose, of course. Ride mechanics need to get to the top of the hill to inspect the chain and do regular maintenance. There is also the occasional walk down, when there is a mechanical or electrical problem and the decision is made that it's better to walk guests down from the hill than to have them sit in the coaster train for an unknown period. Ride operators on the Magnum must be willing and able to deal with heights and open-style steps and frightened guests.

As you reach the top of the hill, the train feels like it's slowing. Indeed, as often claimed, you can see Canada on clear days: Pelee Island and Middle Island, only about 17 miles away to the northwest. Kelleys Island, the largest on the U.S. side of the lake, is clearly visible, five miles out in the lake. On the far horizon is Put-in-Bay and Perry's Monument, 14 miles away. The lake itself is blue or deep green or even gray depending on the time of day and the mixture of sun and clouds. More than any other ride at Cedar Point, Magnum seems connected to Lake Erie.

The dive downward off the lift hill takes your breath away, especially if your basis for comparison is Gemini or Blue Streak. You cannot really prepare for it. You shoot up instantly into the second hill, which itself is 157 feet high, and then bank to the left and head into a tunnel before roaring into the ride's second signature element, the famous "bow tie," where the train banks sharply on its side and turns on itself and then drops down along the beach and starts to head for home.

The beach and the lake are on your left and ahead of you is a second tunnel. Then the track turns right, and you fly through a series of three smaller hills which push you up from your seat and into a final tunnel, where you hear the sharp hiss of the brakes as the train slows dramatically and you head for the station. You cross the midway at about 15 feet above the concrete and look for guests to wave to, and scream to, as you want to share with the world that you have just had an extraordinary experience: you've just ridden the Magnum XL-200.

There were some in park industry in the 1980s who believed that all future steel coasters would include inversions. Dick Kinzel wasn't one of them. He was not a fan of riding upside down and suspected he was not alone.

By the standards of 1989, Magnum was a very smooth ride. The manufacturer added some padding to the interior of the trains to make the ride experience more comfortable for guests, but essentially nothing of note required modification. With a three-train operation, it could give about 1,800 rides per hour, an impressive number.

All we had to do was manage the phenomenon we had created. The station was like a rock concert, especially at night. Riders screamed and yelled as each train came into the station, holding their hands in the air, shooting fists in the air, clapping and shouting. The guests waiting to ride did the same, especially those who were about to ride. After exiting the ride, guests ran down the ramp which led to the midway and the ride plaza and lined up to see their ride photo.

It made all of us, from CEO to sweep, incredibly proud that we had created something that was so successful.

That August, Dick Kinzel showed me a note he had received from Carl Hughes, president of Kennywood park in Pittsburgh and an industry leader. In part it read: "The promotion job on Cedar Point's new coaster is the best anyone has ever done." Made my day.

Attendance in 1989 was an amazing 3,249,000 visits, a new record, eclipsing the old record of 3,133,600 set in 1986.

We added extra permanent queuing to the ride.

## "Cedar Point Will Move You"

In 1989, we introduced a new theme line: Get to the Point! It had been used before, back in the 1940s and early 1950s, but H&M did not know that and neither did I until I stumbled upon it in some old advertising files months later. The best theme lines MARC had created— "The Amazement Park" and "America's Roller Coast"— would still be used in certain specific applications, but we began using Get to the Point! as our slogan in 1989. It did not have the romance of The Amazement Park or the positioning of America's Roller Coast,

but it was a strong call to action, and it was wrapped around a song—
"Cedar Point Will Move You"—that was an instant brand classic. It
was the best theme music or jingle created in my time at the park. It
didn't hurt that Dick Kinzel fell in love with it instantly. We ended
up playing it on the midway, in ride queues, in stores, just about
everywhere. It was a great pop song. It still plays in my head, and I
haven't heard it in 20 years.

There's no question Magnum was Dick Kinzel's favorite ride. In
later years, he would acknowledge that Millennium Force was a bigger
and more intense ride experience—and when he entertained a visiting
celebrity or important financial person he took them to ride Millennium
Force, not Magnum—but in his heart Magnum was always number one,
and for a combination of reasons. It was the ride that really started the
coaster wars. It generated the biggest YOY (Year Over Year) attendance
increase in the park's history. It was the first great coaster at Cedar
Point built on his watch (the Iron Dragon notwithstanding).

In December, the Investor Relations department started work
putting together the company's 1989 annual report to unitholders and
investors. Dick Kinzel invited me to write a draft of the president's
letter. I know he thought I could do as good a job as the folks at Edward
Howard, our financial public relations firm in Cleveland. I was cheaper,
too. I was flattered to be asked. I met with Dick just before Christmas
break to get an idea of what he wanted to say in the letter.

For 1989, I knew he wanted to communicate how special Magnum
was for the park. My goal was to make the letter a conversation between
Dick and the unitholders—and the employees. Using preliminary year-
end financial data, I worked on the letter over Christmas and turned
in a draft the first week of January. Both Dick and Investor Relations
were pleased with it. Finance updated the year-end numbers and
added a few tweaks and we were ready to go. Both Stacey Frole from
Investor Relations and Bruce Jackson, our CFO, were good writers and
contributed to writing the letter. For the next 15 years we basically
repeated the same process. In December I got input from the Finance
staff and from Dick. I produced a draft letter by early January. The
annual report was printed in February.

## The Disaster

In 1990, we had an impossible task: top Magnum. It wasn't going
to happen, of course, and in fact the park went in a very different
direction. Management decided to extensively modify an existing ride,
Avalanche Run (our Intamin-built bobsled ride, a disappointment from
its first operating day), and market it as a brand-new ride experience:
Disaster Transport, a space-themed coaster ride in the dark.

We failed to pull it off. We hired an Orlando theming company to design the transformation. On storyboards it looked great, even Disneyesque (which is why I think it got approved), but, it did not deliver the kind of ride experience our guests were expecting. Putting a steel shell over Avalanche Run was the easy part. Creating a legitimate themed, thrill ride experience was a much bigger task. Whether we acknowledged it or not, we were setting ourselves up to be compared to Space Mountain at Disney World.

The story line for the ride—navigating various space obstacles to deliver cargo to an ice-covered planet—was not communicated effectively in the queue and most guests had no idea what was going on. Most wouldn't have cared, either. Although some of the individual executions were impressive, we just didn't pull off the critical mass of theming to make the ride successful. As we found out quickly, the audio and other special effects were very expensive to maintain and broke down frequently, adding to guest confusion. To tell the story effectively, you need all the chapters in the book. Guest surveys and quality ratings quickly revealed, especially for a major capital investment of $3.4 million, that Disaster Transport was indeed a disaster. It was a dog; in fact, it was a barking dog.

## Star Wars Joins the Coaster Wars

The best thing about Disaster Transport was the TV commercial we created to sell it.

H&M was anxious to build upon the success of the Magnum campaign. They knew it would be difficult to replicate, although initially they were as excited as any of us about what could be accomplished if the ride delivered the experience the storyboards suggested.

We had the same challenge: how do you pre-sell the ride without being able to use actual footage of the ride? And unlike Magnum, even when the ride was operational it would be very difficult and horribly expensive to film the ride experience.

John Ragsdale and his team proposed a TV spot that didn't use an image of the ride at all, just a suggestion of it. The spot opens with a tight shot of a young boy outdoors at night, sound effects of crickets, etc., starry sky above. The viewer senses something big is going to happen but doesn't know what. Suspense builds for nearly 25 seconds, then the boy is "transported" into the night sky in a blend of sound and light that certainly by 1990 standards was impressive. It broke through. It ended up being the only TV spot ever created for Disaster Transport.

Rather than bid our TV advertising production by individual spot, as was usually done in the business, H&M bid all our TV spots as a package. They knew it would take special skills to create the effects they wanted for the DT spot, and they had a solution if they could make it work financially. It was serendipitous, I believe, but Lucasfilm (yes, the Star Wars guys) had recently created a small division to produce TV commercials. The strategy was to better utilize both the equipment and technology, and the human capital, they owned when in-between motion pictures. The Lucas folks hoped the Lucas brand would be powerful catnip to every agency creative director in the world, not to mention a few clients. We caught them at the right time, as they were launching their business and trying to get clients. In short, they were pricing aggressively, enough so that we could afford them.

It meant a six to 10-day trip to California, as we had plans to shoot three quite different TV spots and record several radio spots as well.

Most of the work was done in studios, but one spot, a second year Magnum spot, was shot entirely outdoors in an enormous green field which bordered a pheasant farm north of San Francisco. It was March and northern California was emerald green, as Ireland-looking as any place in America. The surrounding hills were soft and green and completely treeless. John Ragsdale wanted an open horizon for the spot. The spot never delivered in overall impact, though its individual pieces and parts were executed very well. It was mostly shot in black and white, always a tricky business in the modern age.

A young boy, 10ish, looks at big metal slide, its outline against a clean background looking like a giant coaster hill. The boy slowly climbs up the slide. Quick cuts of Magnum images. The boy gets to the top, sits down, and hesitates. It's the moment of truth. More quick cuts of cresting the Magnum and looking down the first hill. The boy lets go of the rail and slides down the slide. More cuts to actual images of Magnum. The spot was serious in tone and feel, even a bit artsy. Its psychology was sound—conquering your fears of riding a big coaster—but it just didn't feel right when it was all put together. It was not a well-liked spot within park management.

Lucasfilm had assigned us an in-house producer whose job it was to manage the whole project. His name was Lope Noy. He was short, wiry, with black hair down to his shoulders, very personable. He had known George Lucas for many years (they were both part of a company group that got together to play poker) and had worked on all the Star Wars movies. This was 1990, only six years after "Return of the Jedi" had opened. At the end of the week, the day everything wrapped up, Lope took Ed Bailey, our account executive from H&M, Ginny Carmichael, our agency producer, and me on a special tour.

It was designed to impress, and it did. It was the Lucasfilm equivalent of Cedar Point walking a VIP client past the ride line and putting him into the first seat of the Magnum. Lope took us to the one story warehouse which housed all the Star Wars artifacts and props, and then to a tour of Skywalker Ranch, the headquarters of Lucasfilm.

The warehouse was small, unobtrusive and ordinary-looking. It was white I remember, and one story, located in San Rafael just off a commercial street, surrounded by other nondescript buildings. We parked in the back and Lope took us in. No windows, but plenty of overhead lights. There it was in front of us, sitting on rack after rack of standard gray metal shelving: "Star Wars," "The Empire Strikes Back," "Return of the Jedi," "Indiana Jones and the Raiders of the Lost Ark," and other George Lucas films. There were models of the Death Star, models of the Millennium Falcon, models of various space creatures; matte paintings of the background landscapes in the Indiana Jones movies; costumes, including the complete costume of Darth Vader. The most sacred object was Luke Skywalker's light saber, which I got to hold in my hands and wave around in the air. I have the pictures to prove it. At the time I questioned the wisdom of leaving all this stuff just sitting on shelves gathering dust with what appeared to me to be rudimentary security. To me, at the time, they were priceless objects. Looking back, I can see the wisdom of sticking them in some unobtrusive, quiet, unexpected place, a counter-intuitive approach. But more than that, I now realize that what matters are the movies themselves, the visual and emotional experience the objects were a part of. Still, cool to be Luke.

Next stop was Skywalker Ranch, George Lucas' film-making enclave in the green hills above San Rafael. It is well hidden in a quiet valley, almost a bowl, so it is well protected and surrounded by undeveloped land. Lucas' headquarters is a massive Victorian-style ranch house, white and beautiful, with Queen Anne turrets and a huge front porch. The ranch was designed as a workplace first. There are several buildings designed to look like ranch buildings which house studios for creating sound and visual effects. Behind the main house are several cottages where visiting directors and producers can live and work while the artists of Industrial Light & Magic do their thing.

Lope gave us a tour of the main house. As we were walking up the main steps, we passed another group coming down the steps. One of them was Dennis Hopper (our only celebrity sighting). George Lucas was not in town, but Lope took us everywhere, including Lucas' library and the screening room in the lower level, which was filled with massive black leather chairs and sofas. We ended the tour with lunch in a beautiful dining room off the back of the house with walls and ceilings of glass. Lope explained to us that there was always a chef on duty to prepare whatever meals were needed. Just like the white House, I guess.

Lucas was an emblem for high tech, especially in 1990, before the internet, smart phones, and augmented reality. But the visual message at Skywalker Ranch, from the vineyards behind the house to the hidden (underground) garages, to the beautifully paneled library, was a California ranch circa 1890.

I did get a tchotchke out of this, a black sweatshirt which reads Skywalker Ranch and includes the Lucasfilm logo. I still have it. I have worn it seldom. It goes into the will.

## Mean Streak

Cedar Point dropped back in attendance in 1990, as expected in a year following an event like the opening of Magnum. We still were comfortably over the magic three million mark, dropping 147,000 visits to 3,102,000. The plan was to get it all back in 1991 with the introduction of Mean Streak, the highest, fastest, and steepest wooden roller coaster in the world.

The strategy seemed sound enough on several levels. We had the biggest and best steel coaster on the planet, Magnum, which had dramatically increased attendance. Just think about what attendance we could generate with the highest, steepest, and fastest wooden roller coaster? Magnum and Mean Streak would be thunder and lightning, brothers, comrades in arms, Butch Cassidy and the Sundance Kid. Together they would firmly brand Cedar Point as the roller coaster capital of the world.

Mean Streak was a great name, a play on our other traditional wooden roller coaster, the Blue Streak. However, it did not work well as a logo or as a merchandise mover. Don Miears, then VP-merchandise and games, argued forcefully a ride name should have a heartbeat to be successful. Mean Streak was too abstract (of course Magnum was abstract but a successful logo). The best names worked on both the advertising and merchandise levels: The Beast, Wildcat, and Iron Dragon. Even in its opening year, Mean Streak was a disappointment when it came to merchandise, mostly due to a poor logo (for merchandise).

It was a massive project. The ride was located at the far end of the park, at the back of Frontier Town, between the CP&LE Railroad and Camper Village. Perimeter Road, the access road to Soak City and Hotel Breakers, had to be re-routed to accommodate the massive footprint of the Mean Streak. In basic design it was a figure eight. It took 1.7 million board feet of southern yellow pine to build the Mean

Streak. It was a mile long at 5,247 feet of track. It cost $7.5 million to build.

It did have capacity, a must for a major Cedar Point coaster: 1,600 riders per hour on three Philadelphia Toboggan Company (PTC) trains. It was 161 feet high and had a 155-foot first drop. It was designed by Curtis D. Summers and built by an Ohio company, the Charles Dinn Corporation, both out of Cincinnati. I was not part of the negotiations with Summers and Dinn, so I don't have any feel for the contract, but the project did not work for them financially and the Dinn Corporation went out of business less than a year after Mean Streak opened.

The lighting package was a brilliant design, created by Lee Jewett and GE designers and engineers from Nela Park, near Cleveland. The entire ride was up lit from the ground by white light. It was a dazzling effect, visible out on the lake for miles. The first year the lighting package was as talked about almost as much as the ride experience.

How to promote it? How to presell it? How to launch it? The agency came up with a concept for a TV commercial called Lumber Mill. Two teen boys sneak a visit to a lumber mill at night, watching truck after truck leave with lumber, to be used in the building of the world's biggest wooden roller coaster. We decided to shoot the spot in at a mill outside Seattle, Washington, in the foothills of the Cascades. I was skeptical, believing there had to be a location option closer to home, where transportation costs would have been less, but the agency argued that this mill was the perfect location visually and the owner was anxious to work with us and would cut us a great deal. In the end, they wore me down and we shot the spot in Washington.

I remember it was a very cold damp night, and I was underdressed. The temperature was in the low to mid 30s and there was a knife-like wind. It was a long shot list and we had only about 12 hours of darkness, so we had to move quickly. The owner of the mill was there all night and operated some of the equipment for us. He was talkative and a good storyteller. He scared some of the crew with very realistic stories of Bigfoot sightings in the woods behind the mill. There were mountain lions, too.

One of the crew members, a grip, was absolutely petrified and wouldn't walk to the back areas alone. The owner was an older guy, a face full of stubble, a little chunky, probably in his late 50s or early 60s. I remember he seemed impervious to the cold. He wore bib overalls over a flannel shirt and over that a ratty gray lightweight jacket open at the throat. I would assume he was right out of central casting for the owner of a lumber mill.

By midnight, I was freezing. It felt even colder than the night we had filmed Demon Drop back in 1983, which was my standard for cold experienced in the line of duty.

The spot was very "theatrical," meaning it was movie-like. It looked like it was expensive to film, though it was not. Looking back, the storyline was a bit misleading or at least hard to understand. It did not compare to the teaser spots for Magnum and Disaster Transport, which were simple and direct and did not try to tell a long story. In my opinion, the spot was only marginally successful.

The same could be said for the spot we created for the in-season campaign, which featured a lone rider on the Mean Streak. The shots of the ride were exciting and communicated the size of the ride, but it had no magic moment. The focus on a single rider experience did not work, either. Jim Colvin, our director of maintenance at the time, asked me why we focused on a single rider experience when riding was almost always a group event. He also questioned the wisdom of showing a nearly empty train roaring around the track. Two great observations.

The Mean Streak advertising was marginally effective. I don't believe it made a big difference one way or another. Advertising is supposed to make a difference. If it doesn't, it's failed.

I don't recall much about my first ride on Mean Streak except that it shook me like a rag doll and I got off the ride feeling a big queasy. I thought the ride was too long. It was thrilling alright, but not in a completely good way. Some of our guests truly loved it, but most did not. For many it was not fun. Guests came off Magnum pumped and ready to go again. Guests came off Mean Streak glad they had survived the experience.

For the true wooden coaster fan, it did not measure up to the Texas Giant at Six Flags Over Texas. For these fans it was too long and too slow.

Mean Streak had a great opening, a beautiful May Saturday. We all thought we were on track for a record year, a Magnum year. However, attendance soon cooled, and we did not get the traditional post July 4 surge that creates a record year. I remember talking to Don Miears in early August about the lack of an attendance surge. He felt the ride just didn't deliver in terms of guest expectations. In a word: it was not Magnum. Park attendance for the year was 3.1 million, comfortably above the 3 million benchmark but considerably below expectations. I don't recall our attendance budget for the year, but I'm sure it was in the 3.2 to 3.3 million range.

We all scratched our heads on this one. Mean Streak would be the last traditional wooden roller coaster built at Cedar Point.

It did not improve with age; in fact, the ride experience declined as the ride got older. The ride experience usually deteriorated as the season wore on and the wood dried out and the whole structure "loosened up," resulting in a ride that was rougher. Some years we put hoses up on certain parts of the track and watered the ride at night so the wood would stay tight.

Visually, it never lost its allure, even when we added a haunted house as a permanent Halloween attraction in the infield and used a portion of the infield for a maintenance shed and a pieces and parts boneyard.

## Bear Country

In 1992, we needed to take a break from big expensive thrill rides. Even Cedar Point couldn't financially handle a Magnum or Mean Streak investment every year. We all knew that the beast needed a varied diet. Too many Magnums was a bad thing. Many of our guest were not riders by choice or were age and height disqualified. The Cedar Point strategy leaned toward thrill rides—it was our Unique Selling Proposition (USP)—but essential to the mix were family attractions and non-rider activities. They had to be refreshed, too. Several years earlier we had made a deal to bring the Berenstain Bears to Cedar Point. The Bears were the creation of Stan and Jan Berenstain, writers and illustrators whose books were very popular with young families, particularly with children in the three to seven-year-old range. They had a targeted appeal, even within the larger context of the world of animated children's characters. They were not "TV characters," their primary medium was the printed word: books. Cedar Point looked at lots of options, but cost and availability were big issues.

The characters performed in a small show and had a home in an area inside the old Earthquake ride on the main midway. They were first introduced in 1987.

I take some credit for bringing the Berenstain Bears to Cedar Point. I was familiar with the books because we had read them to our boys when they were younger. A couple of titles, like "The Spooky Old Tree" and "The Messy Room," were among their favorite books. Dan Keller had headed up the project of finding the right characters for Cedar Point. He had distributed a list of potential characters to park management and asked for feedback. The Bears were on the list. I called Dan and recommended we look at the Berenstain Bears. Dan had children about the same age as our boys, and he was familiar with the bears and liked them as well. He decided to talk to Stan and Jan Berenstain.

Our primary competitor, Kings Island, had a license deal with the Hanna-Barbera characters, including. Scooby Doo, and then later with Nickelodeon. The Six Flags parks were tied in with Warner Bros, including Bugs Bunny, Superman. Disney was, well, Disney. Knott's Berry Farm was tied into the Peanuts characters. We were an oddity in our park peer group in not having a character association. That said, we seemed to be doing well without one.

In 1992, the park decided to address the young family market by expanding our relationship with the Berenstain Bears. We built an outdoor attraction themed around the bears and their books in a small area on the west side of the Coliseum previously shared by the Sky Slide and miniature golf. At the same time, we ramped up our marketing and PR program to introduce Bear Country and push our very attractive junior price. Bear Country at Cedar Point included a tree house, spooky old tree (with an indoor slide), dinosaur dig, and other activities. Stan and Jan Berenstain were active participants in the design of the attraction. The final product was delightful, a critical hit. Families loved the attraction.

I had the opportunity to meet with Stan and Jan them several times while working on the marketing plan for the attraction. They were fun to work with, though I admit I was a fan as well as business partner. They came to the park twice that summer, once to do readings and book-signings at the new Bear Country. I recall several of us had dinner at the Bay Harbor Inn following their appearance.

Stan Berenstain, the more outgoing of the two, held court for several hours. He was a natural storyteller, as well as a brilliant illustrator, and we gobbled up every word. I remember thinking that most people his age—he was in his late 60s at the time—were content to play bingo at the parish church (a terrible stereotype of seniors, but remember I was in my early 40s then and ignorant about those a generation or two older than I was). He had the energy of someone 30. I was impressed. Retirement was not in his personal plan. I could understand why it wouldn't be.

Cedar Point had a good year in 1992, attendance increased 80,000 visits to 3.2 million without the benefit of a big new ride. I did not believe that Bear Country was the main attendance, but it was a factor. I remember telling Dick Kinzel and others that based on attendance performance Bear Country had the best return on investment ROI of any new attraction in the history of the modern Cedar Point. I do not recall what, if any, significant competitive activity occurred in 1992. Bill Clinton was elected president, I do remember that.

The year 1992 was also the year Cedar Fair, after a long and contentious negotiation, acquired Dorney Park & Wildwater Kingdom, in Allentown, Pennsylvania, a traditional park that had reinvented itself by adding a water park. It was Dick Kinzel's first park acquisition. It had been on again/off again for several months. My boss, Bill Near, was named the new GM at Dorney Park. Bill had been my boss for nearly decade. Our temperaments matched well. We had different skill sets—Bill was a food guy and I was a marketing guy—so we learned from each other. He was about 10 years my senior. His assistant, Bev Ontko, became my assistant. We worked together for 10 years. Bev's sense of humor, her loyalty, and her willingness to adapt were much appreciated.

## Snake River Falls

In 1993, we were back to thrill rides, our natural home, our comfort zone, and our core competency. Cedar Point introduced Snake River Falls, the highest, steepest, and fastest water ride in the world. We liked making "highest, steepest, and fastest" claims for rides. It certainly made the selling job easier. In style, Snake River Falls was a shoot-the-chutes water ride with one massive hill 82 feet high.

The ride was designed by Arrow Dynamics. The big splash at the bottom of the flume hurled huge amounts of water up in the air and directly at the center of a pedestrian walkway which functioned as the exit from the ride. Watching departing riders standing on the bridge and getting splashed had huge appeal. In front of the ride there was a stone bridge that connected Frontier Trail to Frontier Town which offered a perfect view of the main action of the ride. Guests would line up four and five deep to watch both the riders being splashed on the exit bridge and the impact of the splash on the riders in the boat. The splash was truly impressive. If the wind was from the northeast and at least 20 mph the splash reached guests on the stone bridge.

I don't recall very much about the construction of the ride, except that it was a mad rush at the end to get the ride tested, inspected, licensed, and ready to open by opening day. In fact, I remember watching carpenters with power drills still working in the station putting up signs while the opening ceremonies were taking place.

You did get wet when you rode Snake River Falls; no way to cheat it. The splash would get you. It was a fun and exhilarating experience, and a little scary as you plummeted down the flume anticipating the big splash, but it was not a ride I rode often in my career. Mainly because you got wet; it just wasn't fun to walk the midway in wet clothes (the ponchos never really kept you dry). I rode it when I was in the park on my own time, which was a relatively rare event.

Our marketing and advertising campaign for the ride was good, if not great, and did the job for us in building awareness and making the experience fun.

The 1993 season exceeded expectations—by a lot. In fact, Cedar Point set a then new all-time attendance record: 3.350 million. No one expected it. Looking back, it was probably a combination of the new ride, good weather, an expanding economy (the '90s were really starting to kick in) and weaker competitive pressure. All through July and August the attendance numbers were outstanding. This was in the time before Halloween events; the season effectively ended on Labor Day.

The 1993 season reinforced how little we really knew, with any certainty, about the dynamics of attendance. There were so many factors at work: weather, competition (numerous types), demographic trends (which ones really mattered?), consumer confidence, unemployment rate, advertising, group sales programs, good and bad publicity, news events, local economy, regional economy, national economy, new attraction—and trying to sort it all out, including how the various factors related in combination with other factors, was a task beyond any of us. Or anyone else. It still is.

What we knew with absolute certainty was that on a short-term basis, a single operating day, weather had real impact: if it rained, nobody came to the park. The corollary was not so ordained: beautiful weather didn't always translate into great attendance (but often it did). It was enough to drive a marketing guy, or a CEO, or board member, nuts.

The other thing we knew was that the right new attraction, usually a roller coaster, would drive incremental attendance in the short run (one season). Our hope, shared by management groups throughout the industry when they introduced a big new ride, was that it would carry over to the following year, and the year after that and the year after that lifting attendance to a new base level. It remained a hope.

You couldn't control the weather, but you could control the right new attraction.

## Raptor Rules the Sky

All during the 1993 season we were already almost giddy about what was coming after it: another world class roller coaster.

Bolliger and Mabillard (B&M), a coaster design company based in Monthey, Switzerland, had created a new kind of coaster where the train rides below the tracks and riders sit four (or two) across, held in place by an over-the-shoulder harness, with their feet dangling free, like sitting in a ski lift chair. B&M had built two coasters of this type for Six Flags. A group from Cedar Point went to Chicago to ride B&M's Batman at Six Flags Great America. They were impressed with the concept but came away full of ideas on how Cedar Point could do it better.

In what I view as a master stroke, Lee Jewett and Dick Kinzel decided to locate the ride in the front of the park on the south side of the midway, displacing the Midway Carousel, the Mill Race, and a small flat ride, the Calypso. Part of the ride would be erected over the existing Cadillac Cars and the Turnpike, both vintage rides from the 1960s. The ride would cost $12 million, but it would be the highest, fastest, and longest of its kind, and, as Lee said it, "It would change the front of the park forever."

What to call it? Marketing had a working list of names. Senior management had some ideas. The Planning & Design team had a list. Our ad agency, now M&F after acquiring H&M in 1992, had a list. Everyone had a list. We started out with hundreds of names, most of which were quite bad. I wish I had kept the first draft list. But we got things down to eight names and the agency did some rough logo treatments for each name.

Technically, it was Marketing's responsibility to come up with the name, but everyone wanted in on the act. It was a friendly competition, but it was a competition.

One of the names suggested came from an unlikely source: Tom Salamone. Tom was our corporate treasurer, a numbers geek, a person without a creative bone in his body, as he often described himself. The first time I heard it, I loved it. In my mind, it was the clear winner. It was short, aggressive, communicated flight, and would merchandise well. I saved the note Tom had given me with the name "RAPTOR" clearly hand printed on it. I still have a copy. Someday, it should be in the Town Hall Museum.

I suggested we test the final list of names with park guests, easy enough to do. One day toward the end of June we put names and logos on individual sheets and posted them on a wall in the Marketing conference room. We then invited groups of guests off the midway to come in and look at some possible new ride names. We screened the groups by age and sex and whether they were at the park mainly to ride rides, especially thrill rides. We promised the participants the session would be short, and we'd give each of them a voucher for a free soft drink.

Over the course of the day, we met with more than a hundred guests. The clear winner was Raptor. The name stood on its own, but the logo really brought it to life. It had been designed by a young woman in the M&F Art Department. It would go on to become arguably the best logo ever created for a Cedar Point ride. The logo was the face of a raptor, black with an orange beak and below the image the name Raptor in green typeface; the eyes are fierce and stay with you.

Don Miears, Cedar Point GM 1994–2000, coined a word to describe
the reaction of guests after riding Raptor. They had been 'raptorized.'
Over a million per year since 1994. CEDAR POINT ARCHIVES

The endorsement of park guests sealed it for Dick Kinzel. The ride had a name. We added "Rules the Sky" to the logo as a theme line.

Raptor was the first ride name and logo we decided to trademark. We were overjoyed when our intellectual property attorney informed us the name was available. We were nervous about it right up to the day of filing.

"Jurassic Park" the movie was only about a year into the marketplace and for many people the word raptor was associated with the very scary and very carnivorous pack of velociraptors that are the dinosaur villains of the movie. Cedar Point's Raptor had nothing to do with the Jurassic Park raptors. The context of our name was the generic name for birds of prey, nothing to do with dinosaurs.

All of that said, we hoped to borrow some of the popularity and some of the cachet given the name by the movie. As we anticipated, Universal, which owned the rights to the movie, heard about this new amusement park ride named Raptor and assumed, quite incorrectly, that it referred to the creatures in the movie and put us on notice to cease and desist using the name. Our attorney quickly responded that the ride had nothing to do with dinosaurs, but with birds, just birds.

In late August, we announced Raptor with the biggest PR event in the park's history. Robin Innes, Janice Lifke Witherow, and Dan Feicht put together a remarkable event. Both Claude Mabillard and Walter Bolliger attended, flying over from Switzerland. News media and special guests were invited to attend a special event in the Coral Courtyard, the group picnic area along the Cedar Point Beach. As the ride was being announced and described, a yellow stunt plane flew over the lake just off the beach and at a low altitude. The plane, flown by famous stunt pilot Art Scholl (who would die a few years later during the filming of "Top Gun,") proceeded to fly a course duplicating the route of the Raptor coaster train; yellow vapor trails marked the route. It was impressive in every way. Weather was good, we had a large number of media representatives attend, and the crowd was dazzled by the unexpected air show. Several Cleveland and Toledo TV stations led with the story at both the 6 p.m. and 11 p.m. newscasts.

The marketing program for the new ride was off to a great start.

Things only got better with the famous "Raptor Video." The folks at H&M pitched us on putting together a five minute promotional video on the new ride to help build awareness of the coaster during the off-season. This, of course, was pre-internet, pre-website, pre-YouTube. Our plan was to do a mass mailing of the video to the news media (local, regional, and some national), opinion leaders (government officials, sports celebrities), coaster fans, and group sales clients. Our hope with the latter was that they would put the video on their internal networks.

For Cedar Point marketing, this was a new path. We shot much of the video in September, at least the outdoor scenes, then added the animation and graphics in October and November. The initial mailing took place in early December. If I remember correctly, we mailed about 5,000 videos. It was an expensive project, but it was worth it.

The video used animation of a raptor-like creature breaking out of its egg and then flying high over Cedar Point, then diving down to the midway, transforming into a roller coaster. The viewer then goes on a simulated ride on the coaster. A good portion of the video consists of cutaways to various Cedar Point managers making comments about aspects of the ride, e.g. construction, park location, ride specifics, etc. Participants included Dick Kinzel, Jim Colvin, Lee Jewett, Jack Falfas, John Hildebrandt, and Claude Mabillard of B&M. Music and sound effects were excellent. The video was a home run in every way. By today's standards, the animation is crude, but today's standards didn't exist in the fall of 1993 and the winter of 1994. All that matters is what it was in its own time, and what it was then was great.

At the time, we had a promotional relationship with the Cleveland Indians, who in 1994 were opening their new stadium, Jacobs Field. The giant scoreboard included a state of the art Sony Jumbotron. We successfully negotiated a deal where the Raptor video played on the Jumbotron approximately 10 minutes before each first pitch. It was great placement. Jacobs Field sold out every game.

From my perspective, ride construction went smoothly. There were no major delays or problems. This was Cedar Point's first B&M coaster, but the firm's reputation for quality in every aspect of the park versus manufacturer relationship had proceeded them, and they did not disappoint.

I got my first ride on Raptor courtesy of Jack Falfas about four weeks before opening. Jack and several others in Park Operations and Maintenance had already ridden it. I had walked over to the ride site with Bernie Bonuccelli, the director of marketing at Dorney Park, who was at the park for a marketing meeting. My mission was just to show him the ride, but Jack did a lot more than that. Construction by this time was focused on things like queues, concrete, and landscaping. Construction crews had gone home for the day. Park Operations was starting to really learn the basics of operating the ride. This was their time to train.

Bernie and I were standing in the station just taking it all in, when Jack came up to us and said: "Want to ride?"

We jumped at the chance.

Jack rode with us and provided expert and excited commentary on the ride. You could tell Jack loved Raptor and was in the process of making it his own (as he had done with Magnum). Jack was Jack, and no one would know more about Raptor than Jack Falfas.

Raptor has given tens of millions of rides thus far in its working life, averaging well over a million rides every season. If there is common description of the experience of those millions of riders it is this: flight. If you want to feel a little of what a bird feels, or better yet what a pilot feels in a small plane, or in an X-wing fighter, ride Raptor.

When we opened the ride to the news media a few weeks later, we invited several pilots from the Ohio Air National Guard to attend and ride Raptor. They all said it was the closest they'd ever come to duplicating the actual experience of flying.

Raptor is an amazing ride experience. One key is its length. At 3,790 feet, it was designed to give a little breathing space between elements—something missing in the first B&M inverted coasters—and it makes the ride experience significantly better. The individual elements, starting with the breath-taking roll off the first hill and the dive into the 360-degree loop, and including the cobra roll, and the beautiful inverted roll which ends the ride, are put together masterfully.

I believe there is only one way to ride Raptor: front seat. The visual experience is qualitatively different.

The ride sounds large. There is no sand in its support columns. It doesn't glide in terms of sound as do similar coasters where the columns are filled with sand to absorb the sound from the ride. Instead, there is a roar, a steel-on-steel roar that dominates the main midway. For some, it is an irritant; for others it is a great part of the ride experience and adds to the appeal of the ride for spectators as well as riders. Personally, I like it. I think it gives the ride power and personality.

Our TV advertising campaign built off the bird of prey and flight concept. We shot the non-ride footage in a valley north of Los Angeles. That time of year California is very green. It passed for Ohio. The TV spot opens with a teen age boy riding his bike down a dirt path. Then switches to the point of view of something moving in the sky, looking down at the ground. The boy hears a screech and reacts with fear. He looks above and sees something. He drops his bike and starts running, looking over his shoulder. Then the camera switches to the POV of the creature from above as it closes in and ultimately lifts the boy off the ground, grabbing him with his talons, as an eagle would pick up a rabbit. Then a screech and the logo.

Like the Magnum teaser TV spot from 1989, the viewer never sees the actual ride. But it works.

For the in-season version of the TV spot, we cut some of the front end of the spot and added actual ride footage, so that after the boy is lifted into the air he finds himself in the front seat of the Raptor. Shots of the actual ride follow.

At Cedar Point, the actor who played the young man had a difficult time riding the ride so many times in quick succession. He hung in, though, with minimal breaks. As I recall, we had one day to get the shots of the ride we needed, and we had bad weather moving in. We had to push hard to get what we needed. I know I was glad I wasn't the actor. He earned his money that day.

I am not an inversion guy for the most part. I accept the Raptor ride experience as beautiful but stressful. I usually felt dizzy afterward; sometimes I didn't feel right for several hours. I could never ride it multiple times. As I got older, I rode Raptor less and less. However, I'm in the minority; it's a ride that for nearly a quarter century has remained one of the top five rides in the park in popularity and ridership. At the same time, it has been relatively easy to care for.

Millennium Force, Top Thrill Dragster, and Magnum (certainly in its early years) were defined by stats as well as ride experience. Stats, highest, fastest, steepest, etc. converted to specific numbers, are a big part of the conversation of the ride, including the marketing and advertising messages that tried to define them. Not so much Raptor. Initially, we included lots of numbers in promotional materials, but they increasingly got lost in what defined the ride: the unique ride experience. Many, perhaps most riders of Millennium or Dragster could tell you how tall the ride was or how fast it went, but you would be hard pressed to find riders who knew how high the first hill was (159 feet) or the ride's top speed (60 mph) or the number of inversions (six). The numbers didn't matter. The feeling of flight did.

Guests poured through the gates in 1994. Cedar Point attracted 3,617,000 visitors, the most in its then 124-year history. The record still stands a quarter century later. It was an increase of 264,000 visits over the prior year, 1993, which itself had been a record year. Lots of good news.

But there were problems, too. By the mid-1990s Cedar Point was struggling to maintain an adequately-sized seasonal staff. The economy was booming, and high school and college-age students had lots of options. There were increasingly more restaurants, hotels, marinas, campgrounds, and retail stores in the Sandusky area, all looking for part-time workers. Cedar Point traditionally housed about two-thirds of its workforce.

We joked that in the 1970s you had to know someone to get a job at Cedar Point. In the 1990s that someone was now calling you. Times had changed.

Cedar Point was always staffed to open the season but starting in early July attrition became an issue just as attendance was peaking.

Cedar Point began aggressively recruiting international students in the mid-90s. We worked with several different companies, who organized recruiting trips and international job fairs to match students with U.S. employers. Cedar Point started with United Kingdom students, then expanded to include European students, then eventually students from all over the world. The program started with a few hundred student workers and grew to 1,200 or more. The program was a life saver for the park.

## Attendance Counts

We were all proud of our attendance numbers. This was true across the company and the park but especially so within the Marketing and Park Operations divisions. We both received validation from the big numbers. In Marketing, it was simple. It was our job to sell tickets.

I loved walking the midway on a busy Saturday, dodging guests. They were everywhere in those years. I would often take a walk around the park around 6 p.m. My work was largely done for the day.

On big days, the lines for the major rides could be more than two hours long, sometimes, briefly, even longer. We fielded complaints from guests on busy days who told us they had only been able to ride three or four rides all day: two hours at Raptor; two hours at Magnum; 90 minutes at Mean Streak; 90 minutes at Corkscrew. They did not drive here from Kalamazoo, Michigan, to ride the Antique Cars or the Midway Carousel. They were here for the big rides featured in our advertising. Things got particularly difficult when one our stars got indigestion, especially if it occurred on Saturday. I did not envy Jack Falfas' job to deal with disgruntled guests who had waited in line to ride Magnum for 30 or 60 minutes only to have it break down. Fortunately, Magnum was a very reliable ride.

There were lines at food stands. There were lines at restrooms. There were lines to buy tickets. There were lines to buy souvenirs. We worried about lines, but we loved them, too.

In what turned out to be my time at the park, 1974 – 2014, a period of 40 years, Cedar Point, in my opinion, did not face what today we would call an existential threat. We had problems created by forces outside the park's control, but they were non-life threatening to the organization.

I have two close friends, both a little older than I am, who worked a similar number of years for General Motors. Both are mechanical engineers, graduates of the prestigious General Motors Institute (GMI). In their working lifetimes they saw massive, externally driven change transform General Motors: robots, Japanese and other competition, gas prices, labor costs, the quality revolution, the green revolution, the 2009 bankruptcy. For many years we talked through GM's problems over glasses of beer while sitting around the kitchen table. I never had any doom and gloom to report. Our basic strategy of building great thrill rides and developing resort additions like water parks and hotels was never challenged.

## The Texan

The 1994 operating season was also the first season that Don Miears served as GM of Cedar Point. In the fall of 1993, Dick Kinzel conducted an internal reorganization. Don Miears was promoted to GM of the park and to a seat on Cedar Fair's Board of Directors.

Don turned 58 in 1994. By some points of view, he was old to be a GM. However, anyone who knew Don knew he had the heart for the job. I used to tell people—at the time without any experience as a GM—that it would take five seasons to leave a mark. As it turned out, he had seven seasons, retiring at age 65 after the 2000 season. He came in with a bang—Raptor—and he went out with a bang: Millennium Force. Very good bookends. I used to tell people that he was blessed in that his first two years as GM he could concentrate on running the park and not worry about attendance. Worrying and fretting about attendance is something GM's do a lot. It soaks up a lot of time and a lot energy. Don was spared this his first two years, as they turned out to be the two best attendance years in the history of the park (to date).

Don was a Texan, born and raised on a farm outside Arlington on the way to Ft. Worth. He came to Cedar Point in 1971, recruited by Truman Woodworth to run retail operations and games. He had worked for Six Flags before coming to Cedar Point. Don knew a lot about farming and ranching and had ridden the rodeo circuit briefly as a young man. He was middle height, but he was a bear, thick and strong with enormous hands and a big shock of reddish blond hair. He wore a thick mustache of the same color, in style like Tom Selleck's, the actor. He walked with a unique gait; no one can duplicate it. It was purposeful and strong but not quite right because of bad knees (he had both replaced while he was GM).

Don had more pure physical energy and stamina than anyone I've ever worked with. He was a marvel. He could work early, or he could work late. It didn't seem to matter. Even in the off season, he seldom left the park before 7 p.m. He was not bashful about asking you to stop by to talk about an issue at 6 p.m. or later on cold Tuesday nights in February. What was impressive was that he was as fresh and energized then as he was first thing in the morning. On summer Saturdays he played golf early, teeing off at 7:30 a.m. As soon as he finished, he went home and showered and got ready to go to the park, usually arriving before 2 p.m. He stayed until closing, which meant 11 p.m. or later. He didn't hang out in the office. He was on the midway. The next day, Sunday, he would be at the park by 8 a.m. and work until at least 6 p.m.

He was well known in the industry, especially in the merchandise and games area. He had pioneered the import program, the strategy of personally going to Asia every fall to buy souvenir merchandise directly from manufacturers.

Don's outside passions were fishing, golf, and gambling. Fishing was mostly relegated to the time he spent at his condo in the Florida Keys, but golf was part of his life six months a year. Golf took a back seat to the park, of course, but he managed to keep a low handicap despite limited play. When he was in the Keys—usually for two to three weeks in March—he fished as often as he could. He loved poker, and was very good at it; he loved betting on golf, and he was very good at it. At the park, Don was hard, serious, driven; but when he was on the golf course he was funny, relaxed, a different person.

He had lived in Ohio since 1971, but he had not surrendered a syllable of his Texas accent. When you had done something or said something which he felt was wrong, or even stupid, he had a simple question: "You got rocks in your head?" The emphasis was on "rocks" and "head." He would often gesture with an enormous index finger to make a point.

Don asked great questions. He was a burrower, always trying to get you to explain in precise terms why you believed the way you did. In this, he was like Don Dittmann. However, Don Dittmann would sometimes drift off course, Don Miears never did. With Don Miears, there was never a hidden agenda (at least none I could ever detect). He gave it to you straight, and you always knew where you stood.

Every August, the Marketing division was responsible for providing a detailed recommendation for admission pricing for the next season. We assembled our plan, which involved dozens of different ticket categories to include revenue and volume projections. The primary authors were Jan Guthridge and Lee Alexakos. After the three of us did a final internal review, it was time to present it to Don. I enjoyed the challenge, but not everyone on my staff did; most approached the exercise with considerable trepidation. Don wanted to know WHY. Why are you recommending a 75-cent increase versus a $1 increase in Starlight Admission? Why do you believe you can generate an increase of 15,000 tickets in the House Account ticket category? He was relentless. If you gave what he considered an inadequate answer you might discover you had rocks in your head. The presentation usually went several hours.

He invented words on occasion, coining the statement "He (or she) was Raptorized" to describe someone who had just ridden the ride and didn't know what to say.

Don prided himself on his financial knowledge, including accounting, which occasionally drove our Finance division nuts. Don kept his own books, which he would pull out of the drawer to prove his point. When challenged, he would wave his finger and say with emphasis: "That may be what I said, but it's not what I meant."

## Don Meets Lenny

One of the best Don stories involved the famous rock singer, Lenny Kravitz. In the summer of 1996 Kravitz was playing a date in Cleveland. Turns out, he had a love of roller coasters and had heard about Cedar Point's collection, especially the Raptor. One of his management group contacted our PR Department and asked if there was a way Lenny could ride a few of our roller coasters the day after his Cleveland performance. In those days we did not have a formalized VIP program; basically, every celebrity appearance was custom, depending on several factors, including how much time they planned to stay at the park, how many people were involved, and what they wanted to do in the park. One of Don's rules was that he had to sign off on any VIP visit that involved allowing a celebrity to avoid waiting in line with all the other guests. This meant, of course, that he had to sign off on virtually all VIP visits. The PR Department notified Park Operations about the visit and, per protocol, advised the GM's office. Don was a country music fan. He was thrilled when he heard Randy Travis was going to be in the park the next morning.

It's easy enough to see how "Kravitz" and "Travis" might sound alike to some ears. Regardless, Don heard what he heard: Randy Travis. He showed up at the Raptor the next morning looking for Randy Travis. He didn't see him anywhere, so he started asking around. Finally, someone (not me, I think it was Jack Falfas) advised Don that the slender, good looking black guy with tattoos and dreadlocks about to enter the station platform was Lenny Kravitz.

"Who the EXPLETIVE is Lenny Kravitz? Don wanted to know. He had no clue. Jack gave him a quick tutorial while Lenny and his entourage rode Raptor.

In truth, Don handled his disappointment well. In fact, after Kravitz got off the ride Jack steered him over to Don and introduced him. Lenny rhapsodized about the ride and soon Don was all smiles and everyone was laughing about the case of mistaken identity.

There is a postscript to the story. That fall, several of us, including Don and his wife, Diane, and Jack Falfas, were having dinner at Emeril's restaurant in New Orleans as guests of Joe Heflin, an executive with Whitewater, a water slide manufacturer, at the annual IAAPA convention and trade show. We were still on appetizers when Jack Falfas suddenly jumped up and said: "There's Lenny Kravitz!" and gestured toward the door.

It was indeed Lenny, and an entourage. Jack was up in an instant and headed right for Lenny. From where I was sitting I had a clear view of Lenny's face. It was not signaling recognition. The person next to Lenny was taking Jack's measure as he closed the distance and was undoubtedly doing a quick review of the method he was going to use to take Jack down. Jack was talking, and I'm sure smiling, but I couldn't see his face.

At the last moment, Lenny realized the big guy hurtling toward him was the guy from Cedar Point who let him ride the Raptor. He broke into a big grin and soon everyone was shaking hands. Lenny's group was quickly escorted into a back room, but Lenny himself came over to our table. He was a very friendly guy. He complimented us on our coasters, especially the Raptor, and thanked us all again for the VIP treatment when he had been at the park. We all laughed about the Randy Travis versus Lenny Kravitz mix-up. Then he went around the table and shook hands with everyone in our group. He is a class act.

## Christmas in the Park

At the end of the 1994 season we decided to test a Christmas event at the park. Kings Island had done it semi-successfully in the 1980s but had dropped it after several years. The industry talk was that it just didn't make enough money to justify the effort, which included delaying ride maintenance work until after the holidays. The talk was also that it was a huge drag on full-time employee morale.

A group of managers had visited the Kings Island event, and I was a part of the group. We were there on a cold weeknight and attendance was low. You can't escape weather in this business. While frosted breath and falling snow might bring on the Christmas spirit, for most people it means an excuse to stay indoors. We all felt Kings Island had some built-in advantages, the two biggest being its location in a metropolitan area and several large indoor facilities. The Kings Island Festhaus could handle hundreds of guests and had adequate restrooms, food service options, and a large stage. And HEAT.

We approached our event cautiously. We dipped our toes in the ocean. We called it "Christmas in the Park." Our offering was minimal—but so was the admission price: zero. However, we did request that guests bring at least one canned food item as a donation. We opened Park Plaza, the large gift shop at the front of the park. We sold season passes, a few Christmas items (we sold Christmas in the Park mugs and a few other souvenir items), and leftover clothing and such from the 1994 season. The Midway Carrousel, located just inside the main gate, operated. There might have been a few smaller rides as well. At least one food stand, I think it was Bayou Refreshments, sold hot chocolate and snack items. We had a beautifully decorated Christmas tree on the midway. We set up an area with a stage and bleachers for local choir groups to perform. We filled the area just inside the main gate with Christmas lights. We played Christmas music on the park's sound system. Guest were restricted to the area near the park's main entrance.

The offering that generated the most interest was a horse-drawn carriage ride through the park. We used a local provider, who did an excellent job. The carriage was themed out, the driver in full costume. We sold out every night we were open. Guests loved riding through the park at night. The problem was capacity. Each ride was about 30 minutes and could accommodate up to six guests. I forget the number of hours we were open on an operating day, but it was probably four to five. I think we charged $10 per rider, so each ride could generate $60 and we could do no more than 10 rides per day. Do the math: $60 x 10 = $600. The vendor probably got $300, or half the take. Our gross revenue was $300. We generated that much in five minutes in a food stand on the midway during the season. We needed a dozen carriages, or we needed to charge $100 per rider. Neither option was feasible.

Our guests, especially those living locally, thought the event was grand. They didn't show up if it was too cold, too windy, too rainy, or too snowy (which was most days, of course, in December on Lake Erie), but when they did come they enjoyed being in the park. Their only real complaint was that there wasn't much to do (they were right).

Cedar Point, unlike Kings Island, did not have heated interior space of any consequence anywhere in the park, but especially not in the front of the park. There was literally no place to get warm. Our merchandise location had limited space and of course no seating.

We also had a distance perception to overcome in Cleveland and Toledo.

Christmas in the Park operated December 10-30, a total of 20 days/nights.

Most of the staff hours came from the operating divisions: Park Operations, Merchandise and Games, Food Service, Maintenance. Other divisions were pretty much unaffected. In Marketing, we helped generate awareness of the event with some local advertising and publicity efforts in Cleveland and Toledo.

In January, we did a recap. If we included the revenue from the sale of season passes, we came out marginally in the green, though in most cases the pass sales would have come in the spring anyway; it was a timing issue. Guests liked the event. The buzz was good. But they wanted more to do.

Dick Kinzel said no. Publicly and officially, we said Christmas in the Park was a fun experiment, but we were really not in the Christmas business. The event would not be repeated in 1995. The real reason is that Dick didn't feel he could ask his full-time staff to work the month of December. He told a group of us that it just struck him as he was walking the park on a cold, wet night and watching our employees do their jobs that they should all be at home with their families.

"I expect everything out of them during the season. (Which he did.) I can't ask them to do it in December," he said.

True enough. I always respected Dick for that decision. I believe it was the right decision for Cedar Point at the time. But times change, circumstances change, and Cedar Fair has successfully introduced Christmas events at several Cedar Fair parks (though not at Cedar Point) in recent years.

## Cedar Point Celebrates 125 Years

The summer of 1995 Cedar Point celebrated its 125th Anniversary. I was named to chair a committee to integrate the 125th into our marketing program as well as other aspects of park operations. It was an assignment I coveted, given my increasing role as the unofficial park historian. We had a great committee: Dan McManus, Robin Innes, Deb Hessler, Marje Rody, Candy Frankowski, Lee Alexakos, Connie Lewis, John Taylor, Ann Marie Whyte Muehlhauser, Paul Codispoti, and Katja Rall-Koepke. Lots of talent, lots of experience. As I write this, in the spring of 2018, 23 years later, only one of us, John Taylor, is still with the company. Marje passed away in 2015, and the others have all either retired or moved on. Cedar Point is starting to prepare for its 150th Anniversary in 2020.

In late season, 1994, we met with senior management and made our recommendations.

Our headline recommendation was to convert the Town Hall Museum to essentially a Cedar Point museum to be renamed the Museum of Amusements and Thrills. We proposed getting rid of most, if not all, the exhibits that did not tie directly to Cedar Point and adding to and expanding our park exhibits. Included was a hands-on children's exhibit. We proposed setting up a small retail operation to sell postcards, plates, and other collectibles. We estimated a $300,000 price tag to do this. Senior management was sympathetic, but no cigar. It was purely a matter of money, I was told. We could not afford to spend that amount on something which would not directly produce significant revenue; there were too many other priorities. I didn't like the decision, then or now, as I realized the 125th was the time to do it and it wouldn't get serious consideration again, if ever, until the 150th Anniversary when most of us would have left the company one way or another.

However, just about all our other recommendations were accepted: logo, name tags, banners, new ticket designs, souvenir merchandise. We reviewed plans to integrate the 125th into TV, radio, and print advertising. We did not have new ride in 1995. Our calling card was the Summer Spectacular and the 125th. And we were hoping for a strong sophomore year from Raptor.

It all worked. Attendance dropped less than 100,000 from 3.6 million to 3.5 million, despite the lack of a new ride. It was still a great performance, the second best in the history of the park.

In the summer of 1995 Cedar Fair made another acquisition: Worlds of Fun and Oceans of Fun in Kansas City. The company was growing fast.

The Raptor was Don Miears' focus his first year, but he really took ownership of the 1995 new attraction, the "Summer Spectacular," a laser, light, and music show. It was a big investment for a non-ride attraction, a gamble that it could hold interest for numerous seasons. It had worked at Valleyfair, but many were skeptical. The screen was massive, 50 feet by 72 feet, blocking the view up the midway and partially hiding the entrance to the CP&LE Railroad Station. The projection equipment was housed in a permanent tower approximately 200 feet in front of the screen; the building was 15 feet high, two booths connected by an open-air bridge.

The show itself was impressive and successful. The combination of lasers, music, lights, pyro wrapped around a feel-good theme that included a tribute to Cedar Point's 125th Anniversary and ended with Lee Greenwood's anthem "I'm proud to be an American" was a big hit. The show was about 15 minutes in length. There was a lot of senior staff input, but the creative direction was the responsibility of Marje Rody, who did a masterful job balancing all that input.

The viewing area took up most that portion of the midway. Because of the pyro, we had to close the Iron Dragon and a few other rides during the performance. We really didn't know whether guests would sit or stand during the performance, but most of us thought guests would opt to stand. Turns out guests mostly sat on the midway and only stood in the area behind the tower. We were wrong.

Cedar Points 125th Anniversary theme was worked into the show. We used lots of vintage images of the park, and it worked. Guests really liked seeing flashes of the old Cedar Point. Over the 16 seasons of its existence, the show used a lot of Cedar Point theming and imagery in the show presentation. Some of it could have been construed as blatantly promotional or commercial, and some in our management group thought our presentations were too commercial; but our guests didn't seem to feel that way about it. When the Raptor logo appeared on the screen, people cheered. When they saw POV video of the first drop on Millennium Force, they cheered. When they saw the launch of Top Thrill Dragster, they cheered. I think for most of our guests the Summer Spectacular was just a part of their Cedar Point experience. At the end of the day they liked reliving their ride experiences, their shared park experience with family and friends. I think they found it validating to see themselves up on that massive screen. It spoke to the power of our brand, our hold on the hearts of our guests.

Throughout that first season, Don Miears could be seen on the bridge between the two booths before, during, and after most shows. He was constantly tweaking our performance.

## Mantis (aka Banshee)

The 1996 season was another coaster year. This time it was a stand-up, a subset of the standard inverted coaster. In the stand-up riders literally stand up through the course of the ride, held securely in place by an over-the-shoulder harness and an adjustable bicycle-style seat. I had ridden a stand up at Kings Island several years before and it was a definite thrill. Our chosen manufacturer was B&M, fresh off their success with Raptor.

We budgeted aggressively, another 3.5 million attendance year.

Then came the name. We conducted the usual go-around with Marketing, the ad agency (M&F), Planning & Design, and senior management. I forget the names of the other candidates, but we settled on a name: Banshee. The name had come up in the past and had been on the list for the ride named Gemini. A Banshee in Gaelic folklore was an evil spirit or ghost associated with death. We all thought it was a pretty cool name: exotic, short, scary, great for theming. In

August 1995, we proceeded to plan a publicity event to announce the ride and started work on a logo and promotional materials.

Although pure Irish on my maternal side, my only knowledge of Banshees had come from the Walt Disney movie, "Darby O 'Gill and the Little People," I saw the movie as a young child and I recall the image of the Banshee had been very frightening.

The ride was announced September 8, right after Labor Day. The PR Department came up with a great plan. We set up a dais and seating near the ride site—behind the CP&LE Station and between the Iron Dragon and the Red Garter Saloon. Media and special guests were escorted to the area. At a specific point in the presentation, a helicopter appeared over Sandusky Bay headed toward park. As the chopper got closer you could see it was carrying something odd underneath it. As it got closer, the something odd looked more and more like a piece of coaster track, which in fact it was. The chopper flew right over the ride site and then carefully lowered the piece of track onto the midway. Our Maintenance crew unhooked the cables and gave the thumbs up and the cables went back into the chopper and it began ascending. It was a great show. Everyone was impressed. At the follow-up reception we handed out Banshee T-shirts and other promotional items. We were feeling pretty good about ourselves.

The euphoria didn't last long.

The next day, late in the afternoon, I got a call from Don Miears that Dick wanted to see us in his office right away.

"There's a problem with the ride name," was all he said.

I expected Dick to be angry and upset, but he was cool and even a little dispassionate. If he had gone through the anger stage, he was now past it. He was, however, determined. He told us at the outset of the meeting, smiling as I recall, not to waste any time trying to change his mind. He had made his decision. It was our job to manage things going forward.

"We have to change the name of the ride," he said. He held up a copy of the Sandusky Register. In their page one story on Banshee they had noted that according to their research a Banshee was a ghostly figure from Irish folklore who appeared prior to the death of someone in the family. "We can't have a roller coaster with a name associated with death," he said.

No one was to blame for all this, he said. We had all signed off on it. However, he had not been aware of the death association prior to reading the article.

Banshee was a great name for a coaster, but it would have to wait another 18 years.

Neither of us tried to talk Dick out of his decision. There were arguments to be made, but we didn't make them. We both knew nothing would change.

There was an immediate PR issue: we had to announce to the world we were changing the name of the ride within days of announcing it. There was precedent. Before it was the Corkscrew, the Corkscrew was the Great Lake Erie Roller. We survived that and we'd survive this. As we talked, my mind was racing as to how best to do get this accomplished. I knew the sooner we came up with a new name the better.

Word spread quickly in the park. Most employees thought Banshee was a good name for a high thrill roller coaster. The Marketing staff and the agency vented for a short time, then moved on.

Very quickly, all the Banshee promotional material we had created jumped in value: buttons, media kits, hats, T-shirts (especially T-shirts). Coaster enthusiasts of all types were particularly interested in the T-shirts. They would sell at a premium on eBay for many years (and probably still do). I have often joked that mine goes in my will. For years Dick kept a supply of Banshee T-shirts in his office which he had great fun handing out to VIP guests.

Our official reason for dropping the name was guest and media feedback on the death association with Banshee.

We were accused, of course, by the media and some guests, both publicly and privately, of manufacturing the whole thing just to gin up publicity on the new ride. Anyone who knew anything about our company culture knew that theory was nonsense. It irritated me that people were half serious about it.

Our PR staff, Robin Innes and Janice Lifke Witherow, did a great job handling the issue with the news media, which faded rather quickly. There was no social media to worry about. I was not involved with the damage control; my job was to get the coaster named.

We started from scratch. Again. We did a lot of field-testing in the park. We sent out groups of researchers who tested names and logos with park guests. Eventually, a few weeks later, we ended up with Mantis. I don't think anyone, in or out of the organization, ever thought Mantis was a great coaster name. It was not Magnum or Raptor or Iron Dragon or even Gemini. It was a "B" at best. But it was good enough. Yes, we probably settled.

On many levels, however, Mantis worked. In the bug world, the mantis is a cross between a great white shark and a T-Rex. Nasty animal. Carnivore. This was the mantis of the roller coaster, not the slow-moving, often stationery, light green stick insect children collect in backyards. The logo focused on the dark side. Many people fear large bugs. (Small bugs, too.)

When we announced the name, we got a "B" reaction. It fit.

To replicate the great success, we had had with the Raptor video, that fall we went full speed on a successor, a Mantis video. The folks at M&F came up with the story of a crazed scientist who accidentally creates a giant Mantis. It was about five minutes in length and very dark in tone and feel, almost a mini-horror film. It was beautifully filmed in an old building on the near west side of Cleveland. It had a very theatrical feel. However, the jump at the end from mad scientist and giant mantis to Cedar Point and roller coaster just did not feel right.

Dick Kinzel hated it. Absolutely hated it. He was expecting a dog, and he got a cat instead. Don Miears was cool to it. None of us were in rapture over it. On the park side, I was closest to the project and had been on site for the shoot and the edit. I appreciated what went into it, and I understood where M&F was coming from: Mantis was not Raptor; it would be a mistake just to replicate the formula; we needed to do something different; this approach would work well with the target market (12-24 with a male skew). However, Dick and Don were both looking for something more like the Raptor video. I did what I could to re-edit the video to make it more "Cedar Point" but it was a lost cause. It was not a dog, it was a cat. In the end, we distributed it just before Christmas and moved on.

Dick never did. He blamed M&F for creating a terrible product and, I believe, started looking forward to the day when M&F would no longer be our agency of record.

The 1996 season was perceived as less than successful, as attendance slipped to 3.4 million. The expectation was that with a big new coaster we could climb back up to the 3.6 million level.

Overall, Mantis performed well, a solid "B," which seemed to be its destiny. I confess I rode it only once. Going upside down numerous times while standing up was not much fun for me. There were some operational issues. B&M had designed a three-train operation which could in theory could deliver a significant hourly ride capacity, something Cedar Point required in a major coaster with a $12 million price tag. However, to get to a three-train operation consistently required a near perfect station operation. If the train was not unloaded and loaded very quickly, the following train would set up in the brakes just outside the station, which then meant the third train set up in the first brake (basic safety on multiple train coasters does not allow more than one train in a designated zone at one time). This slowed everything down and put a great capacity out of reach. Working the platform on the Mantis was a high pressure environment for ride crews. Only the best thrived given these challenges. A modification to the restraint system the following season further slowed station time and made it even more difficult to meet intervals. For most of its life, the Mantis devolved into a two-train operation. The third train was not part of the winter overhaul and ended up being scavenged for parts. On all but the busiest days, a two-train operation met demand.

## Second Agency Review

In the fall of 1996 we did an agency review. The folks at M&F were dumfounded, never saw it coming. This was understandable as attendance had been strong for several years. Our advertising program had been effective by any objective evaluation. However, Dick asked Don Miears and I to go out and shake the trees and see what else was out there. We started the process in September and made a final recommendation in mid-December. M&F participated in the review, but I knew in my heart it was a waste of time.

Don involved Jack Falfas in the review, which I guessed (correctly) to be part of his training for when he became a general manager. I assumed he was next in line when we made our next park acquisition. I thought it was a smart thing to do. I enjoyed Jack's participation in the process; he brought a different perspective.

The two finalists could not have been more different in terms of style, history, and culture. Liggett Stashower (LS) was a Cleveland shop, only one office, and officially could be termed a mid-size agency. It had made the finals in our 1988 review. Its roots in Cleveland went back to the World War II era (my mother had briefly worked there as a receptionist). Their offices were in the old Halle Brothers department store on Euclid Avenue. In my opinion their biggest asset was their creative director, Lynn Lilly, who I had first met during the 1988 review.

Their competition was the Detroit office of J. Walter Thompson. At the time, JWT was the largest ad agency in the world. The Detroit office was bifurcated into two arms: Ford Motor Company and everything else. One arm had a lot more muscle than the other. The non-Ford part of the shop was a decent-sized agency in its own right. Its two biggest clients were Kohl's department store and White Castle hamburgers.

JWT's pitch to us naturally capitalized on their strengths: they could leverage the agency's incredible buying power on our behalf; the talent resources of their Ford team could be tapped as needed; they knew the Detroit market (Cedar Point's largest) better than anyone. They clearly believed bigger was better, but they had carved out an agency within an agency that was hands-on and appropriate to our needs. We got the benefits of big, but we also got the benefits of small.

The Liggett Stashower pitch was essentially about passion. They would do whatever it took to bring us great advertising. They were customers, too. They knew Cleveland. They knew our history, our brand. They had their not-so-secret weapon: Lynn Lilly.

We agonized over the decision, bringing both agencies back for a second "final" interview. Don Miears left the decision to me. I went with JWT, mostly, because I thought it would be good to settle the big agency question. I wanted to see if they could really deliver on the media-buying and strategy disciplines. I also thought it would be beneficial to have an agency that was Detroit based after so many years of Pittsburgh and Cleveland.

The most impressive person at Liggett Stashower was the creative director. The most impressive person at JWT was the director of client service.

I chose with my head, not my heart, and it is one decision I would like to have back.

Our relationship with JWT lasted only two seasons, 1997 and 1998. The 1997 season was an attendance disaster by our standards. The advertising got some of the blame (it always does), but probably bigger factors were poor weather, an admission price increase, and the lack of a big new attraction. The debut of Chaos, a small carnival class ride, didn't provide a compelling reason to visit the park. In 1997, we did add a major upgrade to Soak City, including a wave pool, more slides, and new kids' areas. But attendance at City did not have a measurable effect on Cedar Point. JWT was a good shop, but the chemistry just wasn't there.

JWT did help us launch HalloWeekends that fall, even in a lame duck role, and did a fine job.

## Cedarpoint.com

I saw firsthand the power of the internet one July afternoon in 1999. My phone rang, and I answered it. The voice on the other line was male and had what I thought was a Spanish accent. He explained he was calling on behalf of his advertising agency, one of the largest in Europe. He said he was calling from Lisbon, Portugal. Their client, if memory serves, was Volkswagen. They were introducing a new model and the agency had come up with an ad concept for print and outdoor that involved the image of a roller coaster.

I asked if they had a specific coaster in mind.

Turns out they did.

"We would like to use one of your roller coasters in this ad. It is called Mean Streak. I am looking at it right now on your website," he said.

I was shocked, though I suppose I shouldn't have been. This was power, transforming power. He told me they had conducted a search on the internet and found Cedar Point and the Mean Streak.

We ended up cutting a deal. They paid us a handsome location fee for the rights to use the Mean Streak in the ad. In September, they sent a team of four people to the U.S. to do the job. We scheduled the shoot for a weekday, so the park would be closed, and they would have all the time they needed. It was a happy ending for all involved.

I was an internet fan from the first, in part because I believed it would likely become a terrific marketing tool. I pushed hard to get the funds to build our first website. We used a new division of M&F, focused on digital services, to build our first website, which debuted in December 1995. We added visitors every month, an upward trajectory that never ceased. The early editions of the Cedar Point website were informational. We saw the website as a better version of our best park brochure. As time went by we added more and more information.

In the summer of 1997, during lunch at Breakwater Café (located at the very tip of the peninsula adjacent to Sandcastle Suites), my friend Dave Francis, the Cedar Point historian, mentioned he had referred two of his business to business clients to a small digital company in Wadsworth called Website Design & Development (WDD). His clients were very happy, he said. The company principals were a husband and wife team: Katie and Mark Bruno. Katie, he told me, held a doctorate in polymer science from the University of Akron, a world leader in the field.

I was intrigued. I gave WDD a call and a few weeks later I met Katie for lunch at the Breakwater Café. It turned out to be an eventful meeting. She did indeed have a doctorate in polymer science. She got her initial experience putting together a website for her department. One thing led to another and she and her husband soon had a viable business. They had three young children at home; they had a big incentive to grow the company. Katie was the face of WDD. Mark was the programmer and mostly back of the house.

For an hour she dissected our current website and offered ideas on how to improve it. I was impressed. Clearly, she wanted to move past the website as brochure strategy. She saw great opportunities to make it more interactive, including a customized trip planner, and to ultimately develop e-commerce capability.

We made the change to WDD.

I was impressed by Katie and Mark's drive, their ambition to grow, their intelligence, their technical skills. Over a period of 15 years they assumed a major role in managing the websites of Cedar Point and our sister parks. However, nothing lasts forever. With the acquisition of the Paramount Parks, and then the expansion of the Cedar Fair corporate marketing program, it was decided to go in a new direction.

WDD has gone on to become a major website supplier for small parks and Family Entertainment Centers.

# Cross Training Program

In 1997 I got an opportunity to participate in what was called the Cedar Fair Cross Training Program, a corporate program put together by Dick Kinzel to prepare managers with leadership potential to become park general managers. In 1997, we were four parks and soon to be five with the Knott's Berry Farm acquisition that fall. Senior management wisely wanted to develop a bench so that when a GM slot opened there was a pool of qualified people to choose from. I was flattered and grateful I was one of the managers chosen to participate.

I never thought Dick Kinzel was a big believer in academic training when it came to business. His business school was the midway. It certainly worked for him. The training program for future general managers was a series of visits to the Cedar Fair parks and shadowing senior managers in a variety of park disciplines. It made sense for learning the specifics of the business, the grit of it. Spending a day on the midway with a park GM was worth 20 pounds of business books.

In late May I got my assignment. In June, I would spend several days at Worlds of Fun, our park in Kansas City; in July and August I would spend several days at Valleyfair, near Minneapolis and at Dorney Park in Allentown, Pennsylvania. I would also work a night shift in Cedar Point's cash control operation.

The Cross Training experience was one of the best experiences of my 40 years with the company. I learned a lot, and looking back both short term and long term I used the experience to make many decisions. Cross Training also opened a window to the other Cedar Fair parks.

At Worlds of Fun, I got a class in project management from Dan Keller, the GM, who was overseeing the construction of their hyper coaster, Mamba, due to open in 1998. I remember the massive spreadsheet he unveiled, his key to keeping the project on track. He took me through it in detail.

Walt Wittmer, GM at Valleyfair, talked to me about his management philosophy, which for him was all about the difference between being a manager and a leader. Walt told me he aspired to be a leader first. He said leadership was his primary function. He said he wanted to give people the freedom to create. "I try to listen to people," he said. "That's my number one job."

I asked Alan Schwartz, the finance vice president at Valleyfair, if he could sum up for me in a word or two the most important concept in finance. He didn't hesitate: "Documentation. Financial systems are about documenting activity that involves money."

At Worlds of Fun, I asked Phil Bender, director of revenue operations, which was the toughest park discipline. He said food services, in part because of the physical requirements.

I spent much of my time at Dorney Park with John Albino, the GM. He shared with me some his thoughts about being a GM. At that time, he'd been on the job three years. Seven years later, I would literally be in his shoes.

Some of his observations:

- Nothing really prepares you.
- The "loneliness of command" takes some getting used to.
- General Managers need PR training and presentation skills.
- You can delegate authority but not responsibility.
- This isn't a democracy.
- Sign all checks. Sign off on all purchase orders over a specified level. Sign off on all change order on capital projects.

Daryl Smith, a former Cedar Point colleague who now headed up Park Operations at Dorney, when I asked him for a one-word definition of operations, replied: "Procedures. Operations is all about adherence to procedures."

He believed the most critical relationship in any amusement park is between Operations and Maintenance, and he believed it was the GM's responsibility to ensure it was a good relationship. Daryl had good insight.

## Power Tower

In 1998, Cedar Point introduced Power Tower, a creation of Stan Checketts of S&S Worldwide in Logan, Utah. A $10 million investment, we committed to marketing it as we would a major new coaster. It consisted of two Turbo Drops and two Space Shot rides put together, all operated by a pneumatic system.

It was an impressive ride with a small horizontal footprint. The vertical side of things was another matter. The top of the tower was 300 feet above the ground.

You sit four abreast on a tiny seat which is ever so slightly tilted forward so you feel like you could slide off rather easily. If you are unlucky, you sit in one the outside seats so there is nothing next to you but air. The restraint system is an over-the-shoulder horse collar harness similar to what's used on inverted coasters. There is a web-style strap that connects the harness to the seat. The system does not feel adequate for the task at hand. But 35 engineers say it is.

If you are riding the Space Shot, you are lifted slowly off the pad while the ride's brain adjusts for several factors, including the weight of the platform. A moment or two later, as the anticipation is cresting, you and your 15 other platform mates are shot straight upward at 50 mph to a height of 275 feet. Then you drop down, only to bounce (on air) back up again, each subsequent bounce being shorter. It's quite a thrill. I did it. Once.

The Turbo Drop ride experience may well be the most terrifying in the park. From the ground the platform rises slowly but steadily to the top of the tower. At first, it's not so bad, but as the platform gets above 100 feet or so the fear of heights gene starts to do its work. There are great views to enjoy no matter which side you are sitting on. I recall the horrifying feeling that I was sliding forward on the seat. Then I made the mistake of looking to my right and there was nothing, nothing but air, and nothing but air beneath my chair. I was terrified. It gets worse when you reach the top and poise, motionless, for several seconds (or several eternities) until you are shot down at 50 mph, bouncing back up on air just when you feel you are going to hit the ground.

One experience was enough for me.

The Power Tower had a lot going for it: great ride experience, visual appeal (especially at night), good capacity (1,800 rides per hour), good location, unique sound, and relatively low maintenance.

The advertising campaign for Power Tower was a good one, in my opinion, but attendance was soft in early season and into July. We were all getting restless with JWT. The client service director had been promoted and was less involved with our account. I sensed it was becoming a chore for them to make the two hour drive from Detroit to Sandusky for meetings. Don Miears and Dick Kinzel were disappointed in the attendance. It became more and more obvious to me that JWT just wasn't a good fit for our business. I did not see the relationship getting any better. I talked with Don and Dick and at the end of July I made the phone call and ended the relationship with JWT.

They did not see it coming, but they handled the break very professionally.

I convinced Don Miears we did not need to do another major review. We had just done one two years before. I told him I thought we should meet with Liggett Stashower and update one another and talk about the business and see if we could come to an agreement that worked for both parties. Don agreed. The meeting was a success, and Dick blessed it as well. By Labor Day, Liggett Stashower was on board.

## Magnum Turns 10 / Camp Snoopy

In 1999, we celebrated the 10th Anniversary of Magnum. We had learned in our experience with the Cedar Point 125th Anniversary, and the way Disney had successfully milked anniversaries for years, that anniversaries, if done right, are great marketing hooks. The public, and the new media, love anniversaries. Without a new ride, the Magnum 10th would be our ride message. Although pushed by Raptor, guest surveys showed it was our most popular ride, a brand treasure. Liggett Stashower and the creative team at Planning & Design came up with great advertising and promotional materials for the anniversary. The PR Department created a number of special events and media events, especially in early season, to promote the Magnum anniversary. It all worked. Magnum led the way in 1999 for our ride messaging.

Cedar Point introduced Camp Snoopy in 1999, a Peanuts-themed area located off the Gemini midway. It was Cedar Point's first major capital addition with Peanuts branding since we had acquired Knott's Berry Farm and had negotiated a license to use Snoopy and his friends at Cedar Point. Camp Snoopy was modeled off Camp Snoopy at Knott's; we freely borrowed ride theming, signage, and actual attractions. Camp Snoopy opened with nine rides, a show area, themed food stand, and a retail shop. I recall the effort to get it open by opening day was legendary. Delays from some of the ride manufacturers was the biggest problem. Jack Fletcher, our ride maintenance supervisor, oversaw the project. Jack was a pusher and not one to back away from a challenge. He made it work.

Our advertising messaging that year was classically bifurcated: one set of messages for teens and young adults focusing on Magnum's 10th Anniversary; the other set for young families focusing on Camp Snoopy. We also had a whole park/resort message we used for our direct response and distant market programs.

The decade ended with another three million attendance year. In fact, Cedar Point attendance topped the three million attendance mark for the entire decade, a new record and one still intact. The 1990s had been great for Cedar Point. We turned the corner into the new millennium with a full head of speed.

In fact, we had plans to own the year 2000.

## Chapter 14
# Glory Road-Part 2
**Millennium Force, Top Thrill Dragster,
and David Letterman**

## There's No Force Like Millennium Force

Millennium Force is a ride like no other. It is the world's best steel roller coaster; in my opinion it is the best roller coaster yet built, steel or wood.

After four years without a new roller coaster, it was time. Dick Kinzel, and really all of us in management, wanted to extend the Corkscrew-Gemini-Iron Dragon-Magnum-Mean Streak-Disaster Transport-Raptor-Mantis bloodline. It was what we did: build another coaster, cementing even stronger our claim to be the best coaster park in the world. It was an old, but successful strategy: roller coasters and resorts.

It was not an automatic slam dunk with our board of directors, especially with a $25 million price tag. I was fortunate enough to be part of the team that pitched the ride to the board in November 1998. The meeting was in a conference room in the offices of Squire Sanders, a large law firm located in the Key Bank Building in downtown Cleveland. We were up high, near the top of the very tall building and we were in a corner conference room which overlooked the new Cleveland Browns Stadium. The room had glass, way too much glass, on two walls, and floor to ceiling. I was more than a bit unnerved. It was a gray, overcast fall day, common to the Great Lakes in November. But our job was to talk about summer.

My assignment was to present the product strategy—why we needed another world class coaster and why we believed the marketplace would reward us for building it. With assistance from Planning & Design, we put together a beautiful hand out with charts, graphs, images, and good clear copy that made our case very well. I was able to stand with my back to the glass, thank God, while I did my part of the presentation. The eyes of the board were mostly friendly, and I think they could sense that I was a true believer, which I was. There were some skeptics, at least at first. The questions were good and mostly, I remember, focused on what could be alternatives to such a huge investment. In the end, there weren't any. Mary Ann Jorgenson, a lawyer with Squire Sanders & Dempsey, and a leader on

**Millennium Force.** CEDAR POINT ARCHIVES

the board, asked a lot of questions but finally called for a vote and we got our coaster.

What Dick wanted was a ride that would surpass Magnum but would carry the same genetic code: steel structure, tubular steel track, no inversions, high capacity, world class stats: highest, steepest, fastest. Lee Jewett had identified a potential location for the queue and the station: the bay side of the park, utilizing the area where the Giant Wheel then stood behind the CP&LE station. The course itself would include parts of the Frontier Trail and the Island. It was a very tight fit. There were some at the park who feared cramming a huge coaster in this space would kill the ambiance of the Frontier Trail, though the ambiance had been in decline for years.

There were two manufacturers considered for the project: Intamin, a European firm that had designed Thunder Canyon and Avalanche Run and some smaller rides at Cedar Point; and D.H. Morgan, whose principals had been involved in the design of Magnum, Gemini, Corkscrew, and several rides at other Cedar Fair parks. B&M was not considered because their expertise was really restricted to inversion coasters (also, as I recall, they were committed to several new coaster projects that would make it impossible for them to do the project within our timeline).

A 300-foot plus lift hill—one of Dick Kinzel's specs—required a certain amount of real estate. The height of the first hill largely defined how long the ride had to be. The energy created by a 300-foot drop had to be dissipated in a proper way. The combination of speed, angle of descent, height of secondary hills, track design, track layout had to all come together to provide a great ride experience—but in a defined space. The biggest issue in some ways was the lift hill itself. Traditional coasters like Magnum used a chain lift to get the trains to the top. There are practical limits on the speed the chain can move a train up the hill.

Magnum coaster trains take almost a minute and a half from the time they engage the chain to the time they drop off the first hill. The rest of the ride, until the train hits the trim brakes outside the station, is a flash in comparison. No one is complaining. The ride to the top is thrilling, and the view is spectacular, but adding another 105 feet to the lift hill would mean a much longer ride up. It would significantly impact the capacity of the ride.

Morgan's solution to the problem was to utilize two lift chains rather than one monstrous chain. Still, it would require a long ride up the lift hill, and it would use all the space and then some we had allocated for the ride.

Intamin approached the site limitations and the lift hill challenges with a more creative solution, which also provided some added benefits.

Intamin proposed utilizing elevator technology to solve the lift hill challenge. Instead of the train attaching to two different chains which circulate up and back, it would attach to a steel cable which was wound around a massive drum at the bottom of the hill. The cable could be wound much faster than the chain could move up and down the hill. It was smoother, easier, but mostly it was faster. And it took up less space. And it allowed the climb up the first hill to happen at a much steeper angle.

This new strategy for coaster design impressed the Cedar Point team, including Dick Kinzel, Don Miears, and Lee Jewett. As things turned out, this would be the last coaster for Lee and Don. Don retired in 2000 and Lee in 2001. The new guys, directed by a Hungarian engineer named Sandor Kernacs, got the order. Construction began in August 1999 with the removal of dozens and dozens of trees, some of them old cottonwoods probably 200 years old. It was painful watching these grand old trees turn into pulpwood, but big old trees are somewhat problematical in a place like Cedar Point. An amusement park is not an old growth forest. The loose sandy soil on the peninsula has poor holding power and cottonwoods especially are prone to splitting. Cedar Point is often hit with severe summer thunderstorms that can kick up near hurricane force winds for brief periods. Tornados are less common but do occur. In my 40 year career we experienced three tornados. The safety issue is a real one.

The character of Frontier Trail did change with the construction of Millennium Force, but the Trail had already changed from the pristine themed area it was in the 1970s. But enough trees and foliage were left to still make it a respite from the main midway.

Millennium Force was the son of Magnum, and an attempt to duplicate its success. It succeeded. The son eclipsed its father, certainly as a revenue-producer and a brand-builder. Millennium Force generated 3.4 million visitors in 2000, its first year. To some on the staff it was a disappointment, as they believed a ride as great as Millennium Force should generate Raptor-type numbers. But there were several factors working against a big attendance surge.

One was that the introduction of Millennium Force was accompanied by a $5 increase in the admission price. The increase was covered extensively by the media. The regional economy was reasonably strong in 2000, but it was starting to weaken in advance of the 2001 recession. Finally, and perhaps more importantly, 2000 was the year our northeast Ohio competitor, Geauga Lake, was rebranded by its owner, Premier Parks, as Six Flags Worlds of Adventure (SFWOA) and introduced four new roller coasters and conducted a massive advertising campaign to go with it. Some Cedar Point visits, and some second and third visits, were lost to SFWOA simply out of the market's desire to see what it was all about. But as Bruce Jackson, our CFO, stated when anyone bemoaned the fact that we didn't hit the 1994 and 1995 attendance numbers: "Don't let anyone ever tell you 2000 was a disappointment. It was an incredible year."

Liggett Stashower had the opportunity to help launch Millennium Force. Like Raptor and Magnum before it, Millennium Force was a dream assignment. I told the creative team the advertising had to match the ride. It had to be equal to it. We needed a campaign that generated incredible buzz in the marketplace during the construction period and during the pre-season, and then gave our guests a compelling taste of the ride experience once the coaster had opened.

The agency created a logo, and a backstory to go with it in the form of a short video. The logo was elegant in its simplicity: a line drawing, slightly exaggerated, of a coaster hill. It looked and felt smooth and free-flowing, very current, like good-looking cursive. It did not have a "heartbeat" but it still worked. The logo also reflected the look of the actual ride, with its wide sweeping curves.

The video backstory showed the logo popping up mysteriously all over the globe. The video was a success. We sent it to our usual lists, plus some new ones.

From my perspective, the construction of the ride went relatively smooth, though as the marketing guy I did not sit in the weekly construction meetings chaired by Don Miears. My focus was selling it, not building it. The station design differed significantly from Raptor, Mantis, or Magnum. In these coasters, riders entered and exited the ride at the same place, what was termed a flush station. With Millennium Force, riders exit the ride at one end of the station, the unload position. The train then moves empty to the load position, where riders board the train. There are benefits to this design in terms of capacity, but a major problem is that, unlike Raptor for, example, guests do not have an opportunity to put loose objects (hats, backpacks, purses, etc.) in a storage bin to retrieve after they have returned to the station. What this meant was that guests were required to place loose objects in a locker or with a non-rider before getting in line. We of course provided lockers proximate to the ride and we of course charged for their use (which was resented by many guests as they were used to the Raptor-Magnum-Mantis system.) The revenue was considerable, as were the complaints, but there was no going back.

Millennium Force was a $25 million project and included moving the Giant Wheel from its original 1972 location to an area along the beach close to Disaster Transport.

# First Ride on Millennium Force

I got my first ride on Millennium Force on a clear, cold Saturday afternoon in early April. The ride was undergoing testing and I got word from my good friend Rich Helzel, then vice president of park operations, that Saturday might be a good day to stop by and grab a ride. I was anxious to ride and anxious to compare it to Magnum.

The speed of the ascent is amazing, especially for a rider used to the Magnum. The Millennium Force covers 310 feet in 18 seconds; the Magnum covers 205 feet in 90 seconds. You are also going upward at a severe angle, heading, it seems, straight into the sky. On that first ride it was a bright and sunny day and I remember glancing below and to my left at Sandusky Bay and noticing dark spots underneath the water which marked objects on the bay floor.

I had the good fortune to ride in the front seat (the front seat is always the best seat in my opinion, though others claim the middle seats or more commonly the back seat). I rode with Rich Helzel, who kept up a running commentary on the technical aspects of the ride structure. He was already a veteran rider.

As you reach the top the train slows down and the angle flattens and the horizon opens up: Kelleys Island, Marblehead Peninsula, and Lake Erie. There is a brief slow down as the train goes over the lift and the weight of the train is evenly distributed between the two sides of the hill. But then gravity takes over and the train quickly accelerates. There is the visual sensation that you are going beyond 90 degrees, that the track is tucking back under the hill, but then it straightens out and your eyes are focused on the bottom of the hill which looks like it is going to smack you in the face and then carry you underground.

Riders are exposed on Millennium Force. The seats are raised up, and the second seats in each train as well, a kind of modified theatrical design. The restraint system is a T-bar that flattens against your mid-section. There is a seatbelt across your lower waist. You have no sense of being enclosed in a shell; rather the opposite, you feel like you're riding on top of a telephone pole. All this is by design, beautiful design.

I have, in easily more than 75 rides, never once raised my hands going down the first hill.

At the bottom of the hill, the train hits 93 mph, and your body reacts appropriately. It's quite an experience, as they say, like no other.

To me, the best parts of Millennium Force are the big sweeping curves at high speed, as the train roars out onto what is now Adventure Island and then shoots back through the tunnel toward the station. The track route is inspired with just the right amounts of sweep, airtime, and twists (the train banks sharply several times but never inverts). It is a big experience: visually, physically, and emotionally. And it is all delivered on a track that is incredibly smooth. In some ways, that smoothness is the ride's biggest achievement, especially considering its immense size. The difference in smoothness between Magnum and Millennium Force is stark. Magnum feels almost Stone Age after riding Millennium Force.

It all comes together: the edginess provided by the exposed seating, the ascent, the drop off the first hill, the beautiful high bank, the big sweeping turns, the roar as the train comes out of the tunnel and runs past the station to the half helix ahead of the station brake. Millennium Force is the most elegant roller coaster ever built, and also the most thrilling. Hard to be both. The ride is a work of art.

Millennium Force was the first coaster to top 300 feet; it was the world's first giga coaster.

## Media Day and Vanderbilt Graduation

Naturally, we planned a big media introduction for Millennium Force. Our challenge was to top the effort we had done for Raptor. One major difference was that there was no internet in 1994, but there was in 2000. But our launch strategy was still built around saturation TV coverage: get as many media outlets as possible to come to the park just before opening day and do stories about this great new roller coaster. Get as much reach as possible, which only TV (mainly broadcast) could really provide. We knew we could get media coverage throughout the season on a one-to-one basis, but there was only one grand opening. We wanted to be on the news in Chicago, Atlanta, and Tucson as well as Cleveland, Detroit, Toledo, and Columbus. The goal: everywhere.

For TV stations, we hired a Cleveland production company to set up shop at Cedar Point by Millennium Force, taking over the interior of the Red Garter Saloon. We reserved satellite time so that TV news reporters could transmit their stories back to their home stations right from Cedar Point. Essentially, we created our own editing studio. Some TV stations brought their own trucks, but most relied on the facilities we provided for them. We did everything we could to make it easy for the media to come to the park to cover the opening of the ride. For radio stations, we put together a kind of motorcycle helmet that could accommodate a small microphone and transmitter, so a station could conduct an interview on the ride itself. Dan Feicht did his usual magic working with Maintenance and Safety to design and create a mounting system for the coaster train that would accommodate a digital TV camera.

Our PR team—Robin Innes, Janice Lifke Witherow, and Dan Feicht, made it all work and did a splendid job. They were true pros. Looking back, I think it was the most successful media day we put together in my years at the park. My job was to manage senior management, be available for interviews (which I loved doing), charm any VIP guests, and stay out of the way.

We scheduled Media Day for the Thursday before the park's opening day on Saturday. This gave Park Operations and Maintenance a day to recover from Media Day, finish up last minute construction issues, and fine tune training of the ride crew.

It also fortunately provided a window for me to attend our sons' college graduation, which was scheduled for Friday, May 12, 2000, sandwiched in between Media Day and Opening Day. On Tuesday, Marie and I drove down to Nashville. On Wednesday afternoon, I flew back from Nashville to Cleveland, so I could be at the park for Media Day on Thursday. Late Thursday afternoon, I flew back to Nashville. Graduation was Friday. On Saturday Marie and I drove back to Sandusky. Crazy.

Don Miears was very supportive of my travel schedule and my attempt to be in two places at almost the same time. He approved the company providing me a driver to and from the airport on Thursday and Friday, which I greatly appreciated. I admit I threaded the needle between family and work that week.

Graduation Day in Nashville was hot and humid, as expected, a touch of July in May. There were thunder storm threats all morning, and we saw the occasional blue/black line on the horizon, but our part of Nashville was spared. There is no graduation or commencement speaker at Vanderbilt. The Vanderbilt tradition is for the chancellor to hand out each diploma to each graduate as the graduate's name is announced. It is a nice tradition, but it makes for a long ceremony.

I wore a light-colored summer suit, and a white fedora to protect my head and face from the sun. Marie wore a blue and white dress she had bought for the occasion. We carried umbrellas. The boys wore robes, of course, and underneath shorts and a shirt. It was not a long walk from the hotel across campus to the main quad, where hundreds and hundreds of brown wooden folding chairs had been set up in front of the stage. We made sure we got there early enough to get seats.

I remember the sky that day, perhaps because we were concerned about the thunder storm threat. I remember it was very blue. The sun was quite warm, but clean, and the air did smell good, a combination of all those Southern flowers blooming everywhere. Marie and I talked quite a bit, rambled in conversation over the lives of the boys and our visits to Nashville the past four years. We followed the ceremonies (the class of 2000 came last), checking off sections in the program as the morning wore on. We were both relaxed and happy.

We did hear Mike and Tom's name announced as they received their diplomas. I tried to take their pictures, but we were far away, and they pretty much got lost in the shuffle. We got plenty afterward.

After graduation, the mother of one of the boys' friends hosted a dinner at a local Italian restaurant not far from campus and graciously invited us to attend. While we were waiting for our table in the restaurant bar I glanced up at the TV monitor on the wall. There it was: Millennium Force. POV shots of the first hill, then various shots of the structure, basically the story our PR staff had put together and put out on the satellite. I heard the voice-over talk about the stats and the fact it was now open at Cedar Point in Sandusky, Ohio, near Cleveland. I cannot remember now if it was a local station or a network like CNN. But I was thrilled. It was a great day.

The author with Stan Cheketts, creator and manufacturer of Skyhawk, the park's new ride for 2006, at Media Day. The author is smiling. The ride manufacturer is not. COURTESY OF SANDUSKY REGISTER

The ride was an instant hit. The ride lines the first two weekends were perhaps the longest I can ever recall for a ride, once or twice stretching down the Frontier Trail as far as the Candle Shop. The news media reported six to seven hour waits. This was crazy, of course, but it probably was more than three hours at times. Overall, the ride performed very well the first part of the season, but even minor hiccups caused guest problems because demand was heavy and constant. Everyone wanted to ride Millennium Force. There were no disappointed riders. In fact, looking back I cannot in all the time Millennium Force and I shared the park ever remember a guest feeling the ride did not meet or exceed their expectations. It is fun being associated with a product that good.

## The Running of the Bulls

In those days, we held guests outside the turnstiles until the park officially opened. This was true at all admission gates: Main, Marina, Beach, and Resort. Shortly after the season started, we noticed a new guest phenomenon: as soon as the gates opened, guests began charging down the midway to get in line to ride Millennium Force. It wasn't just a few guests; usually it was hundreds, on some days it felt like it was all guests. They ran as fast as they could; it could rightly be called a charge. Most were young—but certainly not all. There were lots of families that seemed to be all dragging one another, balls of yarn tumbling down a hill. And they were all happy. Their faces had big broad smiles as their fists pumped in the air.

Many were giddy and laughing. It was not a stampede; they had a single purpose and remained fixed on the goal to the extent we had the occasional slip or fall or an inadvertent bump along the rail. The distance from the Main Gate to the entrance is about one quarter mile. Some did not make it and geared back to a fast walk.

Between the Cedar Point Cinema and Coaster's Restaurant, on a wide part of the midway, the four streams of guests from each entrance came together in a river that flowed past Iron Dragon and over the railroad tracks and into Millennium Plaza.

We called this phenomenon "The Running of the Bulls," a reference to the annual event in Pamplona, Spain, where hundreds of people run down the streets of the city with the bulls which have been selected to fight in the arena during the annual festival. I don't remember who coined the phrase, but it stuck and has been used for many years within the employee world at Cedar Point.

Guests ran as if bulls were chasing them for one reason: to avoid waiting in line for two to three hours to ride Millennium Force. The coaster was the king of the midway.

Millennium Force had good capacity, approximately 1,400 riders per hour, and it could run in a drizzle or light rain (though with fewer trains). In its first year it gave over a million rides and would average more than 1.1 million per year going forward. Its biggest ongoing maintenance issue in its first year was the need to constantly replace wheels. The combination of heat and speed was hard on the wheels. We always had enough replacement wheels on hand to keep the ride open— and Jack Fletcher and his crew got expert at changing them out quickly, but it required the ride to shut down for a period of time, usually 20 minutes, which is not a good thing on a warm sunny afternoon when there is already a more than two hour wait to ride the ride.

Finally, our Maintenance team and Intamin found a supplier who suggested a different spec for the wheel and the problem was solved. The biggest single downtime issue was a broken lift cable on Labor Day weekend. The cable broke about 30 feet from the top of the hill on Saturday morning. Fortunately, the problem occurred during a test run so there were no guest issues. Intamin thought a cable would last two seasons, not one. Our Ride Maintenance crew did a herculean job getting the spare cable installed in time for the following weekend.

In my time at the park we had to take guests off the train and back down the lift hill to the station a handful of times. It was never a fun activity for either guests or employees, but under the guidance of the manufacturer we had worked out procedures so that it could be done safely. There are no steps going up the lift hill on Millennium Force. Instead, the manufacturer had provided a small (two-three person) car called a funicular, which could be powered up and down the track, parallel to it. The common purpose of the funicular is to provide a way for maintenance crews to get to the upper reaches of the hill to work on the ride. But it was dual purpose.

It also provided a way for guests to be safely evacuated from the ride if need be. Guests were tied off to the ride structure and then assisted into the funicular, and then taken down to the station. It took more than an hour to unload a full train. We only did it when we felt it was the only option. There are always issues: weather, time of day, the time it will likely take to fix the problem so that the lift cable can be restarted, and the train can get to the top and drop off the hill.

Guests were usually very understanding. The timid ones never got on the ride to begin with. We offered guests immediate boarding on other coasters, which was always well received, though it seems counter intuitive at first. However, for guests we were giving back time, a valuable commodity. Getting immediate boarding on Top Thrill Dragster and/or Maverick effectively meant adding two to four hours to their day in the park. Plus, it felt good to get escorted to the front of the line. Depending on the circumstances, we usually made an offer of a courtesy return visit as well.

Over the years, Millennium Force has received many accolades, including receiving the Golden Ticket as the World's Best Steel Roller Coaster a record 12 times. It consistently is voted the park's best coaster in in-park surveys. If Dick Kinzel wanted to impress a VIP guest, whether it was a Wall Street banker or a famous athlete, he walked them out to ride Millennium Force. I did the same. So did every other senior manager at the park.

In my opinion, there have been four great signature rides at Cedar Point over the past 50 years: Blue Streak (1964 – 1975); Gemini (1978 – 1988); Magnum (1989 – 1999); and Millennium Force (2000 -?). Blue Streak, Gemini and Magnum each enjoyed a reign of 10 seasons as the kings of the Cedar Point midway, a decade each when they were unquestionably the park's best rides. Millennium Force is at 17 seasons and counting. The new coaster for 2018, Steel Vengeance, is serious competition. It delivers an outstanding ride experience, but in my opinion Millennium Force is still the King.

## IAAPA Summer Meeting, Wicked Twister

Don Miears retired after the 2000 season. He was 65. His successor was Dan Keller, who had been the GM of Worlds of Fun since we had acquired the park in 1995. He and I were the same age, 51, though his tenure in the company was two years longer. A Sandusky native, he had worked seasonally at the park in college and started full time in the Foods division in 1972. He became the VP of food services in 1980 and later senior VP of operations under Dick Kinzel. Dan was my boss for three seasons, until I transferred to Dorney Park in 2004. He was intelligent, organized, analytical, focused on metrics and quantitative measurement. He was a planner and a manager; he ran good meetings. He had a cool head. He was easy to work for. His expectations and his standards were high, but there were no left hooks that came out of nowhere.

On October 25, 2000, at the annual conference of the Ohio Travel Association (OTA) at Sawmill Creek Resort in Huron, I received the Paul Sherlock Award. The award recognizes ongoing contributions to the promotion of travel and tourism for the state of Ohio. The late Paul Sherlock was Ohio's first travel director. I found out after the presentation that I had been nominated by Joan van Offeren and Lee Alexakos. The award was presented to me by Bill Schwartz, a longtime friend and fellow past president of the OTA. This recognition was the most significant of my career, and one I treasure. It was also a surprise.

The OTA is the umbrella trade organization for the travel and tourism industry in Ohio. I had been active with the OTA for many years, including service as a board member and then going through the chairs to serve as OTA president in 1996.

I had hired Joan as my administrative assistant in 1979. She was from Milan, only 15 miles south of the park, and had gone to school to become a radiology tech; however, she discovered she was misplaced in healthcare. Perhaps the most naturally outgoing person I've ever worked with, Joan quickly earned a promotion to PR representative.

In 1985 she left Cedar Point to become the executive director of the Erie County Visitors and Convention Bureau, a position she held for more than 30 years, until shortly before her death from cancer in 2017. Joan had become a leader in the tourism industry at both the state and local level. Joan was also a good friend as well as a colleague. She was also close to Marie. Marie had done free-lance work for Joan, and they bonded as Master Gardeners, too.

Marie and I dedicated our 2014 book on the history of tourism in the region, "Lake Erie's Shores and Islands," to Joan.

In 2001, there was no new ride; Millennium Force had soaked up a lot of capital dollars, certainly enough for two seasons. But Cedar Point never stands still. In 2001, we opened a Johnny Rockets restaurant in the former site of Fascination on the main midway. We also opened Lighthouse Point out near the old Cedar Point Lighthouse, a development featuring cabins and cottages and upscale RV sites. The long-term strategy of being both a resort and an amusement park required feeding both beasts.

In 2001, Cedar Point was scheduled to host the International Association of Amusement Parks & Attractions (IAAPA) Summer Meeting on September 13-15, an event which would attract 200 or more industry leaders to the park. It had been in the planning stage for nearly two years. Dick Kinzel wanted to showcase Cedar Point to his peers in the industry. The event packed in a number of social events, including a chartered boat trip to Put-In-Bay and a dinner and special presentation at the Rock Hall in Cleveland. The keynote event was a dinner and dance in the historic Cedar Point Ballroom on Saturday night. In preparation for the dance, we decorated the Ballroom in the art deco style that made it the place to be in the WWII years. We even stripped and refinished the Ballroom floor.

However, all that would all have to wait a year.

On Tuesday, September 11, two days before the Summer Meeting was scheduled to begin, the attacks on the World Trade Center and the Pentagon shocked our country. As many others have noted, it was a beautiful late summer day for most of the eastern United States. That certainly was the case at Cedar Point. We had just come off the run-up to Labor Day and the park was newly quiet. I was in my office preparing for an update meeting on the IAAPA event, when Deb Hessler came into my office and said the World Trade Center was on fire. I flipped on the TV in my office and saw smoke billowing from the spot where the first plane had hit. Along with millions of others, I saw the second plane hit a short time later.

The decision to cancel the Summer Meeting was an easy one. After a flurry of calls with IAAPA officials, it was rescheduled for 2002.

That night, Dick Kinzel hosted a dinner at his home for everyone on the internal committee, several IAAPA officials, and a few early arrivals. It was a somber evening. The skies were still empty. The sunset, I remember, was spectacular, as they often are that time of year.

Two weeks later HalloWeekends started. There was some internal discussion about toning down the atmosphere of the event and its dark imagery considering what had just happened in New York. We pulled back a few things—but we were not loaded up on blood and gore to begin with. We wondered what impact 9/11 would have on park attendance the balance of the season. Speculation went both ways: the marketplace would retreat to the basement, dial back from entertainment venues; or, the marketplace would be looking for escape from all the bad news, and a trip to Cedar Point would be the perfect anecdote. Actual park attendance was somewhere in between. It was the first year the park stayed open until the end of October.

In 2002, we introduced Wicked Twister, the world's largest linear induction shuttle coaster. The summer before Dan Keller and I were dispatched to SFWOA by Dick Kinzel to ride a similar but slightly smaller ride. It was technically a roller coaster (it went up high, and gravity brought it back down), but it was as different from Millennium Force or even Magnum or Raptor as a surface ship is to a submarine. Still, it was certainly a thrill ride and scared the hell out of me when I rode it.

Dan and I rode it twice, as I recall, once in front and once in back. Riders sit four abreast on a train similar to a Raptor train. The massive electric motor blasts you out of the station and straight up about 200 feet. Then you roll quickly back down to the station where you get another blast that sends you back and up at terrific speed 200 feet. When you reach the top, the train holds for a few beats, increasing apprehension, before it roars back down toward the station. The pattern is continued for three passes until the ride slows and stops.

Our version of the ride was of course bigger and better, setting records for height and speed. Rob Decker, the successor to Lee Jewett as director of planning & design, located it on the beach between the Oceana Stadium and the Giant Wheel, an area of the park which needed some traffic-building. Since the ride was mostly open, it did not mar the view of the lake and the beach. There was an interesting view up the Hotel Breakers boardwalk. It had acceptable capacity at 1,000 per hour.

I rode Wicked Twister only once, when I got shamed into it on Media Day by a TV reporter.

The Media Day launch went well except for an embarrassing incident where the managing editor of one of our important newspapers was unable to ride because of his size. It was close, but he was just too big. At first, he was quite perturbed, but after he better understood that our decision was based on the need to provide for his safety, he came around and was making jokes about the whole experience. The inability to accommodate larger guests on some of our headline rides was, and is, an ongoing problem for Cedar Point and other amusement parks.

Wicked Twister was not a big draw to the park. This was evident in guest surveys and on the midway and outside the park where there was just no buzz. We did not have huge expectations for Wicked Twister, it was never going to be Raptor or Millennium Force, but we had hoped it would be a difference-maker. It had maintenance problems its initial year and was down mechanical much more than we would have liked, but even when it was down we did not have to handle many guest complaints, if any. The joke on the midway was that nobody cared. It was not like one of the big three: Magnum, Millennium, and Raptor. When they were down for mechanical, the guests howled. We heard about it.

Still, 2002 was a good attendance year. And we were very excited about 2003, which we hoped would be a repeat of 2000, headlined with a magnificent world class coaster: Top Thrill Dragster.

## Top Thrill Dragster

I do not recall much about the birth of the idea which became Top Thrill Dragster (TTD). However, it was a natural outgrowth from the Intamin launch coaster which debuted at Knott's Berry Farm in 2002 called Xcelerator. TTD had a long lead. Some of the footers for the ride structure were poured before the start of the 2002 season and covered up with dirt during the operating season.

The structure itself became the pivot point of the whole park. The station was located essentially across from Power Tower and the track and hill stretched about 1,000 feet down the midway to the entrance to Magnum and what was then the Paddlewheel Excursions entrance. The entire ride was visible from the midway. There was nothing hidden, unlike Magnum and Millennium. Walking up the

Top Thrill Dragster at the moment of truth: 122 mph (minimum).
CEDAR POINT ARCHIVES

main midway you see Power Tower first, then Top Thrill Dragster. The perspective is deceiving, as Power Tower looks taller at first, though it's 125 feet shorter. There were, and are, lots of jokes about the Dragster structure being a 420 foot-high phallus. It doesn't take a lot of imagination to go there.

The action of the ride was simple enough. Using hydraulic power, each train is launched at tremendous speed down a straight track. The track then heads straight up a 420 foot hill. At the base of the hill, the train separates from the catch car underneath the train and heads up the hill, hitting 120 mph as it starts its ascent. The train crests the hill at a much slower rate of speed, of course, and then gravity takes over as it heads straight downhill with a half twist and 420 feet or so later reaches the run out where it flies toward the station until it hits the brakes. The time from launch to hitting the brakes is only 19 seconds. But that's just about right

I don't recall the of the naming exercise except that it was non-controversial and settled early on. Given the action of the ride, the name fit perfectly and created all the backstory we would ever need. It was relatively easy for Planning & Design to create graphics and branding for the ride. Top Thrill Dragster was a winner.

Pieces and parts of the ride started showing up in August 2002. Site preparation was in high gear before Labor Day. There was no hiding anything. Dick Kinzel believed a "deny the obvious" was the best strategy to keep the buzz going in the off season, especially in the fall, so we refrained from officially announcing the ride until early January 2003. Dick liked to joke to both reporters and guests that maybe it was going to be a restaurant, which always got laughs.

"Maybe it'll be the tallest Golden Arches ever," he told one reporter.

No more videos, we announced Top Thrill Dragster by mailing a CD with animation of the ride, interviews, stats, etc. to the news media, coaster enthusiasts, group sales clients, local and state government officials, and other influencers. Then we posted most of the same information on our website.

The construction company used two cranes to build the tower. The second was a specialty unit—there were only five in the U.S.—which was needed to lift into place the top 100 feet of track. That winter, while the crane was still there, Dan Feicht went up in a basket to take some incredible images of the ride from the vantage point of the top of the ride. The vistas from every point of the compass were incredible. It was late December or early January. The lake was nearly ice-covered. The ground was white. The images got picked up everywhere.

The countdown to the first ride was more intense than any other ride we had ever built, even Gemini, Magnum, and Millennium

Force. When you looked at the track and then the 420-foot hill, your first reaction is one of fear. Top Thrill Dragster looked like no other ride. It really didn't even look like a roller coaster, though it handily met the Merriam Webster definition: "an elevated railway (as in an amusement park) constructed with sharp curves and steep inclines on which cars roll." There were a few naysayers, who thought Dragster was a one trick pony—but what a trick!

## First Ride on Top Thrill Dragster

I remember my first ride on Top Thrill Dragster very well. It was one of those overcast, cool, breezy spring days that make you despair of good weather ever coming to the Cedar Point Peninsula. It was late April, probably two weeks before opening. We had all watched the ride run empty, of course, which was impressive. There were a group of us in the station waiting to ride. The usual crew: Intamin folks, CP Maintenance and Operations staff, a few miscellaneous executives, PR staff, construction and contractors.

After an afternoon of successful unmanned launches, the senior Intamin person, Sandor Kernacs, gave the okay to launch with people in the train. This would be, truly, the first ride. I believe Sandor sat in the first row. Dan Keller, our GM, sat next to him. I sat a few seats back with my good friend and colleague, Monty Jasper, then Cedar Point VP-maintenance and construction. I was crazy scared. I remember pulling the seat belt tighter and tighter. The restraint system was like Millennium Force, a T-bar that pushed up against you about waist high.

The ride operator, one of our rides managers, took delight in making sure the T-bar was pressed tight against me. On a rational level, I knew the restraint system would do its job. I knew I wasn't going to come out of the seat. On an emotional level, I was missing an over the shoulder harness system very much. My heart was pumping. I had a death grip on the bar. I had an urge to urinate. I was rapidly descending into the psyche of a 10-year-old about to ride his first coaster. I was back on the Wild Mouse. This was not fun. Not at all. I was sweating under my jacket.

Monty was not having fun, either. He was the guy at Cedar Point who knew more about the ride than anyone else. He had overseen its construction. He was a mechanical engineer with decades in the business of roller coasters. And he was as white as a wedding dress. I'm sure I was, too.

We looked at each other. The train released with a slight hiss and moved out onto the track. We knew the sequence of events from watching unmanned launches. After stopping in place, the train rests for a few seconds, then it moves backward ever so slightly as ⸱ car engages under the train. This is the moment of truth.

We had to wait, of course, while the Intamin people fidd. something in the control booth. I thought my bladder was g explode. I needed this experience to be over.

Monty was more sanguine (not). "John," he said. "I reall⸱ ᵤₒₙ t want to be here."

We waited a few more seconds, and then we launched.

It is fast motorcycle speed. The thing I remember most was thinking it was going to be impossible to make the transition to vertical. Going up you feel the momentum slowing as the weight of the train pushes against my favorite scientific law: gravity.

At the top you slow and natural forces push you upward in your seat. It is VERY UNNERVING, but it is short in duration. Your view is to the southwest; you see the bay, Sandusky, the tops of trees—but only for an instant.

The ride down is quick and a blur. I did not feel frightened. The half twist is disorienting but within a second or two you are on the straightaway to the station. Our hands were in the air and pumping. We had done it. Top Thrill Dragster's first ride was in the books.

I was often asked that first year to compare the two rides: Millennium Force and Top Thrill Dragster. I still am. There really isn't much to compare. Visually, they are very different. Their ride experiences are quite different, too. Millennium has more great moments, but Dragster has four—the pre-launch anticipation, the launch, the ride to the top, and the crest—that are perhaps the best coaster moments yet created. I believe in totality of experience Millennium offers more for the rider, but on fear factor and those first 10 seconds Dragster offers more.

They both cost about the same: $25 million.

Like Millennium Force, I never talked to a guest who was disappointed in the Dragster ride experience.

As park operator or owner, if given a choice, I would favor Millennium. It appeals to more people, has a bigger market base.

Together, they are the best one-two punch in the industry.

The technology behind Dragster was simple in some respects; hydraulic pressure has been around a long time. However, this was a unique application.

Our advertising campaign for Dragster was straightforward: show the ride. Liggett Stashower was able to create some spectacular images of the ride using a miniature, remote-controlled helicopter fitted with a film camera, essentially an early version of a drone.

The first year, and even the second, Dragster had unacceptable amounts of downtime, especially compared to Millennium Force. It was frustrating for the manufacturer, Intamin, and for Cedar Point, ut most of all for the guest. The guest had invested a day, or more, of his life, and his money, to ride Dragster; but mostly he had invested his heart, his anticipation, his bragging rights, his fear, and his love of the park into riding Dragster.

After telling all his friends he was going to Cedar Point to ride Dragster, after a five-hour drive from Grand Rapids or Buffalo, after laying down nearly $100 for tickets, after all the emotional investment, after waiting in line for more than an hour . . . well, it sucked to be told by a kid in a uniform that the ride was shutting down for mechanical reasons. No, we can't tell you how long it will be down (mainly because in many cases we don't know how long it will be down, and it would be disastrous if we told you 15 minutes and it became two hours). Yes, you have the option of remaining in line, but if you leave the line you must re-enter at the end of the line.

It did not help that Dragster was so visible to so many guests. When it was running, the midway was electric. Crowds gathered in the stands we had built next to the ride to watch the ride operate. The sounds of the ride—the rock music soundtrack, the throbbing noise from a high end dragster as each train exited the station, the big click as the train rolled back as the brake fins dropped down for the launch, the incredible high decibel whoosh as the train roared down the track, were palpable, infectious, fun; it was life at its best at an amusement park.

From a mechanical and, especially electrical perspective, Dragster was a huge challenge for Monty Jasper and Jack Fletcher. They were given permission to hire three additional ride mechanics, which helped, but much was new territory for them. There were over 1,500 proximity switches on the ride, the failure of one could shut the ride down. It wasn't always immediately obvious which had failed; you had to hunt them down, which sometimes took hours.

For the first time we began to use our website—after a lot of demand from guests—to give updates on the ride's operating status. We also put up signage at the front gate basically telling guests before they walked into the park that riding Dragster might be problematical. The downtime got lots of media coverage as well. The PR staff spent a lot of time explaining what was wrong with the ride instead of what was right. The ride was a success in every other way, but it just broke down too much.

Monty Jasper, Bill Spehn (vice president, park operations) and I were the three guys on the line when it came to Dragster. Monty's job was to keep it running. Bill's job was to run it. My job was to tell its story. We worked well together and knew each other well, and we spent a lot of time together that summer on the Dragster platform dealing with ride issues of various kinds. There was even a bit of gallows humor when things got very frustrating. Monty would lament that he should have followed his original dream and become a librarian. I seconded his choice of careers and said I should have been an English or history teacher.

When things got really bad, Monty would laugh and say: "If I left right now, I wonder if I could get to Texas before they knew I was gone."

Despite all the problems, Top Thrill gave more than 800,000 rides in 2003 and more than 900,000 in 2004. It hit a million rides in 2005. And has given at least a million rides every year since.

LeBron James rode Dragster in 2000. He was at the park with his classmates from St. Akron Saint Vincent who were there on their senior class trip. By all accounts, he liked it.

## Cedar Point Nation

The 2003 season was also the year of Cedar Point Nation.

In January, I started working on an idea to increase Cedar Point's attendance through geographic market expansion. I called it Cedar Point Nation. I spent most of the month working on the proposal, knowing it would need Dan Keller and Dick Kinzel's blessing and knowing it would need to be included in the 2003 advertising budget. I had a short window to get it done. I didn't want this to become a 2004 project. The introduction of Top Thrill Dragster had opened the door.

My pitch was that the best opportunity to grow park attendance was to embark on a marketing program that positioned Cedar Point as a "Super Regional" or even national destination and to specifically target Cedar Point's existing distant markets like Chicago and the Middle Atlantic (NYC, Philadelphia, Washington-Baltimore). My argument, buttressed by a lot of data, was that growth from our traditional markets, such as Cleveland, Toledo, Detroit, Columbus, was going to be increasingly difficult in future years (they were mature markets and in Cleveland's case newly competitive with the transformation of Geauga Lake into Six Flags Worlds of Adventure).

Cedar Point measured guest origin through collecting zip codes and had been for many years. Our database was huge and valid. It clearly showed a trend of increasing attendance from distant, even national markets over the past five seasons. In the proposal I noted the factors driving this trend: growth of the internet (and cedarpoint. com); national publicity (Discovery Channel shows, USA Today features); Millennium Force and our collection of world class thrill rides; growth of our resort offering (Hotel Breakers expansion). In

1997, the "Other" category accounted for 8.1 percent of visits; by 2002 it had grown to 15.9 percent, essentially doubling.

I shared my draft proposal with Lee Alexakos, who helped pull a lot of the hard data together and who created the charts and graphs that gave the information context. Lee made significant contributions to the proposal. She believed in the strategy.

At bottom, it was all about using advertising as an investment tool, like introducing a new roller coaster, to increase sales/attendance. I have always thought advertising's highest and best use is to help grow the business. Many managers tend to view advertising more as a cost of doing business, almost a necessary evil.

The proposal called for an investment of $400K the first year and an objective of 20,000 incremental visits from markets we identified as "Other," or outside our existing markets. Year two proposed an investment of $1 million and a 50,000 attendance increase; year three was $2 million investment and a 100,000 attendance increase.

Our strategy would be based on increasing our PR/publicity effort in Chicago and the Middle Atlantic market by contracting with a PR firm with experience in the travel industry. We would look for affordable opportunities to do some targeted national advertising, including the Travel Channel, USA Today (travel section), magazines, internet/online (Expedia). We would also look to expand advertising in Chicago and the Middle Atlantic market using direct response messaging on local cable TV. I believed strongly the PR effort, if executed properly, was a huge opportunity and would produce measurable results. We had a great hook with Top Thrill Dragster.

## David Letterman and Doctor Phil

I had shared some of my proposal with our son Tom, who was at Rutgers University in New Jersey pursuing a doctoral degree in psychology. One of his advisors and mentors was Charlie Maher, the noted sports psychologist who had worked extensively with the Cleveland Indians, New York Yankees, and several Olympic athletes. He also taught organizational psychology and had a great interest in how businesses innovate and grow. Tom mentioned to him the proposal I was working on and he was fascinated by it. He loved the idea of an amusement park in Ohio using roller coaster superiority to establish a beachhead on the East Coast.

Through Tom, he invited me to come to Rutgers and share my Cedar Point Nation proposal with his graduate level class in business organization. I jumped at the opportunity and Marie and I decided to drive to Rutgers for Presidents Day weekend. It was mid-February. I shared with Dan Keller that I was going to speak to the class about Cedar Point and roller coasters.

I was also excited about another opportunity: the chance to be in audience for the "David Letterman Show." Tickets to the show were free, but I learned most were allocated to local CBS affiliates around the country. Andrea Beck and Susan Preisler from LS helped get me two tickets. When we I left for New Jersey I had a letter from the "Late Show with David Letterman" with confirmation of two tickets reserved for the Monday night show, February 17.

The drive to Rutgers was uneventful, but as we drove across Pennsylvania we were being flanked by a low pressure system starting to head up the East Coast. We spent Friday night in State College at Marie's brother's house and got into Rutgers on Saturday afternoon. Sunday, we drove from Rutgers to Glen Ridge to see my sister, Mary Frances, and her family. The snow started early Sunday evening and the 30 minute drive back to Rutgers on the Garden State was a bit harrowing. We were staying at a small hotel on campus (no restaurant). We woke up to more snow. The room had only a small window and we kept track of the accumulating snow as it piled up against the trees behind the building. Classes were cancelled on Monday morning; the university was shut down.

The snow continued all day. A lot of public transportation was not operating. The roads were terrible, of course, but I was determined to get into the city to the Ed Sullivan Theater, where Letterman's show was taped—if there was even going to be a show. Marie called the show (it wasn't easy getting through) and the message was that the show would go on.

Without the high clearance and all-wheel drive of the Rendezvous, we wouldn't have gone anywhere that morning; but we picked up Tom before noon at his apartment on the edge of campus and drove to the train station in New Brunswick. The trains were running but were behind schedule. The platform was nearly empty of passengers. We had a long wait and it was very cold. When the train did get there, it was nearly empty, too. The ride in was other-worldly. The snow was more than a foot deep at this point and the buildings, the houses, the streets were covered and still. Nothing was moving.

Penn Station was far from empty but not its usual craziness. We stepped outside into a side of Manhattan I'd never experienced. We managed to get on the subway which took us relatively close to the theater. The streets were rutted with snow. Some of the side streets were blocked with drifts. We saw people on cross country skis. Traffic in mid-town was less than half of what it normally would be and moving like an old man on ice skates. It was still snowing steadily.

The Letterman show is at the Ed Sullivan Theater on Broadway, and for many years was the home of the "Ed Sullivan Show," a Sunday night staple when I was growing up. My parents were fans. What significance it had for me was that it was the place where the Beatles had made their U.S. debut in 1964.

We got to the theater about 4 p.m. There was a large crowd out front, which we found encouraging: the show was going to go on. We walked up to young woman in a down jacket and stocking cap with a name tag and a clipboard. I introduced myself and gave her my letter, courtesy of CBS's Cleveland affiliate. I told her we needed one more ticket for our son. This was the moment of truth because we only had reservations for two tickets. We planned to try to bluff our way for a third. Tom was prepared to hangout in mid-town and drink coffee for two hours if need be.

She looked down at her clipboard and looked up. I could tell she wasn't sure about something. "How many tickets do you need?" she asked.

"We need three tickets," Marie said, holding up three fingers.

"Okay, here they are," she said, smiling, and handed us the tickets. We were in. The show was on.

The interior of the theater was very small, pint-sized compared to how I had pictured it. It is a common observation. I guessed the size of the audience at around 400. The set looks small on the stage, which is below grade; it really isn't a stage at all. We ended up in good seats, right on the rail of the balcony. We had about a half hour before taping began. One of the assistant producers gave us a rundown on what to expect. It was clear what they wanted from us was enthusiasm, lots of cheering, even screaming, all at the appropriate times.

Letterman came out to warm us up a few minutes before the show began. He joked with the audience, mostly about the weather. He thanked us for making the effort to attend in the middle of a snowstorm.

His opening monologue was mostly about the snow. He cut to one of his staffers, a young woman, who was positioned on the roof of the theater with a yardstick. Letterman asked for a reading, and the woman fired back with a number, which drew cheers from the audience. The cutaways to the woman on the roof continued throughout the show. I think the last one was 23 or 24 inches, a lot of snow.

His guest that evening, for the first time ever, was Dr. Phil, who was just starting his climb to the top. I remember they played well off each other, but I do not remember at all what they talked about.

It was dark when we left the theater, but the snow was letting up. It was impossible to hail a cab, so we just started walking down Broadway toward Penn Station. We were starving—no food since breakfast—but most restaurants we passed were closed, along with most other businesses as well. It was cold and with all the snow it was tough walking. About halfway to Penn Station we came upon Rosie O'Grady's, a restaurant fixture in the Theater District for many years. Amazingly, it was open. We couldn't get in fast enough. We viewed it as an oasis. The three of us had a leisurely dinner, got warm, and talked about the day. The train ride back to New Brunswick was beautiful with all the lights of the city.

The next day Tom and I did our good deed for the day and helped dig out the driveway of an older man who lived next door to the hotel. I also got the news that classes at Rutgers were cancelled for a second day, so no appearance in Charlie Maher's class. I was very disappointed. We all outwardly agreed that there would be another opportunity, but I knew in my heart there wouldn't be.

We left early the following day in brilliant sunshine and followed it all the way across Pennsylvania on Interstate 80. I needed to get back to have a meeting with Jim McCartney, the head of the production company we were going to use to film our 2003 TV spots. We met at Fridays in the early evening. Jim and I went way back. I first worked with him in 1982 and he had directed the Demon Drop spot in 1983, one of the best TV spots we ever produced. I shared with him the Cedar Point Nation strategy and he shared with me his plan to film the ride. He was a recent convert to a strict vegan diet, even to the point of eating only raw, uncooked food. I thought he was crazy, but he had become a true believer and continued to calmly and logically make his case.

"We didn't evolve to eat Big Macs," he said.

The Cedar Point Nation proposal was dated February 7. I hand-delivered copies to Brenda Lakner, Dick Kinzel's administrative assistant, and Corinne Casali, Dan Keller's assistant, and hoped for the best. Reaction came quickly: they liked it. In Dick's case, so much so he asked for enough copies to share with each of the board members. There was a Cedar Point board meeting that month to approve the budget and he wanted to put the Cedar Point Nation proposal on the agenda. Dick was a notorious hard sell on increases in the advertising budget, so I felt particularly pleased with his reaction. The board members liked the proposal, too; in fact, I received a phone call from one board member who was particularly impressed.

We got approval to spend the media dollars but not the addition of staff to do the PR work. I was disappointed because I thought a national PR effort would really bring benefits not just to Cedar Point but to our other parks as well. It would have been a good return on investment. We had a very good PR staff in those years—Robin Innes and Janice Lifke Witherow were top drawer professionals —and they were successful in generating a lot of national stories on the park.

We ended up running full page ads in USA Today, featuring Top Thrill Dragster. We put together 30 second and 60 second TV spots with a direct response message. The coasters were the hook, the waterpark, beach, campground, and hotels were the barb. It worked very well, and we achieved the attendance goals we set for our distant markets. I got an increase in the budget for 2004 but not what the plan had called for.

Looking back, I think I was at my best as a marketer during this period, roughly the five years between 1999 – 2004, corresponding to my early to mid-50s, and, interestingly, corresponding to the launches of Millennium Force and Top Thrill Dragster. I was in a sweet spot. I had had lots of experience in all the marketing disciplines. I was current with new technologies that came with the internet. I had confidence in my ability to solve marketing problems and to recognize marketing opportunities (like Cedar Point Nation).

I moved into general management just as social media was emerging as a marketing tool. I had a Twitter account my last year at the park, 2013 (I was the first Cedar Fair GM to have one), but I tweeted irregularly. I viewed tweets as the opportunity to write haiku. I cleared my account when I retired. I got a Facebook account early on, but we have it only to see pictures of our grandchildren.

## Chapter 15
# Chasing Boeckling's Ghost
### Dave and Diane Tell the Story of Cedar Point

The person who knew the most about Cedar Point's history was the late David W. Francis.

David was a cool and dispassionate observer, a professional historian. There was no rah-rah in him. He loved the park, but it was a kind of matter-of-fact love, not the passionate affair I saw on the faces of coaster enthusiasts and park fans. Yet there was no question he loved the park as much as they did.

I first met Dave in 1975, shortly after I started at Cedar Point. We had talked several times on the phone when he had contacted the PR Department for access to several vintage photographs he wanted to use for an article in a historical quarterly. I could tell right away he knew a lot more than I did about the park's history, especially the early history. His area of interest as a historian was the Gilded Age, the period from the end of the Civil War until about 1905 or 1910 (some would say until the start of World War I). Cedar Point's earlier years as a local resort fit neatly into that time frame, including the golden age Boeckling created with the building of the Hotel Breakers, the Coliseum, and the new, electric-powered midway.

Dave also knew quite a bit about George Boeckling. (Dave Biechele, a Sandusky realtor and descendant of Boeckling, also knows a lot about his famous great uncle.) In writing and researching "Cedar Point: Queen of American Watering Places," Dave Francis had no choice but to get to know George Boeckling. It is hard to over-estimate Boeckling's impact on Cedar Point. He acquired a local resort in 1897, built it into a regional destination, and then operated it very successfully for more than 30 years. After his death in 1931, his heirs attempted to operate it using his template—and did keep it alive, if just barely at times—for the next 20-25 years, until George Roose and Emile Legros acquired Cedar Point and put in place a new way of doing things. In short, he was the primary influence on Cedar Point, even from the grave, for more than 50 years.

In my opinion, George Boeckling, George Roose and Emile Legros, and Dick Kinzel, were the most significant men in Cedar Point's history. Bob Munger, who was CEO (and a significant

shareholder) for 12 years (1975 – 1987), was the bridge between Roose and Legros and Dick Kinzel.

I'm not sure David really liked George Boeckling. He admired his success, but I think there was a ruthlessness about Boeckling that was a turn-off. There was no question Boeckling was a remarkable man. He was highly intelligent, logical and practical, but also a dreamer, a visionary, a risk taker. It was a gamble, at least to most of the world, to build Hotel Breakers in 1905. Ditto the Coliseum. And the electric midway. And roller coasters. And the Cedar Point Roadway aka the Cedar Point Chaussee. However, I don't think Boeckling viewed these endeavors as gambles. He had great self-confidence, the surety of an entrepreneur. He saw them all as opportunities.

Dave collected a lot of information about Boeckling. He told me once over lunch that he just about had enough to write a small biography, and that he was tempted to do it. However, he never did, moving on to other projects. We both acknowledged there wasn't a big market for biographies of regional business tycoons who had died 75 years ago. The thing he created, Cedar Point, was of course a different matter.

There are lots of Boeckling anecdotes floating around Sandusky, though fewer every year as those who had known him personally have died off. Children who might remember seeing him at Cedar Point in his last years would now be in their mid-80s. There are stories that he was a womanizer and secretly, or not so secretly, had affairs with a number of local women. Boeckling never married and never had children, though legend has it he had been married and then divorced back in Indiana. He made sure Cedar Point was well stocked with booze during Prohibition, making deals with whomever he had to make a deal with to ensure his guests would not get thirsty. He lavishly entertained

David Francis and his wife, Diane DeMali Francis, historians of Cedar Point, authors of three editions of "Cedar Point: Queen of America's Watering Places." And good friends.
COURTESY OF DIANE DEMALI FRANCIS

representatives from the steamship companies, the railroads, and other organizations, with private parties that included gambling, liquor, and friendly females.

He loved music. He worked deals with the New York Metropolitan Opera to stop overnight in Sandusky on their annual summer trip to Chicago. He brought the cast and crew to Cedar Point's Hotel Breakers, where he cajoled them into giving impromptu concerts in the Rotunda of the hotel.

George A. Boeckling in his later years. He led Cedar Point into its first golden age.
CEDAR POINT ARCHIVES

George Boeckling was the son of German immigrants, born in 1862 in Michigan City, Indiana. His first job was as a grocery clerk at age 12. He later became a traveling salesman and then was involved in a wholesale lumber business. How he arrived in Sandusky in 1897 and acquired the capital to eventually own a majority of shares of the company is a bit of an unknown. But he did.

Boeckling was his own PR man, and very good at it. He had more than a bit of P.T. Barnum in him. He staged championship boxing matches, brought in a group of supposed "head hunting" tribesmen from the Philippines, and in 1910 promoted the first long distance flight over water. Glenn Curtis flew non-stop from Euclid Beach to Cedar Point on August 31, setting a new world record. George Boeckling was there on the beach to greet him when he landed. He was a first-class promoter.

By all accounts, he lived large, active in the Sandusky community and generous to many local charitable and civic organizations. In 1914, he built a large home on Columbus Avenue in the second Renaissance style, quickly adding a ballroom for entertaining. In the 1950s, it was sold to the local Knights of Columbus. I have attended weddings, graduations, and even political events in the house. As of this writing, it has become a German restaurant.

My good friend Kevin Terrell, who was manager of cash control at the park for many years, found a large, vintage picture of George Boeckling. It had turned up in a closet somewhere stuck behind a pile of junk. It was probably taken in the 1920s. It was not a summer image—Boeckling is wearing a wool coat and a fedora. Kevin told me he had decided to give Boeckling his due. He hung the picture in the Cedar Point vault, and ever since George has watched over Cedar Point's money. Kevin claims he never experienced it, but some of the college kids who have worked there in the summer claim Boeckling's eyes move on occasion. One kid refused to enter the vault again after experiencing "the eyes."

I liked telling stories, Dave liked finding facts. He was a graduate of Baldwin-Wallace College, where he majored in history, and received his M.A. in history from the University of Memphis. He made his living as an adman. He and his wife and co-author, Diane De Mali Francis, owned a small advertising agency in Wadsworth, Ohio, near Akron. Most of their clients were business to business. Earlier he had worked for Loos, Edwards, and Sexauer, a small Cleveland agency, and prior to that for the Richfield Coliseum and for Chippewa Lake Park, where he had been VP of marketing. He and Diane married in 1981. She was a former advertising copywriter who had worked in New York City. They were a strong team.

We first met in person in 1975 when Dave was at Chippewa. We were competitors, of course, in the Cleveland area, especially for company picnics and group outings. We had dinner at the Bay Harbor Inn at Cedar Point, and talked Cedar Point, Chippewa, coasters, Civil War, amusement parks, a long list.

His historical interests went beyond Cedar Point and amusement parks. He collected toy soldiers. He read deeply on the Civil War. He published numerous academic articles on the 19th century shipping industry on the Great Lakes.

Dave's interest in Cedar Point sprang from stories his grandmother told him about visiting the park as young girl in 1909. In the late 1970s and early 1980s Dave and his wife, Diane DeMali, began collecting Cedar Point memorabilia and information about the park. Their interest blossomed and in 1988 Daring Books published "Cedar Point: Queen of American Watering Places." Although most readers (and buyers) were probably more interested in the numerous vintage photographs David and Diane had collected for the book, it also told the story of Cedar Point in text that was well written and comprehensive. For the first time, the story of the park from its beginnings in 1870 to the current day was in one place, and put together by a professional historian.

David and Diane put together a second edition in 1995 to coincide with Cedar Point's 125th Anniversary celebration, and Diane wrote a third in 2009. The later editions are updates and include some new photographs.

Dave regularly sent me historic images, newspaper and magazine articles, books—anything he thought I might have interest in seeing. I reciprocated.

Dave and Diane usually came to the park once or twice a summer and always stayed at Hotel Breakers or Sandcastle Suites. They were beach people and liked nothing more than to hang out at the Breakers beach with a good book and a cool drink. David and I usually met at the Breakers for an extended lunch. Our conversations were wide-ranging. Cedar Point, of course, was usually the first topic.

Dave and Diane were unitholders, so he tracked the company's financial performance carefully, though he respected the strict rules of financial disclosure I had to observe as an employee of Cedar Point. We also talked about books we were reading, or had recently read, the business environment in Cleveland and NE Ohio, the agency business in Cleveland, the state of the state of the amusement park business overall, his most recent collectible acquisition (he and Diane's collection of Cedar Point memorabilia was very impressive), a bit of Ohio politics, and he and Diane's current amusement park book project. We also swapped Boeckling stories. I would sometimes ask when he was going to finally write George's biography.

David developed cancer in late 2005, my first year as general manager. His emails mentioned regular trips to the Cleveland Clinic, but his attitude remained positive. However, he did not make it to Cedar Point in 2006 and died in July. Marie and I drove to Wadsworth for Dave's wake. I remember how green and lush the countryside looked, the rolling landscape of Medina County. I had not left the bubble of the park in several weeks and it felt good to be on the road, even though the destination would be painful.

The funeral home was packed. Dave had been an active member of the Wadsworth community for many years. Diane was very gracious and thanked us for coming such a long distance. As I recall, he was dressed for eternity in a blue blazer and a tie, a Cedar Point tie.

I told Diane that we would do something at the park to honor Dave, but I didn't know what it would be. I spoke the truth. We had a kind of unwritten policy against memorials in the park for understandable reasons. Jack Aldrich was the only exception to the unwritten rule. There wouldn't be a plaque mounted at the entrance to a ride or a brick on the midway. Diane, I think, understood, and did not press it.

Seven years later, as I was quickly approaching retirement, I knew I had to do something or it never would be done. I was the link to Dave at Cedar Point. Working with John Taylor from Planning & Design and with Diane, we created a remembrance of Dave and the contribution of Dave and Diane to celebrating the history of the special place called the Queen of American Watering Places, and it is now in the Town Hall Museum.

George Boeckling died of complications from kidney disease on July 24, 1931. As David and Diane wrote in their book, he went out in style. The Sandusky Boys' and Girls' Band played at his home the night before the funeral. Flags at the park and on the steamer that bore his name dipped to half-staff. His portrait in the Breakers lobby was draped in black.

Boeckling's final resting place is under an impressive stone peristyle just inside the entrance to Sandusky's Oakland Cemetery. It is the largest monument in the cemetery. The monument is on a slight rise of ground on the west side of US 250, the main highway approach to Cedar Point, just yards away from the road. Hundreds of thousands of cars and their passengers unknowingly pass within sight of Boeckling's grave every summer on their way to the park. He's close enough to count the cars.

## Chapter 16

# The "Mad Men" of Cedar Point

### Selling Roller Coasters from A to about Y

I spent 40 years selling Cedar Point. In all those years we used the services of an advertising agency to create and place most of the advertising for the park. I worked with seven different agencies during my career and dozens of sub-contractors and hundreds of individuals: copywriters, film editors, broadcast producers, creative directors, media planners, media buyers, research directors, art directors, account executives, direct marketing planners, strategic planners. It was an endless list. I am very proud of the body of work we produced for Cedar Point. I believe the advertising we created was a significant factor in the long-term success of the park.

To me, advertising comes down to the message: what you say is ultimately more important than who you say it to or where and when you say it. You need to nail the whole package to be consistently successful, but the thing you absolutely must get right is the message.

There were four people I worked with in my career who really got the message right: Ed Fine, John Ragsdale, Sarah Venizelos Malamed, and Lynn Lilly. They produced some of the best advertising messages ever created for Cedar Point.

Ed and I worked together at the beginning and at the end of my time at Cedar Point. He started at MARC Advertising in Pittsburgh as a copywriter about the same time I started at the park. MARC lost our business after the 1988 season, and spent 18 years in the wilderness, and then had a second go from 2006 through 2011 with Yellow Submarine Marketing, a spin off from MARC. Ed was there for all of it.

John Ragsdale was the creative director for Hesselbart & Mitten, the Akron agency which succeeded MARC. Sarah Venizelos was his creative partner. They were a powerful team. H&M merged with a Cleveland firm, Meldrum & Fewsmith, in 1992. John left Meldrum after a few years due to health reasons. Sarah stayed with Meldrum and eventually became president of her own agency in Cleveland.

Lynn Lilly was the creative director for Liggett Stashower, the Cleveland agency which had our business from 1999 through

319 *Always* **CEDAR POINT**
**A Memoir of the Midway**

2005. Lynn loved the midway, and understood it, and brought real passion to her work for the park. She left Liggett in 2004 and moved to Georgia where her husband had taken a teaching job. She was a great loss.

I always thought Ed felt it was a privilege to work for a brand like Cedar Point. He understood our customer and appreciated the power of our brand. Ed came up with the two best Cedar Point brand-defining theme lines of the past 50 years: The Amazement Park, and America's Roller Coast. He and some of his colleagues at MARC formed their own company, Yellow Submarine Marketing, in 2006.

All these folks were creative directors at their agencies, the people responsible for creating and then crafting the messages which would deliver customers to our door. Their partners were the media planners and buyers, the numbers guys (though most were women) who worked to put together the plan to reach our customer. The third group were the account service team, whose job it was to define the customer to the creative and media teams, and to maintain the relationship with the client. Within the agency, they were the client's advocate. They were also responsible for keeping the whole enterprise on track.

As the client representative, my loyalties were clear: Cedar Point. I had no competing issues and no other clients. It was my job as VP of marketing to utilize the agency in the most efficient way to produce great advertising that would sell lots of tickets to the park.

Despite my liberal arts background and lack of interest and aptitude in math and science, I never took a mass communications, advertising, or public relations class in college. Given the requirements of ROTC, theology/philosophy (one class of one or the other every semester), and my major (English), I didn't have a lot of options for electives. Still, I considered myself a purist and opted for classes on Victorian Novelists or Early American Writers rather than mass communications. I don't endorse this strategy. After four years at Notre Dame I was prepared to go to graduate school, but nowhere else.

I learned the advertising business on the job, so I had no choice but to learn it if I wanted to survive and hopefully thrive. As I noted earlier, Don Dittmann was my primary mentor, and he was an excellent teacher. Jack Goldsmith, the co-founder of MARC Advertising, was also a mentor. Don got me involved in advertising in 1975, shortly after he started at Cedar Point. He brought me along to agency meetings and planning sessions.

I didn't know the jargon, the unwritten rules (or the written rules), or the internal politics of agencies. He debriefed me after meetings, challenging me to defend the actions taken, or not taken.

He recommended books on advertising, which I devoured. He sent me his copy of Advertising Age, the weekly newspaper of advertising, which I also devoured. A lot of it was agency/client gossip: is Ford Motor Company losing its love for J. Walter Thompson? But I learned from the gossip reporting, too.

## Advertising Heroes

My two advertising heroes were Leo Burnet, founder of the Leo Burnet Company in Chicago, and David Ogilvy, the founder of Ogilvy and Mather. Leo Burnet was the person behind some of the most successful campaigns ever, including

"Tony the Tiger," "Charlie the Tuna," the Marlboro Man," "Good Hands," and "Fly the Friendly Skies." Many are still in use. He died in 1971, the year I graduated from college.

A Brit, Ogilvy was best known for using product knowledge gleaned from research to drive the creative product. He believed advertising's job was to sell stuff, not to change the world. He retired in 1973 from management duties but stayed active in the business until his death in 1999. The book I consider the Bible of advertising, "Ogilvy on Advertising," was published in 1985.

I was a learner, not a decider, until Don retired in 1982, so I served a six-year apprenticeship. I think that was about right. I know I felt ready to go when the time came.

## My First TV Edit

Don retired around June 1. The 1982 campaign, which featured the introduction of our new flume ride, Whitewater Landing, was fixed in place by then. However, we still had to edit our TV commercials. These would be the first TV spots I would sign off on. I was looking forward to the experience. The director the agency hired to shoot the spots, Jim McCartney, had a special relationship with someone at the Osmond Studio in Provo, Utah. It seemed like an out of the way place to go, but the price was very good so we opted for Provo. It was scheduled to be a very quick trip. Fly out in the afternoon, spend the night, start work early and work all day and then catch a late flight back home. As it was, we didn't finish until late and flew back early the following day.

Our group was small: myself, Ed Fine, Bob Griffing (art director), and Jim McCartney.

This was my first visit to the Far West. I had been to Colorado for a few days after ROTC Summer Camp in 1970, but that was it.

I was surprised to see snow on the mountains around Salt Lake City and along the drive down the interstate to Provo. I remember how clear it was and how the blue sky dazzled like jewelry. We stayed at a non-descript motel outside the city. Each room was a free-standing cabin. We were told at check in to watch where we stepped, especially at night, because of the prevalence of rattlesnakes. We had dinner at a rustic steakhouse. The director had been there many times, and as I remember it did not disappoint. Conversation was easy and fast. Ed and Bob were fans of the Old West. We talked like a group of kids about Indians, grizzly bears, the Mormon settlement in the 1840s, famous gunslingers, mountain men.

Bob Griffing or "Griff," as he was usually called, is a gifted artist. A few years later he would retire to a cabin in the Allegheny forest north of Pittsburgh and paint scenes of frontier and Native American life primarily from the 18th century. I have a book of his paintings. They are extraordinary. His originals hang in the homes or the rich and famous across the U.S. He has painted some Western scenes as well.

In the morning, it was all business. The studio was cold and quiet and dark. Our editor was a friendly guy, originally from California, and he asked a lot of questions about the park as he loaded all the visual elements of the spots into the editing equipment. Editing, especially in the stone age of 1982, was a tedious process. I had some idea what to expect, but I still found it a bit maddening at times. As the editor put in various pieces of the film shot at the park two weeks prior, the spots began to really take shape and I began to feel ownership. The spots were what we called "Whole Park," aimed at a general audience and visually a series of cuts of a family enjoying a day at the park.

All day and into the night I had to give approvals as we progressed through the editing process. In the end, we had something very good, and I felt confident I was doing work I knew I could do.

I enjoyed working with creative people and I like to think I was successful in getting them to do some of their best work for Cedar Point.

Cedar Point's core customer or target market was bifurcated. The first group we called Riders, which we defined as those 12-24, whose interest and motivation was rides, particularly thrill rides and coasters. Over the years and with various agencies we modified the 12-24 to 18-34 or 12-30 but never the interest or motivation to visit the park. The second group we called Families, which we defined as adults 25-49 with children. These were guests who typically had a broader range of interests at the park reflecting their age differences. Sometimes it was modified to 25-54, reflecting the increase in older mothers. Families enjoyed roller coasters, but they also liked live shows and less stressful rides.

There were subgroups within these two groups. Younger Families were a subgroup: families with at least one child under 48 inches, which is someone who doesn't ride adult roller coasters. This is the Camp Snoopy, Planet Snoopy, Kiddy Kingdom crowd. I can attest from personal experience they experience the park quite differently than the other groups.

The Holy Grail was a TV spot, and a campaign, that served all groups. Very hard to pull off. The most effective Rider spots had some scare in them, and they used younger actors. This didn't always work for Mom.

Most years, with most agencies, we created two campaigns, sometimes three: Riders, Families, and Young Families. The Young Family campaigns were usually created in seasons when we were introducing a new attraction, like Camp Snoopy, Planet Snoopy, or "Snoopy on Ice," (the Peanuts-themed ice show) aimed at increasing attendance from this segment. From a budget perspective, we had to cover Riders and Families. Most years, we did not have enough media dollars left to provide the coverage we would have liked for Young Families.

If someone mandated that we could only make one spot, it would have to be a Family spot that was ride heavy.

I spent the most time with the account services team. Cedar Point was a large enough account that we had a client service person assigned full-time to our business. I spent more time with this person than any other team member and considered them an integral member of my staff. I worked with some outstanding client service managers in my career, including Tony Bucci and Michele Fabrizzi from MARC, Ed Bailey from Hesselbart & Mitten and Meldrum and Fewsmith, and Susan Preisler at Liggett Stashower.

Ed and I worked together from 1989 to 1994, when he left Meldrum to take a key marketing position with the Rock and Roll Hall of Fame and Museum in Cleveland. Although Ed has relocated to Austin, Texas, where he has become a leader in the music industry, we remain good friends. We worked together to launch Magnum, Disaster Transport, Mean Streak, Snake River Falls, and Raptor. We thought alike. He was a marketing guy first, and advertising guy second. I always thought he would have been an excellent VP of marketing for Cedar Point.

Michele and Tony were an impressive team. Incredibly hard-working people, and they have enjoyed significant success in the ad world. Michele went on to become president of MARC and Tony led an acquisition effort to acquire other agencies, dramatically increasing the size of MARC, which he serves as chief executive officer and board chairman. Low key, analytical, an excellent judge of talent,

**EVEN WHEN YOU SEE IT, YOU WON'T BELIEVE IT.**

No place on Earth comes close to the fun of a family vacation at Cedar Point.

**Unbelievable Thrills**

Take on Magnum XL-200 - the highest, fastest, steepest roller coaster on Earth - and only one of nine toe-curling coasters at Cedar Point. Challenge through Thunder Canyon. Whirl on the Witches' Wheel. Dare the Demon Drop, then cool off at our 5-acre, 10-slide Soak City® water park. All the rides you can imagine, and then some.

**Unbelievable Attractions**

IMAX 7-story giant-screen movies. The dolphins of Oceana® Frontiertown. Theatre after theatre of live shows, music and lights keep the excitement going.

**Unbelievable Kid Stuff**

Fill their days with the wonder of Berenstain Bear Country, Kid Arthur's Court, Kiddieland Rides and the Petting Farm.

**Unbelievable Location**

On a magnificent Lake Erie Beach where you can make it a weekend at the historic Hotel Breakers. Or Camper Village, the RV campground closest to the fun. There's always something new happening at Cedar Point. But you've got to see it to believe it. So c'mon. Get to The Point.

**Call 1-800-BEST-FUN and save on your Cedar Point Getaway.**

Or send in the coupon below for your Great Vacation Planner. It's packed with hundreds of dollars of savings on Hotel Breakers, Camper Village, Park Admission, Restaurants, Food and Merchandise.

**Get To The Point.**

There's always something new at Cedar Point. But you have to see it to believe it. For details on all the fun waiting for you and your family, mail this coupon to: Cedar Point Marketing Department, P.O. Box 5006, Sandusky, OH 44871-8006 or call 1-800-BEST-FUN (1-800-237-8386) now!

Name

Address

City                State            Zip

**Get to the Point.**

**PARK OPENS MAY 6TH. OPEN DAILY. CEDAR POINT**

Sandusky, Ohio

Cedar Fair Limited Partnership. All Rights Reserved.

A print ad developed by our agency, Hesselbart & Mittten, to launch the 1989 season. CEDAR POINT ARCHIVES

Tony is a very impressive executive. Tony is also a marketer as well as an adman.

The agency business is a very tough calling, not for the weak of heart. There are very high highs—when you win the big new account in an eight-agency competition—and there are corresponding low lows—when the client brings in a new VP of marketing and you get fired just because he or she wants to bring in a shop he knows from his previous job. It is fluid, ever-changing, worrisome, and insecure— but it is also sexy, exciting, and cool (sort of like working for an amusement park).

I occasionally wondered how I would do if I were placed in an agency environment. Not sure. I could fantasize about being a copywriter or a broadcast producer—my heart would be there—but knew I had no visual or art talent. Little interest in media buying or planning. I liked market research and believed in it, but I didn't like it enough to do it every day. I would probably end up as a "suit," as an account executive in client service.

There is variety in the agency world—many different clients with different products and services and with different advertising needs. This is not a bad thing. I had only one client: Cedar Point. I only knew one thing, but I knew it very well. I thought of myself as a brand manager, the model used by the big package goods companies like Procter & Gamble, where one manager is responsible for a brand and all that goes with it.

Part of my role with the agency was to be the guardian of our brand, Cedar Point, to know what was acceptable and what was not. I had to be a cop sometimes. And I had to be Scrooge. Agencies are just not set up to be savers. Given the choice, they tend to gravitate to whatever costs more. Not out laziness or malfeasance, more the desire to do a great job.

Broadcast TV production was always the most difficult cost issue. A radio spot, even one produced for a major brand and with all the trimmings, including top tier talent, can often be executed by a small group of people: writer, producer, talent, audio engineer. A TV spot, on the other hand, usually involves dozens of professionals. I was always amazed, and sometimes frustrated, by the number of people who touch a TV spot from start to finish. In my time at the park, TV production was typically 10 to 15 times the cost of radio production in any given year.

The 30 second TV spot was king in my advertising lifetime. Everything revolved around it. For many brands, including Cedar Point, it drove the messaging and for many agencies the right answer to any advertising issue was the right 30 second TV spot.

Most everyone consumes TV and is exposed to TV commercials and thus it follows that everyone has an opinion on TV advertising.

The advertising guy is like the food guy, who also must deal with the fact that everyone eats and has an opinion. There is a lot of second guessing. Consumer reaction to TV spots is very subjective. You learn to live with it.

One of MARC's biggest contributions to Cedar Point's advertising was developing and executing our trade strategy. MARC convinced stations to give us air time (30 or 60 second spots) in exchange for Cedar Point tickets (valued at the Funday or retail ticket price) on top of our cash buy. This strategy really stretched our media buy and was used effectively by Cedar Point for many years—and is probably still being used. Both sides benefitted.

Radio stations especially needed prizes for on-air promotions and giveaways, and Cedar Point tickets were in demand and easy to manage administratively. From the park's perspective, we benefitted from the increase in our effective media buy; but we also benefitted from the in-park spending when the tickets were redeemed. I always wanted every trade ticket to be redeemed, but redemption rates for trade tickets were low, usually averaging only 60 – 70 percent.

## Big Joe Moticik

On the bookshelf behind the desk in our home office is a 1988 National Championship Notre Dame football in a plastic display case. After almost 30 years, the leather is starting to crack, the colors are getting weak. On the football there is an inscription that reads: To John Hildebrandt, Happy 40th Birthday to a Notre Dame man for all seasons – Lou Holtz. It is one of my most treasured possessions. I joke with my sons that it will go in my will. The football was a gift from Joe Moticik, the account supervisor at Hesselbart and Mitten in 1989, the year of the Magnum and the year I turned 40. Joe had played football (tight end, I believe) at Northwestern in 1963, the last year Ara Parseghian had coached the Wildcats before moving on to Notre Dame in 1964. Joe had remained friends with Parseghian over the years. He contacted his old coach and asked him to intercede with Lou Holtz, then the Irish head coach, to get the football inscribed as a gift for me, a Notre Dame grad (Class of '71). It was pure Joe.

When I met Joe he was about 50. He was still a big man, but now his shoulders sloped downward and he was thick in the middle. After back surgery, he could no longer walk like an athlete; but his arms were still muscled and his grip strong. He stood about 6 foot 3 inches and had curly salt and pepper hair and a raspy voice.

In personality, he was friendly, outgoing, positive, always smiling, and a natural storyteller. Unlike some former athletes, he enjoyed talking about his time on the football field.

He had had a successful career in Chicago advertising. He was a good client man and had worked on some big brands. I forget the details of how he came to a small but growing agency in Akron. He was a city guy and very old school in many ways. We were a decade apart in age and of different generations. He came of age in the 1950s, as did Dick Kinzel, Bill Near, and Don Miears. He worked in advertising when agencies still worked Friday hours in the summer (you get to head to the lake or the beach at noon), when client lunches were of flexible length and often fueled with alcohol, and when everyone wore suits, even on Fridays.

Joe was immensely likeable and a good bridge between the creative and media worlds and the client point of view.

Joe supervised several accounts, but Cedar Point was his key responsibility.

Joe and Jack Falfas formed a bond, based on their shared football experience and their admiration for the legendary Green Bay coach, Vince Lombardi. In fact, at the start of the 1989 season Jack invited Joe to speak at the employee pep rally on opening day eve. He did a fine job.

Joe was a mentor to Ed Bailey, the young man H&M put on Cedar Point as account executive.

We were all cruising into the 1990 season when I got a call from Bill Waldman, the president of H&M, that Joe Moticik had been let go. I was shocked. Advertising is a risky line of work.

## Jack Goldsmith

One of the finest men I ever worked with was Jack Goldsmith, one of the co-founders of MARC Advertising. He qualifies as a second mentor. We knew each other for more than 40 years and I valued his counsel greatly. Jack was 48 when I met him in 1974. I was 25. He was a master of self-deprecation. I felt he was often underestimated but rarely bested. He was always poking fun at himself. Every holiday season for decades he sent out a card that was in some fresh way a joke at his expense. I have saved most of them.

Behind the small stature and white hair was a first class business mind. He didn't hide it necessarily. But in meetings, or afterward, his voice would change inflection and he would speak slower and everyone would listen.

He was single and his wife and his life were his work. He kept friends for a long time. He had a great filter for people and he divided the world into two camps—good guys and jerks. He could respect the ability of some jerks, but in the end, they were jerks.

He loved Pittsburgh and his knowledge of Pittsburgh sports was truly impressive. He was what today we would call a shooting guard in high school and claimed he was the last person to shoot a two handed set shot in official competition.

In the mid-1980s he sold his interest in MARC and became a solo marketing and advertising consultant. He was highly successful. He died in 2017. He was 90.

We did not talk that often after he left MARC, perhaps two or three times a year. But that was the way it was meant to be, and it worked for both of us. Jack had nicknames for everyone. He called me John Victor Hugo (I assume in some association with the French novelist Victor Hugo), but mostly it was just, Johnny.

## Chapter 17

# The True Believers

### Coaster Riders of the World, Unite

I have many friends who are coaster enthusiasts.

By coaster enthusiast, I mean a person who spends a serious amount of his or her leisure time and discretionary income visiting amusement parks riding roller coasters; a person who belongs to one of the enthusiast organizations, like ACE (American Coaster Enthusiasts) or their local and regional counterparts like GOCC (Great Ohio Coaster Club) or even RCCGB (Roller Coaster Club of Great Britain); a person who keeps careful records of the number and types of coasters they have ridden and keeps lists of favorites; a person who can manage the bodily stress of riding a big coaster like Millennium Force eight times in a row and ask for more. I mean...

You know who you are.

## ACE

There were no coaster enthusiast groups that I'm aware of prior to the 1970s. The American Coaster Enthusiasts (ACE) was officially born at Busch Gardens Williamsburg in 1978—the same summer Cedar Point hosted its first Coastermania. In fact, I had arranged for Nancy Steinmuller of my staff to attend what was called Coaster Con I, so we would be better prepared to host our own event a few weeks later. The idea for a coaster enthusiast club was the inspiration of three men, Richard Munch, Ray Brashears, and Paul Greenwald, who had met at Kings Dominion the summer of 1977 for a coaster riding marathon event tied to the release of the movie "Roller Coaster."

Today it is an organization of more than 5,000 members, many from outside the U.S., dedicated to the knowledge, enjoyment, and preservation of roller coasters.

Most amusement parks, including Cedar Point, have had an interesting relationship with roller coaster enthusiasts over the years. At heart, we love them; how can you not love people who tattoo the logo of your best coaster on their arm? People who have pet names for your coasters? People who call themselves Raptor Jo? Ultimately, they are family.

It is the same everywhere. I think I understand at least the basic psychology of the enthusiast, as I am one. My "enthusiasm" is the study of the American Civil War. For others its Corvettes or Model T's, black powder rifles, duck hunting, the novels of Charles Dickens, postcards, World War II. The list is forever long. Enthusiasts are often also collectors, but not always. The Civil War community is basically divided into three groups: reenactors, collectors, and students of the war. There are subgroups within these groups, as some people focus almost exclusively on either the Confederate or Federal experience; some collect only artillery artifacts; some are interested only in military affairs while others are students of the entire Civil War era. When I am asked about my interest in the Civil War, I am usually first asked if I am a reenactor (I'm not) or a collector (I'm not, unless you count a few books and some artwork).

For coaster enthusiasts, it is more targeted. Relatively few, in my observation, collect coaster stuff—it is hard to put coasters in your basement—but most collect promotional material, bits and pieces off coasters, such as signage, seats, etc.

Mainly, coaster enthusiasts collect ride credits. Experiences. It is not about owning or possessing something, it is about experiencing it. And they collect lists: Top Ten Steel Coasters; Top Ten Wood Coasters, Top Ten B&M Coasters, Top Ten European Coasters. Numbers and lists are very important in their world.

Some of it is inside versus outside. If you're a coaster enthusiast, the opportunity to stand inside the launch room of Top Thrill Dragster is pretty heady stuff, a major bucket list thing. For a Cedar Point ride mechanic, it's one more thing to do before heading to Magnum and then to lunch.

I have always maintained that coaster enthusiasts are physically self-selected before anything else. You've got to have the gene for it. It's certainly not dangerous or unhealthy to ride roller coasters, but you must have a physical tolerance for it. The going upside down is a deal-breaker for many, myself included. I don't enjoy it at all—it's not fun—and the older I get the less fun it is. If I ride an inverted coaster, for example, the Corkscrew or Raptor or even Maverick, I am feeling dizzy when I get back to the station and my head is not right for several hours.

The fact that some people can ride coasters like that numerous times in a row, even at what I consider a very advanced coaster age of 60 plus, is just amazing to me. At nearly every coaster event held at the park I used to watch enthusiasts ride again and again and again without the least distress. Just joy. I marveled at it. I was happy for them.

## NAPHA

There is an equivalent organization for those who are passionate about amusement parks, including roller coasters; people who love the midway games and cheese on a stick and cotton candy and the show in the Red Garter in equal measure to coasters. The National Amusement Park Historical Association (NAPHA) was founded in 1978. Its mission is the preservation, documentation, and enjoyment of both traditional amusement parks and modern-day theme parks.

ACE tends to have a younger membership base and it certainly enjoys a much higher media profile. NAPHA is perceived as associated more with preserving the history of parks than anything else, which is a very worthy cause but not nearly as sexy as Top Ten lists.

Cedar Point has hosted dozens of ACE events over the years, both large and small. I think the highest attended Coastermania event attracted more than 2,000 enthusiasts. ACE and NAPHA have participated in a number of new coaster launches and Media Days at Cedar Point and other parks. It is almost a competition among parks to see who can have the most enthusiast events.

The relationship between the parks and ACE and NAPHA is classically symbiotic. The parks have what ACE members passionately desire—access to roller coasters—and ACE members have what parks passionately desire: media attention, which means marketing benefit. Both groups win when they come together.

## ERT

The nexus of any roller coaster event is Exclusive Ride Time or ERT, a period, usually 60-90 minutes before or after the park is open to the public, when a coaster(s) is open exclusively for a group. Participants can ride as many times as they want in every seat position they want. To enthusiasts, it doesn't much matter how early it starts or how late it goes, it's all good. Back in the 1980s and 1990s, Cedar Point was more restrictive but as the seasons passed and we got more and more comfortable with these events, and the events grew in popularity, we expanded the number of coasters with ERT and the length of time it was available.

ERT is what the enthusiasts live for. They couldn't get enough. Typical morning ERT would start at 6:30 or 7 a.m. and run until 9 a.m. ERT in the evening usually began a half hour after the park closed and went until 1 a.m. We would try to offer two to three different coasters both in the morning and evening and stagger the operating times.

The cost to the park to provide ERT was minimal: the labor cost to operate a few of the coasters for an extra hour or two. Usually a bigger issue was maintenance time. Our coasters very much needed their beauty sleep. The timeline for Ride Maintenance to do their daily and nightly tests and inspections on our coasters was very tight. Scheduling several hours of ERT on the big guys like Millennium Force and Magnum in a 24-hour period was very inconvenient for our Maintenance staff. To their credit, they always found a way to get it done, usually with minimum overtime. To the average ride mechanic, coaster enthusiasts were a pain in the ass, though their benefit to the park was certainly understood and appreciated.

Most ride operators loved working ERT because it was fun, and very validating, to watch guests ride with such enthusiasm, such joy, such love. Lots of high fives in the station. If you work Millennium Force or Magnum or Top Thrill Dragster, you get used to seeing enthusiastic riders, but ACE members and other enthusiasts keep it up ride after ride after ride. It is something to witness. Coastermania was mostly a one- day event. The number of coaster rides a dedicated enthusiast could amass in one 24 or 36-hour period and still be ready for more was amazing. Some enthusiasts probably got in 50 rides in two or three sessions of ERT.

Cedar Point, like most parks, showered enthusiasts with lots of perks when they attended Coastermania or similar events: low admission fees, a hosted lunch, access to park officials, buttons or patches, complimentary commemorative T-shirts (or even sweatshirts one year), backstage coaster tours, merchandise and food discounts. However, what really mattered to them was ERT. That's what it was all about. That's why they were here.

They are a colorful group of people. All ages, but the average age is probably around 30. A male skew, as might be expected. Mostly white. A wild mix of professions and trades, from ministers to bus drivers, architects, IT managers, college students, teachers. Friendly, easy to talk with. When they are at events like Coastermania, they tend to dress for the occasion: old sneakers; baggy cargo shirts or well-worn jeans; a worn T-shirt or hoodie that is a souvenir of a favorite ride or park or event; a jacket that sports buttons and patches from collar to sleeve.

With a few exceptions, they were not risk takers and had little in common psychologically with people who climb mountains or go skydiving or whitewater rafting. I do not know the percentage of ACE members who own or ride motorcycles, but I am betting it is below the norm.

Coaster enthusiasts are often labeled thrill seekers, and indeed they are, but riding a roller coaster, even an extreme ride like Millennium Force, is a very safe activity. It is a much, much safer activity than driving a car, for example (much less a motorcycle), or walking across the street in New York City (140 - 180 pedestrian deaths a year, on average). Millennium Force gave approximately 18 million rides in the period I worked at the park. There were no serious injuries. It's safer than a microwave and a bag of popcorn.

But it doesn't feel safe. And it certainly doesn't look safe. Creating the illusion of danger, and all the psychological and physical stress that goes with it, and doing so in a way that is very safe is what riding a roller coaster is all about. It is fun to be scared, especially when you know you are not in any danger. You know you are going to die, but you know you won't. A similar psychology is at work in a haunted house during Halloween.

For most enthusiasts, park management and representatives from coaster manufacturers were treated as minor celebrities (or major celebrities in case of Dick Kinzel or the late Ron Toomer from Arrow Development). I can relate to the enthusiast, as I am that way around Civil War authors or historians like James McPherson or Harold Holzer, two rock stars of the Civil War world. I get nervous, tongue-tied, and worry about asking dumb questions.

Dick Kinzel posed for quite a few photographs at ACE events; I even posed for a few myself.

I was often impressed with the amount of knowledge some enthusiasts had about both coasters and amusement parks, especially coasters. Many were content to just ride and enjoy the experience and talk about it with friends. Others made a study of it, and really knew a lot about the technical side of the business. They could explain how G-forces worked; they understood track design, safety systems, controls systems; they knew how coasters were manufactured and how they were built. Some had encyclopedic knowledge of all the stats of every coaster ever built. Many of them knew more about coasters than we did.

Enthusiasts loved to talk about their riding experiences. Some of them were really good at it, and certainly Cedar Point, and other parks, took advantage of what they said about coasters and how they said it. For the unveiling of a new coaster, we generally invited several hundred ACE members and other enthusiasts to the park, along with media representatives, important sales clients and sponsors. They were a good mix. The enthusiasts were very appreciative of the invitation.

They took vacation days or sick days and sometimes traveled considerable distances, and at serious cost, just to participate in the event. They liked talking to the press, and even sought them out. They tended to gush—after all, this was a first shot at riding the big new thing in the coaster world. They gave up great quotes about the first hill experience on Millennium Force or the moments before the launch on Top Thrill Dragster. The other good thing was that they kept riding. All day long. It's a lot more fun riding a big coaster if you do it with other people. We would have news media wandering in to the park all day. They were looking for people to interview, to ride with, to talk to. ACE members and other enthusiasts didn't disappoint. Our PR staff was very good at matching media reps with coaster enthusiasts, so that the reporter from the TV station from Buffalo, could stand in front of Millennium Force or Top Thrill Dragster or GateKeeper with Joe Smith or Jane Smith and look into the camera and say:

> *"Here I am standing in front of the first hill of the world's tallest roller coaster. Millennium Force is the newest record-breaking ride at Cedar Point in Sandusky, Ohio, a park known around the world—and here in western New York State—for its collection of thrill rides.*
>
> *Alongside me is Joe Smith, from Buffalo, who with his girlfriend and some other friends made the four hour drive to Sandusky today to be among the first to ride Millennium Force.*
>
> *Joe is a member of the Western New York Coaster Club.*
>
> *Together, we took Millennium Force for a spin. But I'll let Joe provide the commentary. He's the expert."*
>
> *(Footage of Millennium Force with Joe's commentary)*
>
> *"This is just an amazing roller coaster. It's incredible. You go so fast! I mean really, really fast! The first hill feels like you're sticking your head in the clouds. You're over 300 feet in the air! The first drop I was breathless—I thought we were going to dive into the earth!"*

It was not just media exposure. ACE members and other enthusiasts were big users of social media and loved to talk and write about coasters.

It was part of their job, and mine too, for our PR staff to be friendly to coaster enthusiasts. It was good for business, of course, a view shared at the highest levels of the company. Dick Kinzel went out of his way to make himself available to ACE members. He knew the park benefited from a positive relationship with ACE.

# EastCoaster

Janice Lifke Witherow in our PR Department became our unofficial liaison with ACE from the mid-1990s until she left the company to raise a family in 2005. Janice was our point person with ACE. She embraced the opportunity and was a terrific translator between the park and the enthusiast community. ACE loved Janice, and Janice loved ACE.

The best evidence of that special relationship I ever witnessed was at the 2005 EastCoaster. EastCoaster is an off-season gathering of coaster enthusiasts from New England and the Middle Atlantic states, usually held in a community center in Northampton, Pennsylvania, not far from Allentown. It usually attracts several hundred enthusiasts who spend the day learning about what's new in the coaster world and attending a swap meet. Parks are invited to make presentations. I was there as GM of Dorney Park to help with our presentation of Hydra, our new B&M coaster. Janice could not attend but sent a video addressed to the group, letting them know she was leaving Cedar Point to care for her young family. She brought the entire room to a standstill. Tears in the video and tears in the room. Genuine affection on both sides. It gave PR a good name.

One coaster group that loves Cedar Point without equivocation is the RCCGB, or in plain English: The Roller Coaster Club of Great Britain. England has its share of great coasters. I have not ridden any of them, which I know is my loss. Every two years the RCCGB organized a 12-14-day tour of U.S. amusement and theme parks, attracting a group of about 75 coaster enthusiasts from all over the British Isles. Their leader and organizer is an outgoing Englishman named Andrew Hine.

In 1998, Amusement Today magazine, an industry trade publication, initiated the first Golden Ticket Awards, what has developed into a kind of Academy Awards for the amusement park industry. The program was the brainchild of Gary Slade, the magazine's publisher. Golden tickets were awarded in numerous categories from Best Park to Best Steel Roller Coaster to Friendliest Employees. Over the years the Golden Ticket Awards have grown in visibility and stature.

Winners are determined by the votes of a group of park experts. The group of experts was highly confidential. No park people were in the group. We had no idea how many people participated, what their qualifications might be, where they lived, or how many or which parks they visited in a given year. Our working assumption was that many Golden Ticket Award voters were ACE or NAPHA members. We believed, led by Dick Kinzel, that it was a good business strategy for Cedar Point, and all Cedar Fair parks, to maintain a good relationship with ACE and NAPHA and the enthusiast community.

There was a dark side, too. A few enthusiasts sometimes became too enthusiastic and pushed the safety issue. In a quest to get more air time, they would try to get a looser fit for the lap bar or other restraint or even loosen or undo the seatbelt. Our ride operators were trained to spot these actions and react appropriately. Fortunately, it was a very rare event. A more common concern was riders, both enthusiasts and regular guests, who could not resist the opportunity to try to document their ride with their camera. As cameras became smaller and smaller, and social media became bigger and bigger, the problem became more acute for parks. Guests always underestimate the difficulty of safely holding a camera while riding an aggressive coaster, or any coaster.

Many guests try to capture selfies while going up the lift hill; others try to document the rider's point of view as the train runs through the course. The dangers of metal objects like cameras flying over the midway are real. Our ride operators could usually spot an open camera on a lift hill. They would shut the ride down on the hill and walk up the steps and deal with the issue. Safety always came first.

To ACE's great credit, the organization has developed a code of conduct for their members when they are visiting parks. ACE's leadership in this area has been much appreciated by Cedar Point and really all amusement parks. I think it's made a difference.

For us, for the parks and the manufacturers, it's business. Coasters are our livelihood. We are not fan-boys. That doesn't mean we don't enjoy riding roller coasters or that we aren't a little in awe sometimes about what we have collectively created, but at bottom, for us, Millennium Force is a meal ticket as well as a work of art. (Millennium Force is indeed a work of art.) The expression, "Baseball (or any sport) is a business first" has application. Fans (the word is derived from fanatic) basically have an emotional relationship with the sport or the team. The owners operate a business but that doesn't mean they don't love it, too. The two drivers are not mutually exclusive. Ask the Dolans, who own the Cleveland Indians, or the Rooney family, who own the Pittsburgh Steelers.

## Point Buzz

Not long after Cedar Point launched its website in December 1995, up popped the "Unofficial Cedar Point Website" the brainchild of Jeff Putz, a Cleveland park fan who was also a professional IT tech. Jeff's creation, Point Buzz, launched in 1998. In 2004, Point Buzz merged with Virtual Midway, another fan site, created by Walt Schmidt. Other fan sites devoted to Cedar Point cropped up over the years, some quite good and others very amateurish, but in my opinion Jeff and Walt's site has always been the gold standard.

At first, park management, including myself, viewed Point Buzz and other fan sites with decidedly mixed feelings. It was great seeing so much information about the park shared with so many fans, but it had a dark side, as Point Buzz provided a forum for everyone or anyone who had any kind of a beef with Cedar Point. We knew we weren't perfect, but we surprised to find out we were that far from perfect. Point Buzz predated Facebook by several years. It was really our introduction to social media. Fans posted their thoughts, feelings, likes, dislikes, fears, predictions, speculations, and opinions on just about every aspect of the Cedar Point experience. Nothing was sacred. Favorite subjects were speculation about future attractions (usually wrong), insights into management's motivations (also usually wrong), and trip reviews (the good, the bad, and the beautiful).

A visitor would offer a comment about Cedar Point Fries (good or bad) and in 30 minutes it might generate a dozen posts.

To their credit, Jeff and Walt created guidelines for posting which discouraged bad internet behavior and have continued to refine those guidelines.

## Cedar Point Love

There were many people who were more than ACE members or unaffiliated coaster enthusiasts or members of NAPHA. These guests were Cedar Point fans first and all else was secondary. Many did not regularly associate with any of the fan groups. For these guests the Cedar Point midway was a part of their self-definition. They understood why Dave Francis was buried wearing his Cedar Point tie.

Over the years, I got to know many of them. Many I knew through letters and guest comments. Many I met at Coastermania and other events at the park. Most I met randomly on the midway in the years I was general manager of Cedar Point. Usually, they sought me out. I might be standing on the porch of the Candle Shop on Frontier Trail and a couple, perhaps middle-aged, would walk up to me and ask if I was John Hildebrandt. After I replied in the affirmative, they would introduce themselves and tell me where they were from (it could be anywhere) and how much they loved Cedar Point.

The conversation then galloped along: favorite coasters; favorite shows; a favorite food item; the number of visits so far this year; the rumor about a new coaster; their first visit to the park as a child;

the lament that Fascination was gone from the midway; the cost of midway fries; how much they loved staying at Hotel Breakers. The mixture of rides, games, lights, music, singing and dancing, sugary and fried foods, warm concrete, coaster chain clicks, crazy T-shirts and people mostly from everywhere had worked its way into their hearts and would always remain there.

The conversations would go on for several minutes. I enjoyed them. I marveled that the park was so important to these guests; the park was like a member of their family. The bond was emotional, and it was very deep. The park was part of their family history. We always parted wearing smiles. I would invariably forget their names the next time I ran into them on the midway, but it didn't seem to matter. We would start the conversation again.

Cedar Point is not the only business that builds bonds like this with people simply by doing what it does, simply by existing. Many entertainment businesses or sports organizations create similar relationships, which I understand well. I plan to stick Indians pennants into the ground next to the graves of my grandmother and my aunt when the Indians finally do win the World Series.

We received a few requests to spread Dad's ashes at the park, usually at a specific spot like the Hotel Breakers beach or around one of the footers on the Raptor or in a flower bed on the Main Midway. We always said no. I know we disappointed people, but we operated an amusement park, not a memorial park. They usually understood. Did they do it anyway? I think they did. I once saw a small group of people—youngish, probably in their 20s or 30s—standing alongside the Gazebo in Frontier Town early in the day. The park had just opened. It was odd for me to be there at that time of day, but I had some business at the Mean Streak. It was 2006. One of the group was down on one knee and she looked like she was putting something in the ground. By the time I got close to them she was standing and the whole group was looking down. They looked very serious.

I immediately suspected they were burying or sprinkling someone's ashes. I kept walking. Some of them looked at me as I walked past them. I said "Good Morning" in a cheerful way, and several responded in like manner. Over the years, as I walked past the spot, I sometimes thought about that morning and wondered what it was I had seen.

There is only one memorial at Cedar Point (HalloWeekends not included). It is on full view near the entrance to the Jack Aldrich Theater. It honors Jack Aldrich, the father of live entertainment at Cedar Point in the modern era.

We got many more requests for in-park weddings. Our issue always came down to inconveniencing other guests. If we could

Sam and Kathy Meland, the ultimate Cedar Point fans, with the author on
October 27, 2013. AUTHOR'S COLLECTION

handle it without holding up the Millennium Force line for more
than a few minutes we'd do it. Guests loved to get married on roller
coaster platforms or, ideally, while stopped halfway up the lift hill
(something we really couldn't accommodate). Other guests were
always entertained by weddings—if it didn't seriously interrupt their
day at the park. We also hosted larger groups for weddings in the
Ballroom and the Coral Courtyard overlooking the beach and the
lake. Cedar Point is a great place to get married.

The Cedar Point family I remember best was Sam and Kathy
Meland from Olmsted Falls, a Cleveland suburb. We first met back
in the early 1990s at a Coastermania event. Sam and Kathy were my
age, or close to it, and had a large family. All were big Cedar Point
fans. They were avid collectors of anything Cedar Point but especially
promotional material. Sam was a safety consultant who traveled
all over the country and the world. Kathy was an extrovert, always
talking, always smiling. She was her own energy source. She talked
her way into my office one day and begged for any kind of promotional
material for their collection of Cedar Point "stuff." She was not very
interested in old, collectible souvenirs; she wanted the new stuff: flags,
cups, mugs, press kits, media giveaways. I gave her some of whatever
promotional materials we had available in the office that day and it

was quickly apparent I had made a friend for life. Sam and Kathy had a large family, and all were Cedar Point fans. I have known the Meland family for more than 20 years.

Two or three times a season, Sam and Kathy spent the weekend at the Hotel Breakers. It was a big deal for them. They would hang out in the bar at TGI Fridays in the evening. I would be walking through the hotel and see a gaggle of arms waving at me and it was the Melands. Their enthusiasm for Cedar Point was boundless, but they could also be critical and always told me when we screwed up. They were coaster people, but they were, are, Cedar Point fans first. Much of their leisure activity for six months of the year was spent visiting Cedar Point. In the off season they pined for the park and counted the days until it re-opened.

As the late Harry Chapin sang in "Mr. Tanner," "Music was his life, it was not his livelihood." For Sam and Kathy, Cedar Point is their life. For me, the park was my livelihood. I walked in two Cedar Point worlds.

## Chapter 18

# HalloWeekends

### Scaring Things Up at Cedar Point

I was never a Halloween person. I stopped trick or treating in the seventh grade, as was customary in our neighborhood, and never looked back. Though I had loved the fall and the harvest season, I was neutral at best on Halloween itself. I did take our boys out to trick or treat when they were young kids. I remember their first costumes, made by Marie, were the Lone Ranger and Tonto. In those early years my friend Art Mirtes joined me, as he had two boys about the same age as Mike and Tom. We worked the local neighborhood hard. We always had a couple of beers in our jacket pockets. We consumed discreetly.

In the early and mid-1990s, Halloween started to grow as a holiday. Not sure why. Free-standing haunted houses began popping up everywhere. People began decorating their homes in Halloween props. Halloween for amusement parks was created by Knott's Berry Farm in 1973, and then several years later by Universal Studios followed by several Six Flags parks.

Knott's called their event "Knott's Scary Farm" which eventually included branding as "The Haunt," and aimed its appeal at teens and adults, not kids. Knott's introduced "Monsters" who roamed the midways in scary costumes to frighten guests. Word started to get out in the general industry that Halloween-themed events at amusement parks—not just stand-alone haunted houses that operated only 30-40 days a year—were big time attendance-builders. I remember hearing at an IAAPA convention in the mid-90s that Six Flags Great Adventure had attracted more than 40,000 guests on the Saturday before Halloween. You couldn't ignore that kind of performance.

In the fall of 1996, Dick Kinzel decided the Cedar Fair parks needed to take a long look at a Halloween event for the 1997 season. Cedar Point would be the test park. For Dick, I think Halloween was purely a business decision. I don't think he had any particular interest in Halloween as a holiday or as an event. I think he enjoyed Christmas at Knott's much more than the Haunt.

Since it would be a promotion, it was decided to budget the event in Marketing. Don Miears, our GM, got his orders, but Don was not a reluctant soldier: he knew this was something we had to

do, and he approved. As is usually the case with new products there were lots of naysayers, especially within middle management. In those days, the park was open weekends after Labor Day, usually closing after the first or second weekend in October. As it was, staffing was stretched to the limit. How would we ever get enough people to put on special events and entertainment and to decorate the park? Going any later into October brought with it loads of weather risks, too.

There was an open question about the appeal of Halloween in late September and early October, more than a month out from October 31.

There were lots of it-will-never work employees, but they were eventually converted.

Don appointed a committee to look at the challenge and come up with a plan. We all laughed because we knew there was only one conclusion that was acceptable to Don and to Dick: Just do it. Don appointed two co-chairs, John Hildebrandt and Jack Falfas. Our committee included representatives from around the park, including Monty Jasper, our VP-maintenance; Marje Rody, our VP-live entertainment; Dan McManus, our director of Food Services; Peggy Bertsch, the training manager in Park Operations; Connie Lewis, our director of Merchandise; and George Richmond, manager of Animation.

We called ourselves "The Eight Ghouls." (Roughly 20 years later only Monty Jasper is still with the company.) We met and put together a plan, very modest in scope, designed to be a test. We got it approved and were given a very modest budget. I remember we had a park-wide meeting to kick-off the event, something very rarely done at Cedar Point.

One of the first things we needed was a name for the event. I can't remember now the other contenders, but Monty Jasper coined the word HalloWeekends. It was a brilliant name: it was unique, it said Halloween, and it said the event was all about weekends. It has evolved into a very memorable and effective brand name.

We had budget to do two haunted houses, I think at $60K per house. I got on the phone and talked to two potential suppliers, one who owned a company in the haunted house business in Texas and Myrtle Beach, South Carolina, called Elm Street Hauntrepreneurs; and the other, a young guy who owned a successful haunted house in St. Louis and did business as Halloween Productions. We decided to do a whirlwind visit to both operations, starting in St. Louis, then going to Myrtle Beach, all in a 36-hour trip. Our group: myself, Jack Falfas, Monty Jasper, and George Richmond.

## Visiting a St. Louis Haunt

It was late February, still very much winter, and St. Louis, at least the part where the haunted house was located, was a poster child for urban blight. It was cold and windy and bit rainy, overcast, and the streets and sidewalks had the look of late winter: beer cans run over so many times they are imbedded in the street; newspapers scattered around, but not in, trashcans; ice-split sidewalk cracks; even a dead rat.

The Halloween Productions attraction operated out of an old, abandoned factory near downtown. It was built of brick and several stories high. It looked to be Civil War vintage.

It was very cold in the building. There was no heat and the outside temperature was probably in the upper 30s at best. I was shivering five minutes into the visit. It smelled, too, a unique odor of mold, dirt, damp brick, old wooden floors, and air that did not move frequently enough. There was some natural light which filtered through a few windows just inside the entrance.

The owner took us on a tour, starting with his souvenir and food locations at the entrance. He talked non-stop. There were no actors, of course, which he kept apologizing for, but he would point out the spots where they lurked when the attraction was in operation. This was the first "haunted house" I had ever really been in. Without theatrical lighting, just a garish white overhead light, the scenes and the props looked junky more than anything else. I was not impressed. Then he started turning off the lights and directing his assistant to turn on some of the special lighting and everything changed. I got it.

The scenes were gross, macabre, even disgusting, or even a little disturbing: two or three people being burned alive, a few missing arms and legs. One scene led to another led to another led to another. It was dark and quiet. We had twisted and turned so many times we were all disoriented. It was cold. All of us, myself included, tried to keep things cool and professional, asking lots of questions. But there was just enough edge to the whole experience that, as Monty said later, "They would have looked for a long time, but they never would have found us."

The owner seemed quite knowledgeable about a lot of technical details, e.g. electrical systems, building materials, capabilities of various suppliers.

He was all business, but he also said stuff, like he had always wanted to spend a night in a coffin, that gave you, well, pause.

Finally, the tour was over.

## Visiting a Myrtle Beach Haunt

We were running late for our flight to Atlanta. Our host kept talking but we finally managed to get away. When we got to the airport, we discovered our flight had been cancelled. Jack took over and got us booked on another flight and somehow got us all upgraded to first class. It was the first, and only time I should add, in my life that I have ever flown first class. I liked it a lot. Instead of Atlanta, we flew to Charlotte, and then to Myrtle Beach. When we finally got to the haunted house in Myrtle Beach, it was dark and it was late.

The owner met us in front of the attraction, which was in a commercial enclave just off the strip, very close to the beach itself. It was themed as a standard haunted house: Victorian-looking, a few pointy towers, dark in color.

He had no actors, he explained, as the attraction was closed until spring break, so he was going to wear all the hats and move around inside the house from spot to spot. He disappeared into the house and told us to give him a few minutes to get set up. When we went inside the house, we found ourselves in front of a framed image; I don't remember what it was, but as we looked at it, trying to figure out what it was we were suddenly startled by the owner himself, wearing a mask, appearing in the space and screaming. We all jumped back. It was a simple trick, some would say a cheap trick, but it was effective. We were all quite startled. It worked.

The owner's operating philosophy, of which he was quite proud, was summed up in a phrase: high startle, low gore. He believed scaring people was all about startling them, hitting them with the unexpected in a sudden and unnerving way. The best scares were scares that dropped you to your knees. He was not big on gore. A little, he believed, went a long way. After a while, it just gets boring, and while it may be gross and disgusting it is not inherently scary. In this, he was going a bit against the grain, as most operators, we discovered, were in a competition to deliver the most blood per experience.

As we went through the house, the owner used various kinds of misdirection to startle us. They all worked to some extent, but we were now looking for it and none were as effective as the first encounter. One simple trick he used was a room with two racks of clothing. The visitor must walk between the two racks, an intentionally narrow track. You were unable to walk without brushing against the clothing. Very scary when you know something or someone is hiding in between the coats and shirts.

Afterward, we adjourned to dinner and talked through the day.

It was plain to us that both companies wanted to do business with Cedar Point. They knew it was a big deal that amusement parks, including a giant park like Cedar Point, were starting to get in the business. They wanted to partner with us, get a foot in the door, and be our haunted house supplier. There was big-time potential for them.

We did resolve to adopt an operating philosophy that was similar to what we saw in Myrtle Beach. We would focus on scaring people in our attractions, not grossing them out. It also fit with Cedar Point's squeaky-clean family image. We believed our guests would not relate well to seeing buckets of blood at Cedar Point. We were a family park.

That philosophy carried the park for many years and is still largely intact, though in recent years, and even in my time as GM (2005 – 2013) more blood has worked its way into the park's Halloween attractions. This has largely been the trend in the Halloween business, both as practiced by amusement parks and by stand-alone haunted houses and mazes.

## The Point's First HalloWeekends

For the first season, we ended up buying two haunted houses, one from Halloween Productions and one from Elm Street Hauntrepreneurs, an opportunity to compare two industry suppliers. There was no IBM or General Motors in the haunted house business. We located the Elm Street house in Frontier Town, incorporating it into the shell left behind when the Frontier Town Carousel was moved to Dorney Park. It was their standard house, very similar to what we had experienced in Myrtle Beach. We decided to locate the Halloween Productions house within a portion of Disaster Transport, in an area of the queue that was seldom used. The attractions would be at opposite ends of the park, which we thought was a good thing.

HalloWeekends was a learning experience for all. Jack handled all the construction and operational plans; I oversaw the marketing, live entertainment, and miscellaneous issues. The budget was extremely tight, especially for the haunted houses. Don Miears scrutinized every penny we spent.

We did get permission to attend the annual Halloween trade show in Chicago in March. Aisle after aisle of booths where you could buy every ghoulish thing you could think of, from racks of zombie heads to very life-like rubber snakes to some very sexy costumes for adult Halloween parties. Lots of animatronic monsters. If you needed to buy large quantities of material to make fake blood, this was your place. If you needed a disemboweled mannequin for your haunted house, this was your place. If you needed 75 rubber werewolf masks, this was your place. It was an eye-opening experience for me; I found it fascinating.

Our HalloWeekends committee met bi-weekly in the spring but in June we switched to a weekly schedule and expanded the membership.

We were determined to essentially decorate the whole park—we felt strongly we had to do this—and we divided the park into zones or areas and recruited groups of full-time staff to be responsible for the decorations. In an effort to hold down labor costs, management dictated we were essentially not allowed to utilize any seasonal labor to decorate the park. This put quite a burden on the full-time staff, but they rose to the occasion and for the most part enjoyed doing it. We had very little money to give them to work with, but they came up with some very clever vignettes and displays utilizing junk from the park boneyard, old clothes and costumes, stuff from home, and dozens and dozens of Styrofoam tombstones. They turned out to be a very creative group.

We relied on John Taylor, Cedar Point's resident genius, to work with each group to make sure whatever the group did worked. John defined the areas, oversaw the budget, and approved their overall look and feel, and helped them locate props. From that first season, John assumed the leadership role in decorating the park. It was his vision on display in the park every HalloWeekends.

We did some general theming with cornstalks, pumpkins, cobwebs and lighting effects and attempted to give the park an overall Halloween look. Looking back, we had to leave a lot of holes, but John Taylor did his best with the resources available to give the whole park the Halloween treatment.

One issue we struggled with was how much pre-event publicity we should do in the park. We needed to build awareness of the event— and the nearly one million visitors from the first of August through Labor Day was an important market—but at the same time we were sensitive to showing lots of Halloween themed decorations on the midway in the heart of the summer. To some in our committee, it just didn't feel right. The first year we compromised on August 15. We put a hearse on the midway with promotional information and added some additional signage in the park. We also printed a flyer with HalloWeekends information and passed it out to every car as it went through the toll booths and into the parking lot. We anticipated some negative guest comment on the Halloween props, but we never received any. The next year we started in-park promotion on August 1.

The 1997 season was also Cedar Point's first real season with a website. We created a special section promoting the event, launching it right after Labor Day. We learned quickly, however, and in subsequent years the Halloween site became a site within a site and was available much earlier in the season.

HalloWeekends was a great opportunity for our Live Entertainment division. As the event evolved, it became mostly about live entertainment. The first year we added a magic act, a children's show, a hay bale maze, a troop of gypsy fortune-tellers, and re-themed our Red Garter Saloon show. Using local actors, we created several one-person shows that were very successful, the most famous being a young man who alternatively performed Edgar Allan Poe's "The Tell-Tale Heart" and "The Raven." I do not recall his name, but he gave a mesmerizing performance.

Marje Rody created the live entertainment package for the event and managed it exceptionally well through the 2008 season, when she retired from the company. One of her great finds was Jimmy Foreman, a local theater person who created Halloween-themed vignettes and recruited talent to staff them.

Marje created a group of performers—witches, fairies, mimes—who wandered the midways on their own interacting with guests and posing for photo ops. One of the most successful was a reincarnation of the Wicked Witch of the West, played with green face, long nose, and black hat by Ann Marie Muehlhauser from the Marketing division. Ann Marie could do the laugh and the "my little pretty" even better than it was done in the movie.

Getting the two haunted houses constructed, inspected, and licensed was a huge effort. Jack Falfas made it happen, as did Monty Jasper and the Maintenance team.

From a business perspective, the event was certainly successful. Overall, the 1997 season was a disappointment in terms of attendance, but the nice increases we saw during the three weeks of the event helped end the season on an up note. The event generated approximately 150,000 visits over nine days. We knew Cedar Point was now in the Halloween business and would be for a long time. Our guests loved the theming and decorations in the park and in our surveys rated their whole experience very highly.

## Buying Knott's Berry Farm

That fall, Cedar Fair announced that it was acquiring Knott's Berry Farm. The Knott's purchase would be the biggest single park acquisition in the history of Cedar Fair until the Paramount Parks purchase in 2006 (which included five parks). Knott's was the king of Halloween, the largest and most successful Halloween event in the country, probably in the world.

I was a member of the Knott's due diligence team, and I had an opportunity to visit the park. It was November, post Halloween, but we were still able to learn a lot about the Knott's version of Halloween.

In early December, at the company Christmas Party at the Radisson Harbour Inn, Dick Kinzel announced that Jack Falfas was going to transfer to Knott's Berry Farm and become the park's GM. As Cedar Point Christmas parties go, this was one of the better events.

After the dinner and the corporate announcements, much of the crowd headed upstairs to the lounge which overlooked Pipe Creek and Cedar Point Drive. The bar was not large and soon it was packed with a lot of people in a very good mood. We were no longer on the company's tab, but it didn't seem to matter. Music, dancing, a crowded bar, the anticipation of the annual Christmas shut down, the continued growth of the company, people happy for Jack—it was all working.

The bar kept a bottle of Louis XIII cognac in a big beautiful bottle at the top of the bottle display behind the bar. It was clear glass, round, and looked impressive. And it looked expensive, which it was: $120 per 1.5 oz., served in a large sniffer, so all your friends could see. I don't know whose idea it was, but someone yelled we should all throw down $20 and pass the sniffer around and we'd all get a taste. This is what we did—to cheers and clapping, of course—and I do remember it tasted special. Jack announced that he was going to buy another shot of Louis XIII and pass it around (lots of cheering). Standing next to Jack was one of our Maintenance guys, a fan of Jack's, and at that moment well on his way to inebriation. (He had just returned from the dance floor where he had danced solo like Anthony Quinn in "Zorba the Greek," which caused a bit of a stir). Jack took the sniffer and handed it to the guy and said, "Taste this. It's the nectar of the gods." The tech took the sniffer in his hand and held it out with a well-what-the-hell-do-I-do-next look on his face. Everyone at the bar was looking at him as his face then changed to a what-the-hell look as he downed the entire sniffer in one gulp. We all went nuts, of course, and Jack shook his head and laughed.

Jack made sure the tech got home safely that night. That was Jack.

With Jack gone, I became chairman of the HalloWeekends committee going forward. I chose Monty Jasper as vice chairman. I saw it as a huge opportunity.

## HalloWeekends Takes Off

The first time we knew we really had something special was the second season, 1998, the year of Power Tower. The first half of the season had been a disappointment in terms of attendance, but the second half was an improvement, especially in the fall. The third and final weekend of HalloWeekends, on a beautiful fall Saturday, we did over 45,000 in attendance, a number none of us could have anticipated before HalloWeekends. We were stunned.

In 1998, our second, we added a third haunted house, the Toxic Tunnel of Terror, in the picnic shelters at the front of the park, an urban apocalypse concept we borrowed from Knott's. In 2000 we re-themed Cedar Point Cemetery into Pharaoh's Secret, a kind of aliens meet mummies theme. It was wacky, but it worked. Thanks to John Taylor's efforts, and the work of the decorating committees, we improved the look of the park each season. Guest surveys validated our belief that many guests came to the park just to see the decorations.

In 2000, we expanded to five weekends. In 2001, we expanded to seven weekends, basically remaining open through Halloween, depending on the calendar and the day of the week the holiday fell. We were in it for good.

The marketing focus, especially in the early seasons, was a value message, almost a two-parks-for-the- price-of-one message: Cedar Point AND Halloween, or Coasters AND haunted houses. We also very deliberately developed messages that worked to address both the younger thrill-seeker and the young family. Our goal was to build an event that was as inclusive as possible. We wanted everyone to come to HalloWeekends. If anyone could pull it off, it was Cedar Point. We never considered creating both a daytime event and a separate gated nighttime event. Our strategy was the right one, at least for Cedar Point. The numbers spoke for themselves.

We also learned a few things. While it certainly peaked in late October, the public's Halloween interest was ready to be stoked in mid-September. Actually, once Labor Day passed it was officially fall and okay to talk about Halloween. We started our event the second weekend after Labor Day. No one ever complained that we were starting too early.

Another thing we learned was that after a few HalloWeekends guests adjusted quickly to riding rides in cold weather. Amusement parks were not just summer experiences anymore. For a northern park like Cedar Point, this was a big jump in thought, something we never would have considered 10 years before. Riding Millennium Force in 45-degree weather is an interesting experience, even if you're dressed for it.

The Knott's influence on HalloWeekends was open and welcome, even though there were as many differences as similarities between the two events. At Knott's, the Haunt was considered a special event in terms of pricing and product. The regular park day ended late afternoon and the park was cleared of guests. It reopened as the Haunt in the evening, staying open on some nights until 2 a.m.

Most tickets were sold in advance through various partners, including local retailers (and eventually online through the Knott's website). At Knott's, haunted houses were called mazes. All were heavily and, in many cases, quite beautifully themed. All the actors were elaborately costumed with theatrical make up and/or masks. On most nights, Knott's costumed hundreds of actors. The park employed more than two dozen makeup artists.

Knott's tilted to the adult. Their mazes featured lots of blood and body parts. Many of the female actors gave their characters a sexual aura. The highlight of every Haunt night staged twice a night in Calico Square (the largest open space in the park) was a spectacle called "The Hanging." I had never seen anything quite like it. Each year Knott's "hung" a local or national celebrity, whose identity was kept secret until the Haunt opened. The show is merciless in its attacks, accompanied by so much fake blood you could paint a house with it. It moves at warp speed with actors flying across the stage, dropping down on trampolines, and jumping into the air. Costume changes are constant. The commentary is full of sexual references, politically incorrect statements, and character defamations. All in good fun, of course. And it is fun.

It always amazed me and it still does, that Knott's, proud of its family image and proud of its relationship with Snoopy and the Peanuts gang, could also produce something like The Haunt and have the public accept both. Didn't it violate classic marketing theory? Perhaps, but it worked. The Knott's brand is big enough and broad enough to encompass both things: Snoopy and Elvira. The park's market got it.

The feel of The Haunt is a nighttime party.

With its Southern California location, Knott's had a great employee base of actors, techs, and designers. Many of the Knott's actors created very specific characters with names and back stories and costumes. Actors returned year after year to play their character. Not all monsters were struggling actors; some were lawyers, EMT's, business people, homemakers, people who just loved performing, and scaring, for a month every year.

There was a hierarchy, starting with the actors who worked from set positions within the mazes to roving characters who wandered the midway in pairs or small groups, to the "Sliders," the top of the heap. Sliders were actors who had mastered the technique of sliding, which involved running up to a guest or guests and suddenly dropping down on your knees and sliding toward them and at the seemingly last moment jumping up in front of them. Done properly, it usually dropped guests to their knees in fright, the ultimate startle.

The monster appears out of the fog, looking like something out of a bad video game, and comes right at you. When he drops down to slide, the sound is piercing, and when he, or she, pops up in your face you scream involuntarily. It was not easy to be a Slider. It required extensive training and some natural athletic ability. Sliders wore special protective gear on their knees, legs, and hands. Monsters who showed interest or aptitude were typically assigned a veteran to help them learn the proper techniques, and the proper attitude, to be a Slider.

In 2001, Cedar Point introduced "Screamsters" as our version of the Monsters at Knott's. It changed our event dramatically, and for the good.

**The author as Screamster.**
**The Fright Zone, 2002.** CEDAR POINT ARCHIVES

The name was coined by one of my marketing colleagues, Ann Marie Muehlhauser, who felt we should differentiate between the two groups; we all felt Cedar Point deserved its own name.

John Taylor went west to Knott's to learn the basics of the makeup operation. Our park operations staff learned from Knott's how to recruit and organize our Screamsters and how to train them to perform for our guests. Over the years, Knott's had developed sophisticated training manuals we put to good use.

At Knott's, the Entertainment division ran the show. At Cedar Point it was the HalloWeekends committee, a more blended responsibility. Since Park Operations recruited and staffed the existing haunted houses we decided to make Operations responsible for operating the new Fright Zone. John Taylor, from Planning & Design, would be responsible for the Screamster makeup and costuming operation, as well as his theming and design responsibilities. In hindsight, I have sometimes questioned our decision to put the hiring, training, and supervision of the Screamsters under Operations. Live Entertainment might have been a better home, especially over the long haul.

The Screamsters and the characters in the houses were essentially performers, not operators; they were actors putting on a show. However, Operations had the staff infrastructure in place to get the ball rolling and they were more experienced in managing large numbers of seasonal employees. We ended up going with Operations. As many things go, once you head down a path it becomes difficult to change. In succeeding years, as we added more scare zones and haunted houses we stayed with the same management structure.

We considered several potential scare areas for Screamsters but decided quickly that we should designate a section of the Frontier Trail as "The Fright Zone," specifically from the Millennium Force tunnel to just past the Grist Mill. The Trail was a natural choice for many reasons. It was an asphalt midway, black, which would help immensely with lighting. It was heavily wooded which would help to hold fog and create shadow. The buildings were small and angled. Finally, it was already themed. It was a spooky area at night even before it was converted to the Fright Zone. We decided to utilize many of the characters, masks, and costumes that Knott's had developed over the years for their "Ghost Town" area of the park. It was a natural fit. What can be accomplished with the three basic elements of sound, light, and fog still amazes me. Our Live Entertainment tech crews did a marvelous job creating an atmosphere that was both scary and fun.

My bias is probably a factor, but I believe the Fright Zone at its peak was the best outdoor scare zone Cedar Point ever created.

We converted part of the Frontier Town Arcade into a combination Makeup and Costume Shop. John Taylor used the Knott's model but adapted it to Cedar Point's needs. We made the commitment to using quality prosthetics for masks, all of which were hand-painted in advance. John recruited our makeup artists, an interesting group which included local art teachers, self-taught theater people, and several others who just showed some interest and aptitude. One of the artists was my wife, Marie, who had worked as an artist at Dorney the prior year. She liked doing it, was good at it, and we needed the help. Technically, she worked for Planning & Design (John Taylor) which reported to Corporate, so she did not work for me. She ended up working seven seasons at Cedar Point as a part-time makeup artist.

As HalloWeekends expanded, adding more outdoor and indoor attractions and upgrading the presentation in all venues, we outgrew the space in the Frontier Town Arcade and moved the operation to the PEANUTS Theater in 2006, then finally to the Cedar Point Ballroom in 2009, where space was not an issue. We started with eight artists in 2001 and had more than 20 when I retired after the 2013 season. In 2001, we put 30-35 Screamsters through make up and costuming; by the time I retired we were doing more than 300 every night.

It was, and is, an amazing production, all pretty much invisible to the guest. The wardrobe and costuming effort, led by Herbe Donald and his assistants in the Costume Shop, started in July. The Costume Shop was in the Ballroom near my office. I used to stop in sometimes in the afternoon to watch them work, and perhaps grab a snack (they snacked well in the Costume Shop).

We recruited Screamsters from a variety of sources, including the theater departments of local colleges and universities. I think we hired 35 or 40 the first year. Nearly all were young, certainly under 30, and most were male. Several were paramedics or EMT's. We did our best to train them, but we were novices as well and it was mostly on the job training, out on the midway.

## Scare Tips

The idea was to be a specific character, and to develop a back story that defined you, even though as a practical matter you really wouldn't be sharing it with anyone else. Screamsters were taught to lurk in the shadows, to glide along the edges of the midway or to stand behind a strobe light (which made you invisible to people approaching you), then suddenly jump out with a scream. Another technique was to approach from behind and suddenly appear over the guest's shoulder. This strategy, when executed properly, was very effective.

Many Screamsters used shaker cans (a smallish can filled with a few stones or metal pieces) to save their voices. Some Screamsters never talked, and let their visual impact do all the work. Some talked a lot—some talked too much.

Inspired by the Sliders at Knott's, we developed our own team of Sliders, led for several years by Rob Larock, then a part-time controls tech in Maintenance. He poured his heart into it and did a marvelous job. When he became a full-time employee in the Maintenance division he had to give it up due to his new responsibilities.

The scare subjects ran the gamut. The easiest to scare, if you didn't scare them they'd probably want their money back, were teenage girls, especially the 12-17 age group. It really wasn't much of a challenge. Older women were second. Couples were a good target, too. Screamsters were taught to focus on the girl; in fact, many of the guys loved to get the attention of a Screamster and point to their wife or girlfriend. The hardest to scare were males 18–34, who took pride in their manliness and refused to play the game. Most Screamsters didn't invest time in trying to scare them with so many other targets readily available.

The worst guests in the scare zone were boys in the 10-12 age group. Screamsters avoided them at all costs. As a group, they were nasty, mean, and vicious.

Many guests took off running if a Screamster got too close. This always got a reaction from fellow guests. It was hard to resist the temptation to run after them, but Screamsters were trained not to do it for safety reasons. Screamsters occasionally forgot their training when caught in the moment.

Children in strollers were off limits, as were toddlers or young children. Old folks, too. Screamsters were taught to break character and talk to children who appeared to be badly frightened and offer them a high five. Most of the time, it worked. In theory, children were not supposed to be in the Fright Zone, but of course that guideline was wildly violated from the beginning. This was Cedar Point, the ultimate family place.

## I Am a Screamster

I decided early on that I would have to go out at least once as a Screamster and see what it was all about. I had so much fun I did it a couple of times each HalloWeekends for several years. My character was Mountain Lion Man, a feline mask with nasty fangs. I was dressed as a cowboy and wore a black hat and gloves.

It took the makeup artist (not Marie) 10-15 minutes to do my mask. Masks are carefully fitted and then glued to your face. Then paint was added. My mask was relatively simple; others were practically works of art.

It was physically impossible to eat and drink wearing a mask. The best you could do was to drink using a straw. Visibility was impacted as well.

The moment I left the Makeup Shop and began weaving through the crowd as I headed for the Frontier Trail I felt transformed. I was now invisible. I felt a little like Frodo wearing the One Ring. No one knew who I was. The rule was no scaring until you reached the Fright Zone, but I could see guests looking at me and backing away. I had a clear path. I had to resist the urge to suddenly jump at them. Once in the scare zone, I became Mountain Lion Man. I never screamed. My favorite technique was what I called the side startle. I approached my victims from behind and to the side, as actual mountain lions do, and then suddenly jumped in front of them and shook my shaker can in their face.

I of course took the easy route and scared teenage girls and young couples. It was great fun. I really had to laugh when some of the girls would flirt with my character. I was asked to the prom several times. If they only knew they were flirting with a bald 50 plus guy the screams would have been truly impressive.

It is hard, physical work being a Screamster: jumping, running, lunging, waving your arms, waving the shaker can, constantly moving around changing directions and speeds. It reminded me of playing basketball or racquetball. We had a Screamster break area behind one of the cabins and I found myself there frequently. After two hours, I was shot, soaked in sweat. The rest of the group worked for four hours. However, I was in my 50s and nearly all of them were in their 20s. I thought I did pretty well for my age.

Our ironclad rule was no touching of guests. The expectation was that no one touched anyone, guest or employee. Every piece of advertising stressed the "please don't touch the monsters, and they will not touch you" message. There were, of course, accidental bumps. Guests would sometimes react wildly and you got accidentally hit. Screamsters rarely got whacked, even when mixing with large crowds. When they did get wacked, it usually came from 10-12 year old boys, usually working in pairs, who would come up behind you and kick or punch you in the leg or back, make a silly comment, and run away. Screamsters hated the little miscreants and I couldn't blame them, especially after I got whacked a few times myself.

We made sure we had a strong Cedar Point Police presence in the Fright Zone. We usually had at least two officers working the area at all times, sometimes more on Saturday nights. They were there mostly to protect the Screamsters, all of whom had a whistle to signal if they were having problems with a guest. On Saturday nights we would occasionally need to deal with guests who had consumed too much beer, usually males in their 20s and early 30s.

Over the years, we expanded the number of outdoor scare zones until we had six, adding Werewolf Canyon in 2003 (later re-themed as Cornstalkers), CarnEvil in 2004, Fear Faire in 2006, Terror Island in 2008, and Blood on the Bayou in 2011. Our themes included werewolves, pirates, clowns, Renaissance fairs gone bad, and Cajun crazies. Compared to an indoor maze, an outdoor scare zone was much more economical. All you needed was sound, light, rough theming, and actors. There are no buildings to build, no fire protection systems and indoor sprinklers, no queues, no permits. However, they were very weather sensitive, as a hard rain pretty much ended the party. To be successful, we needed both indoor and outdoor experiences.

At the same time we added and upgraded our indoor mazes or haunted houses. Over the years, we naturally got better and better at it, or mostly John Taylor got better and better at it. After a few years we were no longer dependent on outside suppliers or even Knott's Berry Farm.

Recruiting, training, supervising, and motivating several hundred Screamsters is not easy. Screamsters were paid the same as a base rate employee (basically minimum wage or slightly above). They had to be personally interviewed and take a drug test. Most were college-age people, many in-between jobs or school or looking for a second part-time gig, but there was a sprinkling of older folks, would-be singers and dancers, even mother/daughter or father/son combos who wanted to scare together. Some Screamsters were simply a little weird. The turnover rate per year was high, on average about

50 percent. We did pretty much wave the dress code since Screamsters are supposed to be scary looking and their faces would almost always be covered in some way. So, lots of beards and novel-looking facial hair, tattoos, and piercings.

## A Pep Rally Warm-up

The person who was responsible for managing the Screamsters for more than 10 seasons was Bill Spehn, our VP-park operations. He ran the show from 2001 – 2003, then was transferred to Geauga Lake, then back from 2008 – 2012. Bill had been a college football player for Grand Valley State in western Michigan. He was an imposing guy, probably six feet five or six and 275 pounds. He liked sports metaphors and football analogies and in his previous and future lives he had been and would be a football coach. Managing and coaching were almost the same thing in his mind.

He was an ardent believer in the pep rally. Before leaving the makeup room, whether it was in the Frontier Town Arcade, the IMAX theater, or the second floor of the Ballroom (since 2009), he called all the Screamsters together and did his best to whip them into a frenzy, getting them ready to perform and scare at a high level for the next four hours. Bill's rallies reached their zenith in 2008 – 2012. They were something to see, and to hear. At about 7:30 or so, the music would start to play "I'm Shipping up to Boston" by the Drop Kick Murphys. On cue, the Screamsters started gathering from the seating area of the Ballroom and headed down to the center of the room. Many of them started dancing in tune to the music; some just jumped up and down, shaking their prop (if they used one with their character). They danced alone and they danced together: vampires, witches, crazed clowns, wild-eyed pirates. The Screamsters sorted themselves out by location, cheering and screaming and waving.

They were all Screamsters but they were all loyal to the zone where they worked. The veterans led the way. This was their first show of the evening. Bill would stand to the side and watch with a smile. These were his people. On an average night, there were about 150 Screamsters participating in the rally. As the music peaked, Bill would wade into the center of the crowd and do some dancing himself, which always pleased the Screamsters.

Then the music stopped, and Bill took the microphone and began to talk to the Screamsters. He did more shouting than talking, as he exhorted them to scare as never before. He reminded them that thousands of people were outside waiting for them, that the only reason they came to the park tonight was to experience the scare zones, to see them (not the roller coasters). He screamed questions: "Who's here to scare?" and pointed the microphone to the Screamsters as they roared back: "We are!"

Bill had written a Screamster manifesto of sorts, a short oath which they shouted out together to conclude the ceremony. Then he led them out onto the midway for the Screamster March to the center of the park, where they assembled in front of the laser show booth to hear more scare orders from the Overlord, a character created to serve as the leader of all the Screamsters. It was great theater, especially when combined with chilly air, fog, red lights, a great soundtrack, and a huge crowd.

Not everyone reacts well to the Pep Rally strategy. In my observation, it works for about half the population. The other half thinks it's whacko, cringe-worthy, in fact. (My wife, Marie, counts herself in that half.) Some of the Screamsters did not participate in the rally. It was just not their thing. I'm sure there were a few guys in Knute Rockne's locker room who tuned him out (and who still played well).

I gave Bill credit. He put his heart into it and he was good at it.

Our HalloWeekends entertainment offering had five main product lines: outdoor scare zones like the Fright Zone or Terror Island; indoor haunted houses like Zombie High School or Eerie Estates; daytime children's activities, even a haunted house for kids, Magical House on Boo Hill; Halloween-themed live entertainment in our theaters; and park decorations. On top of this we added Millennium Force and Top Thrill Dragster. It was, and is, a very powerful product.

## A Mistress Named Elvira

Another gift from Knott's was Elvira, Mistress of the Dark. In the summer of 2001, blessed by Dick Kinzel, we negotiated a deal to bring Elvira to Cedar Point for a special appearance and meet and greet. Elvira had been a major part of the Haunt at Knott's for many years. The unofficial Queen of Halloween, she had become famous hosting a TV horror movie show in Los Angeles and had parlayed her notoriety into personal appearances, product endorsements, and various Halloween tie-ins. She had put together a persona (Valley Girl speak, wacky, a little goofy, flirtatious) and a look (big black hair, lots of make-up, tight black dress, cleavage like the Grand Canyon) that appealed to a surprisingly broad cross section of the marketplace, though led by 15-year-old boys. She was sexy, but in a comedic, flirty style.

I worked with Charles Bradshaw, then the director of live entertainment at Knott's and the lead person on the Haunt, on the main deal points. He had worked with Elvira many times and knew her peculiarities and demands, which were many. In "real life" Elvira was Cassandra Petersen, a native of Manhattan, Kansas, who had run off to Las Vegas to be a dancer as soon as she graduated from high school. In Vegas, she had allegedly dated both Elvis Presley and singer Tom Jones, albeit briefly. She was a minor actress and singer for many years until her Elvira transformation in 1981.

In 2001, her career had probably plateaued, but she was still a big deal.

I was with the group that welcomed her and her husband and an assistant to the Radisson after a limousine ride from the Cleveland Airport. She of course looked different (pretty good actually, especially for someone 50 years old; she was light-haired and still had a dancer's body). She was not in character, and she seemed friendly enough. Her character was packed away in a half-dozen suitcases of various sizes.

Dick and Judy Kinzel took Elvira and her husband to dinner at the Bay Harbor Inn. Dick said later that no one had recognized her (not surprising). He said she seemed to know a lot of famous people and shared some Hollywood stories with them.

Her appearance on Saturday night on the stage in front of the laser show screen drew a nice crowd. She didn't say much, mostly just smiled and waved, but the crowd loved her. We arranged for her to leave the stage and step into an appropriately themed horse drawn carriage for the ride out to Frontier Town for the meet and greet in the Golden Palace. The Live Entertainment staff had created a special chair (throne) for her to sit on during the event. The crowd was large, enthusiastic, and respectful. Elvira handled it well; she was a professional.

I had my picture taken with her, as did my brother-in-law, Ben Martilotta, who drove all the way from State College, Pennsylvania, for the chance to meet Elvira.

## HalloWeekends Parade

The HalloWeekends Parade, officially known as "The Monster Midway Invasion Celebration" made its debut in 2007, an idea that originated with Dick Kinzel. The Paramount Parks had a Nickelodeon-themed parade which rotated among the parks. Dick saw it and liked it and thought a parade might have traction at Cedar Point. We acquired a few floats and started work. It turned out to be a brilliant theft of an idea. Cedar Point was an ideal park for a parade with its long and wide midways. We needed a Halloween attraction with broad family appeal given the size of our crowds.

The Halloweekends Parade on the main midway. CEDAR POINT ARCHIVES

Dick charged John Taylor and Charles Bradshaw with creating the parade. They executed brilliantly.

We scheduled the parade for 4 p.m. on Saturdays and Sundays. On Saturdays the parade assembled just outside the park in the Planning & Design parking lot and entered the park between the restrooms and the back of Gemini. The route ran down the Gemini and Corkscrew midways past Top Trill Dragster and under the Corkscrew helix (the pinch point on the route, both in terms of height and width) before coming out on the main midway. It continued down the lake side of the midway past the Coliseum and Kiddy Kingdom. It exited the park close to the front entrance between the Ice Cream Parlor and the Lotszapalozza and then disassembled in the Merchandise and Games parking lot. In all, it was nearly a half mile long parade route. It took about 20 minutes to go door to door. Before the event, we painted the route on the midway to help with crowd control.

The trickiest part of the operation was getting the music and sound right. The music and song for the parade were created by Brandon Knoechtel, a former Live Entertainment staff member who had left the company to freelance. It had the right mix of whimsy and energy. It was a good song to march or walk to; it played in your head (I can still hear it).

The parade was led by two high school marching bands (the bands received free admission in return for performing) to warm up the crowd, then came the parade proper, an amalgamation of costumed characters, Gypsy fortune tellers (who danced to the music), floats with giant inflatable spiders and various "monsters," tricked-up vehicles, and as a concluding act a float with Snoopy as the parade grand marshal.

The parade required lots of staff, both as participants and as escorts and marshals. The latter wore bright yellow HalloWeekends jackets. It was their job to work as crowd control with the Cedar Point Police. We recruited several community organizations to provide marshals in exchange for a donation to the group.

The HalloWeekends Parade was an instant success. Our guests loved it. There was no specific role for the GM, but I wanted to be part of it, so I just walked along as though I were a member. I floated up and down the length of the parade, which probably stretched 200 yards when everyone was at their proper interval. I did do some crowd control, especially on busy Saturdays. (I was proud of the fact that we managed to stage the parade efficiently even on days with more than 50,000 in the park.)

The experience of walking the parade I can only compare to the experience of being on the platform of Top Thrill Dragster or Millennium Force. And by "experience" I mean the impact on your soul. Perhaps that is too strong, so not soul but rather psyche or attitude or heart.

The parade attracted mostly families, but not all. Even 19-year-olds love a parade. They would line the route five and six deep. For 20 minutes, you looked into 10,000 faces, all smiling, all happy, all waving, all holding up cameras or cell phones, all with friends or brothers and sisters or parents or grandparents. So much purely positive energy directed at you, at an activity that you played a role in creating, is an amazing, amazing feeling. You, of course, must smile back. And you're better for it. I loved walking the parade. I loved seeing so many happy people and knowing I had something to do with it.

I often saw people I knew from the community, friends and neighbors, season pass holders I knew from walking the midway.

## HalloWeekends Musings

As the seasons passed, we observed that the huge increase in September and October attendance came at price: a steady decline in July and especially August attendance. For many years, August was a lock for at least one million visits; in strong years we did a million visits in July as well. HalloWeekends wasn't the only factor in the August attendance shift. The steady and seemingly inexorable trend toward starting school earlier and earlier was a factor. Summer now ends in mid-August.

In the 1970s and 1980s, even into the 1990s, weather permitting, the second or third Saturday in August was always the biggest attendance day of the season. HalloWeekends would change all that, now it was the second or third Saturday in October, two months later.

For decades, the calendar (Labor Day) created its own impetus for getting to the park before it closed for the season. With Halloween, the season became much longer, not just in the raw number of additional operating days but also in terms of perception that there's still time to do the Cedar Point thing.

With HalloWeekends, there was no going back. The genie was out of the bottle. We just had to admit to ourselves that not all that October attendance represented new Cedar Point visits, that a significant amount were in-season visits that we had moved to September and October. Of course, many were season pass visits, too. The real trick would be replacing the August visits, something which in my time we failed to do.

Weather was always a dicey thing with the potential to lift you up on a cloud near heaven or grind your face into the ground on the way to hell. Every day that passed took you closer to winter. By the time you got to the last two weekends in October you ran the risk of really bad weather: temperatures in the 40s, wind, rain, even sleet.

We were open Friday nights from 6 p.m. until midnight; Saturdays from 11 a.m. until midnight; and Sundays from 11 a.m. until 8 p.m. Over the years hours didn't vary much. On Friday nights we offered lots of Halloween activities, but a reduced ride offering. We priced the park accordingly. The reduced offering was driven by two factors: lack of employees and lower attendance. However, the bigger issue was staffing. Friday night attendance averaged 8,000 – 10,000. Most were either season pass holders or guests staying at one of our resort properties. Compared to most other parks, the Cedar Point Friday night crowd was older and family-oriented. There were strollers everywhere on the midway. In fact, we often fielded complaints from guests that there was not enough for families to do on Friday nights. We did not open Camp Snoopy, for example, due to staffing issues.

Sunday it wasn't a staffing issue, it was a guest issue: there just weren't enough of them. Attendance averaged 12,000 – 14,000, even though virtually all of the park was available. Several factors worked against us on Sundays: football; church; the fact that there were no nighttime events or attractions (haunted houses are just more fun at night); the need to get homework done and the kids organized for the week; a 90-minute drive home on Sunday night in the gathering twilight; the fact of Monday, a work day for most, which for many cast a pall over Sunday starting about four in the afternoon. We tried everything over the years: deep discounting, special events, staying open later so we could add some nighttime attractions. However, nothing really worked, even spectacularly good weather. To grow the event over the long term we knew we needed to attract more visitors on Sunday, but we never found the key.

## It's All About Saturday

Saturday was king, the monarch of attendance, the emperor. On a typical HalloWeekends weekend, Saturday represented more than half of the weekend attendance, some weekends 60 percent or more. It was, of course, classic good news/bad news. We loved the huge crowds on Saturdays, but the dependency on Saturday created huge weather issues. A rain-out on an early October Saturday might result in the loss of 30,000 or even 40,000 visits, almost impossible to make up. We all dreaded the year that might bring two or three rainy October Saturdays in a row. Conversely, rain on Friday or Sunday had much less negative impact on attendance.

I think the guests who came on Saturdays knew what they were getting into.

Big Halloween Saturdays stretched us to the limit: traffic control, parking, food service, park cleanliness, ride efficiency, security, and overall guest service. At the same time, they were energizing. It was our Super Bowl. We wanted to show the world, and each other, that we could do this. Everyone chipped in. To use a sports metaphor, we elevated our game. From my perspective, as a GM, and even before, when I was the marketing VP and chairman of the event, I believe we largely succeeded in delivering a great product at a good value.

The park hung together, our systems held. Ride lines were long, but Millennium Force gave thousands of rides. The restrooms stayed clean. If not as spotless as a Tuesday in June, the midways were still in good shape. The trash cans were full, but never to the point where garbage was piled up on the ground beside them. In my last seasons at the park I was able to access park attendance in real time on my smart phone. I remember walking the park on those days. They were long, but they were sweet. I was proud of the staff and what they had accomplished. Never underestimate the Cedar Point employee.

The attendance growth in September and October was real enough. Scary sometimes. We were much better equipped to handle big crowds in July and August, both in terms of guest service and revenue opportunities. Seasonal staff typically peaked in mid-July and then began a steady but gradual decline. On our big Saturdays in October we operated with about 55 percent of the staff we had available on the Saturdays in July and early August. How did we do it? Fortunately, many international workers were able to extend their time into early October.

We also actively tried to hire as many local high school students and seniors as possible. We provided incentives to draw our college students back for the weekends. And we recruited non-profit groups to work food stands and to do other work. The volunteer program was very successful, a credit to our HR staff and the managers in our operating divisions. The program was simple in concept. A non-profit group, for example a church in need of a new roof, would agree to work a food stand at Cedar Point for specified weekends. Instead of hiring individual church members, we hire the church. We cut a check to the church based on the number of hours their members worked. Some non-profits raised significant funds for their group.

We could not have operated the park during HalloWeekends without these non-profit groups. They made the difference, especially in revenue operations like food stands and retail shops. It was not perfect. In most cases, a trained, experienced seasonal employee was more productive than a volunteer. The long hours and physical effort required, especially in food locations, was tough on older adults. Younger groups, especially college groups like fraternities and sororities, could be undependable: calling on Thursday afternoon or Friday afternoon with the news that they were terribly sorry but they wouldn't be able to work the weekend after all. Some groups wouldn't even call.

HalloWeekends was hard work for the full-time staff, but there was a big payoff at the end: We closed! The seven, or sometimes eight Halloween weekends were draining for the operating divisions. Most full-time employees took off Monday and Tuesday, but working every weekend, basically open to close, wears you down mentally and physically. Saturdays were particularly tough with many employees working 12-14-hour days.

On paper, we were working five-day weeks, but those five days might translate to 50 or more hours, mostly concentrated in three days. Being off weekdays is different than being off on weekends. A lot of entertainment and recreational opportunities are not available on weekdays. For families with school-age children, it was difficult to schedule time together. There was simply no way we could operate the park effectively without asking our full-time staff to work very long hours during HalloWeekends. The Cedar Point culture demanded it. I had great respect for my staff for the sacrifices they made to make the event work. In my last years at Cedar Point we did provide more time off for the full-time staff using some creative staffing techniques, and we were able to cover more special requests. Senior management was supportive, which I greatly appreciated.

The way I looked at it, they were paying me to be here. The guidelines didn't apply to the GM. And in truth I really didn't want to trade the excitement of a big HalloWeekends Saturday for a leisurely drive through Amish Country. That drive could wait.

## Chapter 19

# Dorney Park

Rookie GM

O n Monday, April 7, 2004, I think about 10 a.m., I received a call in my office from Dick Kinzel. He told me he had just received a call from John Albino, the general manager of Dorney Park. John was going to retire. And soon.

He offered me the job.

"Take a day to think about it," he said. "Talk to Marie. Make sure she's on board with this."

I called Marie immediately, in less than five seconds. It wasn't a long conversation. We both jumped at the opportunity. I called Dick back within five minutes, maybe less. He seemed a little surprised at the quick response, but he also seemed very pleased. He put out a memo to the company with the news that day.

Dorney Park happened at a good time for us. We were both 55. The kids were gone to the East Coast and the West Coast. My mother had died four years previously. My in-laws, Tessie and Ben, lived in Sandusky and were still living somewhat independently, but under Marie's care. They would have the option of moving to Allentown with us or to State College near Ben, Marie's brother. I had been at Cedar Point since I was 24 years old and had moved up the ladder about as far as I thought I could go. Dick Kinzel didn't seem inclined to create a corporate marketing chief, and I was perceived strictly as a marketing guy, or so I thought. Marie had recently finished 12 years as a Perkins Township Trustee. She was ready for a change.

At 55, a lot people are being put out to pasture, or are cruising toward retirement. I was being given the opportunity to change my professional life. Dorney Park was a great opportunity, and a significant challenge. I will always be grateful to Dick Kinzel for giving me the opportunity to be a general manager of an amusement park.

John Albino called me later that day. He seemed pleased that I was going to succeed him. We had always worked together well in his days at Cedar Point. I knew he would be a tough act to follow.

The other good thing about the move was that Lee Ann Alexakos would succeed me at Cedar Point. She had been my go-to person for many years. She had the talent, the knowledge, and the leadership

skills to excel in the job. She had earned the opportunity; I knew she would do very well.

It was April. Things had to happen quickly. The next day I received a packet of Dorney information from John and a call from the John Barnum, the Dorney finance guy, who said he would start sending me financial reports every week.

Marie working as a makeup artist at Dorney Park, 2004. AUTHOR'S COLLECTION

I had been to Dorney several times and knew the park a little. We acquired it in 1992; it was Dick Kinzel's first park acquisition. My old boss, Bill Near, had been transferred there as general manager. The first years of the new Dorney Park were difficult. Attendance did not meet expectations and there was resistance among some of the staff to accepting the Cedar Fair/Cedar Point culture and the business strategies that went along with it. Cedar Point's old agency, MARC Advertising, had been brought in by Bill Near to help get the marketing program refocused. I made several trips to the park in those years to assist on marketing issues. I had also spent four days there in 1997 when I was going through the Cedar Fair GM Training Program.

The Dorney opportunity came at the same time we acquired Six Flags Worlds of Adventure, the old Geauga Lake/Sea World property east of Cleveland. I had been very involved in the marketing due diligence for the acquisition. The deal had just closed a week or two before. My sales manager at Cedar Point, Jan Guthridge, had just been transferred to the new Geauga Lake as the director of marketing. Things were happening fast.

Marie and I spent two weekends at Dorney before I moved there permanently in mid-May. The first trip we flew from Cleveland and stayed at a Comfort Inn across the street from the park. Marie stayed at the hotel and looked through real estate magazines while I drove over to the park to meet with John. I remember it was an overcast, cool, drizzly afternoon. I spent several hours with John driving around the park in his golf cart. As he drove, he talked about the park with obvious pride.

He had been general manager for nearly 10 years. The park had been transformed in that time, and John had made it his own. He had made his mark. There was great pride in what he had accomplished, yet at the same time I had no doubt he was anxious to move on. He had always aspired to retire young. We had talked about it often when he was at Cedar Point. John was only 59 and in good health, so he had won the game.

Dorney opened the first week in May, so there was a lot of pre-opening activity in the park. We stopped to talk briefly with ride mechanics, carpenters, and groups of seasonal employees who were stocking stores or cleaning food stands. John was a man of opinions, and after we talked with each person, as soon as we were out of earshot, he volunteered them.

Dorney was an old park, like Cedar Point. Its first operating season was 1884, making it one of the oldest in the country. It had been essentially family owned for all its existence until Cedar Point acquired it in 1992. It had a rich history, which naturally appealed to me, including three rides that dated from the 1920s. When it first opened, it was in the exurbs of Allentown, but over the decades the City of Allentown and Whitehall Township had grown up all around it and now it was surrounded by Interstate 78, a four-lane commercial strip, a veterans hospital, and lots of residential housing. The opportunities for physically growing the park were extremely limited and very expensive, something that had frustrated Dick Kinzel from the beginning. Cedar Point was surrounded, too, but by water instead of houses, pizza shops, hotels, and roads. There was a difference.

Topographically, Dorney was two parks, an upper and lower park, connected by a midway. The difference in elevation didn't seem like much until you have to walk it several times a day. The employees called it Cardiac Hill. The water park, main entrance and main midway were in the upper park, which was the newest section. The lower park had an eclectic collection of rides, including three great vintage rides—the Whip, a flat ride; Thunderhawk, a traditional wooden roller coaster; and the Zephyr, a one-of-a-kind train ride, all anchored by the Steel Force coaster station. A beautiful stream wound through the lower park which emptied into a small lake. In heavy rainstorms, the creek would overflow its banks and flood large sections of the lower park.

Dorney attracted approximately 1.3 – 1.4 million visits annually, so it was much smaller than Cedar Point; however, for its size it had significant financial impact. It was the most profitable Cedar Fair park outside of Cedar Point. It was also really two parks, not one. In the 1980s, Dorney made the risky decision to build a large water park adjacent to the amusement park and market the new combined park as Dorney Park & Wildwater Kingdom. The gamble paid off. Wildwater Kingdom proved to be very popular and Dorney's attendance jumped accordingly.

The owners had made a good decision: Dorney Park & Wildwater Kingdom became the largest water park on the East Coast. The water park was a huge attendance driver, especially in July and August. By the early 1990s, Dorney was more a water park that also offered an amusement park experience rather than an amusement park that offered a water park experience. And it wisely marketed itself accordingly: two parks for the price of one. At the same time, the owners looked to cash in on what they had accomplished. They found an eager buyer in Cedar Fair.

Dorney's attendance came from Allentown, Bethlehem, and Easton, and the greater Lehigh Valley, but also from Philadelphia (only an hour away) and New York/New Jersey (less than two hours away). Within a two-hour drive lived 30 million people, a huge base of potential attendance—the competitive offerings of Hersheypark, Six Flags Great Adventure, and the Jersey Shore notwithstanding. Certainly, at first look, it would appear there were people enough for all the parks.

At Cedar Point, most of our neighbors were about a mile away across Sandusky Bay. On soft summer nights when the wind was out of the north city residents could hear the train whistle; it was far away, beautiful even, nostalgic. The lights from the rides and the midway were a sparkling necklace on the horizon. At Dorney Park, the park was in your backyard and sometimes screaming in your face.

The next day Marie and I spent time with Keith and Ronda Koepke before flying back to Ohio. Keith was a former member of the Marketing division at Cedar Point. I had known him for many years. He was from Oak Harbor, near Sandusky, and had gone to Findlay College and then was hired full-time at Cedar Point as our Detroit sales representative. He had an opportunity to go to Dorney in 1997 as the number two guy in the Marketing department and had moved to Allentown. His wife, Ronda, was a medical equipment sales rep.

I remember the drive out into the country to the foot of the forested mountains to a country inn where we had lunch. I remember thinking how beautiful it all looked, the rolling blue hills and the huge Pennsylvania barns and thinking we were going to like living in the Lehigh Valley very much.

Keith was an invaluable help to me in learning the Dorney culture and getting to know the community. He had been at Dorney for seven years, but in many ways he was still a Cedar Point guy. We shared a culture and a successful history at Cedar Point. He was a good man and I trusted him completely. I knew he would always tell me the truth.

Ann Jones, also a Cedar Point alum, would be my admin at Dorney Park and invaluable in my Dorney education.

The next weekend we looked at houses. We looked at dozens, but finally found one, a little west of the park, only a 15-minute drive or so, all on surface roads. From our parlor window we could see the beautiful ridge line of South Mountain, the first ridge of the Appalachian Mountains. Another mile west and the landscape became increasingly rural. Black bear occasionally wandered along the fringe of our neighborhood. We were excited to be living there.

## Welcome to Dorney Park

I had a grand send-off party at Cedar Point. I received many gifts and well wishes. Two old Cedar Point colleagues from the 1970s, Preston Taylor and Don Ingle, flew in from Chicago for the party. The park was open, of course, so things did not go too late. I had invested 30 years in Cedar Point, but I couldn't wait to leave. It was a strange feeling. In a lot of ways it felt like a retirement party. In a way, I guess it was. Given my age, no one, including me, ever expected me to come back to Cedar Point.

I flew Kinzel Air to Dorney a few days later. Dick often chartered out of Sandusky's Griffing Airport for day trips to the parks. We flew twin engine, two-pilot, five or eight seat planes. Dorney was about a 70 minute flight; Michigan's Adventure even less; Worlds of Fun and Valleyfair were two hours, even longer depending on weather. You needed a trained bladder for the Valleyfair and Worlds of Fun trips. We all used to joke about the first time someone would have to use the bathroom contraption in the back of the plane. It was labeled for true emergencies only. I don't think it had ever been used, but we all knew that someday it would be. On most flights it was a mixed passenger group. It would not have been pretty.

John picked us up at the Lehigh Valley Airport. It was about a 12-minute drive back to the park. It was a Monday, a weekday, and the park was not open. We talked park talk: the past weekend's attendance and weather, staffing levels, ride performance. I remember it was a cool but sunny day.

When we pulled into the area in front of the administration building I saw that my parking spot already had a HILDEBRANDT name plate. Classic John Albino. When we walked into the building and headed down the hall, I saw that the name plate outside the GM's office had also been changed.

John had already ensconced himself in a tiny guest office in the back of the building.

The three of us talked for a while in the GM's office, now my office. I do not recall anything specific that we talked about. The official passing of the torch took place a short time later out in the park at the Red Garter Saloon. All full-time staff, approximately 75 people, were in attendance. Dick spoke first. He thanked John for his efforts and acknowledged how much the park had grown under John's leadership. John spoke briefly, thanked his staff for making him look good and said they should be proud of what the park had become. I spoke last, also briefly. I thanked John and Dick. I know I acknowledged the long history of the park, that it was a great institution, and that I looked forward to learning more about Dorney's history and that I was very glad to be here. Then it was time for lunch.

Dick left shortly after lunch. He looked to say goodbye to John, but John was already out in the park somewhere.

Now it was my turn.

## John Albino: Mentor

John's official last day was not until the following Monday, so we had a week to manage the transition. I appreciated every hour of it. As I look back on my career, it was my great fortune to succeed John. He left me a park that was extremely well run. He also took the time to guide me and mentor me that first week. He had strong opinions on everything, and always gave reasons for his opinions, but he respected my point of view as well. I did a lot of listening. We spent hours walking the park.

Every 10 feet, there was new information to absorb. He gave me the maintenance history of every ride, its capacity, what kind of manufacturer's support it received, what the guests thought of it. Every game and food stand we passed John would rattle off its financial performance. He showed me the not-so-obvious places to look for trash. In every park there are places employees like to hide, when they think they need to; John pointed them all out to me.

The midways sparkled. There was more concrete, especially new, good-looking concrete, at Dorney than any other Cedar Fair park, including Cedar Point. It was not by accident. John explained to me how he had used every dollar he could from larger capital projects like Steel Force and Talon to replace the old black top midways with concrete. It showed. The midways of the entire park were washed down every morning. John had acquired an old water truck which was small enough to navigate the park.

We spent a lot of time in the water park, even though at this time of the season attendance was minimal.

There are no end of things a general manager of an amusement park can worry about. No end. It is not a job for someone who worries a lot. Unchecked, worry becomes paralyzing and breaks your spirit, and your heart. But that doesn't mean you don't think about things, including the dark side of things. It's part of the job. They pay you to worry.

John was candid in his evaluations of staff members, both seasonal and full-time, which I appreciated very much. I remember one evening when we were walking the park we ran into our merchandise manager, Mike Fehnel. Mike was one of our youngest full-time employees, out of college only a year, a local kid who had worked at Dorney every summer in high school and college. He was 23, I think, but looked 16. The three of us talked for several minutes. Afterwards, as we walked away, John gave me his evaluation of Mike: "He's one of the best young managers in the company. If he stays in the business, he'll run a park someday." John was prescient: 11 years later Mike Fehnel was named general manager of Dorney Park.

It had been John's job to finish what Bill Near had started in terms of bringing Dorney Park up to Cedar Fair or Cedar Point standards: make the park sparkle; improve training and the quality of seasonal employees; improve ride capacity; introduce more live entertainment; add more fiscal and audit controls; repair relations with the local community, and make the park look good: replace blacktop with concrete; improve landscaping and lighting, add better and more attractive signage.

The other piece of the product mix? Roller coasters. Cedar Fair, and especially Cedar Point, had been successful by adding thrill rides, mostly coasters. It was the formula: build good roller coasters, attendance—and profits—would follow. The success of Magnum at Cedar Point was the blueprint. Cedar Fair's strategy, championed by Dick Kinzel, was to build a Magnum style coaster in every Cedar Fair park. Magnum opened at Cedar Point in 1989.

In 1996, Wild Thing opened at Valleyfair in Minneapolis. In 1997, it was Steel Force at Dorney Park. In 1998, it was Mamba at Worlds of Fun in Kansas City.

Magnum, Wild Thing, Steel Force, and Mamba were all the same species of roller coaster. They shared a genus—hyper coaster (200 feet or higher)—and a manufacturer (for three of four). Magnum was built by Arrow Dynamics and Wild Thing, Steel Force, and Mamba were each built by D. H. Morgan Manufacturing. They were the definition of Big Steel, especially for their time, each designed with a 200 foot or better lift hill and essentially an out and back track design. These rides were not clones, each delivered a unique ride experience, but they were siblings.

Key to the appeal of each of these rides was the fact they had no inversions. The lack of inversions was a big plus, definitely broadening their appeal. Riders who like inversions also like rides without inversions. However, riders who like rides without inversions often do not like rides with inversions.

Based on the success of Magnum and Wild Thing, there was a great deal of confidence that Steel Force would deliver for Dorney (and it did, boosting attendance significantly in the year it opened and helping to set a new attendance base of 1.3 million), but it was still a huge investment for a smaller park. The pressure to get it built on budget and on time was significant. When it opened, it was the highest, steepest, and fastest roller coaster on the East Coast.

Dick Kinzel was always amazed, but thankful, that competitive parks never jumped on the Magnum strategy. He would often comment on it. I'm sure the cost of these hyper coasters had something to do with it. Only the very successful, like Cedar Fair, could afford to play in this league. But it was not just a money issue.

I could tell walking with John that he felt closer to Steel Force than any other project he had managed at Dorney. It really defined Cedar Fair's commitment to building a new Dorney Park. The ride became the signature ride at the park and twenty years later it still is. The ride experience is similar to Magnum, and better than Wild Thing or Mamba, in my opinion. With Lake Erie as a background, Magnum is more visually thrilling, but Steel Force feels faster.

John added a small touch, which I think pleased Lehigh Valley residents. On the back side of the last car in each train, there was a message, which everyone in the station could read as the train left the station and went up the hill: "Steel Force, Allentown, PA."

When I arrived at Dorney Park there was a new coaster under construction: Hydra, The Revenge. It was a B&M floorless coaster and located on approximately the same site as the giant wooden coaster, Hercules, which had been removed at the end of the previous season.

Getting ready to ride Steel Force with Louis Koglman in 2004. At the time he was 90 years old and the oldest member of the American Coaster Enthusiasts (ACE). I was glad that his doctor was along for the ride. COURTESY OF THE ALLENTOWN MORNING CALL

## Dorney Park Routine

I rented an apartment in Emmaus, a small town about 10 miles south of the park. I only had to sign a 90-day lease, as we hoped to move into our new home by the end of July. It was about a 10-15 minute drive to the park. For the first time in our married lives, Marie and I were essentially living apart. She stayed in Sandusky to get the house ready to sell and help get her parents ready to move to State College. She flew to Allentown twice for brief visits.

I got to the park early, usually by 7 a.m., and left late, usually not before 8 p.m. In the first few months I did not take a day off but did leave early some afternoons, mostly to take care of something involved with the move. I did not know how else to do it, and in truth I just wanted to be there. It was my park. I had to learn it. I wanted to learn it. It would be easy to say that now, in hindsight, I look back and see that summer of 2004, especially the first two months, as the happiest I ever was in my professional life. But in truth I didn't have to wait to look back. I knew it then.

Many times, I remember coming out of the entrance to the administration building and walking down the steps to cross the road to the employee entrance and telling myself that no matter what it took I was going to be successful in this, that I was going to learn how to do this job and learn how to do it well. I was not going to fail. There was no going back. I would repeat this little mantra out loud.

My savior was Joe Greene.

Joe's title was VP-maintenance and assistant general manager, which meant that in addition to running maintenance and construction he was also my designated back up. Joe was 62 in 2004 and looking forward to retirement. He was of average height and weight and had a full head of gray hair; he had a serious face; he looked like an engineer. Joe was from the Sandusky area and had worked for Ohio Edison for many years before starting work for Cedar Point in the early 1990s. In 1993, when Dorney Park was building Snake River Falls, its first major ride under Cedar Fair ownership, he had gone to Dorney to assist with the project and ended up transferring there permanently. He was a veteran of 11 seasons at Dorney and knew the park well. But scratch the surface and he was still a Cedar Point guy, an Ohio guy.

Our personalities and business styles meshed. I sensed he wanted me to succeed and was going to help me be successful. He knew he was a short termer, perhaps only one or two more seasons, and he did not covet my job.

Joe was an excellent engineer, an electrical engineer by academic training, and a very good project manager. Maintenance was my weakest area, as befitting an English major. My technical mentor at Cedar Point had been Monty Jasper, the VP-maintenance, and we had developed a strong friendship over the years. I was blessed to have a good relationship with Joe Greene at Dorney.

Joe was a good communicator. I always knew what was going on in his area, and, as I quickly learned, the maintenance function touches just about every aspect of running an amusement park. Joe gave me the back story on people, systems, rides, just about everything. He had worked closely with John Albino on getting park projects approved through the township or the county, so he was a great help on the political and regulatory front. In my year at Dorney Park, I spent more time one-on-one with Joe than with any other manager.

Joe held my hand as we moved through the construction of Hydra. He had created a massive spreadsheet that detailed the project down to the smallest elements. The first time I saw it I was a bit intimidated, but then I compared it in my head to marketing and advertising plans that in turn might have intimidated someone like Joe. He walked me through it, line by line, answered all my questions. He had great trust in the manufacturer, a trust well founded, but there were still a thousand things that could go south.

## Red Hat / Blue Hat

In my time at Cedar Point, I had never managed more than 18 or 20 full-time employees or perhaps 25 or 30 seasonal employees. Now I was responsible for about 75 full-time employees representing dozens of different skill sets and approximately 1,800 seasonal and part-time employees. I was responsible for the safety of almost 1.5 million people during the season.

The seasonal staff at Dorney was much different than Cedar Point's seasonal staff. It was much younger, many more high school kids, and more ethnically diverse, including more Hispanic kids. It was also overwhelmingly local. At Cedar Point, two thirds of the seasonal staff lived in company housing.

I talked a lot to the seasonal employees. I figured it was part of my job. I stopped in food stands or walked up onto ride platforms or talked to games hosts and sweeps on the midway. At Cedar Point, many full-time employees ate in the Employee Cafeteria during the operating season, in part, I think, because it was very time consuming to get in your car and drive off the peninsula just to get lunch. That wasn't the case at Dorney, where you could get to McDonald's or Panera in five minutes or less.

The Employee Cafeteria was a seasonal employee hangout at Dorney. I didn't do it every day, but I often went into the cafeteria at Dorney to buy lunch or a snack. I started buying lunch for whomever happened to be right behind me in line. It wasn't a big deal, but it had high perceived value to the employee, who almost always acted shocked and surprised but also grateful. I often ended up sitting and eating with the employee. Word got out, of course, as I knew it would, and after a few weeks I could sense employees would angle to get behind me in line.

Dorney had two colors of employee ball cap: bright red and dark blue. I always wore a hat in the park for obvious reasons. I got into the habit of wearing a blue hat, as I generally favor the color blue, no other reason. I was aware that the Wildwater Kingdom and Operations staffs were issued blue hats and the Foods, Merchandise, and Games staffs were issued red caps, but I didn't think much about it one way or another. In mid-July, while sitting in the cafeteria, a Foods employee came up to me and asked me why I never wore a red cap. I told her I never thought about it.

"The Foods employees think you favor Operations because you always wear their hat," she said, and she said it like she meant it.

I started alternating red and blue caps.

June went fast, and July faster. Attendance was basically on budget, or slightly behind, and the weather was so-so. Construction on Hydra remained on schedule. The first steel arrived. July Fourth fireworks went down to the wire as the supplier had a sudden staffing issue and we almost disappointed more than 20,000 people. The water park was now in high gear.

In late June, Dick Kinzel and Rob Decker came out to Dorney. The plan was mainly to visit two of Dorney's competitors, Great Adventure and Hersheypark. Dick was also very interested in riding the new ride at Hershey, called Storm Runner, an Intamin launch coaster, essentially a smaller version of Top Thrill Dragster.

We were impressed by Hersheypark. It was large, clean, and well maintained, a good mix of rides and attractions. It was not as ride centric as Six Flags Great Adventure. The food offerings were decidedly upscale compared to Dorney Park. I had been told by my colleagues at Dorney that Hershey was the land of soccer moms. It was true. The crowd could have been scooped up off a Saturday morning soccer field in suburban Philadelphia or outside Baltimore and softly put in place on the Hersheypark midway. I saw far fewer groups of older teens. There were more college hats and T-shirts. From what I had heard, Hersheypark drew strongly from the Washington-Baltimore market. In terms of attendance, it fell somewhere between SFGA and Dorney Park, certainly north of two million. With its resort component, it was a destination, not just a day trip.

Again, we were positioned as the value alternative. I had to re-train my thinking. I wasn't Cedar Point any more, I was like the old Geauga Lake.

All four of us rode Storm Runner. The launch was impressive. I did not particularly care for the inversions (not my thing) but they added to the thrill level of the ride and created disorientation through the back half the ride. It was a good coaster for what it was, but I did not see it making any top ten lists.

I made a note to go back to Hersheypark.

The drive back to Allentown went quickly. Dick and Rob were anxious to get back to Sandusky. We talked about our observations of the two parks, and Storm Runner, but I sensed Dick and Rob were mentally starting to check out of Pennsylvania and move on to whatever was waiting for them back in Ohio. I drove with a purpose because I wanted to get back in time for Dick to take at least a quick walk through the park. We didn't end up with much extra time but enough that I could spend about 30 minutes taking Dick through the park. We looked at the Hydra construction site, then did a quick tour. It was my first experience walking the park with Dick when you are in the position of being responsible for everything he sees.

I remember it was a good weather day and a good attendance day, a combination that always put Dick in a good mood. I had warned the staff ahead of time that we'd probably be taking a park tour when we got back from Hershey and the park had to look good. And it did.

"John, the park looks beautiful," he said when the tour concluded. He meant what he said. After 30 years of working with the guy, I usually knew when he meant it.

It was a good day.

I learned to walk the park, looking at guests, looking at employees, trying to think about what they were thinking about, seeing what they were seeing. I liked to walk up on ride platforms on the big rides—Steel Force, Talon, and Thunderhawk. I watched how guests loaded and unloaded, how they reacted as the train came back into the station. I was there as much for the employees as the guests. I wanted them to see me. I liked to think if they saw me there it must mean that what they did and how they did it was important. I loved being up high, up on the platforms. From the Talon platform you had a commanding view into the water park.

In the big picture, rides mattered less at Dorney, especially in the water park season from mid-June to late August. This went against all that I had experienced for 30 years at Cedar Point, where rides were king. Always. On hot summer afternoons, Dorney could nearly be a ghost town and Wildwater Kingdom a mass of humanity. Steel Force was a walk-on. The midways were empty. But the wave pool was shoulder to shoulder and the line for tacos was 30-minutes.

There was less emphasis on ride capacity and ride performance at Dorney. It did not approach the focus that existed at Cedar Point. By mid-season, I understood better why that was the case. I never was really comfortable with the Dorney approach, and I did some small things to reinforce a Cedar Point focus, but it was an uphill climb.

In the evenings, the in-park attendance flowed out of the water park and into the ride park. For the last several hours of operation, Dorney would be hopping and the lines for Steel Force and Talon were long. That was when the Rides Department needed a Cedar Point focus, but it's hard to serve two masters.

I had to acclimate to the heat. A GM is outdoors much more than a vice president of marketing. I ruined the collars of numerous shirts from sunscreen and sweat. At Dorney I inherited a 90 degree rule, which meant managers and supervisors could lose the ties and wear a logoed Dorney Park golf shirt when the temperature was forecast for 90 or above. I had no problem with others doing it, but after 30 years of wearing a tie at Cedar Point I could not give it up, so I suffered. I compromised a little by wearing looser shirts, but I always wore a tie.

The third week of July we had our first hurricane of the season. We got hit a glancing blow, it was mostly rain not wind, but a big enough event that the lower park started to flood in spots. There weren't enough people in the park to field a baseball game. I called Dick Kinzel and explained the situation and recommended we close the park for the day. He didn't object (he was good about not second-guessing weather or safety calls) and we closed the park about 2 p.m., offering a return ticket to any guests who were still in the park.

Dick managed Dorney with a light touch, which I took as a compliment. We spoke two to three times per week, including a mandatory late Saturday afternoon or early evening call when he did the rounds of all his parks and GM's. In the year that I was at Dorney he visited the park only four times. In fairness, he was preoccupied with other things that summer.

Cedar Fair was attempting to digest the acquisition of SFWOA, now re-branded as Geauga Lake. Cedar Point was rushing to finish the conversion of the Radisson Hotel in Sandusky into Castaway Bay, an indoor water park. I was on my own hook, and I loved it. That said, I often called back to the park to the people I had worked with for so many years for advice and information, including Jack Falfas (now at KBF), Monty Jasper, Lee Alexakos, Don Miears, Katja Rall-Koepke, Dick Collingwood, Bill Spehn (now at Geauga Lake), Candy Frankowski, Rob Decker.

## Hawk Mountain

In late August, I took off a Sunday afternoon and Marie and I visited Hawk Mountain, an internationally known raptor sanctuary on Blue Mountain less than 30 miles west and south of Allentown. Marie had visited Hawk Mountain several times as a child on trips from Long Island. Her parents were avid birders and I had often heard about Hawk Mountain. Raptors of all types, but primarily several species of hawks, migrate along the edge of the Appalachians in spring and fall. They are easily visible from Hawk Mountain, especially from a giant granite outcrop which crowns a cleft in the ridge and faces east, about a half mile from the road.

The view from the outcrop is breathtaking and worth the walk whether you see a hawk or not. To the north is the spine of Blue Mountain, green and sharp. On clear days you can see the edge of the Poconos, including Camelback Mountain, a green lump on the distant horizon. Looking straight east you look down into the Lehigh Valley; the downtown buildings clearly visible. With a good pair of binoculars you could count the hills on Steel Force.

We sat for a long while, until we saw a hawk.

I recall thinking I loved it there on Hawk Mountain, and I loved being there with my wife and its ties to her childhood. We were heading into a new life at top speed.

In February, everything changed at Cedar Fair. Dick Kinzel announced that Jack Falfas was now the chief operating officer. All the general managers would begin reporting to Jack. A few weeks later I was on my way back to Sandusky as general manager of Cedar Point.

I was only at Dorney about a year (actually May-March, 10 months), so I left no real legacy. I have not spent time going back and thinking about what I might have accomplished had I stayed. I know I was happy there, personally and professionally, and even if I didn't make a difference at Dorney Park, I believe Dorney Park made a big difference with me.

## Chapter 20

# Cedar Point GM
### The Best Job in the Amusement Park World

In February 2005, I was happy and content at Dorney Park, relatively certain I would be there until I retired, some eight to 10 years in the future. I was looking forward to the launch of Hydra and what I thought could be a record year. Marie and I were very happy in Allentown, Pennsylvania. Very happy.

In January, Dick Kinzel had announced that Jack Falfas, the GM of Knott's Berry Farm, was being promoted to the newly created position of chief operating officer. As part of the new order, all the park GMs would report to Jack. Finance, General Services, and Resorts would continue to report to Dick Kinzel. Shortly after the announcement, Dan Keller, who had been GM of Cedar Point since 2001, decided to retire from the company.

Dick and Jack needed a GM for Cedar Point, the flagship park.

In mid-February, at a senior management retreat at Disney World, the Boardwalk Resort to be specific, during a break in the meeting, Jack told me I was being considered for the job. In fact, he told me I was his first choice. I was surprised, and obviously flattered. I told him I would be interested. He said he would set up a meeting with Dick. Fortunately, Marie was traveling with me. We talked about it. We loved living in Allentown, but the chance to return to Sandusky as the GM of Cedar Point, especially after having spent most of our adult lives in Sandusky, was the more powerful call.

I believe I was Jack's first choice for the job, and I believe I was a relatively easy sell to Dick. They both had known me for more than 30 years. I had done a good job so far at Dorney. They both knew I would be accepted easily by the Cedar Point staff and by the Sandusky community.

I had some misgivings. I knew I was giving up a lot of independence, a lot of autonomy. There's nothing sweeter than running your own park and being 500 miles away from the corporate office. I had learned that in my time at Dorney. I knew the corporate office would always be at Cedar Point as long as Dick Kinzel was CEO. Although Dick and Jack both travelled frequently, they both would be based at Cedar Point and they would spend a lot of time in the park. They were both park guys, operations focused; they would be on the midway and looking over my shoulder. I knew Dick, and probably Jack, too, would always feel he was the GM of Cedar Point.

But the opportunity to run Cedar Point, the best amusement park in the world, is a siren song. No park person can resist it, especially one who had already spent thirty years walking the midways. I was 56. I had visions of retiring at 62. This would be a great way to cap a career. Also, in the back of my mind was the fact that at Cedar Point my earning potential for the last years of my career would be better than at Dorney. How can you say no to Cedar Point? You can't.

There was no question in my mind that I could do the job. I knew the park, the staff, the community, the competition, the guests, the markets.

The meeting with Jack and Dick took place a few hours later in a gazebo in one of the outdoor areas between wings of the hotel. It was a relatively short meeting. Both Jack and Dick were warm and friendly and made me feel part of the new executive team. The announcement would be made on Monday, five days hence, at Dick's staff meeting (with Dan Keller's retirement, Dick had been overseeing the park).

Dick called me from the staff meeting and conferenced me in to his meeting. He announced that Cedar Point had a new GM. He paused for several seconds. Then he said: "John Hildebrandt." A big cheer went up from the room. I could hear it plainly. I was one of them, of course. It was a great way to begin.

Dick added that Greg Scheid, VP-merchandise and games, would be moving to Allentown to be GM of Dorney Park. Another cheer.

Then it was time to talk to the Dorney staff. I had set up my weekly staff meeting to coincide with Dick's call, so all my direct reports were gathered in one place. I walked from my office into the conference room and made the announcement. No cheering, but lots of good wishes. I think they were still in recoil, as Greg would be their third GM in less than a year.

I was disappointed I would not get a chance to open Hydra, my first coaster as a GM. It would have three fathers: John Albino, John Hildebrandt, and Greg Scheid. However, I think John Albino's name belongs on the birth certificate.

## Cedar Point 2005

Less than two weeks later, I was back at Cedar Point. Most of the key decisions for 2005 had already been made. The budget was set. The 2005 season was on its way. My job was to oversee the completion of our new ride, maxAir, a German ride generically called a giant top spin, basically a wheel which swung like a pendulum while the base rotated independently. It was an in-between ride.

I inherited Dan Keller's office on the second floor of the Coliseum. Prior to Dan, it had been Jack Falfas' office. Dan had had it enlarged slightly and redecorated it. The best parts of the office were the view up the midway; the location in the Coliseum, probably the most iconic structure at Cedar Point; and the fact it was located inside the park itself. I thought it was the best office space at the park. Most of the outside wall was glass, and the view up the midway was spectacular.

I could look down into Kiddy Kingdom or up the main midway to the fountain and beyond. The window faced east and it was extremely bright in the mornings. I always left the curtains open if I could, but sometimes I had to close them, at least partially, when I had meetings at the table in front of the window. I gave no concern to the light possibly fading the colors in the room. It was a fair price to pay for seeing the midway.

I had an impressive view of the Raptor, especially the lift hill and the 360-degree vertical loop. The sound of the Raptor was impressive, too: wheels on steel; a tremendous metallic whoosh that penetrated the stucco and wood walls of the Coliseum; a scream along the midway. I always knew when the Raptor was running—or not running.

The formal access to the office was up a winding steel staircase from the Park Operations Office. It was installed in 1972 or earlier, when there was far less concern for accessibility. I guess it was assumed that anyone going to the second floor could navigate the stairs. It wasn't a good assumption. You didn't have to be wheelchair

Opening Day 2005. William Hunsdorfer, representing Huss, the ride manufacturer, and the author get ready to take a spin on our new ride, maxAir. CEDAR POINT ARCHIVES

The author with NASCAR great, Jeff Gordon, who appeared at the park courtesy of Pepsi. Nice guy. Loved our coasters. CEDAR POINT ARCHIVES

bound to be unable to access the stairs. Lots of older people, or visitors with various knee, ankle, hip, or leg issues, temporary or permanent, had difficulties with the stairs, both going up and going down. I used to worry a lot that someone would eventually get tangled up in the steel rails going down the stairs and end up like a pretzel. I always cautioned visitors about the stairs. Fortunately, I had good legs and good wind and the stairs were never an issue for me.

After the window, which almost all visitors commented on, my favorite aspect of the office was that it had a back door which led into the Ballroom, certainly the grandest indoor space in the park.

I also inherited a new administrative assistant, Corinne Casali, a longtime Cedar Point employee who had worked in Park Services and Park Operations before becoming Dan Keller's assistant in 2001. Over the next nine seasons she would prove to be a good friend and an invaluable assistant. She did an excellent job managing Cedar Point's charity ticket program. But most important, I knew she always had my back. We shared a love for the Cleveland Browns, so we did a lot of commiserating over the years.

As COO, Jack Falfas traveled a lot visiting the other parks. I think most weeks he was in Sandusky only one or two days. Conversely, Dick traveled less. I think he was happy to turn a lot of the traveling over to Jack.

One of the things I had liked about Dorney was the use of golf karts rather than cars and trucks to tour the park pre-opening and during the downtime. At Cedar Point, senior management always drove vehicles around the park; it was in part due to geography, but also just tradition. I asked Jack if I could buy a golf kart. He approved it. It was a big help getting around in the park to places unfriendly to cars and trucks, and it was certainly easier to get in and out of, which I appreciated. It was not well suited for rain, of course, or cold and windy weather. However, it became one of my trademarks, at least in the early years. Over time, I used it less and less for a variety of reasons.

I also started wearing a black Cedar Point baseball cap. It became my signature for nine seasons. I needed to wear a hat most of the time anyway. I thought I might as well wear something distinctive, something the seasonal employees could recognize and make fun of. I would typically go through four or five hats a season. Hats of any kind were not part of the management look at Cedar Point. I was an outlier, as was Monty Jasper (another bald guy). Most managers opted for sunscreen exclusively.

In hindsight, I wished I had switched at least some of the time to a brimmed hat which would have protected my neck and ears and more of my face than a ball cap.

I have few memories of my first opening day at Cedar Point as General Manager. We did shoot fireworks as a test to see if it would goose attendance (mixed results, at best). I stayed at the fireworks location and I remember being vastly relieved when the last shells had been shot and guests started to leave.

In July, we undertook another agency review. Liggett Stashower in Cleveland had been our agency of record since the fall of 1998. They had performed well for six seasons. However, they were victims of a change in senior leadership on the client side. Also, at mid-season Cedar Point attendance was disappointing. Dick and Jack had no particular loyalty or attachment to Liggett. I think Jack was already thinking ahead to a time when all the parks would share a single agency. He did not see Liggett in that role, which was probably the biggest driver in the decision to conduct the review. The creative star at Liggett, Lynn Lily, was no longer with the agency (she and her husband had moved to Georgia) and her loss concerned me.

Lee Alexakos ran the review and did an outstanding job. MARC was included in the review and hit a home run, a combination of appeals: history, track record, creative excellence, commitment, and market and industry knowledge. They wanted the business badly. Of the agencies we interviewed, they were clearly the best and it was ultimately an easy choice. As the VP-marketing, it would be Lee's job to manage the agency, but I looked forward to working again with a core group of people I knew well and respected.

Most of the 2005 season was a blur. I had a great staff and together we managed the park. I worked hard at being visible. I walked the midway, stopped in the break areas, wandered through the back of the house from Maintenance to the Food Warehouse to the CP Police Station. Once when Jack and I were on a park tour he mentioned that employees told him they saw me everywhere. Made my day.

In August, Dick thought it would be a good investment of my time to spend two or three days at Michigan's Adventure learning how a small park is managed, particularly on the expense side, basically some extended GM training. I had always had a good relationship with the GM, Camille Jourdan-Mark, and the experience was very worthwhile. Jack came in off the road for a few days and got to be GM of Cedar Point. I know he was hoping to watch over a big August Saturday, but rain got him and killed what should have been a big day.

Media Day 2006 I rode the new Skyhawk with its creator, Stan Checketts. Riding a ride with Stan was always an interesting experience. He talked constantly and enthusiastically from the moment you got on board until you stepped off. He was a great salesman for his products. Skyhawk was an excellent ride in my opinion.

## Purchasing Five More Parks

From the perspective of the company, and its investors, the most significant event that took place in my time as GM was the acquisition of the five Paramount Parks from Viacom in the summer of 2006. It changed the company irrevocably. Cedar Fair doubled in size, becoming a billion dollar company. We now operated 11 parks, not six, and acquired a company with a different park culture and operating philosophy as well. My main responsibility was operating Cedar Point, but as a member of the Corporate Planning Committee I was privy to much of the discussion and debate involved with integrating the former Paramount parks into the new Cedar Fair Entertainment Company.

The acquisition was Dick Kinzel's baby. The Cedar Fair board gave him a five year contract extension to make sure he was around to make the acquisition work. This was understandable. He had a great track record with Cedar Fair. It was a natural move; Dick's involvement would calm any jitters from investors and lenders who might have pause at the amount of debt Cedar Fair was taking on with the acquisition.

The former Paramount parks: Canada's Wonderland (Toronto); Kings Dominion (Richmond); Carowinds (Charlotte); Great America (San Francisco); and Kings Island (Cincinnati) were all going concerns, though some were going more than others. Dick Kinzel often said they were all beautiful parks, well maintained and profitable. As we quickly learned, the staff at the former Paramount Parks strongly believed they were good operators and took pride in their culture and operating philosophy.

What was the difference between the two groups? Cedar Fair was more profitable, its parks had better margins, and it had better cost controls. It believed the right capital investment, particularly new roller coasters, drove attendance. Paramount had better technology and infrastructure, especially in IT. It believed its season pass strategy was the best way to grow attendance. They embraced a more liberal guest service philosophy. While coasters had an important role, Paramount invested in more family and soft attractions than did Cedar Point and other Cedar Fair parks.

## Lee and Monty

I lost two key staff members to Corporate. Following the acquisition, Lee Alexakos was named corporate VP-marketing and Monty Jasper was named corporate VP of engineering and safety. They would remain based in Sandusky, which was a consolation, but I missed them both. Lee and I had been colleagues for 30 years. She is a person who gets things done and a terrific project manager. Lee had been my back-up in Marketing for many years. She had the organizational skills, knowledge, and the experience to succeed at the corporate level. Tim Walsh succeeded Lee, and when Tim transitioned to back to sales, I brought in Clark Culbertson to run the Marketing division. Lee and I had known Clark for many years in his role as an account planner with Meldrum & Fewsmith. Clark brought a fresh perspective to the job.

Monty was a good friend as well as my bridge into the technical side of park business. I was very fortunate that in my GM career I had strong maintenance chiefs who were also good communicators. Gary Gast succeeded Monty but decided to leave the company less than a year later. When we began the search for his replacement, Maverick was under construction. I felt it was critical we find the right person. There were no internal candidates. Jack Falfas recommended Ed Dangler, the number two maintenance person at Kings Island. It turned out to be a great recommendation.

Ed brought three decades of experience; he was ready to run his own shop. Ed had been at Kings Island for 10 years, following a successful career with Six Flags, where he had worked at Six Flags Great Adventure and Six Flags Magic Mountain. He was very strong electrically, a skill set we needed at Cedar Point. Ed told me he considered it an honor to have the opportunity to head the Maintenance division at Cedar Point. We worked together for six years. I believe one of my best decisions as GM of Cedar Point was transferring Ed Dangler from Kings Island to Cedar Point, and I thank Jack Falfas for making it happen.

As the company absorbed the Paramount Parks, and as Corporate grew in size and responsibility, I felt at times Cedar Point was losing a bit of its identity. Corporate was naturally on the prowl for ways to create standardization and consistency, which ultimately meant saving money. One of the first ideas from Corporate was to consolidate employee uniforms among parks, dropping the park name and substituting "Cedar Fair Entertainment Company." I hated the idea but kept my mouth largely shut because I knew I would lose the argument in the end. You have to pick your battles. As others have noted, Cedar Fair is not a brand, rather it is a collection of brands. Park guests did not relate to Cedar Fair Entertainment Company, they related to Cedar Point (or Valleyfair or Kings Island, etc.). To me, things like employee uniforms were basic to the brand.

## Maverick

In 2007, Cedar Point stepped back into the coaster world with Maverick. It was my first opportunity to launch a coaster as a GM. Maverick broke a lot of coaster conventions, the most significant being that height makes right. Maverick's lift hill was only 105 feet high. Cedar Point was known for sky-scratching coasters. It was the park with the first coaster to break the 200, 300, and 400 feet levels. Our tradition was bigger and better.

The decision to retire White Water Landing and build a new coaster in its place was made in the fall of 2004. Next came the decision as to what sort of coaster to build. At the Corporate Planning Retreat in February 2006, held at Universal's Hard Rock Hotel and Resort, Dick Kinzel led a discussion on the two main options for Cedar Point in 2007: a four-seat floorless coaster like the Kraken at Sea World Orlando; or an inverted coaster, designed by Intamin, combining a traditional coaster lift with two LSM launches. Rob Decker presented the case for each coaster.

The floorless option was a safe bet. It would essentially be modifying the Sea World coaster to fit our site and adding enough changes to allow for some "new world records" for marketing purposes. I think the proposed lift height was 200 feet. Some in the group did not like the fact that it was essentially a bigger version of two existing coasters. We were going to invest $20 million in this project—it should unique.

The Intamin coaster was radical, or "creative" as some would say. Only a 100-foot lift hill (but a 105 degree drop), a layout that essentially hugged the ground, a tunnel, a second launch. No question

Maverick. It showed you didn't have to be tall to be great. New in 2007.

this concept broke new ground, especially for Cedar Point. But it was a risk; it was new territory.

We debated the issue for a long time, until Dick Kinzel called for a vote. I am guessing his heart was with the new concept. This was not a democracy and the vote was certainly non-binding, but it felt good to act and declare a choice. My vote: Intamin. However, it was not unanimous. Dick gave the order to proceed with the Intamin coaster.

Site clearing had begun at the end of the 2005 season. To meet a May 2007 opening, we had to demolish White Water Landing before the 2006 season began.

The marketing plan was pre-ordained: Western. The ride would be in the heart of Frontier Town. It needed a Western name, theme, and back story, all relatively easy to create given all the emblems, tokens, conventions, visual icons, and well understood cultural myths and legends associated with the Old West.

We talked about the fact that the ride's target audience was young and much more interested in video game characters and space and science fiction themes than things Western. But we felt we could get away with an Old West theme given the inherent excitement of the product. We had no choice.

The name was brilliant: simple, direct, instantly understood. It communicated independence, strength, uniqueness, power—all good associations for a roller coaster. The logo, an image of a single, powerful-looking horse, had a heartbeat.

I was now in a different role than I had been in the launches of Magnum, Raptor, Mantis, Millennium Force, Wicked Twister, and Top Thrill Dragster. I was now the GM, responsible for the entire project, not just the marketing.

Maverick opened two weeks late. When the ride was going through its pre-opening testing the manufacturer, Intamin, discovered one 20-foot track section that was problematic. It was located on the back side of the ride. The bad news was that the section of track would have to be replaced; the good news was that the section was accessible, and a replacement section could be manufactured in Europe and flown to the U.S. and then trucked to Cedar Point within two weeks. With some luck involved, we were able to open the ride Memorial Day weekend. At Dick Kinzel's suggestion we gave away 500 commemorative T-shirts to the first 500 riders.

At the time we were all concerned the late opening of Maverick would hurt attendance. It didn't seem right that a ride two years in the making should break a leg just before opening. In the long run, it didn't seem to matter. We had a strong attendance year and the ride performed well. Maverick was a very complex ride electrically and some of the ride issues had to be fixed remotely by engineers in

Europe. When it came to roller coasters, and many other rides as well, we knew we were in a world market.

Maverick proved that a coaster does not have to be tall to be great. I think by then we knew it wasn't the case with wooden coasters, but Maverick sealed the deal with steel. Maverick is a great coaster and it's only 105 feet high.

With my aversion to going upside down, part of me dreaded the first ride on Maverick. However, things happen so fast you are not sure when you are in an inversion and when you're not. Maverick is about speed and constant change. It is an antithesis experience to Millennium Force and its big sweeping curves. It's a two-part ride experience, as halfway through the train slows and enters a tunnel, then explodes forward with a second launch. Out of the tunnel the train goes up and to the left, then races downward past water geysers and into a series of quick inversions before heading toward the station.

Our guests fell in love with the ride and it has proven to be a great asset. Many guests rate it the best ride in the park, at the least a strong number three after Millennium Force and Top Thrill Dragster.

## Shoot the Rapids

Maverick was great. Shoot the Rapids was not so great.

When Whitewater Landing was demolished to make way for Maverick, Cedar Point was down to two water rides: Thunder Canyon and Snake River Falls. We developed a plan to get back up to three—water rides are second only to roller coasters in guest popularity—and set aside land in the center of the lagoons area for a new water ride, a flume ride we named Shoot the Rapids (the original Shoot the Rapids, which opened in 1967, had been replaced by Whitewater Landing in 1982). The entrance to the ride was on the Frontier Trail between the Candle Shop and the J.W. Addington Grist Mill. Its key feature was an 85 foot high hill, the tallest of any log flume ride in the world. The new Shoot the Rapids was a $10.5 million investment.

The ride experience was good, but not great. In my opinion, it was a one trick pony. The 85-foot hill was a thrill, but the rest of the ride was mostly a yawn.

Jack Falfas and I rode together on the first ride. I remember we both got wet.

The ride seemed snake bit from the start. When contractors began to dig into the sand on Adventure Island to prepare for pouring footers, they discovered they were building over a massive landfill which dated back as much as a century. Next, shortly before our scheduled opening we discovered the manufacturer made a design error which required extensive modifications to each boat, pushing back the opening of the ride even further into the season. Shoot the Rapids finally opened on July 26, 2010. There were many ongoing problems, and the ride never really clicked with our guests. It had a relatively short life, closing after the 2015 season after only six seasons of operation.

In my 40-year career, Cedar Point introduced 27 major new rides (major defined as a ride costing $1 million or more). We missed the mark with only two, Avalanche Run/Disaster Transport and Shoot the Rapids (2010 version). It translates to a 97% success rate.

One of the toughest things for me to handle at times was the fact that Corporate resided at Cedar Point. From the moment I was offered the Cedar Point job, I knew there would be days when I would fervently wish they would perhaps all move to Paris, France—or at least Charlotte, North Carolina. I had had a taste of independent command during my year at Dorney Park; the taste was very sweet. I did understand what I was giving up; it was an informed decision to take the Cedar Point job. My fellow GMs understood perfectly what I was experiencing, and sympathized.

To their credit, so did Jack and Dick. Dick had spent eight years as GM of Valleyfair, one time zone and 725 miles from Sandusky. Jack had spent seven years as GM of Knott's Berry Farm, three time zones and 2,100 miles from Sandusky.

On numerous occasions, Dick would comment to others, in my presence, that I had the toughest job in the company; I was under the microscope every day. He spoke the truth.

There were days when I wished I was back at Dorney Park, but there were more days when I was glad to walk the midway of the world's best amusement park. In truth, the "colonies," as we called the other parks, grew less and less autonomous as Corporate grew, which was inevitable with 11 parks and assorted properties to manage. From Corporate's perspective, and I can appreciate the perspective, the drive for consistency and standardization across parks is understandable and powerful.

Being a GM is a tough job, as you have a lot of responsibility (P&L, guest and employee safety) but, limited authority. It is a 24-hour job. Like being the captain of a ship, sometimes people have a legitimate need to talk to you at 3 a.m. Even when you are not there, you are there (as the saying goes). I never felt the 24 hour issue to be overwhelming or unfair. It came with the territory.

There is a brotherhood/sisterhood, a club, made up of GMs of amusement parks. It is mostly unspoken, but we all knew it was there, a connection, a mutual respect. I suspect GMs of sports teams share something similar.

# The Cornerstones

One of the things I am most proud of accomplishing as GM was the redefinition of the Cornerstone program.

Cedar Point's guest service philosophy was, and is, based on five core principles—Safety, Service, Cleanliness, Courtesy, and Integrity. The Cornerstones pre-date my time at the park, going back to the early 1960s. Actually, the fifth Cornerstone, Integrity, was added after we acquired Knott's Berry Farm in 1997, where it was one of their guest service principles. The principles themselves are universal and easily understood.

Our international employees, though they came from dozens of different cultures, had no problems understanding what we meant by Courtesy and Cleanliness. Seasonal employees earned points toward achieving each of the Cornerstones. When they had achieved them all, they received a Cornerstone Pin to wear on their uniform. The buy-in to the Cornerstone Pin program varied widely among the operating divisions. However, in a typical season upwards of a thousand employees earned a pin.

Too many. I wanted the Cornerstone Pin to be something special, a way to provide recognition for the very best employees. It should mean something.

Working with Katja Rall Koepke, VP-general services, and later with Leslie Bradshaw, her successor, we put in place a new program. This was one of my first initiatives as a GM. The initial first step to getting a Cornerstone Pin was a nominating letter written by fulltime staff member, essentially a sponsor. Second step was a review by HR. The employee had to own a narrative of service, either guest or employee, over a period of time. In theory, no one could earn consideration for a Cornerstone pin until at least a month into the season. There were exceptions for employees who did something truly extraordinary, some kind of singular action, but that was rare.

With Corinne's help, we tried to award Cornerstone Pins on a weekly schedule, usually after lunch on Mondays. I made the awards in my office, so we had to limit the group to no more than five or six; but there were times when we did more.

I used to show the early arrivals around the office, including my escape door into the Ballroom and of course the view out the window down onto the midway. I sat in a chair by the table. I always invited one of the almost recipients to sit in my chair at my desk. A few of them didn't hesitate for a millisecond before parking their butt's in the chair and spinning it around. Other times the group would hesitate, and I almost had to order someone into the chair.

I spoke briefly to the group. I thanked them for choosing to work at Cedar Point. I thanked them for making a difference. I thanked them for taking such good care of our guests and/or their fellow employees. I told them they were the best of the best. I told them this was a big deal that I considered it a big deal and I hoped they did, too. I reminded them we awarded relatively few pins every year, perhaps 70 – 90 in a season out of a potential pool of 5,000 or more. The Cornerstone Pin was the highest form of recognition a Cedar Point seasonal employee could earn.

When I awarded each pin, I also gave each recipient a copy of the nominating letter written on their behalf. All the recipients then put on their pins. HR always sent a wrangler to the meeting to make sure everyone showed up on time, etc. They also helped recipients put on their pins.

Then it was time for a picture. I always let the new award winners pick the spot, provided it wasn't at the far end of the peninsula. We posed as a group, sometimes as a division or a department. Each Cornerstone recipient received a copy of the picture. It was posted at various employee locations in the park and ran in Behind the Lines, the employee newsletter.

Cornerstone Pin recipients were hard to categories. They were all ages, 16 or 17 up to 70 or 75. Men and women, about evenly split. Many, perhaps most had outgoing personalities; evident even in a short conversation. I was particularly impressed by the number of international employees who earned Cornerstone Pins. It made me wonder how many U.S. college students could go to Poland or Bulgaria or Singapore and work in the local amusement park, successfully interacting with guests to the level that they would be recognized as the best of the best? Probably more than you might think.

Matt Ouimet used to comment when talking about certain individuals that they possessed the service gene, that they were programmed to read people, understand people, like people, and to get real satisfaction from solving people problems. The service gene was strong in the Cornerstone Pin group.

Looking back, some of my best times as GM of Cedar Point were awarding Cornerstone Pins. And I do miss it. I do.

For many years I was a trustee of Providence Care Centers, a Sandusky nursing home and senior living community sponsored by the Sisters of St. Francis. One day I saw rack card in the lobby of the nursing home which read "Hey Stacy!" I picked it up. It was an invitation for the visitor (or resident) to communicate directly to Stacy, the administrator of the property, on any issue that concerned them. It was set up as a self-mailer and Stacy's invitation included the promise that she read every "Hey Stacey!" guest comment.

I stole the idea, with the approval of the Sisters, and had the card modified to fit the Cedar Point environment, and soon we had "Hey John!" cards in racks at Guest Services and various retail locations around the park. Guests sometimes included contact info, but it was not required. Comments ran the gamut of the amusement park experience. It was a great way to get a feel for the concerns of the guests on the midway. I did not promise a response, but I often wrote a quick email to "Hey John!" writers. Interestingly, the majority of "Hey John!" comments were about our employees, and most were stories of seasonal employees doing good things for guests. My practice was to write a hand-written note to the employee thanking them for making a difference and including the "Hey John!" card with the note.

I was not so naïve that I didn't realize that some employees were not above creating their own "Hey John!" notes. I'm sure we got burned a few times, though Corinne was very good at filtering out the illegitimate cards.

## GM Duties

As a GM, you are a generalist surrounded by specialists. I did find the variety of the job exhilarating. Every day I would bounce from an HR issue to maintenance or marketing problems to finance or food service. You got the opportunity to see how it all fit together. In fact, you were paid to make it all fit together as well as it could, balancing lots of needs in search of the greater good, which at bottom was financial performance.

As a marketer, I was used to objective measurement (see Chapter 7). As a GM, I was measured against a greater number of objectives, including attendance, in-park spending, cost control, management of capital expenditures projects, and management of seasonal labor costs. Cost control was always a major issue with Dick Kinzel. He hated waste. He was fixated on it and made no apology for it. Marketers often get branded as spendthrifts, sometimes deservedly so, but I did not believe I fell into that category.

Cost control did not come naturally to me, but I worked at it and got better at it over the years. You could not survive for very long at Cedar Point or Cedar Fair if you wasted money or failed to manage your budget.

Shortly after I retired a friend of our son Michael took a job with a West Coast tech company, a startup. He described what I considered an alien work environment: complimentary juice bar, massages, on premise gym, first class airline tickets, open expense accounts. No one gave a second thought about saving money. It was not my world.

I had an informal group of people I used for advice and counsel during my GM years. The group included Jack Goldsmith, the founder of MARC Advertising; Ed Bailey, the account executive with H&M who went on to work for the Rock Hall and then Austin City Limits; Don Miears; Dick Collingwood, our retired corporate VP-administration; my friends Bud Greene and Art Mirtes; my brother Tom, a partner with Accenture. Marie served as chair of the group.

## Walking the Park Style of Management

Perhaps the most popular business book of the 1980s was "In Search of Excellence" by Tom Peters and Robert Waterman. In their view, one of the key traits of a successful company was called "Management By Walking Around," which argued that successful managers should move about, even wander about, their operations on a regular basis, that this was how a good manager kept his fingers in the pot, that wandering around the shop floor and talking to employees or visiting with customers on their own turf beat reading the Wall Street Journal any day.

I suspect that George Boeckling was a walk-around guy. We have no evidence one way or another, but I'd bet good money he was. I don't have a feel for Emile Legros or George Roose. Bob Munger was not. Dick Kinzel was. So was Don Mears, Bill Near, Jack Falfas, Dan Keller, and John Albino. It was expected of a GM, and I'm sure it was the GM protocol at Six Flags over Georgia and Sea World and just about every other amusement or theme park.

Each of us had our own style. Some GMs walked the same route around the park every time they walked the park. Others took pride in mixing it up every time, just going wherever they felt like going. Some took lots of short walks, others fewer but longer walks. Some tilted toward being morning walkers, others leaned to late afternoon or early evening.

I walked the Cedar Point midway with Dick Kinzel many times. In terms of pace, we were compatible (a good thing). When he went on his tour, we usually left his office mid-afternoon and walked over to Sky Ride west and then slid toward what was once called the Million Dollar Midway, which led past the Iron Dragon and the CP&LE Railroad entrance and onto the Millennium Force Plaza. After a quick look inside the Red Garter, it was down the Frontier Trail.

We often walked on Saturdays, the special day in our world, the day we hopefully kicked ass. Both Dick and Jack were energized on Saturdays. We all were.

Dick's walk focused on the midway; his eyes focused on what the guest saw. We rarely went up on ride platforms or into food stands or into break areas. As we walked, we talked about business issues that related to what was in front of us: the music in the Red Garter, maintenance issues on Millennium Force, what to do with the Town

Hall Museum. From the Frontier Trail we crossed over the stone bridge into Frontier Town. We always stopped for some water at the drinking fountain outside the museum. For whatever reason, it had the coldest water in the park.

Dick was often recognized. Guests liked to shake his hand. They sometimes asked for a picture, which Dick gladly obliged, always with a smile. To nearly all the coaster enthusiasts and many of the season pass holders, Dick was a genuine celebrity, and more importantly, the man who had made all this possible, especially the coasters.

Dick liked the attention, and you couldn't blame him.

We stuck out: two middle age guys in ties. And one with a long-sleeve shirt.

Dick was a sunscreen user. I never once saw him in the park wearing a hat. Like Jack, he favored short sleeve shirts on warm days. I went back and forth on short versus long sleeve but in general favored long, especially the second half of my career when I was more aware of the bad things the sun does to human skin.

If it was a busy day, and the weather was good, and park attendance was running ahead of the comparable day from last year, Dick was in a very good mood.

Whenever we ran into an employee, full time or seasonal, we exchanged greetings. In a Cedar Point environment, you become name tag dependent by default.

"They think you know more than you know" was one of his bits of advice he offered about managing seasonal employees.

In Frontier Town, we watched the basketball game for a while, always checking to make sure they were operating with the right amount of labor, then cruised toward Lusty Lil's. Like the Red Garter, we made a brief stop (or no stop if the show was on break), then rounded the corner and crossed the tracks into the Mean Streak Plaza. We were now at the back edge of the Cedar Point galaxy. We never went up the ride platform, instead did a 360 and headed back into Frontier Town, which we followed to the Gemini Midway.

We picked up trash and on a busy Saturday there was always something to pick up. We checked out the appearance and demeanor of our employees. We looked for sweeps. We checked out restrooms. We listened to park music. Dick was very sensitive to park music: volume, content, content mix.

I did not walk defensively. I knew we were good operators and I had confidence in my staff. But I also asked Corinne to call my direct reports and tell them Dick and I would be on a park tour that afternoon.

When we walked past Gemini we both laughed and talked about its opening day, June 17, 1978.

When we reached Magnum, we turned left and went through the tunnel and exited the park. Next stop was the water park, Soak City.

The water park was Dick's baby. He had introduced water slides as an extra charge attraction at Valleyfair, a very bold move at the time, and had done the same at Cedar Point in 1988. Now, 20 years later, Soak City was a major stand-alone attraction.

It was a quick walk through Soak City, a blur of all manner of people. We always stopped briefly at Bubbles, rested our hands on the fence and took it all in. To me, the swim-up bar was the height of getting away from it all and I envied the guests sitting at the bar or standing in the in the pool, their hands on a cold beer, the Magnum overhead, Lake Erie in the background. Once, in the 1990s, when we had out of town guests, on my day off, my friend Tim McCarthy and I went to Bubbles for a few beers. Our wives were not interested in going with us. I didn't enjoy it at all. I felt guilty being in the pool while my colleagues were all working. I have never been back, even in retirement, though I think about it.

When we left Soak City we left the park and headed into the Resort. First, we had to walk past the Soak City parking lot. Invariably there was at least some trash. It was a kind of no-man's land in terms of which division was responsible for cleanliness. Sometimes I had to make a call.

Dick liked to walk through Lighthouse Point, including a walk out on the pier. There was usually at least one kid with a pole, oblivious to the sounds and sights of the park behind him. Most of the cars parked in front of the cottages hailed from places other than Ohio: Illinois, Michigan, Indiana, Kentucky, Pennsylvania, Canada, Georgia, Florida, North Carolina, New York, and Wisconsin. We didn't say it, but I'm sure Dick felt good thinking about how he had helped create something that attracted people from all over; and I know I felt good knowing I had been part of the effort to create awareness of the park in places like New Jersey and Illinois.

We cruised through the Sandcastle Suites lobby, another spot with cold drinking water. The view of the lake was spectacular from here. Generally quiet, too, as most guests were in the park. Then we headed down the esplanade (or walkway) that led to Hotel Breakers and eventually the Coral Courtyard and the Beach Gate entrance to the park.

Most of the time, we walked through Friday's on the Beach, the Breakers Lobby and Rotunda, and then out to the pools and back out onto the boardwalk. On warm sunny Saturdays the beach was full of guests; dozens of boats, from small outboards up to 40-foot yachts were anchored just past the buoy line which marked the official swimming area. Our guests in the pools and on the beach and on the boardwalk looked happy. I liked what I was doing at that moment, but I also would have traded places with them. It's a hard thing to understand.

Last stop outside the park was the Coral Courtyard, our main location for hosting company picnics: trees, tents, a beautiful view of the lake, the background dominated by the Coral Dining Room and Convention Center, the building that had started it all in 1888, once known as the Grand Pavilion. While the basic structure of the building remains, most of the façade is gone; you have to know what you are looking at to have an idea what it was in its glory days.

Late afternoons in July and August the Coral Courtyard was full of people attending company picnics. It was close enough to dinner time that the smell of barbecuing chickens was like a gift from heaven. I looked around for one of our sales reps and arranged for a quick hello from Dick to the client.

We entered the park at the Beach Gate, giving a wave to the three older Sandusky women—Sue Link (a George Boeckling descendant), Virginia Newman, and Sally Shenberger, who managed the gate operation, and managed it well. On cold and rainy days in the spring fall, with a fierce wind off the lake, working the Beach Gate was like working in northern Canada. It was not for the weak of body. These three ladies, all in their 70s, dressed for it and never complained. They were legends at the park.

But this was mid-summer, early evening, and walking into the park you smelled the flowers and the fresh cut fries.

At this point Dick often headed back to his office, which was quite close by. However, some days he continued past the Coliseum and up the main midway to the front gate to mark a complete park tour.

Because of his travel schedule, I had far fewer opportunities to do park tours with Jack Falfas. I regretted this very much because Jack knew Cedar Point very well and I know I could have benefitted from his knowledge and experience. He had midway smarts. He had built the operating structure for many of the key departments at Cedar Point and Knott's Berry Farm.

## Knute Rockne Worked Here

Many football fans, and certainly most college football fans, are at least generally familiar with the Cedar Point – Notre Dame connection.

In the summer of 1913, two young men, Knute Rockne and Gus Dorais, took jobs as lifeguards at Cedar Point. Both were members of the Notre Dame football team. Dorais was the quarterback and Rockne the end and captain of the team. At the time the forward pass, though legal in college football, was seldom used by the offense.

However, Dorais and Rockne believed that if utilized properly it could be an effective weapon. The team that could throw the ball as well as run the ball would have a decided advantage.

Rockne and Dorais went to Cedar Point with a plan: to perfect the forward pass. They did not run around the Cedar Point Beach with nothing else to do and somehow discovered the forward pass. They arrived with the objective to develop the passing skills they would need to beat Army that fall, a game they knew would receive national attention.

The tradition is that Rockne and Dorais spent all their football time on the beach. However, anyone who's ever tried running and catching footballs in sand knows it's nothing like grass. While they did spend some time practicing on the beach, most of their throwing and catching took place on a grass field next door to Hotel Breakers, the area where the Bon Air addition would be built in 1926. The football in use in 1913 was more like a basketball than a modern football, and more difficult to throw.

However, Dorais learned to throw it effectively by adjusting his grip, just as Rockne learned to catch the ball with his fingers rather than his body. The single biggest innovation they brought to the passing game was the concept of leading the receiver when throwing the ball. It was a big step. In the existing passing game receivers mostly stood and waited for the ball, and then hugged it to their body. On the beach and on the grassy field, Dorais practiced leading Rockne, throwing the ball not to where he was but to a spot where he would be. Rockne learned to run to the ball, to catch it at on a dead run with the fingers of his outstretched arms, with soft hands. Throwing and catching a football at a distance and at speed is one of the most beautiful actions in sport. And it all started at Cedar Point.

Rockne and Dorais did more than lifeguarding. They also worked as bellmen, room clerks, night watchmen, and checkers at the Breakers' restaurants. Rockne met his future wife, Bonnie Skiles, a server from Kenton, Ohio, 80 miles south of Cedar Point, at what became known as the Coral Dining Room. (I would meet my wife in the same dining room 61 summers later.) They would marry a year later, July 15, 1914, at St. Peter and Paul Catholic Church on Columbus Avenue in Sandusky. In 2010, the Erie County Historical Society erected a marker near the church to commemorate the event.

In the fall of 1913, everything came together for Knute Rockne, Gus Dorais, and Notre Dame. On November 1, 1913, Notre Dame, a huge underdog, beat Army 35-13 on the West Point field using a strong passing game and ushered in a new age of football. Although Dorais' first two passes had sailed over Rockne's head, the third did not. Rockne caught it in stride for a 30-yard touchdown. The crowd was in disbelief. Dorais finished the game completing 14 of 17 pass attempts for 243 yards and two touchdowns. More than a century later, still impressive numbers.

Knute Rockne would go on to football immortality as the inspirational coach of Notre Dame from 1918 until his death in a plane crash in Kansas in 1931. He still holds the record for the highest winning percentage of any college football coach. When he died he was one of the best-known sports figures in the country.

My last year at Cedar Point, 2013, coincided with the 100th Anniversary of the Forward Pass and the Notre Dame versus Army game. I admit I took full advantage of the moment. I directed our then PR manager, Bryan Edwards, to put together a commemorative event on the beach. Bryan contacted Notre Dame and put together a reenactment of Rockne and Dorais throwing passes on the beach. The reenactors were two local high school football players (one a quarterback and one a receiver), both wearing vintage uniforms.

Descendants of both Rockne and Dorais attended the event, and their two great grandsons, Mike Rockne and Charles Dorais, also reenacted throwing passes on the Cedar Point beach.

## Wildwater Kingdom

In 2004, Cedar Fair purchased Six Flags Worlds of Adventure (SFWOA) from Six Flags. We closed the animal section of the park (the old Sea World) and re-branded the property as Geauga Lake. Bill Spehn, who had been VP-operations at Cedar Point, was tapped to be GM. In 2005, the park added significant water attractions and re-branded again as Geauga Lake and Wildwater Kingdom, basically assuming a Dorney Park model.

However, attendance never met expectations and the Geauga Lake side of the park was closed after the 2007 season. The company decided to continue to operate Wildwater Kingdom (WWK) as a stand-alone waterpark starting with the 2008 season. It was also decided to operate WWK as a division of Cedar Point, so it became one of my responsibilities. Bill Spehn transferred back to Cedar Point into his former job as VP-operations and Colleen Murphy was named GM of the waterpark.

Colleen and her staff, and then Bill Spehn in a return engagement, gave it their all but we could not operate it profitably. The decision was made to close the park after the 2016 operating season, three seasons after I retired.

The old SFWOA property totaled more than 700 acres. For comparison, Cedar Point's total acreage is about 400, including the causeway. In 1999, there were two parks, Sea World and Geauga Lake, each of which drew more than one million visitors. When Wildwater Kingdom was shuttered in 2016, the two million visitors had become none. Where did they go? Some went to Cedar Point but not in the numbers we had anticipated. Some went to Kennywood or Waldameer or one of the other Western Pennsylvania amusement parks.

Where did they all go I asked a friend of mine? He had a baseball story. When the Brooklyn Dodgers and New York Giants moved to California in the 1950s there was a consensus that the Yankee box office would benefit greatly. Giant fans and Dodger fans would still need to go to baseball games. Actually, not. They found other things to do: picnics, visits to museums, fishing, shopping, TV, visits to grandma, whatever. Most of the SFWOA customers acted similarly.

My habit was to visit Wildwater Kingdom on Sundays during the operating season. It was about an hour and forty minute drive from Cedar Point. The park was an interesting amalgamation of people and attractions. Some of the staff went all the way back to the Anheuser Busch days of Sea World. The park was a tiny several acre speck surrounded by 700 acres of near wilderness, which in turn was surrounded by upscale suburb. I watched as Mother Nature quickly took over. Each visit, the property grew a little wilder. We sold off the rides or moved them to other Cedar Fair parks.

It was an eerie experience walking through the old Geauga Lake property. It was painful for any amusement park person: abandoned and wrecked, the rides torn from their foundations, empty buildings, vegetation growing through coaster track, the old wave pool now a kind of landfill. I remembered visiting it many times in the '70s, '80s, and '90s when it was a respected competitor. The midways were alive, the shouts and screams ever-present.

From the wave pool deck at WWK, you had a commanding view of the lake with the skeletal remains of the amusement park in the background.

I don't believe Cedar Fair purchased SFWOA only to close it. We wanted to make it go and believed we could succeed in making it go. However, we were not able to do it.

## Getting a New Boss

In the fall of 2008 I got a new boss, Richard Zimmerman, who was promoted from GM of Kings Dominion, a former Paramount Park, to a regional VP of Cedar Fair responsible for several parks, including Cedar Point. A Georgetown graduate, he was a finance guy by training and experience. In style he was calm, measured and thorough. Like Don Miears and Don Dittmann, he liked to ask questions and he expected good answers. He played his cards close to the vest, but I always sensed he knew where he was going.

My last boss was Phil Bender, who I worked with for my last two seasons. Phil and I shared the Cedar Point/Cedar Fair culture. He was a graduate of Perkins High School and grew up in the Sandusky area. He worked full time at Cedar Point for a few years out of college, but then transferred to Valleyfair, then to Worlds of Fun, where he became GM in 2001. His career had largely been spent in the colonies. He was a foods guy by training. We shared a love of history, especially Civil War history. I consider Phil an authority on the guerilla campaigns in Kansas and Missouri.

I had 10 bosses in my working career. All male. Some older and some younger than I was. The shortest tenure was three months, the longest 10 years.

None were bad bosses. I learned from all of them.

## Senior Transition

In the first part of June 2010, Jack Falfas left the company. Only 18 months later, at the end of 2011, Dick Kinzel retired.

In a period of a year and a half the company lost the two leaders who had done the most to create and maintain its culture over the past quarter century. When a company loses its two highest ranking executives, the chief executive officer and the chief operating officer, change is inevitable, especially when those executives had been in leadership for a long period of time, and especially when they are followed by executives who are relatively new to the company and who are products of different cultures.

The Cedar Fair and Cedar Point of Dick and Jack was a very successful enterprise, the gold standard of the amusement park industry. We viewed ourselves, especially in the operating divisions, as an almost military organization, and a victorious one. We were very hierarchical, with status and rank displayed by differences in name tags, parking privileges, perks, uniforms, and levels of organization. We valued order, discipline, loyalty, thrift, hard work, modesty, self-control, consistency, tradition, and the bottom line. We were Romans, not Greeks.

Dick's successor, Matt Ouimet, is the product of the Disney culture. He spent 17 years at Disney. Richard Zimmerman, Jack's immediate successor, is largely the product of the Paramount Parks culture. In January 2018, Matt was named executive chairman of the board and Richard was named president and chief executive officer. They are a strong team.

An organization takes its lead from its leaders. Over time, Matt and Richard are bringing more Disney and more Paramount culture to the company, including Cedar Point. The new culture is a blend of values and people from all three companies. It will be the new culture until sometime in the future, when it is replaced by the next new culture. The laws of the marketplace and human nature apply.

Opening Day 2013. GateKeeper: my last coaster. CEDAR POINT ARCHIVES

## Dick's Retirement

Dick did not get a coaster for his last season. The new ride in 2011 was Windseeker, a Dutch creation that, given my acrophobia, I have never ridden. Rob Decker located it on the beach between the Beach Gate and the Extreme Sports Stadium (Oceana).

The Cedar Fair Board arranged for Dick to go out in style, as he deserved, and the company hosted a banquet and celebration of his career in the Ballroom of the Coliseum on September 10, 2011. Craig Freeman, corporate vice president of Administration, was tapped to head a committee to put it all together. I was assigned the role of Master of Ceremonies. Sometimes things go perfectly and sometimes they don't. This was a case of everything going perfectly.

The Ballroom looked terrific, thanks to the efforts of John Taylor and his team; probably never better, even if considering the IAAPA Summer meeting in 2002 when we re-decorated the room and refinished the nearly century-old wood floor.

Food Service, then headed by Gary Gochenour, did a great job providing an elegant meal, despite the limitations of the Coliseum: no kitchen, no elevator.

The guest list put together by Dick and Judy included community leaders, old friends, family and relatives, industry leaders, government and elected officials, senior management, current and former board members—about 300 of us in all.

I worked hard on my script and I practiced my delivery several times.

The list of speakers was long, but fortunately none of them were long-winded, and I was able to keep everything moving along without too much trouble.

A few weeks later I was talking with someone who had been at the event, an elderly Sanduskian, who told me it was the finest party he had ever attended.

Dick's legacy was a simple one, easy to understand and communicate, and it is significant: he turned a two-park company into an 11- park company with a national footprint; he built a billion dollar company. At Cedar Point, he created the strategy of building great roller coasters as the key to success. By adding hotels, RV campgrounds, and a water park, he returned Cedar Point to its roots as a resort destination.

## Establishing the Fast Lane

In 2012, after a successful test at Kings Island, Cedar Point and the other Cedar Fair parks introduced Fast Lane, an opportunity to dramatically decrease the amount of wait time for major rides—for a price. We couldn't take credit (or accept blame) for introducing the concept. Six Flags was there first with a similar concept. Its apparent success at Six Flags really forced us to pay attention to what they were doing.

The advocate for the program at Cedar Fair was Richard Zimmerman. He convinced Matt Ouimet to test it at Kings Island at the end of the 2011 season. The test was successful. We prepared to roll it out across all the parks.

In theory, Fast Lane was simple. Each ride has two queues, one for Fast Lane guests and one for everyone else. At or near the ride station or platform, the two lines merge and the ride crew sorts things out so there is balanced ridership. The key operational driver is the number of Fast Lane passes sold on any particular day. We knew from the jump we would have to cap Fast Lane sales at some point on some days, we just didn't know what that point would be.

Most rides were built with one queue, so we had to figure out a way to add a second, which was sometimes a challenge.

A Fast Lane wristband allowed the rider to bypass the main queue. In theory, the rider might save 60 minutes or so waiting to ride Millennium Force, a similar time savings waiting to ride Maverick or Top Trill Dragster. Instead of waiting 90 minutes to ride a major coaster, you waited less than 30 minutes. Do this three or four times a day, and you've saved a lot of time, which is a precious commodity at an amusement park.

We offered two price points, a Cadillac option which included all the rides and a scaled-down option which did not include the top two or three. We priced both aggressively, a range of approximately $60 - $90, depending on several factors. Fast Lane purchases were on top of admission. Fast Lane was not a cheap date.

Our biggest fear, naturally enough, was blowback from regular riders who would resent those park-goers who could afford the first class option. However, it never happened, at least not to any measurable or significant degree.

Two observations on Fast Lane. First, its success is driven by the quality of the ride experience at Cedar Point. Yes, Millennium Force is a ride like no other and people will pay a lot of money to ride it. Second, time (convenience) is a powerful thing and people will pay a lot of money to gain even limited or incremental time savings.

The success of Fast Lane showed there was a segment of visitors who loved roller coasters, had significant disposable income, and valued their time at the park (you'll gladly pay a premium to shorten your time in line). If you were going to make a day trip to the park, you were willing to spend another $75 or $85 to make sure you got to ride the big three: Millennium Force, Top Thrill Dragster, and Maverick.

## GM Self-Evaluation

I was GM of Cedar Point for nine seasons, 2005 through 2013. It was 23 percent of my career at the park, excluding my season as GM of Dorney Park.

I have never considered myself a transformative GM. I was not enough of a risk-taker, both professionally and personally, nor did I have a specific vision for the park that I was trying to implement. That is not to disparage my own performance. I believe I did a good job of managing the world's best amusement park. The park was safe. The park was clean. The park made money. We delivered a great product for our guests. However, we were only able to do so because we worked with great people. Cedar Point's staff was deep and talented. We had been a successful enterprise for a long time. We were guided by a collection of policies, procedures, and protocols (both written and unwritten), shared experiences, and shared history that went back decades in many cases. It made a difference.

I am approaching age 70 as I write this in 2018. Most of the people I worked with at Cedar Point have died, retired, or moved on to other endeavors. We had a great run.

## Chapter 21

# October 27, 2013

### Closing Act

I told Phil I wanted to keep my retirement date quiet as long as possible, at least until Labor Day. I had watched several long goodbyes in my career and I hoped not to join the list. Phil agreed to my request, but we both knew it would be decided higher up. I understood; I just hoped for the best.

I told him I wanted to explore other experiences in life while I still could. There's nowhere written that you'll be hiking the Appalachian Trail at 85. The gift of time always stays wrapped and in the box. I had known too many people, Harry Bray being one, who died just on the threshold of retirement. I had things to do and people to visit (including grandchildren) and things to write. I loved the park and I loved my job, but it was a 100-mph job. There's no way you can just throttle back to three quarter speed and run Cedar Point. I have always envied attorneys, architects, accountants, physicians, and family business owners the flexibility most of them enjoy at the end of their careers. Most corporate jobs are just not structured to allow a slow-down.

I had heard from many retired colleagues that one day you wake up and the retirement genie wakes up too and you know it is your time. The retirement genie started whispering in my ear during the 2012 season. Marie and I started to prepare.

I was now always the oldest person in the room, and I could remember always being the youngest. I was the oldest GM in the company by half a decade, and the only one in his 60s.

I had proven to myself that I could survive and successfully adapt to the post-Dick Kinzel world at Cedar Fair.

Per our plan, I would be a few months short of my 65th birthday at retirement. That seemed about right to me. Physically, I could still do the job but there were no guarantees that would last.

I was not on a mission to accomplish some wondrous thing before I retired. But I wanted to go out a winner, and that meant a positive year in attendance, revenue, and profit for Cedar Point. With a big new roller coaster to market, I was as set up for success as I could be.

# GateKeeper

So, I started my last pre-season preparation, my last roller coaster launch, and my last opening day. GateKeeper, and the new front gate that went with it, did not disappoint. Construction of the ride, thanks to the efforts of Ed Dangler, went well. Rob Decker did a brilliant job placing the ride station on the site of the old Cyclone roller coaster and more recently the site of the Space Spiral and Disaster Transport. The coaster track flew right over the main gate, then turned and roared back again as it returned to the station; it was a spectacular visual to welcome guests to the greatest roller coaster park on earth.

I rode GateKeeper for the first time with Jerry Niederhelman, vice president of operations, a week or so before opening. As the reader knows, I was no longer much of an upside-down rider, but GateKeeper was fast with smooth transitions and I pretty much kept my head together. The "sitting on the edge of an airplane feeling" was certainly a good analogy for what it felt like to ride GateKeeper. GateKeeper was not Millennium Force or Top Thrill Dragster in terms of the size of the experience—it was more like Maverick or Raptor, which of course is very good—but I was certain our guests would love it. And it was a B&M, like Raptor and Mantis, which meant it would run and run and run.

I spoke at my last Media Day, which was a great success with media reps, sponsors, assorted VIPs and coaster enthusiasts from all over the region. The weather was beautiful, cool and sunny, and many media representatives stayed late to wander the park a bit. I did numerous interviews, now sporting a GateKeeper jacket and hat. Our PR staff really turned out big numbers for the event, which is their primary objective, since we all knew the coaster, once experienced, would sell itself.

Weather was not so good two days later for opening day. It was cool, borderline cold, with dense, low hanging clouds. The air was watery, the kind of cold humidity the Great Lakes are famous for in spring and fall. But that did not dampen the turnout for the ride. The pre-opening line for GateKeeper, our first new coaster in five years at Cedar Point, wound down past the games area and out onto the main midway. I knew we had a winner. There was an abundance of pent up new coaster demand in the marketplace.

I could tell Matt Ouimet was excited. This was his first experience at Cedar Point with a big new ride. It is heady stuff. I enjoyed working for Matt my last two seasons. He was a positive motivator. I think he grew to appreciate the uniqueness of Cedar Point. His focus is the future. Going to work is fun when there is a new coaster in the Cedar Point skyline.

When I got home that night, Marie and I talked about the fact that this was my last opening day. As much as I loved launching big new rides, it was time to move on.

The next six weeks were normal operation, days filled with all the everyday tensions of running the park but no significant crises. I discovered a spot in the GateKeeper station which offered a great view of Kiddy Kingdom, the Coliseum, Windseeker, and the beach and lake. The ride performed well, and attendance was good despite so-so weather. I started keeping a list of things to review with my successor.

Around July 4, Phil told me that they (Richard and Matt) wanted to announce my retirement and name the new GM as soon as practical, which meant in the next several weeks. The reason was to give the new person plenty of training time while the park was in operation and I was still available. You can't argue with that rationale. However, the passing of the baton would not occur until I retired at the end of the calendar year. Cedar Point would be mine to run until I left.

## Jason McClure is the New General Manager of Cedar Point

The new General Manager of Cedar Point would be Jason McClure, then GM of Dorney Park. It was a great choice. Jason was a Paramount guy; at the time of the acquisition he had been the finance director for Kings Island. Prior to Kings Island, he had worked for several years at Carowinds. He was a native West Virginian and a graduate of Marshall University. He was also very young by my measurement, only in his early 40s. I was more than 20 years his senior; I joked with him that I was old enough to be his father.

I knew Jason from corporate meetings and get-togethers. He had a dry wit and an easy disposition. We of course bonded over Dorney Park, and the fact that we had succeeded at the GM level coming from staff versus operating positions.

The last weekend in July my sister, Mary Frances, drove out from New Jersey with her family for a quick visit. I spent most of Saturday afternoon and evening with them walking the park. My niece Mia and her cousin, Leila, had a grand time riding roller coasters. While waiting for them to ride Millennium Force, my sister and I sat at a table under the huge cottonwood trees across from the Red Garter. I told her about my plans to retire at the end of the year.

She was very supportive. We talked about the long-ago days when our parents had taken us to the Hotel Breakers and we played for hours on the beach.

My retirement announcement was scheduled for Monday, July 29. I was normally off on most Tuesdays and we had made plans to drive to Pittsburgh to visit our friends Ed and Marlene Boas and take in a Pirate game. I made the announcement at my Monday staff meeting. An internal memo went out at the same time. I ducked out early for Pittsburgh.

Jason and I worked very well together the next three months. I was looking forward to retirement and he was looking forward to his new job. We took many park tours together. He had been a successful GM for several years, so he didn't need training as a GM; rather he needed to know as much about the park, including its staff, as he could before the end of the season. The scale of Cedar Point is unlike any other park in the company, and pretty much in the industry. It is a beast, a huge, hungry beast, always scheming to find a way to break free. The GM's job is to hold the reins and direct it in a way that delivers great happiness to both the guest and the unitholder. It is a simple plan: have fun, make money.

August went quickly. The park continued to perform well, both in attendance and revenue. Assuming a normal weather pattern in the fall, we were cruising toward a record year financially. In its second year, the Fast Lane program continued to shine. There was no drop-off in use, instead a big increase despite aggressive price increases. We incorporated GateKeeper into the list of rides for Fast Lane. We got better at managing the program operationally and at the individual ride level. We also got better at merchandising Fast Lane in the park and on our website. Fast Lane revenue made a huge impact on the park's overall financial performance. Fast Lane was made for a coaster dominant park like Cedar Point, and we led the company in Fast Lane performance; in fact, no other park was even close.

Labor Day, my last at the park, was uneventful.

HalloWeekends weather was average at best. Three of seven Saturdays were rainy, including two in October. We did have one record weekend with one "Super Saturday" that stressed our resources to the limit.

My last operating day at Cedar Point was Sunday, October 27, 2013, the final day of the 2013 season. I would not officially retire until January 1, but the months of November and December would mainly be taken up with paperwork and filing and saying goodbye to colleagues.

The week after the park closed there was an employee luncheon at Castaway Bay Ballroom in my honor. Phil said some very nice things about me, which I greatly appreciated. Virtually all of the park staff attended, and I received a standing ovation at the end of the program. It felt very good; that's all I can say.

A day later there was a reception in my honor for family, friends, and community leaders. Also at Castaway Bay. That felt very good, too. I received proclamations from the Ohio Senate and the Ohio House of Representatives, as well as the City of Sandusky and Erie County. Several old friends made the effort to attend, including Jamie and Bob Todor from Houston; Preston and Beth Taylor from Chicago; Jane Duffy from Charleston, West Virginia; Kevin and Kate Terrell from New Providence, New Jersey.

Betsy Kling, the weather anchor for WKYC-TV in Cleveland, drove up between the six and 11 p.m. news, to wish me well.

Lee Alexakos had put all this together and she did a terrific job.

My one regret is that our sons were not there. They were both working. It was the middle of the week. They lived a long way off: New York City and Los Angeles. In Tom's case, he would be leaving his wife alone to care for a three-year-old and a one-year-old. If I could change it now I would.

I was technically GM until January 1, but with the company shut-down at Christmas and unused vacation time I went slip-sliding away on Thursday, December 12, a dark and cold day on the shores of Lake Erie, a very December day. There were corporate meetings that week and it felt very strange to be a participant: not bad, not good, just strange. I sat next to Barb Granter, the GM at Gilroy Gardens, a small park we managed on a contract basis for the City of Gilroy just south of San Francisco. There was a GM dinner on Thursday night at Crush, a Sandusky restaurant. Richard Zimmerman offered a toast in my honor for 40 years of service.

The morning of my last day in the office I finished organizing files and taking personal items to my car. Corinne was off, as was most of the Operations staff, so the Coliseum was quiet. I remember feeling good that I had organized things well for Jason. In the afternoon I took two drives through the park. I drove everywhere I could. I got out of my Jeep several times to walk over to places where I had experienced certain things in my 40 years at the park. I talked out loud a few times, addressing a variety of people. I passed the occasional Maintenance vehicle, but the park was empty, the staff huddled indoors. It was the off-season.

About mid-afternoon, Lee Ann Alexakos called. Marketing wanted to buy me a drink. We all gathered in the bar at the Bay Harbor, overlooking the marina, now empty of boats, right at 5 p.m. Our group was the only one in the bar and this early the restaurant was empty. It was almost dark. The gathering was festive, helped by the Christmas decorations and the Christmas music in the

**One of the best nights of my life.** CEDAR POINT ARCHIVES

background. Lee was there, of course, and Deb Patton, Tony Clark, Carolyn Pankow, Jason Blake, a few others. They told me they had made me an emeritus member of the Marketing division and would make sure I got invited to opening day and all other events. I admit I felt at home.

Of course, I really retired on October 27, the last day I had a park to run.

It was a cool, mostly cloudy day with temperatures in the 50s. Not a bad day for the end of October. I was greeted with a "Thank You, John Hildebrandt" message on the big digital sign above the Toll Plaza, and on the new digital sign which covered the length of the main entrance.

Just before opening, I walked out to greet guests. I saw Dick Kinzel walking across the parking lot from his house.

He greeted me warmly and stuck out his hand:

"Congratulations, Hugo," he said.

We talked for several minutes: weather, football, retirement. I was glad we had a chance to talk and I appreciated it that he made

the effort to wish me well on my last operating day.

Jason McClure walked over, and Dick congratulated him on being the new GM of Cedar Point.

I spent most of the day on the midway, retiring to my office just a few times to get warm and check the numbers from Saturday. We had had a strong day, and we were looking good so far on Sunday. Corinne was off, and the office was quiet.

I was stopped frequently on the midway by season pass holders and others who offered me good wishes in retirement. I posed for several pictures and even signed a few autographs. I walked up ride platforms, I checked out the stores. The park was still in its HalloWeekends finery, of course, but in places the theming was looking a little worn; or, after seven weekends, perhaps I was just a little tired of it.

There were no serious incidents, no emergencies, on my last day.

I really enjoyed my last HalloWeekends Parade. There were almost 20,000 people in the park, so the midway was lined with spectators. I teared up a few times. I recognized lots of faces.

Marie came over about 6 p.m. I took her to the Coral Dining Room. It was empty, damp, and quiet. I walked her to the northeast corner of the building and kissed her, on the spot where we had first met on a warm September evening in 1974.

The PR department had organized a send-off and passing of the baton at Gemini just after closing at 8 p.m. I would take my last ride as GM with Jason (no way Marie was going to ride Gemini, or any other coaster).

Marie and I walked the park, got something to eat, and about 7:30 p.m. wandered down to the station house of the CP&LE Railroad. We were being given the honor of riding the last train ride of the 2013 season. I considered it a high honor. We were the only passengers. It was dark now. The park was emptying fast.

But there were plenty of people at Gemini. The group was festive, mostly coaster enthusiasts, pass holders, a few employees. I thought about the day in June when it had opened in 1978; our boys were born two days later.

The ride was great. We posed for several group pictures. Then it was over.

# 27 Questions

**1—** *What impact did your career at Cedar Point have on your family?*

I was away a lot, not away as in traveling all over the country or the globe and absent for days and weeks at a time, not away as in a military career. I was only five or six miles or 15 minutes away, but I wasn't home, I wasn't with my family. I might as well have been in Wyoming. I missed a lot of things, certainly my loss.

When Michael hit his first home run in high school, the first time in the history of the ballpark a Perkins player hit a ball that cleared the right field fence, I was at the park. I wish I could have that one back.

There are many times when Marie and Mike and Tom share stories and experiences, and I have no idea what they are talking about because I had not been there.

**2—** *What is your favorite ride?*

For a long time it was Gemini. Then Magnum. Then Millennium Force. At the end, it was the Cedar Point & Lake Erie Railroad.

**3—** *Would you do it all again?*

Yes.

**4—** *What is the best ride not at Cedar Point?*

The Beast at Kings Island.

**5—** *What is it like to work all summer?*

Occasionally I complained to Marie and to others, but mostly I didn't mind. It never bothered me to work the three summer holidays: Memorial Day, July 4, Labor Day. They were exciting days to be in the park, each for a different reason of course, and each was a mile post

in the operating season. For our guests, I always sensed they were special days, too: it was a day off work, it was a national holiday, and they were at Cedar Point. I used to think it would have been nice to take a real summer vacation, but even if I had my head and my heart would have been at the park. I learned to love winter.

**6— *Do you dream about the midway?***

Yes, quite frequently.

**7— *Did you ever find the perfect pair of park shoes?***

It was a 40-year quest. Lots of casualties. In the end, I think the best pair I ever found was a pair of Rockports with lots of cushioning but poor styling. I had a pair of Eccos that were excellent. Good shoe options increased over the years. I would go through at least two pairs of shoes a season.

**8— *What was your favorite midway food?***

Two things. Ice Cream Waffle (a chocolate, vanilla, strawberry ice cream blend in between two warm sugary waffles). Messy and magnificent. Also, no longer available at Cedar Point. And Cedar Point fries loaded up with salt and vinegar. On the flip side, I hated cotton candy; I could hardly look at it. Same with caramel apples and hotdogs on a stick.

**9— *What is your favorite park—excluding Cedar Point and Dorney Park?***

Knott's Berry Farm. I love the Ghost Town section; it's unique.

**10—*What park that you haven't been to would you most like to visit?***

Europa Park in Bavaria, Germany.

**11—*Regrets?***

From a Cedar Point perspective, I wish I would have spent more time in the park in the evenings and at night. It's a different place. I wish I had better prepared myself for a career in business while an undergraduate.

**12—*Who was the smartest person you worked with?***

Bruce Jackson, our CFO from 1988 – 2005. Also, Tom Salamone, our treasurer in the 1980s and 1990s.

**13—*Who do you think was the most knowledgeable park person you worked with?***

Jack Falfas.

**14—*Who was the best businessman?***

Don Miears.

**15—*Who was the most visionary?***

Dick Kinzel.

**16—*What parks did you think were Cedar Point's biggest competitors?***

Kings Island to the south and west; Geauga Lake to the east.

**17—*What's your opinion of Disney?***

It's hard to compare Disney and Cedar Point, although we are similar in some ways. I have always admired their operational skills. Unless you're in the business, you have no idea how hard it is to be consistently good. Also, they aren't afraid to price their product. You sense they have a very high opinion of themselves, by that I mean they know they have created an amazing product.

**18—*Who were your mentors?***

Don Dittmann and Jack Goldsmith. I learned a great deal from both men. Both were eager to share what they had learned with me. I had the sense that both cared about me as a person. They were rooting for me to succeed at business (which meant Cedar Point) but also at life. They knew each other and liked each other, but often disagreed. Interestingly, neither was a park person. In terms of Dorney Park, John Albino was a great mentor.

### 19—*Do you have a favorite year/season?*

Probably 1978: A record year, the birth of our sons. 2004, when I was at Dorney. 2000, the year of Millennium Force. 1989, the year of Magnum. My last season, 2013, was good, too.

### 20—*How do employees refer to the park?*

Most commonly as "The Park." Also, as "CP" and as "The Point." Employees from the other Cedar Fair parks often use "Cedar." Cedar Point employees never use that name.

### 21—*What has it been like living in Sandusky?*

A great community. A lot of small town benefits, you see a familiar face almost everywhere you go, but we are less than an hour from the west side of Cleveland and the benefits of a metropolitan area. I consider myself half a native.

### 22—*Celebrities?*

Two that stick out are the actor, Rob Lowe, and the NASCAR driver, Jeff Gordon. Lowe came with a friend to ride coasters. I remember he wore a ball cap, solid colored shirt, khaki shorts, and sneakers. He was dressed like 95% of our male guests. He blended in. He was friendly and polite and couldn't stop raving about our coasters. Jeff Gordon was at the park courtesy of Pepsi. I had a connection. My good friend Bud Greene's first cousin worked for Gordon as his executive assistant. I mentioned this to Gordon and we were instantly friends. He rode Millennium Force with Dick Kinzel. He loved the first drop. I met all seven governors of Ohio who served in office while I worked at Cedar Point: Gilligan, Rhodes, Celeste, Voinovich, Taft, Strickland, and Kasich. Not counting Hollister, who only served 11 days.

### 23—*What gave you the most job satisfaction?*

A 50,000 Saturday. Helping to create advertising that you know made a difference. Managing marketing campaigns to launch world class roller coasters. Recognizing a great publicity opportunity and then cashing in (see "Jaws," Chapter 8). Helping to close the sale on a big corporate picnic. Helping colleagues succeed at work, and at life.

Solving a nasty guest problem, immediately changing Cedar Point's status in the guest's eyes from enemy to friend. Awarding Cornerstone Pins.

## 24—*Coke or Pepsi?*

Both are fine companies. I think their products are at parity. I worked more seasons with Coke (23) than Pepsi (17), but the Pepsi years were some of the best years in the park's history and the years when I was the senior marketing person at the park. I mainly interacted with Coke or Pepsi to create and execute marketing and advertising programs. Over the years, I watched Coke and Pepsi react and adapt to the growth in bottled water and other special products. I felt both companies moved their personnel around too frequently.

## 25—*Did your kids ever work for Cedar Point?*

I didn't think they would, but they did. They both worked in Foods when they were 14. In college, they worked one summer as landscapers and two summers as bellmen, Tom at Hotel Breakers and Mike at Sandcastle. Marie worked as a makeup artist during HalloWeekends at both Dorney Park and Cedar Point.

## 26—*How do I get to be VP-marketing at Cedar Point?*

Go to college. Major in anything but take some basic business and communication classes. Get some experience in sales (of any kind). Get an internship at an amusement park. Develop your writing and presentation skills. Know how to use a computer. Know social media. Volunteer for stuff. Have a positive attitude—don't whine. Come in early and leave late. Find a mentor. Learn the delicate art of touting your accomplishments without being a braggart.

## 27—*How do I get to be GM of Cedar Point?*

See above (26).

# Acknowledgements

My first thank you is to a place, specifically the Sandusky Library, even more specifically the Reference section and the Archives room, where over the course of two winters most of this book was written. It became my daytime home. Beautiful books in every direction. Not a Cedar Point midway, but enough people traffic to keep things interesting when you pulled away from the keyboard and the screen and scanned the room. The library is clean, dry, warm in winter and cool in summer. It is quiet. The bathrooms are clean. There is a coffee machine. There are plenty of places to wander when you need a break. There are reference librarians nearby whose job it is to help you find things. It is nothing short of a wonderful place, especially for a writer.

On Sundays, when the Sandusky Library was closed, I drove an equal 10-mile distance east to the Huron Library, another gem.

You can't remember everything, and sometimes you need help in getting it right. I was blessed with good friends and former colleagues who read different parts of the manuscript at different times and in different ways. My Cedar Point story was the better for their efforts. My thanks to: Lee Alexakos, Ann Marie Muehlhauser, Clark Culbertson, Candy Frankowski, Monty Jasper, Duff Milkie, Jason McClure, Tom Salamone, Melinda Huntley, and Don Miears.

Tony Clark was invaluable in obtaining Cedar Point photos. Ken Miller, who is working on a new history of Cedar Point, fact-checked the manuscript. Eric Pasley and Shelley Bryant provided technical assistance on several photo issues.

Dick Kinzel provided unique insights into the Cedar Point leaders who proceeded him: George Roose, Emile Legros, and especially his mentor, Bob Munger.

Betsy Kling, Chief Meteorologist at Channel 3 in Cleveland, and coaster fan, reviewed Chapter 9, "Who's in Charge of the Weather?"

Jennifer Wright designed a beautiful book.

My brother Greg, a high school art teacher and photographer—and a Western Cruise captain the summer of 1978—assisted with photo editing and provided the back cover photography.

My editor, Tim O'Brien, contributed greatly to this project. Most writers don't think they really need editors. Writing is a solitary

activity; it breeds independence, occasionally even arrogance. Tim is a successful author in his own right (17 books, including a 2015 biography of Dick Kinzel) and can embrace an author's point of view as well as an editor's. He dished out some tough love more than once. It was a great benefit to work with an editor who knows the park and the industry so well. He remains the only journalist ever to be inducted into the International Association of Amusement Parks and Attraction's (IAAPA) Hall of Fame.

My 40 years of the park business was shared with my bride, Marie. There were no secrets between us. She always believed in me, and she always gave her advice in unvarnished words. A journalist by training, she was skeptical of everything and everybody. We made a sweet team.

# About the Author

A native of Cleveland, John Hildebrandt spent 40 years working at Cedar Point. He started as a staff writer in the PR Department in 1974, rising to Vice President, Marketing, in 1993. He was transferred to Dorney Park & Wildwater Kingdom as General Manager in 2004. In 2005, he was transferred back to Ohio to serve as General Manager of Cedar Point. After nine years as GM, he retired from the company following Cedar Point's 2013 operating season.

Hildebrandt is a graduate of the University of Notre Dame, where he majored in English; he has an MFA in Creative Writing from the University of North Carolina at Greensboro.

He is the co-author, with his wife, Marie, of "Lake Erie's Shores and Islands," a history of the tourism industry in the Lake Erie region, published in 2015.

In 2000, Hildebrandt received the Paul Sherlock Award from the Ohio Travel Association in recognition of his contributions to Ohio's tourism industry.

He and Marie live in Sandusky. They have two adult children and four grandchildren (who love to visit in the summertime).

# Index

CPSIA information can be obtained
at www.ICGtesting.com
Printed in the USA
FFHW022207210119
50210225-55179FF